CLIFFORD F. GANT

Why Am I Here?

An Autobiographical Exposé:

Duty, Theft, Murder & Redemption

WHOSONFIRE
PUBLISHING
PHOENIX

Why Am I Here?

An Autobiographical Exposé:
Duty, Theft, Murder & Redemption

A WHOSONFIRE BOOK / DECEMBER 2021

ISBN 9781667822402

Printed in the United States of America

Second Paperback Edition

To my Mother.

Dad already knows the truth.

Now you can, too.

12/24/2017

Life doesn't grant second chances. If you lose, you lose. There is no going back to the starting line and sprinting off the blocks to the same trigger plume of white smoke. You may be able to run another race, but doing your best in a moment past and coming up short will never be erased from the annals of history. Neither from the history writer's perspective, nor your own internal memories where it is only you who knows if, how, or where you went wrong.

WHY AM I HERE?

WHO'S ON FIRE

   I am burning. I'm at a mental hospital, left to stew in the chopped up pieces of my past that contributed to bringing me here. It isn't quite what Hollywood promised. Cigarettes and involuntary electroshock 'therapies' are neither readily available. It is really just a warehouse for those deemed 'Guilty - Except Insane.' It is intended for those who committed a crime while not being in the proper state of mind (when is a committed crime *WITHIN* the proper state of mind, I don't know) and unintended as a safety-net for those Public Defenders who wish to prop up their case stats. Pretty much, except for a few standouts, everyone here is pretty normal in the generic, everyone-has-their-day type behaviors. Some periodically scream to random delusions, some MUST have an equal number of creamers and Splenda in their iced morning cup of coffee and some just stare into the abyss. I wonder what they are thinking about. Unlike most, I am not thinking about getting out. I somewhat like it here. I don't have to worry about where my next roll of toilet paper is going to come from, or meal for that matter. I have a bed with my own personal blankets. I have an MP3 player and a radio. I have my own clothes, which helps in maintaining somewhat of an identity and not fading into the blur of being just your run-of-the-mill mental patient. Not that I want to stand out, but my story has indiscriminately thrust me into that type of responsibility. So here I am, just shy of four years since my "Index Offence," and it seems I haven't gone anywhere, mentally or geographically. Today's entry, here, this moment, marks the end of me standing still. This day marks the end of my surroundings limiting me to inaction. If this is only for me, then I hope you enjoy it, Clifford. If this is for the world, then thank you for your eyes and ears. I hope my vision, still coming into focus, will not disappoint.

PREFACE

On The Value of Human Life:

"That is why We ordained for the Children of Israel that whoever takes a life—unless as a punishment for murder or mischief in the land— it will be as if they *killed* all of humanity; and whoever saves a life, it will be as if they *saved* all of humanity."

Surah 5.32, <u>THE QURAN</u>

      This work is not intended to convince the reader of any guilt or innocence to which I am ascribed. Upon reading this offering, there will be no doubt or denial of my guilt. Rather, the question becomes does this re-examined life warrant society saving *it*, and in turn, possibly saving humanity itself? Judgment lies within your grasp. This is not a plea for help. This is a moratorium on human history and what the "Book of Life" would be compelled to omit, if only to preserve its own integrity. I am not looking to set the groundwork to present myself as any sort of "Special Case." I have lived enough life to have personally listened to hundreds of firsthand accounts of life that, in my view, warrant the spotlight more than mine, but alas, they are not here, I am. So I will make a good faith effort herein, to present my story, with supporting documents, anecdotes and theistic disputes to the best of my ability, recollection and theoretical aptitude. Some pieces of my history have been forever lost to the ether. I omit them only due to time constraints and what I will call 'unintended situational amnesia.' I will never intentionally refuse to disclose information simply to further a point or narrative I am trying to make. This is my life, laid bare. Let the chips fall where they may, most already have.

CHAPTER MANIFEST   PAGE

PART 1: DUTY

Chapter I

South Moves North

North Moves South

<u>Growing Up</u>

To start anywhere other than 3232 N. Woodburne Drive in Chandler, Arizona would be a travesty of justice. I was the firstborn of my mother, Tammy Marlene Gant, maiden name Biddle. Due to a previous marriage, I was granted the honor of being the third born to my father, Clifford Earnest Gant. I was his second son. My mother opted for a midwife and a home birth, which was not completely unique in the 80's, but no doubt nerve-racking as well. A home birth was definitely uncharted territory for a first time mother-to-be. Nonetheless, on December 10th, 1984, I breached the 'Veil of Maya' and was granted consciousness-of-decision. In other words, I was born. Clifford Frederick Gant. My father's hands were the first to touch me. That meant something to him. The few surviving pictures I have seen of that day show a woman, strong in determination and perseverance, physically spent and spiritually renewed at the sight of her nine month burden-of-responsibility. I am still inspired by the sense of achievement tangibly apparent in that 25-year old, on that 3x4 inch, thick, Kodak picture.

I wouldn't be hers alone for long, though. No. Turns out I was just the pole position, the torch-bearer, for a litter that would total six over the next nine years. I think of it now as the "one out, one in" policy. Looking back, it's disappointing they both neglectfully subscribed to, or at least permitted, that scenario. One year and six days later, my sister Melody entered the fray, followed by Jessica, Melissa, Matthew and Mitchell. For those keeping track, it went me, THREE sisters, and then two brothers that weren't old enough to beat up till I was at least 14. Also, every child has the letter 'M' in their name except me. (Jessica's middle name is Marie.) I also find it odd that that whosoever names started with the letter 'M', were born natural red-heads. I'm happy with my dark hair.

In the early days, before our troupe was completed, I remember moving around often. Dad invented a razor that he thought would revolutionize shaving. He called it "The Handle" and later changed it to "The Gant Razor," a possible harbinger of his ever-vain

2

attempt at self-promotion. Mom was involved in a car accident years before and was the recipient of a cash settlement that to this day I've never asked her to monetize. She spent a substantial portion of it on the steep price of a plastic injection mold to realize my father's dream. I can remember being five or six years old and seeing him pumping out plastic and card stock packaging from that machine. With KMLE Country playing on the radio, each completed compression yielded a green-backed, ready-for-display unit promoting a colored razor. His razor was his counter to the Shick or Gillette Model-T type razors.

Think of a toothbrush, with two parallel razorblades on each side. It took your standard-of-the-time, Track-II type blades and was a dream for women who hated elbowing themselves in the gut while trying to shave in the bath. With his razor, all they had to do is flick their wrist while 'combing' their stubbly standards. I still think it's a great product. It was an idea ahead of its time.

Melody and I would tow along with two year-old Jessica to swap meets and trade shows, and, I'm not going to lie, we were kind of the draw of attention. Two young, beauty-pageant winners (not bragging), eating peanut butter and jelly sandwiches that came from Tom & Jerry Cat & Mouse collectible glassware, were quite the sight. But the 7-foot fiberglass-coated bright pink foam razor was the splash point. He would pitch his heart out at every open ear.

"Can you cut yourself?" An inquiring soul might ask.

"Yes. But I wouldn't recommend it." He would say with a wry smile.

They would smile back and move on to the next gadget or marketing ploy in line. His vision never manifested, and although his never-ending quest to make it work would drive a wedge between him and his brood, he was undeterred. I believe, and see now, how his intent may have been pure; wanting to 'make a million' to give his kids everything they needed to succeed, regardless of the temporary sacrifices that needed to be made in the shorter term. Still, I don't see that as an ideal worthy of a turned-up nose. Years after he set aside his 'Enterprise' he would become reclusive. He would spend hours reading self-help books, or listening to an Earl Nightingale selection while nursing a Pabst Blue Ribbon. Perfecting his banjo, as he was an Earl Scruggs super fan, he would leave his kids without direction or much needed leadership. He became the discipliner.

Spankings were a normal for me. It almost became worth the temporary pain, to be able to have contact with him. I would outgrow those feelings eventually. When spankings weren't enough, a tablespoon of cayenne pepper held on the tongue for what seemed like forever, but couldn't have eclipsed two minutes. That was sadistic, but became more of a challenge to me to always try to top my secret

'High-Score'. I'd have to act like it was melting me from the inside, and it was, but pushing the limits of my pain-threshold was me making the best of a spicy situation.

When Melody *and* I were the co-conspirators, he almost relished in cracking our heads together. In his mind, if we were going to hurt or pester each other, he would take one action to have us both hurt each other equally, in one fail clap. This isn't to say he was a deadbeat, he was just ill-equipped to handle what he had created. He would pitch in financially by administering colonic therapy in a small back room to those health-conscious individuals willing to let a healer be a healer in the familiarity of his own space.

By 1993, however, the family was at the end of its run in Arizona. Jobs weren't easy to come by and the money was ever short. Family support was needed and Wisconsin became the destination. Enter the Biddles & the Fixes.

Waupun, Wisconsin

617 W. Main Street. If you went there today, there would be nothing. The City Hospital bought the land in the early 2000's and bulldozed the house for aesthetic reasons. But let me try to paint a picture anyways. The house was a two-story, with light blue siding, almost white. The basement was musty and dim and that's where Dad would work on his new craft, airbrushing. Walking down the wooden stairs, I was always scared that someone was going to reach through the exposed steps and grab my ankles, thus causing me to fall the remainder of the way to the cement ground. No one ever did, but nonetheless, I always made the journey to the washer and dryer by skipping as many steps as I could.

The backyard was amazing. Our Arizona house, in contrast, was merely a small area covered in dirt, bordered with a block wall which gave it a prison-like feel. There *was* a playhouse next to the main structure, but that was only used when privacy was needed, no doubt to do trouble-worthy deeds. Granted, it did have a growing fig tree that Dad had planted for me, and a peach tree sapling he planted for Melody. We wouldn't be there long enough to see either yield any fruit. Even with Arbor Day satisfied, the backyard still wasn't play worthy, boasting just a rickety swing set. But this! It was grass! Luscious, glorious grass!

Behind the house and to the left was a detached one-car garage that sufficed for Dad's workshop. Further left was the backside of some sort of office building that ran along our property line right up to a parking lot that was used for a mix of office employees and Waupun City Hospital patients.

We could see the hospital building right out our back door. It was stoic, in all its glory. At night, there would be a tornado of bats

4

flying out of the smokestack that stretched into the night sky. Munching on that nights take of mosquitos and to a lesser extent, flies, I imagine. The nightly show was surely something to behold.

We would soon have a large trampoline and a swing set for entertainment, complete with a slide and tire swing. The tire swing was hung by three equally spaced chains connected to the tire that was parallel to the ground. It was not the type you practice your football quarterbacking accuracy through. This would be the spot that Melody and I would sit and spin for hours of fun. Digging my foot into the ground would act like the bottom of a toy top, and with a little circular motion, I was able to generate quite the amount of speed. The ground underneath the tire swing would soon become barren of grass and reminiscent of having a little piece of Arizona dry dirt right under my big toe. The goal for me was to spin the tire so fast as to have Melody fly off backwards. It never happened, two of the three chains were always held onto tightly. A few times I would make her loose her grip, nothing more, unfortunately. Regardless, for a second and third grader, getting dizzy was pretty fun. The large trampoline that we got at a garage sale, soon after we arrived, was just a pad for launching her into the sky. If you ever had one, you'll know what I'm talking about. But even that got old after a while. Grandma's house never got old, though.

Out on County Trunk M (that's the road, I didn't name it) lived the root of the family: my Grandfather, Fred Biddle, and my Grandmother, Marlene Biddle. On his 50 acres, he grew heirloom corn, raised a few cattle, a basset hound named Tippy, and later he would add two horses. The cornflower-blue country house was quite spacious. With them lived my Aunt, Uncle and cousins: Jerome Fix, or 'Uncle Jerry', as we called him and his wife, my Mom's sister, Pamela Fix or 'Aunt Patty.' They had four children: Miranda, who was my age, Travis, who was Melody's age, and the last two, Calvin and Chanel, were too young to matter. Melody hung out with Miranda and I took to Travis.

The summer we arrived, Travis would take me out to shoot his BB-gun at squirrels or rabbits on multiple occasions. Once, we went skinny-dipping in the fishless pond that was the hunting apex for deer in the area. We would play his Nintendo NES for days. Mario 3, Duck-Hunt and Skate-or-Die were our go-to games. I was admittedly jealous of his gaming gear, especially because my Mom found me a used Intellevision at a flea market, first. I was initially impressed with its side loading cartridges. The controller was like a telephone pad with a directional dial below it. For every game, you would insert a different thin plastic command strip onto the controller's face. For those who weren't blessed with the good fortune of the best Dungeons & Dragons platform experience one could ever hope to explore, pushing the number 4 on Space Invaders might "Shoot" but in Dungeons & Dragons it would command your avatar to "Move Left." Get the jist? But a Nintendo *with* someone to play with made my Intellevision obsolete, no matter how much I hated playing Luigi. (Hey man, can't argue with 'House Rules.')

When we spent the night, which was as often as we could finagle, mornings were the best. Cereal. Real. Sugar. Cereal. At the Main Street location, breakfast cereal consisted of four main choices:

1.   Oatmeal. I am not going to lie, for all his misgivings, my Dad can cook the shit out of some oatmeal. Boil water, dump raisins, wait. Dump oatmeal, lower heat and cover. When you can spin the pot top you know you got the right cooking temperature. If it starts foaming like a rabies-stricken German Shepard, (RIP Hostle, our dog we had to put down in Arizona), turn the heat down. Then, dish out in child's bowls, add a small pad of butter to 'lubricate your joints,' sprinkle cinnamon, a dash of nutmeg and a splash of whipping cream. The man had a system.
2.   Shredded Wheat. The brown bag containing two 'biscuits' of hearty goodness. (I bought a box years ago for like $8, little did I know back then, how top shelf that was.)
3.   Cheerios. Enough said.
4.   If we were lucky, the morning after a good visit at Grandma's with no fighting perhaps, we got Kix. Just enough sweet to make us feel like we were getting away with something, plus it was acceptable on WIC. Oh, did I need to mention we were a food stamp family? Back when it wasn't in an empowering credit-card form. I'm talking like the look of shame, pulling out that book in front of people and tearing out those ration-denominations. God bless her, my Mother. Faultless.

But in Aunt Patty's Breakfast Bazaar we could get TWO BOWLS of our choice between Lucky Charms, Frosted Flakes, Fruit Loops, Honey Nut Cheerios (if the others were running low), and all sorts of random, never before digested breakfast delicacies. Oh the joys of discovering Fruity Pebbles for the first time or Count Chocula. Dad! Cayenne, please. (It brings me back to real life.)

The Green Bay Packers and The Milwaukee Bucks took projection-big screen precedent. If they are playing, and Uncle Jerry isn't racking 'em up in his bowling league or doing a double at Dodge County Prison (which he would end up spending over 25 years serving faithfully), his ass was is in his recliner, watching his boys get it done. Don't get me started with the dream team. The Lambeau Leaps I've seen on that vinyl screen, the Mark Chumura runs, the Robert Brooks' fingertip catches, the Antonio Freemans' routes-run-to-perfection, the Frankie 'Bag of Doughnuts' Centers touching every play. As for the Milwaukee Bucks... uhhh... Ray Allen and Glen Robinson, perhaps? Ok, they were still rebuilding back then. They have Antetokounmpo now, so ... worth the down years? Yes, I do believe so. Uncle Jerry would concur. Not the fair-weather fan, that Jerry Fix, more like ride-or-die, but not fan boy enough to spring for a shoulder tattoo. Faultless.

Then there was Main Street: no cable. Viewing pleasure revolved around Saturday morning cartoons. Complete with Schoolhouse Rock and reruns of "The Mouse & The Motorcycle." I loved that eggshell helmet wearing rodent more than any ACME Roadrunner skit they could come up with. Animaniacs had to top all on Saturdays, though. If you've seen, then you know. Oh, Dot. What an entertainer!

Elementary School

Alto Elementary, Third Grade. The bus ride was a good 30 minutes from the pickup spot that was 35-yards from the house. The bus driver's name was Tom Straks. His daughter, Beth, was my classmate. We were cordial. I would mentally come to unmask him as a Garth Brooks Doppelgänger, so that was cool to live with. In Wisconsin, unlike Arizona, fireworks are legal. So, at one point, in early spring, I came across some sparklers while snooping in the garage. Now, although you may contest, I hereby deem sparklers as the lamest of all fireworks. They are followed closely by the smoke snake, that box of miniature hockey pucks you stack and ignite to make the image of the earth shitting an ash turd into the sky. I decided, in all of my wisdom, to take my lame fire-sticks to school and give them to my classmates as peace offerings. I was kind of a 'schmuck' and talked a lot when I should have zipped it. But hey, God gave me this talker, better learn fast how to use it. First offering on my journey: Garth Brooks, the bus driver.

With a smile, he thanked me for the two silver sticks. There must have been twelve or so in the slim box so I decided to ration the rest till I got to recess to better determine those worthy of this firepower of friendship. After the second period in Ms. Heinrich's Third Grade class, she gets a note. She then proceeds to take me out to the hall, where our backpacks are hung up, and instructs me to give her the contraband. Slick as a devil, I unzip only an arms width of backpack, and start fishing for the sparkler container, blind. You may ask why? So thought she. She moved aggressively to open the backpack fully and found not only the fireworks in question, but a hefty box of intimidating ten-inch barn matches. I was foiled, caught, exposed, busted, whatever you want to call it, I was in trouble, and not the Travis Tritt kind.

"What is THIS!" And she escorted me immediately to the principal's office.

Now, in full disclosure, I had zero intention of sparking any of these at school, but rather wanted to be prepared to light one the second I got off the bus. I awaited the principal's tyranny, anxiously. I don't remember his name but in music class, we had to learn "Edelweiss," his favorite song. Hopefully he liked my rendition. What I wasn't thinking then, but am realizing now, was that if my teacher's name was "Heinrich", and *his* favorite song was in German, that Alto Elementary must have been some slick low-key Nazi encampment. It's a stretch, but felt accurate. Waiting for the Principal to come in, my mind started racing. New school, new class. Am I going to be the badass 'new guy'? Am I really going to impress Linda Bresser? Nate Daane and Dan Bruins are going to think this is going to be EPIC! I remember the principal, we will call him 'Hans', coming in and closing the door. There was nothing in between us but a vast failure to communicate, totally Cool Hand Luke style. With my back to a wall, he charged me, a 9-year old child, grabbed and twisted the neck of my shirt and lifted me off the ground. He exclaimed something to the effect of "What were you THINKING?!" And I pissed myself. Right there.

Shortly thereafter, shamed and confused at my lack of bladder control, I was escorted to the school bus. I don't know if it was early release or what but it was definitely a morning trip with kids on board, maybe from another school. Waupun was a small town and I'm sure they pooled resources, as there were a few elementary schools along the route home. I was dropped off right in front of my Main Street abode, pants that would make Billy Madison proud, and I approached my waiting mother, who I am sure was briefed on the 'official story'. I was grounded, which meant no Crystal River tubing trip that weekend, and no going to Aunt Patty's house anytime soon. I can't remember if my father invoked any 'corporal punishment' but by that time, punishments were more an inconvenience than a deterrent. I never told a soul, until now, about the Principal and I. Not out of embarrassment, but out of any surefire response of "Who fucking cares?" Maybe soon, you might. This was my first step into distrust of authority. This was never reported, and he was never reprimanded. Until now. I'm over it, but yet I'll leave Ms. Heinrich & Principal Hans with a heartfelt, "Shame on you!"

The following years at Alto Elementary were better. Mrs. Beutien, a wonderful spirit, for 4th grade, and Mr. Scott for 5th. They switched English and Math classes with each other. Mrs. Beutien taught both grades English and Mr. Scott had both grades math classes.

Once a week, he would play a game called "Stump the Grump." It was a weekly review of all of his lessons that was really unique. See, he had a punch bowl of assorted fun-sized candy bars, and he would pick a student. That student could either be asked a question or ask him a question. If you answer his question correctly, he would throw you a treat. If you ask him a question and he gets it wrong, which rarely ever happened, you would get two treats, dealer's choice. We were much more successful at answering his questions.

Mr. Scott, 5th grade teacher at Alto Elementary School, in Alto, Wisconsin, you are the best teacher I ever had. At the time in life when a spirit really comes into his (or her) persona, you warned me fairly and honestly, "If you keep being a shmuck (or smart aleck) they [Middle School] will pound you into the ground like a stake." So to update a 25-year old honest, open, advice communication, from teacher to student, my sincere response is:

"Yes, I kept it up, and yes, they did." Play Tim McGraw "One of These Days."

"Mr. Scott, I may not be any better for not heeding your advice and going about it my own way, but I'd be hard pressed to count me worse off because of my neglect of your intended instilled wisdom. Thank you for your service."

Pro Tip: The school is neighbored by the best cheese factory there is in the state. I don't know the name but if you ever go to the gift shop and don't spring for the TWO POUNDS of cheese curds, Mr. T will 'Pity You,' because you are a FOOL! You have been so advised.

Middle School

I have few memories of the 6th and 7th grades at Waupun Middle School, home of the Warriors. I played football as backup running back for a total of three weeks before I deemed any possible benefits under delivered when compared to the utmost loathing I had for the mandatory workouts. I did get substituted in for a few defensive plays, once they realized I couldn't grasp the offensive play calling codes. Was "I-Tight Right 37-Blue" the first gap on the right or the second on the left? Oh well, Barry Sanders knows and that's somehow good enough for me. I did manage an interception in practice once, but still got chided for not yelling, "OSKIE!" At Alto, I did set one school athletic record. That was my crown jewel. Sit-and-reach champion didn't afford me a shot at a girl, but it did amount to the apex of my sports abilities, and that still carries weight with me.

Middle School was when I landed my first job. In Wisconsin, twelve years old marked the age an adolescent could get a paper route. I applied to deliver the route nearest my house in the spring and Mom took me up to Fond Du Lac, some 30 minutes away, to have my first real job interview. I nailed it! The man provided me with my route subscribers list and a ticket book that was proof of payment for those that chose to pay bi-weekly in cash, and also handed me my prized possession: my delivery bag with "Fond Du Lac Reporter" emblazoned on the side. I wasn't completely prepared for the work ahead, banana-seat bike be damned. It wasn't pretty, but it was just the start I needed. I would soon save up enough to buy a ten-speed from the Pamida on Main, Waupun's equivalent to K-Mart, for under $100. I was on top of the world.

During the winter months, particularly around Christmas time, many customers would tape Christmas cards up on their doors which usually contained a cash-tip. It was a nice bonus for peddling through the fresh powder that early in the mornings. They knew I was worth it. What they *didn't* know was what McDonald's did around that time, but I don't think this would have affected their generosity any. Yes, Waupun has a McDonalds to rival the Hardee's right across the street from it, a few miles east from our house, on Main. When McDonald's had their annual Monopoly Game, there would be a free game insert in the Sunday Papers. I figured I would save my subscribers the trouble of throwing it away and I kept them all. I eventually got sick of all the free hash browns I won, but the free sodas, fries and McMuffins were always good. And in the coolest stroke of luck, I became a slumlord! I peeled off McDonald's gold. Baltic and Mediterranean were mine! And in the days of yore, that meant a cash win of, hold your britches, FIVE WHOLE DOLLARS!

I walked in after the route, boss as hell, threw my stickers down, signed my name on a spreadsheet, and out of the register came a greasy, crumbled Abe Lincoln. What a score! McDonald's money is rare to win. I still consider myself honored to have scammed that moment from life. The only other moment I pull from my time delivering, other than the context of its entirety of doing a good job and being a good representative and neighbor to those I served, was the Don McLean moment when I got the bundled stack of newspapers at 5:00 AM and the headline told me that Dianna was gone. The line was lived live in the moment, "Bad news on the doorstep." Peace be upon her.

Middle School is also when I began my accelerated advancement in scholastics, particularly maths and sciences. I got noticed to the tune of getting invited to Northwestern University outside of Chicago to have my Mom participate in the "What to expect while raising a 'gifted' child" seminar. I just wanted to see the football field where the Wildcats took their snaps, but it was announced early on to be off-limits, due to construction. I was bummed. Mom took a lot of notes as if she was the one now in the pressure seat of responsibility. Afterward, we took a slow ride around the suburbs just to admire the houses. Epic architecture, Chicago. Good times. Little did I know that we would meet again.

Dad was mostly employed by a Quad Graphics plant twenty-five minutes south. It was a magazine printing company, among other services. I was amazed later in life to see a picture of the late owner, Henry Quadracci, showing up to an employee picnic riding a legit elephant. Peace be upon him. What a way to make an entrance, though. And what a way to show up randomly in a leadership book purchased from Barnes & Noble in 2003, some five years later. Hit me to the point of realizing maybe nothing is random. I remember Dad would come home with plastic grocery bags full of empty cigarette packs. It must have been a stressful printing press with deadlines and ink levels and all.

See, back then Big Tobacco could market the hell out of smoking, with no restraint. For every pack of Marlboro's, next to the UPC, was printed "FIVE MILES." Now for those on the mailing list, there was a secret catalog, full of top-notch branded Marlboro Gear. It contained everything from bandannas to sunglasses, and duffel-bags to watches. To me it was an adults only Christmas wish list. He would spend hours clipping, then bundling them into 250-mile stacks. But ONLY after separating the heavy carton-stock backing from the thinner cover print of the purchase code. He told me he saved money on shipping that way. I can't imagine how the cost benefit vs. labor extended ratio ever was truly economically viable, but hey, the man had a system. Hundreds of thousands of "MILES" later, he had successfully amassed quite the impressive collection. The most coveted by me, of his hoard, was the Marlboro-branded Leatherman Tool. Complete with the Red Cap Insignia on the carrying case, I saw it as not only practical, but fashionable as well. I'm sure Phillip Morris had to give an honest thought, at the time, to who the true 'Marlboro Man' was. Cigarette companies no longer can trade merchandise for cancer, and I, for one, think that is bullshit.

If, today, one can enter to win a raffle on a popular soda site by chugging down gallons of liquid candy, and entering the max of ten codes per day to maybe win a T-shirt or a gift card, with no societal concern to the sweet, caffeinated path towards early onset Type-II Diabetes and tooth decay, why can't I wear the branding of a company that I *know* is going to kill me, like a real man? Fuck, we are all on the same death march here, guys. Anyone pompous enough to say I can't "Frank Sinatra" the shit out of my own flesh & bone, needs to get a full-body x-ray. Because if they have broken even a single bone in their body, than be relieved they are NOT the Messiah and need not be listened to or lectured from.

When I finally got a handle on this walking corpse of mine, right around this time, I promised myself that I was going to LIVE. I would be determined to strive for the gritty, while admiringly shunning the shiny, to taste dirt rather than stand ignorantly proud, knowing my time would one day come. However I was to end up, I'd be damned if I wasn't going to do it "My Way."

7th grade would come to an uneventful end, and so would our tenure in Waupun. After five fierce winters, my Mom finally tapped out. The last two boys, Matthew & Mitchell, were born at the hospital behind our house a few years before and were now old enough to feed themselves, for the most part. So I guess they felt that marked the right time to give Arizona another shot. With a new found resolve to start from scratch again, they started planning. With the baby-making factory closed for business, maybe they wouldn't have to worry about any more unexpected eventualities and focus on the job at hand. Namely, feeding six growing children. Problem was, the metro-Phoenix area had grown so much in our absence and not wanting to be part of a thriving metropolis, they didn't know where to go.

Mom liked the midsize town feel, where everyone is friendly, but you keep a certain amount of anonymity. Waupun boasted 5,000 residents, anonymity was not an option. Nor was it a locale decision that would be duplicated under the rising Arizona sun. I don't know how or when the decision to plot the Rand McNally's course to the Arizona/California border at the Colorado River was made, but Lake Havasu City was the new destination.

Lake Havasu City was a town of 50,000 permanent residents, with loads of snowbirds. Snowbirds were your mostly elderly travelers that would spend the winter months in the desert and live out the summer months in the North or Midwest. Housing, tourism and the service sector were Lake Havasu City's main driving economic forces. It was a town that was known, but had not yet exploded, perfect to try out. Two weeks before the move, I went to turn in my newspaper getup.

My boss, who I rarely spoke to, was a bit sad faced as he explained to me that the following month they were going to name me "Paperboy of the Month." The big draw was A) getting noticed for my year-and-a-half of hard gear grinding, and B) a flashy black carrier bag with double padding on the shoulder strap, very desirable. This marked the first instance in a long chain of being on the cusp of promotion, and just barely missing it. I had no time to wallow, though. We were moving!

Out on County Trunk M, near the newly framed house Grandpa was building by hand, a hundred yards from the blue country house, Uncle Jerry, Grandpa, Dad and I worked to customize the chosen trailer frame for the move. From the wood flooring, walls were erected that must have topped six feet. It was a feat of modern engineering, and to be towed by a large Dodge full-sized van, made it even more the spectacle. Loading up everything from the two-story on Main was an all-day event that required all hands on deck. It was a solid ten hours of the sorting strategy, "pack it, throw it away, or do *you* want this?" When all was said and done, you couldn't fit a domino in that trailer. If you tried, by the time we hit the McDonald's on our way out of town, the transmission would have surely seized. We were out of there.

Dad thought he was clever and duct-taped a cardboard sign on the back of the overweight trailer announcing we were: "Getting Out Of Dodge," the county Waupun was nestled in. I wonder if anyone else found any humor in that.

Lake Havasu City

Once the Havasu city limits were breached, we were pulled over before we even got to the hotel parking lot. In Wisconsin, trailers were not required to be licensed. In Arizona, it's mandatory. An explanation ensued and we were sent on our way. The monsoon was alive and kicking. I remember Dad leading us from the van to the hotel lobby, and just then, a gust of wind that was strong enough to make me sway, took his cowboy hat, and never relented. It carried three feet into the air and we watched it disappear over open desert. Dad knew it was pointless to try to chase it. I felt for him, though.

I remember being in that detached garage on Main Street, watching him lace up some sort of ½ inch cylindrical metal bearings of sorts to adorn his prized cowboy hat. Perhaps it was paid for with Quadracci's Marlboro Miles. He would string them together like a ribbon of bullets waiting to be expelled in Vietnam, to which he honorably served his station during the war, in the United States Air Force.

He would cross thin wire inside every hollow metallic tube, pulling the next cylinder, or bullet, tightly parallel. He would repeat this action ad nasuem, the man had a system. He would work on that for days. Finally, he completed the project, and, at the juncture of the brim and the base of the cap, he secured it. I'm sure if he would be reminded about that cowboy hat, he would say, "Yeah, shucks, I liked that one." He has never been one to dwell on what's been lost, a quality I'm proud to say I've also organically developed. We stayed at the hotel for a week before he and Mom found a duplex they could afford and, two weeks later, we started school.

Thunderbolt Middle School

Home of the ThunderCats, the school was pink, even though Mom would insist it was 'mauve.' I am still not quite sure of the difference. I would tragically find out, four years later, that I was colorblind, so maybe that taints the playing field of who sees what correctly. My homeroom teacher was Ms. Matzdorf, the most coveted of all homeroom teachers. She was something nice to look at to start the day. Lisa Ling presented the news on "Channel One." This was before she became a big shot reporter. School bored me. Classes were easy, and I effortlessly chalked up a high school credit for taking Algebra 1-2. This would be a pivotal credit in the years that followed.

Mr. Geinger, who was allegedly allergic to the aluminum in deodorant, taught a mean social studies class. He gave us $10,000 in play money to invest and chart two stock market picks. The cool skater kids would laugh with each other as they bought $5,000 in Playboy and $5,000 in Nike. I took it a little more serious. My picks: $8,000 in AT&T and $2,000 in Morton International. You may not know it by name, but I know you have seen the blue round salt tube with the girl & umbrella walking in the rain. I figured people in the future are still going to want to salt their food, and then they are going to want to talk about it. Dial-up internet was still a new thing and the web was growing even after the end of those AOL disks boasting "1000 Free Hours!" Oh, nostalgia. My takeaway from my 8th grade public education was that because I wasn't a skater, I was relegated to the loser pool, and that was fine. It provided fewer distractions. But, not one interested girl. And I was not a bad looking kid. I was ready for the big leagues, though. High School, here I come! Wait.... WHAT?!

As the long awaited summer began, Mom took to comparing the merits of a public school education versus the charter/magnet school that bore the name Telesis Center For Learning. They pitched it as a "go at your own pace" environment. That struck her as perfect for her underutilized 'gifted' one. I didn't have many friends to miss at Lake Havasu High and was quite the pushover on the topic of switching schools. Melody would have none of it, though. She was into sports: volleyball, basketball and softball. She was quite the social beacon of admiration. If superficial was a gift, she got the lion's share. So summer goes by and I haven't even scraped a knee. I also haven't stepped foot on a skateboard, to try. Life was safer that way. Looks like I'd be a resident of Loserville at the new school, too. What's new? Telesis had just migrated to a hollowed out office building close to the London Bridge. It seemed then, that it was quite a rush job to make it look scholastic. Almost like sheets were draped over clotheslines to mark off the classrooms, but in hindsight they were probably standing dividers. A big dirt lot next to the building sufficed us school kids to play soccer on for forty-five minutes a day.

What made itself overwhelmingly apparent very early on was that "go at your own pace" was for the slower crowd, not me. I was shipwrecked on a metaphorical island, alone, let's call it Patmos. My math teacher made me a deal. Mr. Hendricks explained to me that he didn't have enough time to get the rest of the class attended to while also teaching me advanced algebra and its so-called complexities. So, he gave me the book as a test.

"Let the book teach you, and if you have questions I will be here to help." He said. "I will let you do up to one chapter a day, and if you quiz over 80%, you can go on to the next chapter." I burned through two textbooks in one semester. By the time May came around, I was halfway through the Pre-Calculus text. He gave me one question to tickle my mind. $A^3+B^3=C^3$. He said if I solved this unanswered question he would get me on TV. Without further ado, Mr. Hendricks:

$$A^3 + B^3 = C^3$$

I make a motion to release the
constraints of all XY&Z Axis'

Cubing an integer, to me, brings it into the third dimension:
Length, Width and Depth.
So without constraints of stringent XY&Z axi this becomes
The Tryst of Math & Art

A or ⊲ -> 1, An Eye, Mercury, Man, Time

B or ▽ -> 2, Breasts, Venus, Woman, Love

C or ∪ -> 3, A Smile, Earth, Happiness, Energy

So, Mr. Hendricks, my invalid solution is, $TIME^3 + LOVE^3 = ENERGY^3$

My synopsis is that there has never been a solution, because the ABC's of things are not finite.

Time. Time is said to be an illusion, and quantifying it would mean an end to it. It is as if you were going to try to calculate how long there was nothingness before the "Big Bang." (And how would you denominate it? As earth years would be non-convertible.) So (A) or (TIME) requires an 'about' prefix, '~'.

Love. Love is illusive, it comes and goes and one is lucky to count on it while it is around. One *can* quantify love (or at least try to): sex is the oldest vocation on earth, save salesmanship in Eden. While most print models are valued for a mere *look* of allure, high-dollar escorts exist as public displays of sexual prowess. Love can never be valued for its inherent or true value, which in my calculation is infinite. Love can only be compensated at the moment of agreement, and the market is very volatile. Prices èxist somewhere in the area of 'free' to 'not for all the money in the world.' That's the range most are looking to explore at every bar or club visit. So (B) or (LOVE) also requires an 'about' prefix ,'~', as no two interactions or transactions have ever been equal to another, EVER, Ever-Ever.

Energy. One inch of a Star Wars light-saber (said to be pure energy) has just the same amount of killing power as Darth Maul's Double Red Bow staff. Surface area makes it a little more difficult to kill your enemy with, though. (I'd aim for the femoral, the jugular is overly defended.) You cannot cube, nor add an 'about' to the standard of existence. Energy is inherently infinite, while yielding Infinity, and at the same time, being the product of Infinity. Inherently Infinite as potential energy- in the void of nothingness pre-Bang, stored energy- in its universal current form and constant energy- our implied future.

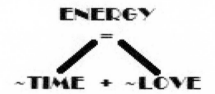

$$\text{ENERGY} = {\sim}\text{TIME} + {\sim}\text{LOVE}$$

Now, I know that this conjecture will never get me any TV time. Novelty, at best, I suppose. I was young.

Chapter II

Make It Yourself

Pizza

On a rainy April evening, Mom dropped me off at Mudshark Pizza. They were a local joint with eight picnic style tables on the inside and a small dining area outside. It couldn't have had more than fifteen employees. They made pizza, salads, wings, and offered wine and microbrews from its namesake brewery, a few miles away. There was also a six-game video arcade for the kids to play with while their pizzas were getting made. It was going to be summer and I needed a job. As there were no bicycling paperboys in Lake Havasu, either due to the distance between houses, or the murderous summer heat, I decided to pursue my fallback, dishwashing. I was hired soon thereafter, at $5.15 per hour. I would show up, and wash the dishes. No one fucked with me and I didn't have anything to do but keep my hands busy, and it was *not* always busy. After a couple months of getting it done, we closed up for the night and I asked one of the workers to make me a pizza to take home.

"Make it yourself." He replied. Not in a mean sort of way, more so phrased as a challenge. The boss, Mary, gave me the eye as if to say, 'Go for it, kid.' Now, I'm pretty good at learning by watching, or even sleeping on books to osmosise their content, so I wasn't particularly worried about completing this task.

I took a dough ball from the plastic container, rubbed the excess olive oil evenly on the ball, flattened it and placed it twice through the sheeter. A sheeter is a machine that flattens the dough for you. Either used out of lack of skill on the pizza maker's part or being in a small space where there is no room available to properly 'spread' or 'throw' the dough. A sheeter was necessary in this small kitchen. I gave it a couple Italian style throws in the air without busting a hole through it, and placed it on a round metal mesh screen. One ladle of sauce, spread to the crust in an even spiral. The proper amount of cheese was distributed fairly and pepperoni and olives were thrown on top, to finish it off. I turned around to put it on the oven conveyer belt. Mary and the delivery driver were staring at me. She looked at him and back at me and said, "Looks like we have our new pizza maker."

Yup, no more pruned hands for me. Now comes the lifestyle change of getting to make people their coveted pizzas on an hourly basis, just what I never knew I always wanted. Wait, no pay raise? No problem. I was moving upward. That's all that mattered. Being in the back of the house, I didn't realize just how much business the little pizza shop did. I mean, it's not like I had to wash pizza *boxes*. Deliveries never had an effect on my work, doing dishes. The new position, however, kept me on my toes for the whole four or five hour shift that I would work. I liked being busy and I liked making each pizza better than the one before.

By the time the summer was over, I had perfected my craft. During a sleepover at my Mom's friend Sherri's house in Laughlin, Nevada in the summer of 2000, I saw the movie that would forever alter the direction of my life. The movie was Men of Honor, with Robert DeNiro and Cuba Gooding, Jr. I knew then, pizza was only a means to an end.

I would visit the recruiting station in Lake Havasu a few weeks later. At the tender age of fifteen, I walked in and told the man behind the desk, who had a knot of chewing tobacco in his lip, that I wanted to fly for the Navy. He smiled and asked how old I was.

"Fifteen, Sir." He told me something to the extent that at sixteen, I could enter the Delayed Entry Program or DEP. I still visited him twice a month until I was able to put my intentions on paper. Summer was nearing its completion and after being at Mudshark for four months I was itching for something new. Not so much because I didn't like the job, I just felt, at that point, I should have been making at least $5.50 an hour. Brass tax, though, I felt that I should have been making more than others in my upcoming class. I would keep my ear to the ground for alternative opportunities.

One day, looking around for some reading material while going to the bathroom, I found Melody's abandoned Seventeen Magazine on the floor under a small pile of dirty clothes. In the back, there was an advertisement section of sorts. I saw a casting call for models at the Fiesta Mall in Phoenix. Now, there was one interlude between my calling as a child model (circa 1990 and the Gant Razor Circuit) and that moment of my life sitting on the Porcelain Goddess: Fond Du Lac, Wisconsin.

Back at 617 W. Main Street, there were no grand shopping adventures to be had, save for the Pamida, a good four miles west down Main. It was nothing to get excited about. To get to an actual shopping mall, one would have to drive twenty-five miles north to Fond Du Lac, Wisconsin. There was a bona-fide mall, complete with movie theater and food court. Going there was a staple for Melody, who would go with Miranda every time the chance arose, but was a treat for me, having only been there a handful of other times. The most memorable was watching "Titanic" on the big screen with Kira Kempfer, un-chaperoned. She was my first kiss (standing on the wood chips of the Jefferson Elementary School playground), first girlfriend soon after that and first breakup, once the realization that thirteen year-olds don't make for good long-distance relationships. Especially with long-distance phone calls being 5¢ a minute, it would have never worked out. But we did get to hold hands for the whole three-hour greatest movie ever made, and that still carries weight with me.

On this particular occasion, Mom drove Melody and I out just to walk the runway for an upcoming JCPenny's Fashion Show. When we got there, right outside JCPenny's, was a congregation of people. The woman running the casting call, Dawn Haase, from M.I.M.E. Productions, would have us all line up, tallest to shortest and have us walk, pivot, and then return to the starting spot. I don't remember being nervous but I do remember being proud of the clothes I picked out myself. It seemed, as a child, I could never dress properly and was surprised that Mom let me come to this outing without telling me what to put on or alter in any way what I chose to wear.

Well, Melody didn't make the cut, but I did. Booyah! Mark one for the underdog! The gig would require five more visits to the mall for rehearsals and one dress rehearsal after closing hours. I got suited up in a Mickey Mouse tuxedo that looked super fresh. Pocahontas was the newest Disney movie and that was the music that was playing when I did my catwalk.

I would come out of a circular turnstile and make my way to the end of the runway, flash the 'Mickster' adorning my vest, and turn around. Now, at this point, the turnstile would have rotated again revealing the girl opposite me in our 'scene'. She would walk out and as I approached her I would take her hand. As she walked by to make her way to *her* runway moment, I was to let her hand go, eye in eye, as if this was the last time we would meet. I would make my way back to the turnstile and they would push the rotate button and three seconds later I was backstage and my work was done. "You have to sing with all the voices of the mountain, you have to paint with all the colors of the windddddd......" Umm... mic drop?

Two months later, Dawn would call me up to recruit me for a cable commercial for the Appleton Mall. With, nonetheless, the same girl I let go in our Pocahontas scene. There was one problem, though; it was to be a Christmas commercial.

Dad was adamantly anti-Christmas, being a 'pagan holiday' and such. But to my surprise, Mom had little difficulty convincing him to allow it to happen. Aunt Patty drove us in her more reliable van with Melody, Miranda, Travis, Mom and I in tow. They weren't allowed 'on set' and hung out at the mall while I changed into the plaid pajama ensemble Dawn had picked out for me. There was a fully ornamented Christmas tree complete with faux presents underneath.

The opening scene would see Lindsay and I run to the tree like it was Christmas morning and shake the presents as if trying to guess what the haul would be. In the next scene, we knelt behind a large box with a big red bow on it, probably a 3x3 foot cube. Problem was she was a good four inches taller than me and was seen clearly over the top of the candy cane wrapping paper that adorned the box. My nose, however, barely made it over the edge of the monstrous gift. They had to call the pet store down the way and retrieved three bags of kitty litter for me to kneel on just to make the scene work. Dawn was making crazy side-to-side jumping-jack actions behind the camera to bring out the pure laughter and joy in us. The six-second scene would show Lindsay and I rifling through the bow, trying to find the tag and who it was meant for. (There was no tag.) They were satisfied with our second take.

The last scene was to advertise that if you showed up to Santa's Workshop at the mall, your kids would each get a free coloring book. So an arm covered in a Santa red and white sleeve and gloved hand, handed each of us a coloring book and we were to point and be super excited at all the 'fun' things that we could color. This was my first bit of real acting.

I felt that coloring was below my skillset, and a Rudolph, Santa's Elves and snowflake book for scribbles, really didn't do much in the way of exciting me. I still made it look good, though. For my 90 minutes worth of work, I received a $50 Gift Certificate to any store in the Appleton Mall and two free rides in the rollercoaster simulator machine that was positioned fifty feet from where we filmed the commercial.

It was a hydraulic ride/mini-movie screen enclosure that positioned up when climbing, and positioned down when falling. It even spun in 360 degrees to simulate the corkscrews. Neither of us dared hit the tap-out button. What a reward! I ended up buying a Green Bay Packer sweatshirt with the gift certificate. Next game, I would be geared up to make Uncle Jerry proud. Go Pack, Go!

So, Seventeen Magazine was on my bare lap with a model casting call staring me in the face, two weeks away. I had to at least try, right? If only just to see if I still had it in me. Mom and Dad weren't interested in taking me the three and a half hours to Phoenix. They both had full time jobs and were doing their best to make ends meet. So I ended up deciding that I would take a Greyhound to Phoenix with Mudshark money and stay at Mom's Cousin, Sue Sullivan's house. They were our first friendly face when we got to Arizona from Wisconsin.

Living in Mesa, a Phoenix suburb, they were on our way through and we stayed there for a few days to stretch our legs before heading out to Lake Havasu. I thought it was cool that she had a parrot, a Scarlet Macaw. When the bird and I first met, Sue was astonished as the bird started regurgitating its food for me.

"She thinks you are her baby." Sue said. I just smiled and thought it was neat. After that unique experience, I would be so inspired as to write an English paper on parrots. They are fascinating creatures. I was excited to see my Momma parrot, again. I wondered if she would recognize me after this little bit of time.

Mom got on the phone with Sue and made sure me staying over for a couple days would be ok. It was. I bought the bus ticket that would have me show up in Phoenix the day before the casting call. Sue's husband picked me up from the station. Nice guy, even though we didn't talk much. It was night out and I went to bed soon after I arrived at Sue's house. We left for the mall at two o'clock the next afternoon. Sue dropped me off and said that she would meet me outside the food court at 6:00 PM. I thanked her, again, for her hospitality. And in the same clothes I rode the bus in, same backpack, too, I walked through the doors of the Fiesta Mall.

The line of people that was set up was immediately recognizable as not being your little Fond Du Lac, Wisconsin 'Cotton-Eyed Joe' production. There were at least 200 people waiting to walk the runway and minders from Macy's walking around asking if anyone wanted a spritz of cologne, or a puff of perfume. Of course, I did. There were not many guys there so I thought this was promising, mathematically. A Hispanic girl behind me caught my eye. I tried to stay focused, but I couldn't help watching her get perfumed.

"Hi." She said as our eyes met with a little smile.

"Hi." I said back. I couldn't just say nothing, there were like a hundred and fifty people in front of us inching their way to the thirty-foot long, raised runway. I was stuck. She was part of a trio. Her name was Veronica, her friend, Erica, and Veronica's Mom, Bea Salas. We talked as the line started moving. She lived in Gilbert, another city in the Phoenix Metro area. She was there just to 'see what would happen.'

"I've never done this type of thing before," she said. I went into a bit of my story, and as much as her talkative friend tried to steer the conversation, I'm sure Veronica's Mom saw exactly what was happening. I couldn't get her shy smile out of my head. My turn to walk came, and the woman with the headset told me to walk up the three stairs and go, on her mark.

"What do I do with my backpack?" I asked nervously. She told me to "use it as a prop." So I did. I strolled down the runway with the backpack swinging at my side. When I got to the end of the runway, I flung it up over my shoulder and gave a turn that would have made Dawn break into cartwheels. "He has got it!" I could hear her say, in my mind.

I walked back and down the stairs, thinking I nailed it. I remember when the woman with the headset got on the intercom and said to the remaining aspiring talent, "Be sure to look at the judges as you walk back."

What! What kind of modeling 'gig' is this? What about the '1000-yard stare?' Oh well, Veronica was up and I watched her float down the runway. She came back, got permission to split from her Mom, and we three kids went off to burn the thirty minutes or so before they announced who the producers were going to pick.

We got to the upper level via the escalator and I saw a rowdy bunch of six or seven guys make their way to the runway. They were, no doubt, there at the just the right time and place. They didn't strike me as being at the mall for a modeling try-out, but they all hurriedly made it to the line, at the bitter end. They did backflips on the runway! "Look at the judges?" Backflips on the runway? I was in the twilight zone. Backflips! Ugh.

It was getting dark outside and Veronica's mom met up with us before the final picks were announced. All of the 'backflip boys' got recruited. While it was a little disappointing to not hear my name called, I did have a good time. Veronica and her friend didn't get chosen, either, and her mom looked like she was in the mood to go. I walked them to their car. When we got to their sedan, I leapt.

"Can I have your number?" She looked over at her Mom and got the nod. '480-545-8154 —Veronica' she scribbled on the back of a Kohl's receipt.

"I'll call you." I said.

"You do that." She replied. I watched them drive off.

6:15 PM… FUCK! Food Court!

Lake Havasu High School

10th grade, sophomore year, turned out to be much a continuation of the 8th grade public school societal hierarchy. I didn't get bullied much, as I was more so just ignored by most of the males in my grade. Exception for the occasional derogatory slight hurled my direction in passing, and I was fine with that. It seemed violence, or the threat of violence was left in Wisconsin.

Chad Donovan was the leader of the skater boys. Kacy Jacobs was student body president, while Kristin Wilson was still cheer captain, and quite deserving if I must say. It was just as I left everything in 1999. I was, once again, relegated to being looked at as the "faggot" friend of the popular girls because I neither participated in sports nor was ever spotted on a skateboard, but I did get to eat right next to Kacy.

Veronica and I would talk for hours each night, which kind of made the novelty of sitting next to the girl I once adored most, lose its luster. With Veronica now taking top billing in the area of my affection, the only one not happy with this scenario was my Mom, when she would get the phone bills. I would lie out on the trampoline, a stowaway from Wisconsin, and stare at the constellation Orion while talking to the girl who actually gave me the time of day, well, night. She would listen to me and my Navy dreams, and I would listen to her and her dreams of being a TV News Reporter. I was ever reluctant to officially 'ask her out' because I was only fifteen and didn't see the importance of having a title but not having each other to hold. I did hatch the plan to invite her to homecoming, though.

I saved up to get a limo for me and a group of three other girls and my one guy friend, Chase. Veronica's Mom drove her in from Gilbert and got a hotel room. I gave the limo driver the addresses of the others to get picked up and we would make our stops, getting out at each residence to take pictures. I had pizza and soda stocked in the limo. Veronica wore a black dress and I had a corsage ready for her. I booked the limo for the two hour minimum so, after all the pickups were made, I had the driver drive the twenty minutes north to the Pilot Travel Center, where Highway 95 meets the I-40, and back. It made for a cool start to the night.

Veronica and I danced for some time, and then we made our way out of the gym. We were briefed that if we left the building we wouldn't be allowed back in, but I really wanted to show her the grounds of my high school. Plus, this was the only night she would be in town, and I wanted to see her under the stars that inspired our sometimes hours-long conversations.

When our walk was done, with thirty minutes of the dance left, I smooth-talked our way back in. I finally mustered the nerve to kiss her, and was received. I remember seeing the proverbial flash of light, but that was just Katie Del La Torre, one of my limo attendees, taking a picture in the darkened gym, not some spirit-shattering moment. I didn't have the limo booked to chauffeur any of us home, so everyone had rides, accordingly. Veronica and I went with Chase and his girlfriend, Stacy Riggenbacker, to Chase's house. Chase's dad was in failing health, and wasn't really interested in what we were doing.

Three weeks prior, when I was scouting for the limo, I paid the owner/driver twenty bucks to pick up Chase and his dad for a 15 minute ride. This meant a lot to Chase, seeing that his dad had never been in a limo before, and that still carries weight with me.

Once at Chase's house, we quickly branched off to our own areas. Mine and Veronica's was the spare bedroom. We innocently made out for a half an hour until it was time to take her back to her Mom's hotel room. We parted ways and I told her that I would call her the next day.

"You do that," she smirked.

Weeks later, she started talking about how her Mom wanted me to go with her family to Disneyland over Christmas break. Her Mom was going to pay for everything and I thought it sounded great. I had never been to Disneyland. I had been to Six Flags Magic Mountain in Valencia, California a couple times, but was under no illusion that Six Flags carried any counterweight to actual Disneyland. Then, the bombshell:

"When we go, we can't do anything though, I have a boyfriend." My blueprint of asking her out on the top of a roller-coaster, maybe the Matterhorn, or while the Ferris wheel was stopped with us in the highest position, was ruined. I couldn't believe what I had just heard. Why didn't I ask her out sooner? I promptly threw away the Build-a-Bear and airbrushed T-shirt she gave me at homecoming. The shirt, made at a fair, heralded "Clifford and Veronica ~ Para Siempre." Forever didn't last like it used to. Well, that was disappointing, I thought. Communication ceased.

So, I just kept pressing on. With my new found 'get out of hell, free' card with the Navy, this state and everyone in it, were just one foregone conclusion. I had to finish school first, though.

I realized, very soon on, that the pre-calculus class they had placed me in would have to be altered. I didn't end my Telesis math blitz by finishing on the bitter end of their textbook. I was closer to the second quarter of their offering. So, when I got to the Pre-Calculus class, which had some Juniors but mostly Seniors in it, they opened to the first chapter. I had to wait until the end of the class to tell the teacher that I had already learned the subject matter. They shot me the next day to the Honors Pre-Calc class. Fashionably late, what a way to make an entrance!

My new teacher, Keri Thompson, was the girls' volleyball coach and I was instantly hooked. Something about smart women, even then, just got to me. The slight rasp to her voice made math **sound** sexy. Mrs. Thompson was Sporty Spice to Mrs. Matzdorf's Baby Spice. I settled in just fine, the only 'jock' in Mrs. Thompson's class was Dusty Lockman, the starting Varsity Quarterback. Come year end, he would pen an unforgettable line in my yearbook, "I think they made the movie Baby Geniuses after you!" It was a shout out to the fact that Keri would let me sleep during her class knowing I wouldn't lower her class's collective GPA any. I was far from being an 'A' student, but maintained nicely at the lower end of the 'B' threshold. The other classes posed no threat to me and were dealt with in B or C fashion. School wasn't really the draw of attention at this point in my life, work was. So when I saw in the newspaper that Papa John's was hiring, I felt it was my position to lose.

Carl Beech, a fair-skinned, Buell-riding, bona-fide badass, was the General Manager. He was a take-no-prisoners type of leader. Papa John's official line was that they wouldn't hire anyone under sixteen years old, but with my little bit of previous experience, franchises have a little leeway to stray from corporate guidance. I was in.

The first thing I noticed was a Little Caesar's plush doll hanging by a noose in his office, a satanic talisman that would come to fruition a mere year later, when Carl would put them out of business. Papa John's in Lake Havasu City was a BUSY store. We ran about $20,000 worth of pizza a week through those front doors and I was immensely proud to be part of something of that caliber.

Over the first few weeks, I wouldn't touch a pizza. Carl had me training on phones, prepping toppings, and the endless and thankless task of gluing coupons on pizza boxes, and then folding them up. (To the tune of hundreds a day.) Carl wouldn't even let anyone clock in till the phones started raging and a sizable backlog of pizza orders were in the queue. This kept his labor costs down. Eventually, I would make it to the make-line where I would portion and top pizza's in an assembly line fashion. Then, I would train to become a decent oven-tender, putting the right pizzas in the right boxes and getting them set for the delivery drivers. Finally, I was brought into the cool kid's club, Carl's baby, the dough station. To toss dough in Carl's Papa John's was the highest honor one could achieve in his store. There were only three, besides himself, that he allowed to be the foundation to every product that left his store.

His 'girls' were Laurie Edziak, a short, blonde, beauty. Stephanie Kutil, a taller, purple-haired punk-rocker who was best friends with Laurie. (While they were on the clock, anyways.) Also, there was Jennifer Thompson, who sat behind me in my math class, but of no relation to the teacher. I think that Carl liked working with girls, and I didn't blame him. Jennifer was on her way out, finding a job at another pizza place in town, which, I believed, made room for me at the dough table. During the shift, Carl and Laurie would take the same smoke breaks and have full on conversations while churning out nonstop crust after crust, not to mention, the occasional cheesestick or breadstick order. Those were the three pillars of the Papa John's system.

I can still remember the commercials making fun of Domino's and their endless gimmicky pizza offerings. "The Hanging Garden Pizza", "The Volcano Pizza," a few other crazy examples, then, "At Papa John's we do one thing and one thing well, that is make hand-tossed Pizza, Breadsticks and Cheesesticks. And we really believe that better ingredients do make a better pizza. Better Ingredients. Better Pizza. Papa John's." Today, the big three pizza makers are, as far as marketing is concerned, indistinguishable. I guess everyone has their price.

Laurie would teach me the tricks of the trade. Her nimble fingers would pull back on the round edge of the dough and then flick and spread the edge in rapid successive movements to make the perfect crust in seconds. For the first couple weeks of my new job detail, she would form the crust and I would stretch the dough to size. Ten inches for a small pizza, fourteen for a large and sixteen for an extra-large. Soon, I would be taking Laurie's place next to Carl, on her days off. He would form the crust and then toss them over for me to stretch, a couple feet to his right. "Fly! Be Free!" he would say in a high pitched voice. Still makes me laugh thinking about it. It wasn't always fun and games, though.

Running a high-volume restaurant meant estimating how busy you would be and how much product you would use. The computer systems have a logarithm to determine the proper amount of supplies to order, but even the best calculations can sometimes go awry. I remember for a period of three weeks he tried to make up for an over-ordered slow week by keeping dough that was two and three days expired. Now, I was never under the impression that it could have made someone sick, you couldn't even tell by looking at it that it was sub-par for use. But as for the integrity of the business, they don't put expiration dates on products as mere guidelines. Dough costs about fifty cents per dough ball and he didn't want to chalk up the loss on his statistics. So, I posed a question to corporate via their website.

"If the expiration sticker on a tray of dough says 'June 13th through June 20th', does it need to be thrown out at the end of day on the 20th or within twenty-four hours after that?" Clearly, the ramifications of this seemingly mundane question were not fully thought out. Two days later, Carl called me into his office, his computer screen lit up with a copy of the email.

"What the FUCK is this?" He asked angrily as he pointed to the screen.

I peered closer and noticed it was my inquiry and answered back, slyly, "It's a question."

"Get the fuck out of my store!" He demanded.

Not really processing what had just happened, I left. Walking out to the parking lot I saw Kim, one of the delivery drivers.

"Carl just fired me," I said in a downtrodden matter-of-fact way. I had made myself an integral part of the team and I trusted everyone knew that it wouldn't be quite the same without me.

"That sucks." She said. "You're a cool kid, I'm sure you'll find more work. It was great getting to work with you." The chilly February air bit a little colder as I got into my '86 Ford Taurus and drove home.

Arizona is a right-to-work state, so there were no ramifications for this controversial firing. However, I do remember the week following when the owner, Rich Goldwater, came to my house and picked me up. We parked off road at a peaceful spot and he expressed his sympathies about what went down and asked me what I wanted to happen.

Naïve to the max I responded, "I want Carl fired."

"I can't do that." He replied. Nor should he have *wanted* to. Carl ran a restaurant that was what turned out to be something like twenty dollars a day shy of being a Million Dollar store. That is a big deal in the fast-food pizza industry. I'm sure there is a Rolex of some sort involved, along with the Goldwater bonus of $10,000 cash. I can't imagine missing out on all that for a few upsold two-liters of Coke and a couple cheesesticks a day. We parted ways not having come to any agreements, but I was respectful of the unsolicited concern Rich showed in asking for my time. At least I didn't try to ask for a severance package.

My unemployment actually turned out to be timed quite well. When Jennifer found out about what happened to me at Papa John's she told me where to apply. She had been working for an old Italian man named Arturo, who owned Arturo's Pizza & Pasta. She had found a new job at a carpet store where the hours were more stable and told me he was hard to understand but nice to work for. She gave me his number and I met with him a few days later.

Arturo's Pizza & Pasta amounted to one single stack brick oven, one four-burner gas stovetop, one Hobart dough mixer and one marble-topped make station inside of a shared kitchen. Half the building was a biker bar. The other half was a sit-down restaurant where patrons could order American cuisine from the main restaurant, The Pour House, or pizza & pasta from Arturo.

It was just him and I that accounted for the pizza & pasta side of things. No delivery. Just dine-in and pickup. He also sold pizza by the slice to the bar, through a little kitchen window. It wasn't a bad setup. It was painstakingly slow, though. To kill the time, we would play chess. Arturo would sit on a bag of frozen peas to alleviate his hemorrhoidal pain. I would learn how to roll Top cigarettes for him, as he would occasionally smoke in the kitchen, usually while simmering a pot of pasta sauce or keeping a keen eye on the baking slices of oiled eggplant, as to not overcook them. Real Godfather-like. We had many worthy matches between orders, even though I could probably count on my right hand the amount of times I actually beat him.

I turned sixteen before I got fired by Carl and by the time I got settled in with Arturo, I was months into the Delayed Entry Program with Aviation Technician 2nd Class Petty Officer Richard Crayne, as my recruiter. I would be required to show up and study the basics of Navy life: ranks of Officers and Enlisted personnel, names of the parts of a ship, and some basic Navy lingo.

A 'wall' is called a 'bulkhead' and a 'water-fountain' is called a 'scuttlebutt,' which I always found amusing to say. Once a month or so, we would go to the track at Rotary Park and do some physical training. I was no feat of modern masculinity, but still managed to do what was required of me. I had taken the practice ASVAB test and scored in the mid-80s which out of a possible 99 meant that I could do just about anything that the Navy offered. My original dream of flying for the Navy took a backseat as Petty Officer Crayne told me that I could apply for Officer Candidate School, or OCS, once I enlisted and got to a command. This is Navy Recruiter fantasy 101. "Get him in and ship him off," that was the bulk of his duty. And, although I didn't see it back then, I definitely understand that now.

After diverting my flight plans, I had my sights set on becoming a nuclear engineer. The main draw was the enlistment bonus. After completing the six month training program, I would receive a $16,000 cash bonus. That was a big deal to me. That could cover the three C's of my new Navy life: car, computer and clothes. The fourth 'C', Christmas, wouldn't be that bad either. I still had to graduate high school, though. I wondered how I could speed this process up.

Mohave Community College, our local College, was offering what amounted to two free classes for high school students over the spring semester. Not only did I take full advantage of this program, I even paid for one additional class. My caseload was Customer Service & Sales, Basic Ground School & Set Production and Design. Customer Service class was taught by Mark Fresh, one of my social studies teachers from Telesis. He ran for city government a couple times, never gained traction, but kept teaching. He was engaging, and a genuinely good human being. Basic Ground School was fun, as I was still fascinated with flying, even though I wouldn't be doing it right away for the Navy. I figured I might as well have some foundational insight if I was to try to go the Officer route, once enlisted. I don't know if I could take command of a plane now because of that class, but I am pretty confident that if I had to land a passenger plane, I would cause minimal damage in doing so. Just stall it onto the runway, no problem.

Set Production & Design was the most involved class, though. We put on a production of "Cabaret" with a local show producer Grace Ann Echajabrea-Jacobs. It was quite the undertaking. By the time the run was ready for audience, I knew every song by heart and would sing and dance to them backstage, to the actual actor's and actress's amusement. I was put in charge of the pulley system that was the center focal point of the stage. One sequined screen for the Cabaret scenes, and a straight black curtain for the other scenes. I donned all black, complete with gloves and a black beanie that I cut eyeholes in and sewed up in back. I looked like a dark Spiderman. I aced all the classes. I remember one review that came in that said that the College's production of "Cabaret" was the best that that California critic had ever seen. Definitely an experience I will never forget.

Summer came and my days would start with wakeboarding early mornings with John Rosenbaum or J.R., as he preferred to be called. He was a real-estate developer opposite my father's tile labor, in town. J.R. would get 'first wake' on his slalom ski, while Dad commanded the decked out inboard machine. Next, Dad would hop on his O'Neil slalom and get his fill. Then it was my turn, with an orange 'Wake-Tech' wakeboard. J.R. told me that by the end of the summer he wanted to see the '69' decals on the bottom of the board, up in the air. He would get his wish. Dad took the picture. Great shot, pop.

When we were done we would pull the boat out of the lake and wipe it down with a mix of apple cider vinegar and water in a spray bottle. It made for no water spots and it didn't smell too bad, either. Afternoons and evenings would be spent at Arturo's, while still maintaining my adherence to the Navy recruiter's office. School would be back in session soon and I started to crunch some numbers. "If I really focused, this could be my last year of school." I began musing. Just the thought of it filled me with a certain amount of duty. "If I can, I must." I was determined.

The high school open house passed and I got my schedule. Honors calculus and honors physics topping the list of intensive classes. Mrs. Thompson would vouch for me to the Calculus teacher Mr. Chisinsky, when he questioned the legitimacy of a junior being in his class. I would visit the guidance counselor soon thereafter.

"I want to graduate this year." I said confidently.

"That's impossible." She retorted. The gauntlet was thrown. I loved nothing like a challenge.

"Look, with the college classes I took in the spring, the pre-requisite Spanish class I took at Telesis (which turned out to be just a second English class), plus the Algebra 1-2 class I took at Thunderbolt in 8th grade, I should only be eight credits shy of graduating. If you give me Senior English and I make up the rest of the credits at Mohave Community College, I should have no problem getting the twenty-six needed to graduate." She didn't have my 8th grade algebra credit in her system, but after some looking, she seemed to come to the realization that it was, at the minimum, *possible*.

"You would need like five college classes." Of which, I had planned to take some low level math classes and just test out of them for the credit and not have to attend.

"I know." I replied matter-of-factly. I had done my homework. I had my eye on a couple of Business Math classes, and a Human Resources class, that I ended up being forced to withdraw from because I couldn't afford the course book. I did get some free knowledge from the teacher though, who used to work for Nestle: "The most expensive part of a chocolate bar... is the wrapper."

"Ok, I'll put you in Mrs. Grey's Senior English." I was already packing my bags.

With a 7AM drama class added to my first semester workload, I would even have a surplus of credits by years end, in theory. Nothing like frontloading an already heavy schedule, right? I have always been a fan of working hard in the present to set yourself up to enjoy the future you are working toward, whenever that time would come. Now, I just kicked it into high gear.

I walked to school on a Tuesday morning ready to give my first drama presentation to Mr. Travsoski when things started to get a little frantic. While the class was gathering, waiting for the teacher, another staff member came in and told us that classes were cancelled for the day. This would have been around 6:45AM Mountain Standard Time on September 11th, 2001. I walked back home to turn on the TV and watch the real life emergency play out, live.

I got home to turn on Fox10 News. (We still didn't have cable.) I was glued to replay after replay of the second tower getting hit by a passenger plane. The ramifications of what cancelled the world that day didn't sink in until the narrative started developing in the days following. Video recordings of the moment President Bush was whispered to, in the middle of a class reading a book about a goat, has always stuck with me. The onslaught of the dog-whistle words like, 'Muslim Extremists' and 'terrorism', were the drumbeats of a script that had seemingly already been written and was now just getting presented. The wave of newfound 'bandwagon patriotism' really irked me.

Over the previous three months, I had developed a rapport with a disk jockey at the local Havasu country radio station, KFLG. We started talking after she recognized how I would routinely call to request Lee Greenwood's "Proud to be an American," on the weekend show. She turned out to be a former service member who served in Desert Storm. I let her know that I was going to be joining the Navy, and from that moment on, every time I called in, we would exchange communications for fifteen seconds more than her normal request calls.

All of a sudden people were calling in multiple times daily to request that song. Whatever. I was proud to be an American before being *told* or *shown* why I should be proud, and that still carries weight with me.

September 11th marked the last time I showed up for drama class. God must not have wanted me to be an actor if he brought down two towers and 2700 people to stop me from presenting an acting bit. Not to mention demolishing WTC #7 (which held its own trove of financial documents), the Pentagon (with all video evidence scrubbed from history) and the incident in Shanksville, PA. Point taken, God. December came around soon enough and my 17th birthday fell on a Monday, in 2001.

After school on Tuesday, my Mom and I were at Petty Officer Crayne's desk ready to sign papers. One thing that struck me, was how he needed both parents to be witnessed signing my enlistment paperwork. AT2 Crayne, once my Mom left, asked me if I could get my father to sign the document and return it to him. I thought nothing of it then, it was almost like my first mission, but upon review of Military Records, seeing my recruiter's signature in the area that explicitly states that the signer had been in the presence of, and witnessed, the guardians of the minor enlistee, sign the document, made me feel uneasy. It was as if the integrity of the entire United States Navy was invalidated from the onset by this falsified oath of witness for this soul-procuring document. "Get him in and ship him off." Right, Crayne?

I would end up dropping Calculus and Physics after Christmas break to lighten my homework caseload. (I think 'Christmas Break' was still politically correct to say, back then.) I would pick up two early morning study hall classes in their place. Mr. Hamilton, the facilitator, once he knew my situation, would let me play chess on the computer next to his desk and help him with the daily Havasu Herald's newspaper crossword when he got stumped. He was the whiz, I was the wildcard. We made a good team. With my five classes at MCC completed or tested out of, second semester was going to be a cakewalk, and it was. Until Mrs. Grey threw a parasitic wrench into my good fortune.

I still don't know how in a publicly funded school system, you can show up and do the work and then have one essay, or one assignment, worth such a portion of your grade that if you fail to complete it, or fail to do well on it, your entire semester of effort will have been for naught. Then, adding more caveats to the fray by qualifying that even a fully completed six page, double-spaced essay would not even be **graded** if not accompanied with a FUCKING COVER SHEET! Well, did I set the stage well enough? By completing a masterful paper, but in a rush of paper-printing, I glossed over the

31

ever-important cover page. My fate was sealed. Unaware that I was handing in a paper soon to be labeled dead-on-arrival, a mere four weeks before graduation, I handed in the last assignment standing between me and the Navy, between me and my future, between me and my fate.

"I'm not accepting this," she spouted as I walked away, in a fit of accomplishment. There should have been a line of people on each side of me, high-fiving me out the door. Real American Hero, coming through!

"Clifford!" Oh, shit, she was talking to me. I turned to face her. "There is no cover sheet, I'm not reading this," she said smugly as she thrust the documents in my direction. I smiled confidently, and held up my index finger calmly, courteously telling her without words to 'hold a moment' while I rustle the certainly uncollected cover sheet from my black JanSport backpack. "Wrong finger," I told myself, as my hand came back empty from the bag. The avalanche of excuses that instantly came to mind, if verbalized, would have amounted to nothing. She was almost *happy* that she caught someone in her snare of red tape. "Stay calm, Clifford, you can figure this out," I thought as I walked, bewildered, down the hall to a seeming uncertain future.

I'll save you the theatrics: For a mere $200 I was able to procure a 'correspondence class' from Brigham Young University in Utah, for English 102. Go Cougars! I had to order two small novels from an online retailer and everything was done online. I had to submit two written book reports by mail to the teacher in Provo, and finish a total of ten or so online multiple choice 'tests' on course subject matter. They were graded online, instantly. With no other homework to speak of from the high school, I focused every spare moment on completing the course. Ten days before graduation, on May 10th, 2002, I brought my guidance counselor the printed transcript on BYU letterhead.

"Well," she said, "You proved me wrong. Congratulations." With all respect due her, and I feel not much was merited in this circumstance, my mental response still rings true: "I didn't prove you WRONG, I proved me RIGHT," and that still carries weight with me.

Although I had told Arturo, in December, that I would have to leave him that summer because I was joining the Navy, his response remains an allegory on why communication is so important.

"Ah, you should have told me before you signed. I was planning on retiring soon and was going to give you the store." Although, even now, looking back, I don't think there was anything that was going to sway my decision to serve. Even something as life changing as being handed a marginally profitable business on a silver platter, to build and grow as I deemed fit, was quite an opportunity, side-stepped.

Working with Arturo on Prom night proved to be busier than normal and I couldn't leave him, in good conscience, without help, so I stayed. I was an hour and a half late to a prom date I had no business asking out in the first place, Devin Molzhan. Her dad owned a masonry company in town and I have no idea how I worked myself into that situation, but prom that year was a train wreck from the get-go.

There was construction going on for the new school gymnasium. The old gym had already been torn down. So the student council, instead of having prom in a hotel ballroom, somehow came up with the brilliant, cost-saving idea of having prom in the, uh, high-school *parking lot*. So, yes, there was a big circus tent and we danced on a graded asphalt floor. It was like hiking Kilimanjaro to get to the punch bowl.

Devin and I still managed to get prom pictures of me in a suit and her in her pretty pink dress. Even writing about this glossed over moment in my life makes me cringe. I'm sorry I was such a bunk date, Devin. But to be fair, you still had Senior Prom to look forward to, at a real venue. That was it, for me.

No matter how much I would like to have the memory of her lips on mine at least once during that night, or at any time, EVER, it never manifested. I had no self-confidence that night, and smelled like yeast, olive oil and tomato paste. *I* wouldn't kiss me. The next day, Arturo had a card for me when I showed up to work.

Knowing that the business of the night before probably messed up my plans for that evening, he thanked me for staying and apologized unnecessarily, and threw in a twenty dollar bill as a supplemental thank you. Arturo would prove to be one of the unsung beacons of inspiration in my life. To live with the only woman you've ever loved, to run the same business that has supported your love throughout the decades, and to have the unwavering support of that same woman, made me realize, at seventeen years old, that is all I would ask out of life. I was eager to watch my future develop.

There was an award ceremony in the auditorium a few nights before the actual Cap & Gown graduation walk. This was used to congratulate and honor those who were receiving scholarships which were awarded directly from colleges, for an athletic scholarship, for instance, or any number of private local philanthropists. Many were the $500 or $1,000 varieties, awarded from a vast array of local businesses. The senior sport class was pretty active and every once in a while you would hear something big like, "Keri Motil, Volleyball Scholarship, NAU, $15,000." And the audience would cheer loudly. After a while, it was my recruiters turn to pimp out his recruits.

There were three other soon-to-be sailors in my graduating class, for those three went an announcement that they would receive

$18,000, the amount provided by the then Montgomery G.I. Bill. The crowd applauded. Then, my turn.

My recruiter unraveled an absurdly oversized check that had my name on it with the denominating value of my enlistment, in regards to college incentives, "$58,000." Consisting of the $18,000 from the G.I. Bill, along with the $40,000 Navy College Fund that I was granted, based on my ASVAB expectation, I remember hearing a few "wows," the rest of the crowd was shocked to silence. A slow applauds followed. Of the entire senior graduating class, I was the one who was promised the most for continuing education. Not a bad haul for a kid who couldn't even vote yet.

Monday, May 20th, 2002, I walked across the stage, erected on the football field, with my purple cap & gown and received my diploma case.   The actual diplomas were handed out after the ceremony, apparently in an attempt to ensure there would be no streakers.   It was the administration's last show of power before releasing us into the electorate. I'll let them have that one. They earned it. Nice try, Mrs. Grey! Still couldn't stop me! Mrs. Thompson, I love you! Class of 2003... males in particular... top this! Maybe they will hand out skateboard scholarships where you can get some new wheels for your dumb wood-planks of injury. Ok, I just now had to exercise those demons.

I hold no ill will toward anyone at my High School.   My yearbook actually did get signed by Chad Donovan, skater extraordinaire, it read: "I used to think you were gay as fuck, but then I got to know you, and I think you are pretty cool. Have a great summer!" I think I helped him in social studies a couple times. But that shit made me cry. What can I say? I've always been me.

Prejudices only block you from expanding your information base. By blocking someone out you think is different and not trying to understand them, on even a basic level, just limits your current personal growth trajectory, and handicaps you in dealing with future people of the same caliber. Always be learning, always be growing. Write that down.

With a handshake and a hug I dispatched Arturo on Monday, August 5th, 2002. He told me I was the best employee he ever had. And if you've never had a career restaurateur tell you those words, you'll never know the feelings associated with receiving them.

I hung out with Kacy Jacobs, one last time. We drove around in my Taurus cranking "Heartbreaker" by Pat Bennitar, or was it Stevie Nicks? I had my seat reclined back and my left foot resting out of the window on the side mirror while maneuvering the winding Havasu streets.   Guaranteeing me a reckless driving ticket, if caught, the laughs I got from her, though, were priceless and worth the risk. To this day, every time I hear that song, I think of that car ride. So many years of poetry that would never see the light of day, dedicated her way. "DTKJ" was code at the bottom of every page I wrote, meaning, "Dedicated To Kacy Jacobs." Just once, I wanted the underdog to get the girl, to be the hero. Maybe one day.

My last week in Havasu was like hearing the clicks underneath the seat of the rollercoaster you're strapped to. As you approach the top, the track starts to disappear from sight and soon you're left looking at nothing but sky. And as those clicks click slower you realize it's all just organized chaos from here on out.

Welcome to the ride.

Welcome to my life.

Chapter III

Getting There

Richard Crayne called me into the recruiter's office on Tuesday, August 6th. The trip to Phoenix to the Military Enlisted Personnel Station or MEPS was scheduled for Thursday, two days away. Located in the center of Lake Havasu, I would show up at the recruiter's office for what would prove to be the last time.

"Request permission to come aboard," I saluted the flag on my left then faced and saluted my recruiter.

"Permission granted." He chimed back with a half-hearted salute. I walked in and sat down at his desk. "You ready for Phoenix?" He asked. He knew damn well I had been ready since the day I walked in, two years prior.

"Yup," I answered nonchalantly. He gave me a small cup with an orange lid and nodded his head to the left to where the bathrooms were located in the building that housed all four Department Of Defense recruitment offices. I got it. You wouldn't want to waste all the time driving me hours away just to have me pop positive for marijuana and make you look bad. On the same token, I *did* have to get a marijuana waiver, saying that once when I was fifteen, at Telesis, I indeed smoked marijuana while hanging out with some classmates. I did inhale. I then immediately went to the bathroom to see if my eyes were bloodshot. They weren't, false advertising. So, with that in mind I took no offense to taking this test.

"On it," I said. In the ten minutes that followed the air changed. He looked at the test strip and asked me if I was *sure* I hadn't been around anyone who had smoked. I didn't know if he was just fucking with me, but I assured him that I, nor anyone I have been in contact with, had been doing drugs.

"Alright. Well, I'll pick you up at 0900 on Thursday. Stay out of trouble." Yeah, you know me, I thought.

Thursday proved to be a big day. I remember not everyone was at home and I wasn't even able to say goodbye to my little brother, Mitchell, who was playing catch with his friends at the high school baseball field. Crayne showed up on schedule and I threw my backpack containing a change of clothes in the back of the government Dodge sedan and made my way to the passenger seat.

Time was tight, and I tried to hold in my laughter as, before we even got to Phoenix, we got pulled over for speeding. No paper ticket or warning was given. The good old boys club, I thought. We finally got to the building and I entered fearlessly.

What followed would be a series of tests. They checked and documented the basics: height, weight, blood pressure & pulse. They had me do the 'duck walk' to ensure I didn't have flat feet or some unnamable syndrome that would prevent me from mounting a proper defense of my country. The core of my visit was centered on taking my official ASVAB test. This would solidify my qualifications and ability to move forward with my training as a Nuclear Engineer. The others and I sat in front of a computer screen which had a keyboard where only four useable letters were displayed. "A B C D" were spaced evenly on the center row of keys. We were given some basic testing instructions.

"If you encounter a problem, raise your hand. Once you proceed to the next page you cannot go back and change your answers. This will be a timed test," and so on. Just give me the questions, already. Not surprising to me, I was the first one done and was allowed to leave the room after the facilitator had ensured I had properly submitted my completed test. An eye exam followed.

I've always needed glasses, but rarely wore them, so I wasn't shocked when my eye exam came back less than perfect. The hearing test came next, where they would sit me in a soundproof cubicle and then they would beam alternating high and low pitched tones into a set of headphones and I was instructed to raise the hand associated with the ear the sound was coming from. Right ear, raise your right hand. Left ear, raise your left hand. Finally, they took me into a darkened room and gave me another eye exam. This one, you may be familiar with, interweaves colored circles with numbers to try to trick you into seeing a number that isn't there. Do I sound jaded?

At roughly 5:00 PM, once all the tests were concluded, I met back up with Petty Officer Crayne. With a little sealed manila envelope, he asked if I was ready for my ASVAB results.

"How do you think you did?" I remember him asking.

"Good. I don't think I did great on the mechanical section, but the rest was a breeze." I replied. I was never one to understand or be curious about how a car engine works. He opened the envelope and shuffled through some papers. Stopping on one page, his face contorted.

"Are you sure you did ok?" He looked concerned.

"What did I get?!" I was getting irritated now, and nervous. Did I somehow blow the test?

Crayne replied downtrodden, "Cliff, with these scores, I won't be able to process you tomorrow." I grabbed for the paper incredulously as he started laughing. Dick move. "You got a 90!" He finally let me know. Later, he would tell me that was the highest score that he had recruited out of Lake Havasu City.

"You're an asshole!" I started laughing, too. As he was looking over other documents, he handed me the ASVAB sheet. Sure as hell, even better than I did on the fifty question test back at the recruiter station. A 90! I was beside myself. Then came a ruffling of a few pages, a half-bend to peer onto the next page. I could tell something was legitimately not right. "What?" I asked.

"It's your eye exam." He said.

"Yeah, I know, I need glasses." I offered, not ashamed.

"No, Cliff, it says that you failed the colorblind test..." I waited, still not understanding the significance, "...and to be a nuke, you cannot be colorblind."

"You mean..." I choked up.

"I'm sorry." He wasn't joking this time and it somehow hit me super hard. I found the nearest wall, sat on the ground with my back to it and started crying. For two years and a sacrificed senior year, all the work I had put into this moment to just have it stripped away because I saw a thirteen instead of an eight on a colored dot test, in a low lit room, was just incomprehensible. In what instance would the fate of the country have ME being the one to diffuse a nuclear bomb? Like, in what world would they tell me to clip the red wire and I instead would clip the blue? Grass is green, sky is blue and blood runs red. But at that moment I had no grasp on anything. This meant no $16,000 bonus, no matter what I signed on to do, FUCK!

"Look, you don't have to go through with this if you don't want to." Crayne said, comfortingly.

"I came to join and that's what I am going to do. What else can I do?" I shot back, not even thinking I could have had a free pass back to Arturo's.

"Let's find out." Crayne found an admin person who welcomed me into their office. My head being in nothing but an all-out tailspin, I remember nothing of the conversation, save the job I agreed to: Cryptologic Technician Communications, or CTO.

Basically, in 2002, when computers were big, slow, and expensive, I figured the next best career to have would be in that field. I would need to pass a background check, as the job required a $60,000 Top Secret/SCI security clearance. So maybe this wouldn't be such a bad thing after all. It was a rather small community, with many different 'CT' varieties. To name a few were CTA, CTI, CTM, CTO, CTT, and CTR all with their respective specialties and all with their compartmentalized top secret info base. A CTO is basically an Above Top Secret Network Administrator. My job would be to ensure that wherever I was, ship or sea, I would be able to communicate with any other command on earth. It sounded challenging, but right up my alley, so the job switch was entered into the system and thirty minutes later I took my oath of enlistment.

"I, Clifford Frederick Gant, do solemnly swear that I will support and defend the Constitution of the United States against all enemies, foreign and domestic; that I will bear true faith and allegiance to the same; and that I will obey the orders of the President of the United States and the orders of the officers appointed over me, according to the regulations and the Uniform Code of Military Justice. So help me God."

I was dropped off at the hotel I would depart from the next day with a parting nugget of wisdom from my recruiter, "Don't jerk off, it'll fuck up your urinalysis tomorrow." Thanks Crayne, thanks for that. The next day, in a group of forty or fifty other new recruits, we were ushered into a bus and taken to the airport. The window seat from Phoenix Sky Harbor to Chicago O'Hare was the last bit of serenity I would have for the next ten weeks. Don't jerk off.

We arrived by government bus at Great Lakes Recruit Training Center in Great Lakes, Illinois, twenty miles outside of Chicago. A uniformed man stepped up into the bus with a stack of paper, "Take one and hand it back. This questionnaire is voluntary but if you don't complete it, you will not get off the bus."

And so it begins, I thought. Five minutes later we all headed off the bus and into the unknown. After the ritualistic yelling at us to hurry up, we got in line for the shaving of the head, we were then stripped and showered. New, temporary clothes were issued, and we were taken to where we would sleep for the night. A few days later, after the obligatory paperwork was processed, they would move us to our permanent barracks. We would spend days stenciling our names on each of our uniformed belongings with a paint pen. Last name, first initial and last four of your social security number. In my case, "GANT, C 2689." Dog-tags were issued soon thereafter. I opted to go with "NORELPREF" as my religion, or "no religious preference."

Dog-tags doubled as the distance you had to go down while doing pushups. When you heard the *clink* of your tags hitting the floor, you've gone down far enough. I thought that was convenient.

Early on, we were taken to the open-air paved-center courtyard of our barracks. This area would be used to practice marching and sometimes basic physical training such as jumping jacks or pushups. The first time we entered this yard our Division Chief took a clipboard and called off a few names. Mine was one of them. She then proceeded to assign us divisional positions that we would carry out for the rest of training. I had a sneaking suspicion that she picked us due to our ASVAB scores, but I never confirmed it.

Another one of our Chief's picks was RPOC or Recruit Petty Officer Chief, who would command us in marches and pretty much be our leader. Not me. Not to say that I couldn't handle the job, I was just not looking to be the standout in boot camp. I just wanted to experience it and move on to what was inevitably next. The other names called were to be the flag bearers. I was tapped to be "Starboard Watch" which meant I had a premium marching position, easily distinguishable from the marching masses, and I would be in charge of writing the "Watch Bill."

Standing 'watch' is a duty escaped by no one in the military. Our 'watch' was to guard the barracks at night. If someone, uniformed or otherwise, was to attempt to enter the barracks where all your shipmates were sleeping, you were to challenge them. Kind of a, "Halt! Who goes there?"-type standoff. The watch rotation ended up being something like once every five to seven days, you would have to lose one hour of sleep to stand watch. The power of the position was too good to pass up. With no one questioning my methods, I didn't schedule myself for a single watch for all of basic training.

After the third week we got our first phone call home. Of course, I call Mom. After talking for five of the allotted fifteen minutes, she had something interesting to tell me.

"You're never going to guess who called for you last week." She prodded.

"Who?" I really had no idea who would be trying to contact me.

"Veronica. She is doing well and asked me to give you her phone number and wanted you to call her." Well yes, I did want to call her, but I had a few questions first. After almost two years, I was convinced, she either just got dumped and I was a rebound, or she gained twenty-five pounds and I was familiar.

After giving her a short call with my remaining phone card time, I asked her to send me a picture. I was not disappointed. A glamour shot from the mall, the Fiesta Mall, no doubt, showed her in all her maturing glory. She was a natural beauty. And she dumped her boyfriend a few months after the Disneyland trip. She said he was controlling. Good thing I wasn't.

As Division 406 made our way through training, my hair grew out, which was the only way of gauging how long the people you would come into contact with had been there for. In the advanced weeks, one would no doubt go into the chow hall and see a group of fresh shaved heads and reminisce as if that was a lifetime ago. And when you would see a group of people having more hair than you, you would wonder how much longer they had been there then you. You were ever conscience of time while you were there. How much longer? It was always, "How much longer?"

I remember the next call, two weeks later, telling Veronica about my gas chamber experience. I didn't bother calling Mom. I'd send her a letter, later.

To instill in us how important our gas masks were, we were all given one to put on. Next, the division was brought into a tent and lined up in rows of ten. There was nothing there but a hot plate next to the instructor standing five feet from the tent flap. He instructed us that on his say-so the first row is to take off their masks and stand at attention. At that time, he will go down the line, one by one, and have each recruit sound off their name and division. If anyone were to fail to sound off or stutter in any way, he would go back to the first recruit in line and start again.

"UNDERSTOOD?"

He dropped a little red pill on the hot plate and the smoke started billowing after five seconds or so. I was in the first row. Through my mask, I could see the white plume and made an active effort to try to get any sense of the smell of what I was soon going to have no barrier against. Nothing.

"Ready! Masks off!" The instructor said. The line of us broke through the unknown, as instructed, yet, fearlessly. Immediate constriction of the throat occurred. The sting of the smoke scorched the nose and soon snot was running down everyone's chins uncontrollably. A thick coat of tears instantly blurred my vision, and being fourth from the beginning of the line, I made sure to not be the weak link. "Gant....Division 406." I could taste my snot and didn't care. You needed to breathe, but every breath made it worse. When our line was done to his satisfaction, he bellowed, "Get outta here! Next row...step up. Go! Go! Go!"

The next fifteen minutes in fresh air were a continuation of the hellfire we had just endured. Instant relief was nowhere to be found. Random voices surrounding the 100-gallon drums of water would yell out intermittently, "Don't touch your eyes!" "Blow your nose!" Some threw up.

When the bulk of us regained our composure, we were asked the somehow hilarious question of the day, "Are you allergic to shellfish?" Some were. Those that were, were instructed to give their masks to another recruit to wash with a sea sponge. We were directed to go to the 100-gallon water barrels and wash out the masks. Looking across the watering hole, Recruit DuPont was still sniffling.

"Well that was fun, wasn't it?" I asked him. He managed a smirk while shaking his head, still in disbelief about what had just happened. It was a rite of passage. The brotherhood was coming into focus.

"That must have been horrible." Veronica replied.

"Yeah, in the moment it sucked, but looking back, it was awesome." I countered.

"Wrap it up, one minute!" Our division Petty Officer announced.

"I have to go, but I'll write you another letter today."

"Good job, Clifford! I'm so proud of you. I remember you talking about this when we were fifteen, and am very impressed you went through with it. Have a good night."

"You too, Veronica. And thanks. I'll call you after graduation."

"You do that." She quipped. I could sense her smile on the other end of the line. The line went dead.

Once the final academic and physical tests were administered, we had our chance to get some liberty. We were dressed in our Cracker Jack dress blues and were let loose on Chicago. We had eight hours or so from the time the bus dropped us off till the time we had to meet for the return trip back to base. I am pretty sure some sort of buddy system was in place. On our way to the city, we were informed that the Art Museum of Chicago would give us free admission, and I did not want to pass that up. There was so much to see.

One of the coolest exhibits was in a well-lit corner of one of the upper floors. There was a huge pile of sugar-free candy, to not exclude the diabetics from participation, and the gig was that it was a 'Never-Ending Pile of Candy.' It would be replenished every week at the expense of the artist. I took two pieces. I wonder if it is still going.

In the relaxing days preceding graduation, I got to talk more in depth to some of the other recruits in my division. One, in particular, I found out, liked chess. He was black. Lake Havasu had a total of three African-American students at the high school, so I had very limited exposure to black culture. I made it my liberty mission to acquire a chessboard to test our skills. So, as we left the Art Museum on a windy October afternoon, I popped one of the diabetic candies into my mouth and set out on my mission.

In walking the historic Chicago streets, I came across a toy store. Shortly after entering, I was able to locate a folding wooden chess set. At $24.99, I had to have it. Getting back on the bus, knowing we weren't allowed to bring anything back, I was a ninja. Prior to our approach, I scrapped the cardboard box and smuggled the folded board, with pieces securely inside, against the small of my back, under my pant waistband. I got on the bus, unchallenged.

Upon getting back to the barracks, I flashed the board in Recruit Adams' direction. His face lit up. We waited till after dinner when the division leaders usually left us to our own devices until bed time. Everyone showered in the mornings, so the tiles were dry in the communal showers. We set it up. He was good. I mean Arturo was a pro, but against any random kid my age, I usually won.

"Good game," I said with an outstretched hand as my king was dead to rights.

"Another?" He asked. Just then our Division Petty Officer came in.

"What the fuck is this?" He asked. (Immediate flashbacks of Papa John's and Carl came to mind.) Better answer correctly, this time.

"Um, it's a war game?" Thinking that phrasing like that would save us. It wasn't like we were playing 'Chutes and Ladders' or 'Hi-Ho Cherry-O' like a bunch of recessed schoolchildren. He shook his head.

"Give me that." We collected the pieces, folded it up and handed it to him. If my chess partner had sucked I would have let sleeping dogs lie. But the fact that we were a good match, my mind started working. Damn you, my mind.

"Wait here," I told Adams. I came back with a pen and a lined piece of paper. I started writing in heavy ink: "K Q Kn Kn B B R R."

"Good idea." Adams caught on quick. There were probably 1 ¼" tiles in the shower and, fuck a chess*board*, we just needed paper pieces and an eight by eight chunk of real-estate. When our Division Petty Officer came back, he was not impressed.

"Get out of here, NOW!" He collected the pieces and subsequently relieved me of my Starboard Watch duties. That stung for a couple reasons: one, I didn't think that I was breaking any serious rules. Secondly, my grandparents, Fred & Marlene, were going to come down from Wisconsin to watch my graduation and I wanted them to see me in my unique marching spot so they wouldn't have to try to find me in a mass of marching bodies. For me, my position was a matter of pride, for me and them. But, there was no repairing that situation.

I stood my first and only watch the next evening, two nights before graduation. Grandma and Grandpa made it down to the base and after the marching ceremony we were able to meet up for a couple photos. My uncle was expected to show up, but couldn't make it, leading to the faux pas that would carry with my grandparents for years.

Immediately after exchanging hugs, I asked innocently, "Where's Uncle Randy?" I would find out, over a decade later, that that statement hurt them because they left early that day to make the drive and that was the first thing I said to them, instead of thanking them for showing up. Uncle Randy was in the Army and I really wanted him to see me cross the threshold of being just some summer labor sorting ratchet sets, to a young man entering adulthood, by service. I didn't think that I would ever get peer respect from Grandpa, but I felt that I *could* have gotten that type of respect from Uncle Randy.

Grandpa didn't like my father from the beginning, so my Dad's offspring, by extenuation, were nothing to be dealt seriously with. We were novelty, at best. I was trying to break out of that, though. We were able to leave the base and found a restaurant just outside the thirty-mile maximum allotted 'radius-of-adventure' limit, set by the base. We talked about what was next.

'A' School in Pensacola, Florida, where I would learn the skills needed for my job. I was excited. Looking through the window of that restaurant, I felt a certain amount of satisfaction for conquering the first hurdle, the hardest part, of getting in. I did it. It wasn't just a promise on a piece of my recruiter's stationary. I put in the work and now had the sea bag to prove it.

For the first four weeks of 'A' School in Pensacola, Florida we were restricted to the base, and had a daily workout routine. It kind of bridged the gap between the structure and discipline of boot camp to the liberty of school and the bona fide Navy. Nothing more than being restricted to base and doing 'Sun-Gods', push-ups, jumping jacks and running for a couple hours a day. "I can handle this," I thought.

School started with me being in the morning Cryptologic Technician class, which sucked because I am a night owl. The other class started at 6:00 PM and went until 2:00 AM, and would have suited me much better. The first day, the night class opportunity came my way. There was a recruit in the night class that wanted to be in color guard, which held practices in the evenings. Mine was the first hand up when the instructor brought this to the class's attention and I was switched. The color guard sailor saw me once and thanked me profusely.

During school, I was at or near the top of the class. I became good friends with my roommate and classmate Brian McCarty, who I thought was really cool. He went to clubs on the weekend while I would stay home and study or talk to Veronica. Veronica and I would talk for at least an hour every night. The only thing that was missing was a trampoline to lie on, for old time's sake. I had expressed my deepest desire to go to Italy, when I graduated. She thought that would be cool for me. There were not a lot of people who did the job I was training for and Italy would come up needing recruits from time to time. The students' positions in class would determine who got first pick of deployment orders, or billets. There were two things that I definitely didn't want. I didn't want to go to Norfolk, VA, and I didn't want to go to a ship. I know, I know, if I didn't want to be on a ship, why would I join the military branch that had ships? I just wanted to ease my way into going out to sea, that's all.

44

As time got closer to graduation, I found myself 2nd in my class. First spot was occupied by a nerdy Marine, and he let me know he wanted to go to Germany. So, if there was an Italy billet available, it was mine to take. Things were looking up. But I had learned that when they start looking up, there is no doubt a hidden cliff just off the horizon. On a Friday, the last exam we had, if I aced it, I would have finished first in my class. It consisted of eight real world networking issues.

Each of us had twenty minutes to diagnose and solve each problem. For example, 'Terminal A4 can't send email.' To which the answer may be that the modem is broken or misconfigured. Or, perhaps the data cable is bad or unplugged. The first seven were figured out in no time. But, I couldn't figure out the last scenario, for the life of me. Often times, the hardest problems have the easiest answers. I know my instructor was just bashing his head against the wall, watching me go from terminal to terminal scratching my head wondering why nothing could connect. The twenty minutes eclipsed. He had to tell me to stop.

My blood was boiling and I was not happy about missing out on top spot by one question. The server was unplugged. The fucking **server** was unplugged! I wanted to challenge the question. The whole premise that all of your users would be down and the whole reason was that the server was unplugged, that just wouldn't happen. Not in the real world, anyways. So, without complaint, I would get second pick. Knowing that the Marine didn't want to thwart my Italy bid, I wasn't worried. Well, billets came around and I saw, and picked, Italy.

"That was picked this morning." My teacher bluntly informed me. To make it rub a little rawer, the person who got the only Italy billet was the one I switched with for his color guard experience. And he finished 5th in his class! No good deed goes unpunished. This was sacrilege.

How is it fair that day class, regardless of position, gets to choose billets before night class? The only shore command available was a Flag Command, Commander Second Fleet, located nowhere other than Norfolk, VA. Everything else was ship duty and I just wasn't ready for that, yet. I was told Commander Second Fleet consisted of soon to be retired senior personnel and the command was in charge of the entire eastern seaboard. Of the choices available, this shore duty was the most promising for a budding career, I thought.

I thought.

Chapter IV

Nor'fucked

CTO3 Jason Barrow picked me up from the Norfolk Airport. He was a married thirty-something, pudgy, and deeply southern, as ascertained from his heavy South Carolinian accent. It was a chilly March evening. He drove me to the base and got me situated in my barracks room. He would pick me up the next morning to take me to building Whisky-5 which would be my station of service for the next three years. Overseeing the piers, which were currently holding four or five docked ships, the Commander Second Fleet building didn't scream power. It didn't scream anything. It was a simple, three-story nondescript red brick building with a key code card reader as its only barrier to entry.

Approaching the building in the passenger seat I found myself looking in awe at the towering floating cities known as ships. As we found our parking spot, I felt a tingling in my stomach. The butterflies I imagine you get in your gut when seeing the New York skyline, in person, for the first time, were hitting me as I got out of the car. The masts contrasting against the overcast skies of Norfolk were almost vertigo inspiring. The sight was truly something to behold.

There were less than ten personnel of differing varieties of Cryptologists at building Whisky-5. Four were my rate, CTO. I quickly found out that this so-called 'Flag Command' was a rampant version of the good-old boys club. Barrow would spend days altering his collegiate fantasy football team, heavy on Clemson players, which went to show why, it seemed to me, he didn't show any motivation on progressing through the ranks. He had a stripe on the forearm of his uniform shirt, letting me know that he had been in the Navy for at least four years. Yet, he was only one rank above me. Maybe he was on the short end of a disciplinary infraction. I didn't care to ask. I was there to do a job. That job consisted of, every morning, processing message traffic in the queue, to the tune of hundreds or even thousands of messages, and answering the eventual trouble ticket.

Being cramped in a small SCIF, or Specially Compartmented Information Facility, you don't have many other interactions with other people outside your skillset. The six or so people you are in the secure room with are the only people you have to talk to. Jason rarely made his way to the SCIF. He routinely hung out in the general non-secure office area with the lower ranking officers and higher ranking enlisted staff. Along with another new recruit, Seaman Apprentice Vanessa Baron, we were the ones that were tasked with getting most of the daily grunt work done. The job was quite repetitive, and the only reprieves were the smoke breaks every 30-45 minutes. I was given my first cigarette, a Marlboro Menthol Light, by Seaman Steven Gagnon on my 18th birthday in Pensacola, halfway through 'A' School, and I had been a smoker ever since. It gave me a generally accepted reason to leave my idle workstation and get fifteen minutes closer to going home. But even 'home' was empty, with only Veronica's voice to fill the void of night.

For her 18th birthday, on May 25th, Bea, Veronica's Mom, bought her a plane ticket to come and visit me. July 3rd-July 9th, 2003. Upon hearing that news three weeks before the date, I put in my leave request and went to the Zale's Jewelry Store at the Mall. I put $500 down on a ring and financed the rest of a serial engraved 1/3 Carat diamond ring and a white gold band for me. I knew what I was going to do. If I got married, I would get extra pay from the Navy to cover rent in the Virginia Beach area code. The Navy would then become my vehicle to sustain a life, a marriage, and after a simple 2 ½ years, I would move on, either reenlisting or using my $58,000 college fund, as a civilian. I wasn't going to waste any time. She flew in on a Thursday, and I picked her up in my primered and duct taped 1982 Mazda RX-7. The rotary engine that would last 500,000 miles (in theory) and the detachable sun roof made it my favorite car. Plus, I felt like a badass driving stick. Like my Taurus, this car also had character. I can't imagine what she thought when I presented this grey hunk of scrap metal as her chariot, but she accepted it enough to get in the passenger seat without complaint. I had rented a Red Roof Inn for the week. We stopped for some take-out and got to the hotel. We made love that night, all night.

Veronica was only the third girl I had ever had sex with. My first time, I was fifteen. While my friend was in his room with his girlfriend making out, I was left alone with her friend, Sam Hill. She had a petite frame and an oversized forehead, but I was fifteen and found a girl who I had never talked to before, just *wanting* me. Looking back, maybe it was just some 'keeping up with the Jones's' in the other room, type shit. The trauma of being that nervous and not knowing at all what to do, made it all the more worse when her dad called me, three days later, accusing me of rape. I unplugged the phone. "Who Wants to Be a Millionaire" was on, and that call made me miss the question. RAPE! Are you kidding me? My dick wasn't harder than a scared two inches and she was super clingy on the car ride home. Rape? This is when Dad and I were forced to have "The Talk."

I still cringe when I recall this man, my father, prefer to use the word "prophylactic" over "condom" when letting me know that if I should continue having sexual relations, I should practice responsible sexual behavior, on his dime. Thanks pop, but I think after having a grown man interrupt Regis Philbin quizzing me on random trivia, to the tune of, "I'm going to cut your dick off!" Yeah, I think I'll keep it on ice for a while. What in the Sam Hill, indeed. Her and her dad moved to Colorado the following semester.

The second girl I had sex with was Annette Wooldridge. We went to school together at Telesis but didn't hook up until a year later while we were both working at Papa John's. I somehow convinced my Mom to let her stay the night, and I guess my waterbed was an opportunity way too appealing for her to pass up. She was experienced, and I was, well, an accused rapist. But she didn't know that, in fact, a few weeks earlier while at her house with her cousin Ashley Powell, she gave me my first blowjob, after I lied and told her I had never been with a girl before. Ashley left us alone, even though I wished she would have stayed. Ashley was a little bigger, but cuter than Annette. That could have been fun.

After round one on the waterbed, once I regained my breathing, she pulled me on top of her again and said, "Now this is how you please a woman." And I go for round two. Looking at my alarm clock recognizing that an hour had gone by, I felt a sense of pride well up inside me. I am a champion! This is nothing like my first time. I guess the partner and emotional connection made a lot of the difference. It is better to give for the collective experience, fearlessly, than to simply take what is offered, timidly. That is something that I have only learned with time.

Annette and I would hook up one other time, at her house. The living room couch cushion was permanently flipped upside down, from that moment on. If her Mom knew, she never let me know, as she liked me from the moment we met. Things did get interesting when two weeks later, Annette called my house and told me that Carl had fucked her at a party, while she was drunk. Not only did it aggravate me because he was a man having sex with my partner. She was also underage. I asked the next police officer I saw what the law was in Arizona regarding sex with minors, and remember being told, to my surprise, that it was fifteen with consent, and being drunk entailed consent. I wasn't mad at her, but didn't want to continue our arrangement after that.

A few weeks after Carl fired me, I was on the internet at Randy Reesha's house. He was a driver for Papa John's who taught me to drive stick on his lowered silver Chevy S-10, when I was sixteen.

My Dad would let me finish learning on his yellow Ford in the high school parking lot, a short time later. I didn't tell him I had previous lessons. I'm sure he thought I was either very coachable at worst or a savant, at best. But, on Randy's computer that day, I got ahold of Lisa, Carl's girlfriend, a lovely lady. She would show up occasionally at the store and Carl and her would disappear into the office and do who knows what, with that one sided mirror and all, no one could see into that office when the door was closed. I defiantly messaged her on Yahoo Instant Messenger and told her simply, "Carl fucked Annette." Within twenty minutes Carl showed up at Randy's doorstep, fuming.

"If you were eighteen, I would kick your ass!" He exerted forcefully. I didn't want to stoke the fire, and after hooting and hollering for a few minutes, he left. I mean, you'll fuck a minor but draw a line at assaulting one? ☺ Randy just shook his head, in disbelief that I wanted to start a war with Carl. I am unaware of any ramifications that happened between Carl and Lisa after that, but I really do wish that they have both had fulfilling lives.

I pressed and held the flash activator button on the Kodak disposable camera I had bought the day before. I was intent on documenting as much as I could of Veronica's trip. Candid pictures only, nothing sexual. It had been years of being deprived of her, and I wanted those moments to last. But it became apparent Veronica was getting annoyed at the paparazzi residing with her, under the sheets. So, I tossed the camera to the base of the TV stand.

We got up later that morning, and had some McDonald's Breakfast. Then we went to Virginia Beach. We walked around holding hands like we were inseparable. Kisses punctuated what seemed to be every other conversation. At dusk, we ventured to find a vantage point to watch the impending fireworks. I had no idea where they would be, and hadn't done much off base traveling to know the layout of the Norfolk area. I got lost. For the two hours or so following sundown, all we could see was the cadenced glow of fireworks that were obscured by the towering trees surrounding the roads we were winding down. We decided to give up and take it back to the Red Roof Inn.

Once satiated with another round of steamy lovemaking which continued into the shower, lying in the bed, I picked up the camera again as she was blow-drying her hair. She smiled back at me, after the flash reflected off the vanity mirror. I reached under my side of the mattress which produced the black clamshell ring holder. I opened it to give it one more look. Is this what I really want? It was a small token of what I felt.

A simple starter ring which would grow with our continued success. To wake up every morning with this young woman as my bride, as my help-mate, next to me, forever, yes. It took one day for me to know that she was the much needed missing piece of my life. She climbed into bed and her hand brushed my back and I flinched. I couldn't believe that this beauty was one simple "Yes" away from being bound to me. I never got to experience love or companionship in my adolescent days, yet, there I was on the cusp of a newly defined 'forever'. Thinking I was getting the camera flash ready for another round of evidence gathering, she tried to reach for my hand. I didn't let her.

"What's in your hand?" She asked cutely irritated. "Give it to me, now!"

"You want what is in my hand?" I inquired. I felt the sweat breaking on my fingertips, moistening the felt on the ring's case.

"Yes!" She replied, not knowing what was coming her way.

"Are you sure?" My heart was surprisingly calm, I mean, she already said "Yes," right? Veronica shot me a 'stop fucking around and comply' look and I gave her the last look of a single man. I took the case in my left hand and rolled over to face her.

Opening the case, I asked her those four, fate-tempting words: "Will you marry me?" Not needing to rush the moment, I took the ring and slowly ran it to the base of her left hand finger. It was sized perfectly. She wrapped me in her arms and whispered, "Yes." Two kids trying to claim adulthood, by deed. I knew though, in that moment, that if my life went to shit, and I still had her, we would be just fine. I would find a way to make it work.

We had the world ahead of us, and a promising new start. I had a guaranteed job and paycheck, and she had free time and a future base of operation to grow into the woman she was going to become. I was in no mood to take it slow. I wanted a new life, now. I wasn't going to give her a chance to change her mind. I gave her the ring on a Friday. The marriage license was bought for $35 on Monday morning, and we hit the courthouse hours later on July 7th, 2003. She flew home two days later. We had no plan of action. We had nothing figured out, save that we belonged to each other, forever, till death do us part. You promised, Veronica, you promised.

Our flagship, the USS Mount Whitney, which had her own assigned crew, was Second Fleet's to come and go as we pleased. This caused a certain unspoken animosity between those that were stationed on the ship for its daily upkeep and Commander Second Fleet, who were living the arguably better life on shore. Arriving on the ship, we would flock to our climate controlled computer spaces to make sure everything was working and then, off we would go. In August, we were tasked to spend a week on the ship for upkeep of our spaces. We destroyed obsolete computers, cleaned the settled

50

surface dust, and put unclassified documents into burn bags for destruction. A short time after our upkeep was complete, Jason asked me during a smoke break if I wanted to come over and hang out after work.

I had never been to his house before and we were close enough in rank for it not to warrant crossing the "fraternization" boundaries, so I agreed. He had kind of taken me under his wing in the four months I had been there, for all that was worth. I even went down to South Carolina once to assist him in moving some furniture for some of his kin. Many times in life you don't get to choose your associates, but you can do your best to work with what you have been given. He was a cool enough guy. But when I got to his house something I saw after the initial tour, tore at the fabric of the clout of integrity I associated with him.

On a wooden computer desk, I saw a laptop. Now, back in 2003, laptops were still emerging as something everyone would eventually want and need to have. Military budgets allowed the branches to get newer technology at almost any cost. Then, when we would dispose of dated technology, there were protocols. Serial numbers would be registered as destroyed and signed off by the destroying party. Hard drives would be de-gauzed and rendered unreadable. Classification labels would be scraped off using razorblades. When we would be engaged to make a purge, I noticed that when we would deconstruct computer towers, Jason would increasingly pocket certain parts. Maybe a memory stick here and there or sometimes even a 32GB hard disk drive, before the towers and motherboards were thrown into dumpsters. Other higher ranking enlistees were periodic witnesses to this, so I accepted it as a perk of sorts. I had no computer tower at home to upgrade, or any use of spare parts, so I didn't partake in the digital buffet. One could argue it was going to just be thrown away anyways, why not use it if you can? To which I would counter, 'if it is signed off as destroyed, it should be in such state.' But after being on the USS Mount Whitney and seeing the hardware that was contained within our space, I recognized that laptop as one from the ship.

From the corner of my eye, I saw the sticker residue in the lower right corner, where a classification sticker had once been. The Navy I joined was an institution of integrity. The Navy I joined was an institution of honesty. Why, Jason, why? Not thinking of ramifications, I resolved then and there that I was going to have to bring my findings up to my chain of command the next day, which I did.

In the military, we all have a chain-of-command. You do not go to the Captain with your complaint until you have exhausted all other means of resolution. So starting with my Division Leading Petty Officer, I made my concern known. CTM1 Smith did not have anything more than a working relationship with CTO3 Barrow, and I felt that if anyone would understand the situation and be able to act accordingly, it would be her. She assured me she would get to the bottom of it. Well, *her* next level in the chain of command was our division Chief, who had been at that command with Jason for a number of years, and they were close friends. The next morning I was brought into the non-secure office and shown the laptop that had been at Jason's house, and told that the laptop in question was never at CTO3 Barrow's house and was, in fact, at building Whisky-5 the whole time. A cover-up. Fuck. Now, as the entire command is concerned, I am the dirt bag snitch sailor who turned in his own. From that moment on, I was on the black-list, ostracized. Not to be trusted. It was the feeling of being contractually required to show up to a workplace, when nobody wants you there. To me, reporting my concern was upholding my oath of enlistment. Stealing from my Navy, stealing from the taxpayer, renders you an enemy, domestic, at least it does in my eyes. And yet, then, I found *myself* to be the enemy. It was a sickening feeling.

Knowing that I was making arrangements to get my pay increase straightened out and get Veronica moved out to Virginia, my command decided it would be prudent to get rid of me for the time being, and perhaps it was a bonus to them that it interrupted my plans of starting my married life. They let me know that they were going to send me to the USS Thorn (DD-988) for Temporary Active Duty, that November. I would be sailing overseas to the Mediterranean Sea, Spain in particular, on the Spruance-Class Destroyer's final deployment before being decommissioned. I was torn about this information. On one hand, I was happy to get away from my shady command, but on the other, I was disheartened that I would have to put off my marriage for six to eight months. This is not what I had intended, nor particularly fair to Veronica, even though, before vows were ever exchanged, she knew that if she married me, she married the Navy also. I made plans to visit Arizona in October, right before my reassignment.

Her household was surprisingly welcoming to the new white boy who snaked his way into their tight-knit Hispanic family. There was no time wasted in taking a drive to California to visit "G," her grandfather. It was my first time in Hollywood. Her uncle and I walked away from the group to check out the Lamborghini's. I had recruited him into a network marketing company, ACN, set to capitalize on the deregulation of telecom that never really manifested, but nonetheless promised him that when our ship came in we were each going to get a Lambo, with side by side plates that would read, "CANYOU" & "BLVETHS." It is great to have dreams.

Somehow the multi-marketing company revoked his membership for allegedly signing up people for long distance service in Florida who never consented to switch. He never did anything of the sort, and our relationship soured thereafter because of that. Shame on you, American Communications Network of Farmington Hills, Michigan! You lost a good person because of your negligent oversight.

We made our way to the flea-market district and I found a unique store selling glass paperweights with laser-blasted 3-D designs inside. After looking for anything eye-catching, I found one with a Navy Aircraft Carrier, detailed enough with fighter jets parked on the deck, and one taking off in mid-air. I paid the woman ten dollars for it. I had no use for it, but it spoke to me.

Next, we were going to make our way down to Ensenada, Mexico. It was my first experience south of the border and I was open-eyed and wait... I can drink, legally? I remember ordering food in a big open air restaurant, but the drinks that followed hit my eighteen year old liver like, well, alcohol to an almost virgin organ, and I was gone.

Before we crossed back into the United States, we stopped at a grocery store and I bought a few snacks, two green bell peppers and a bottle of Correlejo Tequila. Correlejo is the tall blue bottle, great stuff. You could drink the entire bottle and not have to worry about a hangover in the morning, some sort of witchcraft, but I accepted it. The last I now recall, from video of the drive home, was the family laughing at me as I ate a green pepper like it was an apple. My Arnold Schwarzenegger impersonation, while wearing a blue and gold luchador mask, also proved to be entertaining for my new in-laws. To them, I was a shiny new toy that would eventually be cast aside.

Getting back to Gilbert, AZ the next day, we stopped at a pumpkin patch to pick out our carving selections. Halloween was another pagan holiday that was not to be celebrated under my Dad's roof, so this was a new experience for me. I picked a very detailed "Haunted Mansion with Headstones" scene from the pumpkin carving template book, and tore it out. Of the eight or so carving tools, I would not relinquish the finest one even though Veronica needed it for her "Thief Stealing Diamond" outline. I was in the zone, and almost finished. She elected not to wait and with the wider cutting tool, succeeded in debasing the diamond and it fell off. (It was repaired with a few strategically placed toothpicks, but I don't think she forgave me for being so selfish with the tools.) The lighting ceremony proved my concentration worth it. Never before had I seen a more detailed pumpkin scene, the picture I took would eventually be tiled as my Dell Inspiron 8100 laptop background. It was epic.

Knowing I was going to be gone for the next six months or so, I convinced her to let me take my Sony Mini-DV camcorder and get some naughty video for the trip overseas. She was shy though, and insisted a pillow be over her face, and lights off. So I was left with some night-vision amateur porn that was accepted as 'better than nothing'.

I reported to the Thorn on November 6th. I was given the basic tour. Smoke deck, chow hall, SCIF, berthing. The inside of a Navy ship is a fucking jungle. It was awesome. Those cramped spaces floating on a wide open ocean was a completely new experience, and I surprisingly loved it. Upon getting situated I was given the rundown of the communications situation.

Before the long haul overseas, we were scheduled to do a test run, or 'work ups'- a small voyage to Bangor, Maine, around Thanksgiving, to ensure all communications were working. One system was giving two cryptologists a difficult time. They had spent an intermittent amount of time trying to get it online in the months prior to my arrival, but to no avail. Upon learning the situation, unassisted by the SCIF crew, within the first two weeks of me being on the ship, knowing nothing of shipboard communications, I was able to get ahold of IT2 Rodríguez and get our signal out. Our division Chief, upon learning this, told me he was going to nominate me for an achievement medal for my work on that system.

"Wow", I thought, what a departure from the treatment received at COM2FLT. A week or so after I brought the system online, we would eventually make our way to Bangor, Maine. Well, wherever the port city was, *then* we were given a van ride to Bangor.

In Bangor, a group of us ended up at a strip club at noon, and although there were no girls, we were served a drink, and uniquely they gave only $2 bills as change. What a way to: A) Market and B) Increase default strip tip receipts. I thought it was brilliant. Shortly thereafter, we left, to find a pretty nice restaurant for dinner. We were in Maine, so I had to get the lobster. Some of the other customers were dissatisfied that the waiter wouldn't serve me a beer, even though I was in uniform.

"Give him a BEER!" I heard one man shout from two tables away. Thank you, that guy.

Without an alcoholic drop, we would return to Norfolk, validated and ready to embark on the long haul. I was proud of my performance. Shipboard life was cool. I was excited to see Spain.

"I'll call you when I hit port, babe. I love you!" I told Veronica the night before anchors went up. She was going to spend this time planning the formal wedding ceremony, at a venue we had checked out in California, before we went to Ensenada, back in October. Good, I thought, at least she wouldn't be bored.

It takes two weeks to sail to the old world. In the SCIF, there was a monitor with the Atlantic Ocean on display and a blip representing us and our place in it. Slowly but surely, we inched our way across that monochrome screen. There were no boxing matches like in Men of Honor, nor any fishing off the stern, but something was calming about looking around and seeing nothing but ocean, knowing that everyone is playing their part in responsibility. Everyone is pulling their own weight. If there is a fire, you can't call 911. We are trained to deal with every scenario. We are all we got. That is a very unique feeling. I wish it could be bottled and sold, for I miss it.

Before I knew it, there it was, the Rock of Gibraltar. If you know the insurance company Prudential, you have seen the image of the Rock of Gibraltar. It is a towering monolith welcoming you to the Mediterranean Sea. Our first stop was Rota, Spain, but we weren't allowed to leave the base. Next, we were to hit Malaga, Spain for Christmas and were scheduled to hit Barcelona, Spain for New Year's Eve, which would have proved to be amazing if you know the reputation of Barcelona. Instead, we got stuck doing NATO escorts through the Strait and were informed our new plans would include New Year's back in Malaga.

Christmas in Spain was a fairytale. Cobblestone streets, a bullfighting ring, siestas at noon, and every scooter seemed to come with an accompanying supermodel to cling on you. It was surreal. We were briefed before we left the ship that all the orange trees in Spain are owned by King Juan Carlos. We would be subject to arrest if we were to even touch an orange. We were also briefed on the red light district and told that if we were to get a prostitute, to wrap it up. I didn't even think about taking a free pass at some Spanish fly. I had no intention of straying from my marriage vows. It seemed everyone else, was eager to be knee deep in some foreign strange. I had two others in my "buddy" party and we spent an hour or so walking up a long, winding, sidewalk, lined with orange trees, to reveal a legit castle, complete with an indescribable view of the interior rolling hills of the Spanish countryside. Legs sore, we sat for a while to take in the ambiance, and to rest ourselves. Upon returning back to ground level, we found a restaurant. I ordered the bison and our appetizers were five-inch, wild mushroom caps hand-picked from the owner's family ranch, outside of Barcelona. This marked my lifelong palatial shift to liking mushrooms.

Making it back to the ship before our Cinderella cut off time of midnight, I was really beginning to re-examine my thoughts of shipboard life. But I was married now, and owed her somewhat of a normal marital experience. When I got back, she would come first. Calling her from the payphones on the dock, I could hear a different version of her on the other end of the line.

She was overwhelmed with planning the ceremony and wished I was with her. She said that she may just put the whole thing on hold.

I was fine with that. The ceremony was for her and her family, not mine. She wasn't happy. There was nothing I could do. It was debilitating.

Back on the ship, I made it to the SCIF and shot off an email back to Senior Chief Nancy Hobart in Norfolk, telling her that, essentially, it was bullshit that I was sent off right when I got married, and that the Barrow cover-up was akin to the Enron scandal, which was topical at the time. I also made a California wildfire reference, while talking about how fast the truth would spread. December 28th, 2003, I was called into the Command Master Chief's office and took a seat.

He went right into it, "Well, Gant, 2nd Fleet wants me to send you to Captain's Mast for 'Disrespect to a Senior Petty Officer.' Thing is, you've been nothing but a shining star for us, so I'm not going to do that. The way I see it, you have two options. You can either recant, say that you must have been mistaken in what you saw, and was wrong about the laptop situation, or you can fly back to Norfolk and be a part of a JAG investigation." I countered with asking him if I could have a day to think about it. He obliged. I left by thanking him, and went to talk to my Division Chief, CTRC Drummond from Buffalo, New York. The take away from the conversation was that if I didn't finish the cruise, he couldn't recommend me for recognition and the medal I would be up for. This, in case you were wondering, was the Navy Achievement Medal. Some serve upwards of ten years before they have the opportunity to earn one. It's a big deal. I had to smoke.

On the starboard side smoke deck, that night, I saw a Chief I had never met before, and approached him.

"Hey, Chief," this was a rhetorical question, "is it important to stay true to what you know or believe in, even if it means a grave personal inconvenience to you."

"Without a doubt. If you don't stay true to yourself, who else is there to validate you?" He said in no uncertain terms.

"Thanks Chief." Fuck. I mean, the decision was already made, but this just galvanized it. Norfolk, here I come.

When we pulled into Malaga for the second time, my sea bag was packed and I would request permission to go ashore for the last time from DD-988. She was a great ship. Chief Drummond would acquire a military van and drive me to Madrid where I would then fly to Philadélphia, then to Norfolk.

I was in my working blues, and, noticing that, the Delta flight attendant moved me up to enjoy an empty first-class seat, complete with a New Year's celebratory flute of champagne. Once we were in the air, however, they refused to serve me alcohol because I was only nineteen. Oh, law.

Back in Norfolk, it was par for the course. There was no JAG investigation, just an impersonating MP sent to take my statement. Sr. Chief Hobart contacted the USS Mount Whitney and sent me to work with the Gunners Mate's and slandered my name to their Division Officer, which made me seem like a true menace.

"Thirty minute lunches, no cigarette breaks, keep him under constant supervision," et cetera. The first job I was assigned was to be in a bleak, neglected, underbelly part of the ship and was given a brillow pad and some white liquid polish in a spray bottle and told to shine dull copper pipes. So that's exactly what I did, to the best of my ability. The next day, they put me in a harness to clean the foreign debris from a vertical loading bay that nobody wanted anything to do with. I found newspaper clippings from four years earlier, it was a hoot. It was just me, hung down a 100-foot shaft with a hand broom to dust the spider webs away and a plastic bag for trash. Once the shift was done, I disembarked the ship and was walking to my car, when I was stopped by a Lieutenant, whom I promptly saluted.

"Were you the one who was working for me yesterday?" He demanded.

"Yes, Sir." I responded, kind of worried I had misstepped again, somehow.

"Nice fucking job on those pipes." An officer just said 'fucking' to me, and I found that to be very empowering.

"Look, Sir, I don't know all of what they told you, but I am not the dirt-bag sailor they made me out to be. I caught someone doing something they shouldn't have and brought it up. This is them trying to shut me up." Whew, I had said my peace.

"Be that as it may, you'll be working with the Gunner's Mates tomorrow, keep up the good work. And whenever you need a smoke break, let them know." I sensed his imminent departure and saluted with a, "Thank you, Sir."

Working the following week with the gunner's mates was enlightening. They let me polish and assemble some pistols with them. We developed a rapport to the point of them asking if I would cross-rate or 'change jobs' so I could be picked up by the ship. It made me feel proud that even though I wasn't at my owner's command, I was still seen as a value to a different skillset. I was determined to stick with computers though.

I bought Veronica her one-way plane ticket after I acquired an apartment in Virginia Beach on Water Oak Road, off of Independence Boulevard. It was empty when she got there and after a week of sleeping on an air mattress we went to Grand Furniture and bought $3,000 worth of furnishings, all on approved credit. Things got gradually worse at my command.

They passed me up for promotion even though I was more tenured and accomplished than the new CTO that had been received by our command while I was out at sea. I scored higher on my advancement test, as well as participated in many important functions regarding building Whisky-5 that he wasn't around for, and even brought up a NATO channel that Barrow failed at troubleshooting. After two months of being put through the ringer by my command, sent home to shave if I missed a hair and a paper trail of write ups every time I showed up five minutes late, our Captain had to make a move.

I was summoned into his office in March. We had a candid conversation for about thirty minutes where then he got to the meat of the meeting.

"Listen, Gant, I know you are a good guy. I have read your reviews and spoken to your superiors on the Thorn and the Mount Whitney. To be completely honest with you, you've just pissed off too many people here to be successful." Then he asked me flat out, "Where do you want to go." I was confused. He continued, "I will give you my written recommendation as a Captain in the United States Navy [one rank below Admiral] to go anywhere that the Navy is. Where do you want to go?"

"With all due respect, sir, I'd like to talk this over with my wife." I managed to muster.

"Fair enough, take the rest of the day off. Come and see me tomorrow." He said.

When Veronica moved out to Virginia, at the end of January, she went through some emotional times, and would cry often. Turned out, her Mom was having weekly talks with her that ended up making her feel that she abandoned her family for me. I don't know where I got the crazy idea that married people were supposed to live with each other, so fault me for wanting to have her close, now that I was back on dry land. So I guess the writing was already on the wall. The Navy, or at least my initial experience regarding the Navy, left such a sour taste in my mouth that when coupled with my wife's unhappiness, led to the inevitable conclusion. I wanted out.

With a $60,000 Top Secret/SCI government clearance, I could get a job working for any quality establishment and with my skillset, make an easy $100,000 a year. As a newlywed and all of nineteen years old, that sounded attractive. She would be near family, and would feel better too. So I resolved to bring this decision to Captain Adams the next morning.

"If that is your decision, we can make that happen." He said, somewhat disappointedly.

"I brought you something." I extended my right hand and on his desk I placed a rectangular form of glass. He picked it up and observed it. "I picked it up in Hollywood on leave after I got married. She thanks you, too, for helping this situation get resolved."

"Thank you. Wow, this is neat!" He studied it for a moment and then placed in on his desk, to his left. He further explained briefly to me that I would probably have to be written up for not following the direct order Senior Chief Hobart gave me before I embarked on the Thorn regarding the removal of my Mazda from the barracks parking lot.

The electrical system in the car was shorted to hell and it wouldn't start. I didn't have the money at the time to get it towed. Cash flow had always been a problem for me, a recurring theme in my life. I had spent my last $350 on a book library of sales and motivational titles from Barnes & Noble. I was turned onto that type of reading by a SCIF-mate Miguel Curl, who enlisted me into ACN. I bought everything from Zig Ziglar to Brian Tracy and Anthony Robbins. I wish my command displayed that type of leadership. But, nonetheless, upon returning from Spain, Senior Chief Hobart wanted me to show her proof that I had towed the car off property, which she knew I didn't have. I was forced to locate my abandoned RX-7 at the local tow yard and couldn't prove ownership because the VIN numbers were stripped on the car. Having title in hand was a moot point. Apparently stripping VIN numbers from a car is a crime, I didn't know this when I had pliers in hand back in December, before the Thorn embarked.

Upon telling the tow yard assigned to the base the situation, I was told that if I produced the VIN plaque I wouldn't have charges brought, and then could get a paper saying that I relinquished ownership to the tow yard, fulfilling the request of Senior Chief. That whole scenario was the wiggle room that the Captain saw to fulfill my request.

I was sent to Captain's Mast for 'failure to follow a lawful order' and was restricted to the USS Mount Whitney for thirty days, where I would do grunt work with the Boatswains Mates. Veronica used that time to find a job at the Hooters in Virginia Beach. She used my recently acquired Pontiac Sunfire to shuttle her to work and home. She liked working. I even was allowed a visit from her, during my restriction. She came aboard and we fooled around in an abandoned berthing area which no one had occupied for what seemed like years. Once the restriction period was completed they finalized my paperwork.

On my DD-214 separation papers it says reason for discharge was only and generically, "Commission of a Serious Offence." I was not given a stitch of debrief, nor spoken to about what exactly I was giving up by voiding my contract with the military. Even after paying $100 a month for my first fifteen months into the Montgomery G.I. Bill,

I was soon to be ineligible for any of the college money I was promised, or paid into. Also, no amount of VA health benefits would be extended my way. A re-enlistment code of 'RE-4' ensured I would never be asked back, nor could I enter any other military service, even if I wanted to. I was giving it all up to appease the family of the woman I swore vows to. All I had worked for since I was fifteen amounted to this. An unclean break from military service, with marketable skills- at least it wasn't a dishonorable discharge. I received a "General, under Honorable Conditions." That statement seems a little contradictory from the truth, but so were my enlistment papers. By the first week of April, I was officially out and we packed the Pontiac and headed west for the three day trip back to Arizona.

We planned to separate for the first two weeks. I would head to Lake Havasu City to reunite with my family, and her to Gilbert, where she promised to 'calm her Mom down'. I agreed. But when the two weeks eclipsed, she still didn't seem ready for me. I wasn't going to wait any longer. We had to find a new apartment, and I still had to clean out the rest of what we left at the Water Oak Road Apartment back in Virginia. A two-door Sunfire does not have a lot of packing space. I showed up at her house on Tremaine Avenue in Gilbert with eight days left till the end of the month. Her Mom didn't want me there. So I was content pulling around the corner and sleeping in the car. After a few hours of waiting, Veronica came to the passenger door.

"Mom said she can't let you sleep out here. Come in. Please." I obliged, furious at the course of events that were taking place. The next morning, the unthinkable happened. Her dad took me out front and told me in no uncertain terms that he was going to... "Send me on my way."

"Veronica is going to do what she had planned in High School, and go to college." In the two weeks since we had arrived back in Arizona, she had secured a job at a Phoenix-area Hooter's restaurant and was using her Mom's car for transport, but never once did she let me know that she was on board with leaving me. This was a total blindside. My world was falling apart and I had no foundation to start again. Arturo had already retired and sold his store. What was I going to do? My credit was overextended with all the mall credit cards, a car payment, a broken apartment lease, and no bank account to speak of, it was all a wash. All of it. I drove the 26 hours straight and got back to our apartment in Virginia. Along the way, we talked.

The conversation ended with me saying "I love you." Her reply was, "I know." It was over. We had so much passion that burned so fast. We both had a yearning desire to matter to someone other than ourselves and dove in headfirst without thinking. Coupled with what happened with the Navy, we were doomed from the moment I reported Barrow's theft. I played Usher's "Burn" and the "Fuck you, you ho, I don't want you back" song over the phone, till she hung up. I was only nineteen, ill-experienced in love and how to act. I had breezed by life, seemingly succeeding with only my smile and very little effort, but yet I found myself worse off than anyone my age. A failing, if not decimated marriage, a failed military service attempt, no savings, no property, no job, and an overbearing debt load. I needed a place to stage my next move.

Dad was living in Wisconsin at the time, at the home of the parents of Uncle Jerry and Aunt Linda. The Biddle-Fix family has a two wedding bond. At the wedding of Jerry Fix and Pamela Biddle, Jerry's sister, Linda, and Patty's brother, Randy, met and ended up falling for each other, or vice-versa. My Dad was there as a live-in aid to their elderly, ill parents, and was hell bent on changing their diet as a means to cure their diabetes. He did manage for a time to get Jerry's Mom off of insulin, but then Linda came down on him and wanted them to eat whatever they wanted, and damn the results. Or at least that's how Dad explained it to me. He was defeated. I stayed with him for a couple weeks before he left for California to pursue other ventures. In that time, I found a job and got an apartment with Rusty, one of my coworkers.

Granton Marketing in Milwaukee, Wisconsin was a door-to-door sales outfit promoting among other things, the Milwaukee Brewers Baseball Team. In 2004, the Brewers had recently moved into a new stadium and wanted to get more fans in the stands. The 2003 season was the first time they had done exceptionally well, in years, and were finally able to boast a growing fan base. It was like selling, well, baseball tickets to suburban families. Easy money.

We would travel to these subdivisions that had perfectly manicured lawns and the scattered child's bike here or there and would think, "I'm going to profit a hundred and fifty dollars today." Everyone wanted the offering: two club level tickets and a page of buy one, get one free bleacher seats and food discounts, all for twenty-six bucks. The club level tickets were thirty-five dollars apiece at the gate. Of every Brewer Booklet we sold, we got to keep nine dollars. My high-score was thirteen units, which netted me $127 cash at the end of that day. Another not as successful campaign was doing discounted oil changes in Green Bay, Wisconsin. Not quite the moneymaker the Brewers were, but to run around selling in the rain, with the backdrop of Lambeau Field not too far off in the distance, made it worth the trip.

Veronica sent me divorce papers. I refused to sign. I called her new number, and said that I wanted the ring back. Rookie mistake. She sent it back, overnight. I felt that some sort of fight should have been mounted. I refused to accept that I was just going to throw our marriage away along with everything else I had just lost. But, in the great state of Arizona, if one files petition for divorce and neither party is contesting property, it is granted by default, after a period of something like thirty days. I still never signed, yet the state allowed her vows to lapse. Oh, law.

I was jaded back then, but I hope her decision treated her right.

Have you ever loved something so much that you didn't know how to properly show it when push came to shove. I had a lot of growing up to do. I wish I had had someone to climb that mountain with, though. Memories can only take you so far, and certain ones can pull you down just as fast. Then, Katie showed up at Granton Marketing. A much needed uplifting distraction.

PART 2: THEFT

Chapter V

Wild Blackberries

Katie made me forget about my recent turmoil. She looked at me like I was wanted. I needed that. She soon became lover number four. She was two years older than me, taller and blonde. She had an athletic build and I enjoyed exploring it.

Rusty, her and I would commonly drive to the areas outside of Milwaukee and split up to sell the Brewer's Packages. My Sunfire was one of the only three cars that were used for shuttling sellers to their designated turf, and the payments had lapsed, meaning I had to be extra cautious while driving. Mom started getting calls from the dealership.

The Virginia dealership knew I was in Wisconsin and wanted the car back. The car, the job, the apartment and Katie would all be separated from me within two weeks. I parked the car in a Wal-Mart parking lot with the keys inside the gas cap cover and told the dealership where to pick it up. I was depressed and needed some serious reflection time. I was determined, at that time, to follow my father's backpacking adventure. Dad told me, growing up, stories of when he took *his* backpacking journey, decades earlier. I felt that a backpacking trip of my own might just give me the solitude I needed to refresh and reset my mind. Katie took me to a camping store and I spent all the cash I had saved on a backpack, tent, Coleman stove, and all the other gear I thought I would need to last alone in the wilderness. Rusty would be left with an abandoned apartment. He was last to know about this endeavor, at which time, I was long gone.

With a couple bags of rice, oatmeal and ten Clif Bars bought and packed, I was determinedly ready to embark. Katie drove me east across the southern half of the state to Platteville, Wisconsin, fifteen miles from the Iowa State Line. I knew that my food supplies wouldn't last long, so I also acquired a collapsible fishing pole and tackle and I planned to fish for my dinner every night, while sticking to the shores of the great river, Huckleberry Finn style. Katie gifted me a pair of sunglasses and a bottle of Jack Daniels with a flask in the University of Wisconsin - Platteville parking lot. With a couple selfie style pictures and a quickie in the cab of her Jeep, I embarked into the unknown. She selflessly helped me do what I wanted to without trying to dissuade me from following my gut. We were free spirits in the full meaning of the ideal, and that still means something to me.

Crossing through farmland and open countryside was definitely peaceful. I did have to snip a few barbed wires with the trust that I wouldn't be accosted by any shotgun-wielding landowners. The skies were punctuated with a few high clouds, but the mid-80 degree temperature in late June was warming to my soul. On day three, I would find myself bathing in a small creek basin and collecting two Ziploc bags full of wild blackberries, which I polished off while sitting on the top of a two-foot waterfall, a little further downstream. It was not as adventurous as my Dad's story of fighting off a Black Bear that was trying to get his strung up food sack. Unlike him, I didn't have a staff. But I had Jack. I tried to use it sparingly. It was a warm reward for putting solid mileage behind me. Five miles east from where I woke up that June morning, there it was. The tree line opened up to reveal the Mississippi River in all its glory.

I spotted a white bridge not far off and made my way toward it. Upon crossing the bridge, I would be entering the city limits of what turned out to be Dubuque, Iowa. Before I crossed, however, I noticed a little bird hopping around about twenty paces in front of me, midway down the bridge walkway.

As I approached, as history had shown me, the bird would fly away in all its majesty, but it didn't. Perhaps it was injured, I thought. So bending down, I offered it a curled index finger as a perch and it hopped on, fearlessly. Oh my goodness! I am holding a wild bird!

"Hey little guy," it seemed it was just as excited as I was, so I just continued walking with my new found friend in tow. We walked for a good thirty yards and it released. Flying over the handrail of the bridge toward the Iowa Pines, its wings were in perfect working order. What a feeling that came over me, what a moment to share with Mother Nature. What a story that bird is going to have! I recalled Sue Sullivan's Macaw in Mesa. What was it with birds and me? I pulled out my flask and raised a toast in honor of the moment. I took a second pull for good measure.

I found myself veering from the original plan of sticking with the Mississippi River and decided to follow Highway 151 towards Cedar Rapids. It didn't take long for a man in a truck to ask me if I needed a ride. He said he was headed to Des Moines. I really didn't want to shift gears from a backpacking adventure to a hitchhiking journey, but my legs were tired. It had been six days since Katie dropped me off. I had no money, resources were running low and my bottle of Jack had all but three fingers left. I wasn't about to turn tail and run, not just yet, and where would I go anyways? I was wading deep into uncharted waters, but damn the proverbial torpedoes, full steam ahead. I threw my backpack into the bed of his truck and got in. Conversation consisted of mostly me and my history. It was hard recalling wounds that were so fresh and reciting them to a perfect stranger, but it was also strangely therapeutic. Dropping me off at a local gas station inside the city, I offered my gratitude and he wished me well.

"Don't give up. But you know that already." Were his parting words.

With nowhere to go and no money to get me there, I just started walking. I was wearing my blue Navy coveralls, with the "US NAVY" patch ripped off so the only patch visible read: "GANT". An older, overweight woman in a dated Chevy Impala rolled to a stop approaching the main thoroughfare. I raised a hand in acknowledgement as I passed by the hood of her car, and, once to the sidewalk, I heard her holler, "Need a ride?" Midwesterners are so accommodating. No. I didn't. But I had nothing to do so, yeah, why not. She had just crossed town to pick up her prescription medication and talked about how hard it was to manage financially with them costing so much. When she found out that I was just out of the Navy, she was determined to buy me a meal. She picked Carl's Junior, I opted to stick with the least expensive meal they had.

"Medium is fine," I said. Not wanting to add any burden to her already apparent heavy yoke.

"Make it a large," she told the drive thru speaker. Midwesterners, indeed, are very hospitable. She asked how long I would be in town for and I informed her that I didn't know. She offered to take me out to dinner the next night and told me to meet her at the park a few blocks away, the next day at 4:30 in the afternoon. I slept at the park and was there waiting when she pulled up. It was the first time I had been treated, blindly, to dinner at a soup kitchen.

A daily meal for those less fortunate or down on their luck. It was alarming to see the amount of people that needed this help. I never gave mind to this demographic before, and now, looking at one of her male counterparts across the table from us, it was like seeing myself thirty years in the future. And, for a moment, I was surprisingly fine with that. I looked around and realized these people were no different than me. A little down on their luck, but not denigrate. All that was lacking here was opportunity, not drive, capability or desire. Eating there was a truly eye opening experience that I am eternally grateful for. Thank you, Iowa.

The next day, I would make the dreaded call to Mom. She told *me* what was going to happen. Grandma and Grandpa would be celebrating their 50th wedding anniversary over the 4th of July weekend, one week away. Mom would end up getting me a Greyhound bus ticket to Fond Du Lac and would arrange for Aunt

Patty to pick me up from there. Mom and the rest of the family were flying in on the 2nd, and I would fly back with them to Arizona, after the week-long visit. Showing up wifeless after having already introduced Veronica to the extended family in Wisconsin not six months prior, really stoked the embarrassment factor, so I did what I could to keep to myself. If the relatives thought anything about be being solo, they never let on. I was accepted just as the others in my clan were, as family. I did get to meet up with a couple of my classmates from Middle School, so the trip wasn't a total wash.

Tyler Cross was my best, and possibly only, friend growing up. His twin brother, Tim, weighed a little more than Tyler did, so it was easy to tell them apart. Other than that, they were identical. Their Mom, Mary Cross, let me sign her up for ACN long distance with the understanding that her current long distance provider wouldn't charge her for the switch. They did, and I had mud on my face. I didn't even have the cash to cover the twenty dollars they charged her, it was embarrassing.

Tim and Tyler had shown me my first pornographic film, "Taboo", after a 6th grade summer school class, what seemed like a lifetime ago. VHS classics. I wonder if Mary knew her stash was secretly utilized while she was working. Boys will be boys. After Tyler found out I was in town, he invited me to a 4th of July party at their grandparent's farm. There was alcohol, fireworks and girls there. Notching number five on a couch pull-out bed was Melody's old classmate, Kayla, who I was surprised had become good friends with the Crosses. We were all over each other the whole night.

After the anniversary party, Aunt Patty had plans for us all to attend LifeFest, a Christian Music Festival, in the countryside outside Milwaukee. Melody invited Kayla, not knowing that we had just hooked up and that made for somewhat of an awkward festival. Not really the right venue to continue fooling around.

With Christians of all ages and many different music stages, Kayla and I let each other do our own thing. Travis had invited a girl, too. I totally stole her affection. He was furious. I couldn't help it. Danielle was a thin girl, while Kayla was a bit fuller featured. I didn't actively hit on Danielle, but nonetheless, we ended up making out one night in the grass of an abandoned area. Christian tongue, nothing more, I didn't want to spontaneously combust. She told me while we were walking back to the campsite, that she never thought she would kiss a smoker, but she liked it. I was a good kisser. Still am, I like to think.

When I wasn't pissing my cousin off, I made it my mission to collect drumsticks. I had acquired a nice, rare, collection of about six or seven splintered sticks. I got four of them autographed by their respective bands, and as the festival came to a close, I gave the collection to a cute girl who was also trying her best to get some memorabilia. The band Kutless threw out three sticks after their hour long concert that was played to a crowd of at least four hundred people. They were the main draw of the festival and I managed to get one of the sticks they threw out after their set. That was the best score, other than the make out session.

It was all over soon enough and with tail between my legs, I again, threw my backpack on the floor of the garage at 2435 Widgeon Drive in Lake Havasu City, Arizona. The city would come to be known as the 'Black Hole' of my life. I was back in the place that for years I was so desperate to abandon.

Three weeks later, I was able to convince Dad to let me stay with him in Paso Robles, California. Another red-eye Greyhound, and he picked me up in neighboring San Luis Obispo. He was staying in a small studio flat in wine country. Books and fitness gear took the bulk of the floor space. He was working with another real estate person, offering his tile labor in the flipping process that was sweeping the Central Coast in 2004. I was able to offer my assistance as general labor. There was not much to do for a nineteen year old in wine country, so I was able to save up a few hundred dollars within a couple weeks. Then Dad's Mom died. Peace be upon you, Elizabeth.

He left me with the Ford Escort and run of the place until he got back from the small service the family was putting on in Brick Township, New Jersey, where Dad was born and raised. It was the middle of August, and, at that point I felt I was being groomed to be the cameraman for my old man's 61 year old, aging, but muscular body. His vanity shut me off with the quickness. No, I don't want to take pictures of you working out, Dad. He would keep trying to plant the seed and I wasn't having it. So when he flew out to the east coast, I decided to skip town and take a trip to Lemoore, CA, an hour or so away. There was a casino there, Taichi, and I wanted to play poker.

I arrived and bought a $100 rack of chips at the only poker table I'd ever been to that you could smoke at. You may be asking yourself how I was able to gamble at nineteen years old. Well, at that time, gambling on Indian Reservations was an eighteen years or older adventure. It was the only time I felt that my life could change at any moment. Being in any casino meant I had a chance. My past didn't matter, only my odds, which weren't great when playing casino games, but at poker, you were playing other people. My odds of winning greatly increased. And I had attained a certain amount of success online, that I used to convince myself that I could duplicate at a live table. Bad beats and immature play often led to mounting online losses. I tended to stick to low buy-in tournaments, at first. Then to live stakes. Party Poker and FullTilt were my platforms of choice. Money always went in, and I would win, but I never cashed out when I should have. It was a money pit, but it got my shredded heart beating, and that made me feel alive. For that kind of adrenaline rush, I was willing to pay to play. Thing was, I was now playing with all the cash I had, which was usually every time I played.

After winning a number of consecutive pots, I caught the eye of a man who was sitting behind a castle of about $300 worth of chips. He shot me his business card and said that I reminded him of his nephew who had killed himself, a few years prior. Heavy talk for the poker table, I know, but I liked his openness. He left, and I was still there when he showed up the next evening.

Impressed at my card sharking stamina, he asked me if, after we were done, I'd like to come home to a home cooked meal. His mail-order bride from the Philippine Cherry-Blossom catalog had been with him for a few years, helping his successful olive ranch. In the last year, they were able to get papers for her son to immigrate. I couldn't let this pass me up and I agreed to go. Once there, he said he could use a ranch hand, as it was getting close to the olive harvest. I didn't see how that would be a bad idea. After dinner, we all sang karaoke, the kid sung "Bed of Roses" and I sang "That's Why They Call It the Blues." He outscored me ninety-eight to ninety-four. The microphone was rigged, I'm sure.

I would spend a week at the ranch, going out early mornings to clear out clogged irrigation lines. He showed me how to cure olives. That was enriching. Lye. Lye cures olives. It goes like this:

1) Fill a five gallon bucket ½ full with raw green olives.
2) Fill with water to ¾
3) Shake in a heavy dose of lye granules
4) Stir with a wooden stick
5) Let sit for ten minutes
6) Stir again
7) When the green olives start getting red spots, they are done curing
8) Rinse for another ten minutes with fresh water to wash all the lye off the olives
9) Enjoy pitted or un-pitted, with or without pimento.

The problem with this rancher was that he kept pushing me to get back in contact with my Dad, and that irritated me. I wasn't living my newly broken life based on anyone's guidance but my own. I certainly didn't like getting pushed aggressively to go back to be my Dad's camera slave. Dad was entering old age and was desperate to remain relevant. I had a lifetime of experiences ahead of me and didn't want to sell out just to maintain a squalid existence. So, in the middle of the night, I loaded up the Escort with four of the 100 or so twelve-packs of Pepsi that were stacked inside the rancher's front door. It was the refreshment stock for the undocumented labor that would show up in mere weeks to pick the fruit.

I took a digital camera and filled the Escort's gas tank out of the above ground 200-gallon gas tank that kept the ranch's quads fueled up. I was gone. I had no place in this world without seeming to just get pushed somewhere else that I didn't want to be, or forcefully having my dreams diluted. My whole life trajectory was demolished. There was no starting over. There was no mulligan. I had nothing. Everything I was counting on in life had been eroded in a short span of months, and there was no repairing the incalculable damage that had been wrought. I wanted to die. As the dust cloud filled the rearview mirror, I hit the 41. Thirty miles later, I was at the crossroads. Continue on, and I'd be back in Paso Robles in an hour, to await my father's eventual return. My pulse raced, and I closed my eyes. "Sorry, pop." I took the I-5 South onramp and resolved to not stop until I crossed into Mexico.

I had been driving on 'E' for what seemed like long enough to exhaust the majority of fumes I was sure was keeping the grey car moving. The little Ford got great gas mileage but had a small tank. To avoid running out of gas on the highway and being completely fucked, I pulled off at National City and found an empty gas station a mere ten miles north of the border. I got out and opened the hatchback to reveal a big plastic bag full of Gant Razors in an array of assorted colors. There were a handful that were packaged in plastic tubes, complete with a folded, photocopied page of directions on how to use the paradigm shifting razor. I tossed the bag in the passenger seat and returned to the steering wheel.

Just then, a car pulled up on my left and a man started shaving with a Bic-style razor. Really, God? Really? I watched him repeatedly run the t-style razor down the same part of his face in the glow of his visor light and flip-down mirror and surmised that he was using a dull blade. I grabbed a clear plastic tube containing a red razor from the bag and headed over to his open window. This can't be any different than door-to-door sales, I told myself. I have a product and this man obviously has a need. Best $5 I ever earned.

Maybe God was answering his prayers, too. Another sale, fifteen minutes later, netted me ten dollars for two Gant Razors, once I showed the woman pumping gas the matching name on my Driver's License and my sob story about running the car down to empty. I entered the gas station and bought a Snickers and put the rest of the money on pump three. Was I really about to do this? Was I really about to push myself to the limits of life? I took a quick mental inventory.

Unhappy... Check.

Depressed... Double Check.
Ready to give up on life... Obviously.

Back on the highway, I didn't have much time to second guess my actions as the entrance to Mexico was directly ahead. I had no plans on taking the "LAST AMERICAN EXIT" before the cars started jockeying for the quickest entrance. I joined them.

No money to speak of. No plan. Purely the uninhibited: "Throwing caution to the wind" moment of my life. Adding a little Robert Frost to the narrative: one road diverged into ten lanes in a sea of head and brake lights, I took the path less traveled by and that has made all the difference.

Vivo Mexico!

Chapter VI

United States & Mexico

The Imaginary Line

As I approached the slowing traffic in San Ysidro leading to the corrals that you had to pass through to enter Mexico, I recalled my recent past. I was following the same brake lights that I was with Veronica's family, that past October, and my heart broke a little more as I pulled up to the official border line. What was I doing? I didn't even know Spanish. In Dad's now stolen Escort, I got a green light. That was all that stood in the way of this American and Mexico, one red and green light.

Getting a red light upon entry meant you were asked to be searched upon entering by the police presence directly to your right, under a large metal canopy. A green light meant you were free to continue. More security is certain for anyone heading north into the States from within Mexico, if my drunken recollection of returning from Ensenada served me. Something didn't sit right with me about that. Why were Americans allowed to run amok throughout our neighbors house, but our neighbors weren't welcome in ours? Money? Yeah, it's probably about the money.

It was dark. The traffic was like a school of mackerel in the ocean. No one used turn signals, there was barely any braking or distancing, just a go-with-the-flow type feel. "Get off the highway," I told myself, and found a littered parking spot in front of a shuttered business with a brightly painted sign, reading "Palletas." I wouldn't know it was an ice cream shop for any other reason than the popsicle decals adorning the metal security shield, protecting the storefront. I gave a quick once over to my surroundings and promptly locked the doors. I would explore in the morning, under the safety of sun. I reached into the back seat and grabbed a can of Pepsi from the open twelve-pack. Forgive me, Dad.

The morning sunlight glared through the windshield. There were cars driving by and people walking the streets, not particularly interested in the gringo moving about in a hatchback. I pocketed the keys, grabbed another Pepsi and locked the driver side door from the inside before I closed it. The air smelt of breakfast burritos, coffee, seasoned beef and gasoline. I was in awe of the bustling city streets of Tijuana. There were people everywhere. There were lines of people waiting to get their orders placed at any number of food carts, at least four of them were in my immediate field of vision. There were health code violations everywhere. But this wasn't your mother's America.

Every storefront, packed tightly together, seemed to run one right into the next, and each had their own unique offerings. I saw taco stands connected to cell phone stores. A one door entrance to a hidden hotel above what was labeled a "Carneceria", a meat seller, confused me. The best way I could think to explain it now would be to say that my first taste of solo Mexico made me think of a Tetris of businesses. Nothing franchised. No stockholders. Just a rented space and a public offering, and boy, business was booming.

I ventured a few blocks away and sat next to a storefront on a corner, content to watch the day play by. My eye ventured across the street and to the right. "Camera Y Photo," what luck! I jogged back to the car and took out the digital camera and returned to the camera store. The owner was standing outside, enjoying the morning air, as well. Making eye contact with him and carrying something shiny, he could tell I was coming for him.

"Buenos Diaz," he greeted me.

I managed a quite American, "Hola." I held up the camera with a quizzical look on my face as if to say, "Are you interested?" He looked it over and offered back, "Quarenta Dollares."

Now, I knew the basic numerical system, Veronica had taught me well during my last trip, and I wasn't going to accept the first offer simply because I didn't know how to counteroffer. "Cinquenta," I shot back. Fifty dollars would give me a few days' worth of food, at least. He looked over the camera again and shook his head in agreement. He headed into his shop. He came back with two twenties, a five and five ones.

"Gracias, Senior," this Spanish thing was coming easy to me. When in doubt, I thought to myself, just think of it as 'immersion charades.' It's a lot less intimidating that way.

I found a taco stand and ordered four. Having nothing else to do, I went back to my corner to await inspiration. On the way, I found a cigarette stand and bought two packs and a lighter. About a half an hour went by and I was content just chain smoking my Mexican Marlboro Menthol Lights. I couldn't taste a difference, but they were half the price they were in America, which surprised me. I was trying to figure out my future food to cigarette expenditure ratio when a shadow stopped in front of me.

"Hey, you," a voice directed my way. I looked up. "Do you have a driver's license?" The brown man asked.

"Yes." I replied timidly. Am I about to get robbed?

"Do you want to make some money?" He asked. I tried to contain my excitement.

Yes, random English speaking Mexican man, I would much like to earn a side income to counter my recent string of thieving, I thought.

"Yeah?" My interest was definitely piqued. How can I earn money with a driver's license? He asked to see it. Apparently, the plastic card passed muster and he hailed a cab. The white and orange Taxi Libre pulled up and the man opened the back passenger door for me. After paying the cabbie and giving him a rapid set of directions in Spanish, he told me I was going to a hotel and was to wait outside the lobby for a white boy named Kevin, who would be wearing a Hawaiian shirt. I looked at the street sign; I had to remember where the car was parked. "F. Martinez & 2da," Spanish street signs, I thought rolling my eyes, figures. What the fuck is "2da"?

Arriving outside the Placio Azteca to wait for 'Kevin' was anti-climactic. I mean, the hotel itself was majestic in comparison to the surrounding real estate jungle. This was a far cry from the no-frills top floor of that random carneceria downtown, calling itself a hotel. I tried to go in to use the bathroom but didn't pass the dress code for entry. I was not getting in wearing a white tank top. So I was stuck outside in the September humidity, just waiting. Thirty minutes later, I spotted the Hawaiian-shirted American walking my way. I had to pee.

"Are you Cliff?" He asked. I said yes and extended my hand for shaking. "They won't let you in with that shirt."

"I know." I informed him. Opting not to let him know my bladder was about to explode.

"Hold on. I'll bring you down something." He jogged to the doors that were flanked by two men with "Securidad" in bold yellow letters blazoned on their black T-shirts. He emerged moments later with a blue button up and I put it on. He walked me into the lobby past the rent-a-cops and we took the elevator to the top floor. Penthouse, I thought... neat.

As we entered the room, Kevin pointed to the bed and told me to sit. I did as I was told. There was what looked like a young brother and sister on the other bed who would switch their attention from the TV sitting on a cheap dresser, to the window overlooking the pool. They seemed well behaved.

Kevin went over and started speaking to a woman on the other side of the bathroom door. The conversation escalated and it seemed that they were on the brink of yelling, when the door opened. The woman, Olivia, was a tall, rather large Mexican woman who strode toward me and held out her open hand.

"Ju license." She demanded. I handed it to her. "Ahrezhona." She said as if I wasn't aware. "OK, OK, es Ok." She handed it back.

Kevin and Olivia started speaking in tongues again and I just made a funny face at the kids who were staring at me for whatever reason. They giggled. The boy appeared to be about twelve years old and the girl looked a few years younger, possibly eight or nine. Kevin broke away from Olivia and she retreated to the bathroom and promptly locked the door. He came over to me to let me know that we would cross later that night.

"Do you have any money?" Kevin asked.

"Yeah, I got like twenty bucks on me." Although it was closer to fifteen in low-denomination American bills and Mexican Pesos, Kevin knew it was more than enough to get us a couple beers at a strip joint and the cab ride to and from said club. Given the unknown situation I was soon going to find myself in, I had made it a point to hide away one of the twenty dollar bills the camera man gave me, while I was waiting for Kevin earlier in the day, just in case I found myself getting robbed. Those fears were somewhat alleviated once I realized that there was some semblance of a plan in place. We walked out of the Placio Azteca and Kevin hailed a taxi.

"Adilitas, Centro." He directed. He briefly laid down the game plan in the five minute cab ride to the club. "I've got a girl at this place that I am going to say hi to, we are going to grab a couple beers and chill until tonight. When we make it across you'll get $500. No drugs. It's easy. I've been doing it for over a year now."

Hanging out with someone who knew the ropes of the underbelly of Tijuanian society, somehow calmed my nerves. I told myself I had nothing to worry about. We showed up at Adilitas and I gave the cabbie a fifty Peso bill. The foreign money was something to behold. The fifty Peso bill was completely plastic, with a bi-colored butterfly that when held up to the light, inverted its colors. I would have been more distracted with the awesomeness of Mexico's financial anti-counterfeit measures, but the purple building with unlit "Adilitas" signage appeared and signified the first time I would see strippers in action and all of a sudden I was in a hurry to pay the cabbie. Back in the Navy, in Bangor, Maine, it was midday when I showed my face at my first strip club but the American strippers were nowhere to be found. Not the case in Mexico. Sex was everywhere.

We entered without showing identification to the bouncer, and Kevin led me to a table. The music was loud, but not irritatingly so, and the stage was empty. Within seconds, a man was wiping down our table with a cloth and looked to Kevin for further instructions. Kevin ordered two Tecate's and added a couple other sentences in Spanish to the runner.

"He is going to go find her," Kevin informed me. Apparently, 'she' was his on-again off-again girlfriend, and I use that term loosely given our, then, current surroundings. She showed up moments later and shook my hand. A short, portly female, I didn't see anything too attractive about her other than her friendly smile. Over the club noise, I didn't care what they were talking about, in a language I had yet to dip my toe in. I was focusing on my beer, admiring the ambiance exuded by the tattered upholstery of the high-backed half-moon enclave we were seated in. Character.

I no sooner look up from my beer to see Mexican flesh. A stripper had found her way to Kevin's girl, who at this point I understood to be in management, and she was looking my way. Now, to preface a couple things...

1. I have had very limited experience with females at this time
2. I had just been divorced, as per the State of Arizona
3. My self-worth was at an all-time low
4. I was in a foreign country I knew very little about

All of which would make you think that I would have nothing to lose by maintaining this sexy stripper's attention. Now, in contrast, Veronica was a Hooter's girl, smoking hot in her own right, but the smooth molasses skin and hard petite body of this scantily clad skin-seller, instantly crushed my heart. "Where were you when I had a promising life?" I thought, as a wide eyed boy who never even had seen the red-light district in Spain. All my sailor buddies went to fuck working girls when we docked in Malaga. I was a faithful husband, leaving me with no regrets. However, there remains a heaping pile of disappointment I will never shed. The stripper whispered to Kevin.

"She said she wants to fuck you for free." He bluntly relayed. She looked at me and smiled. I had been in a foreign country for less than twenty-four hours and found myself about to smuggle souls across an international border, and had a Venusian Goddess offering herself to me, a complete stranger, and my young, immature mind thought, and I quote, "How many others has she offered this to?" I offered a polite "No, thank you" to Kevin to pass along and she looked at me like it was my loss.

The song changed and she immediately took notice. She gave me a sexy frown, and perkily proceeded to the stage. Kevin looked at me in disdain and shook his head. Then, she danced. With no one else to move for, she was grinding her body into my memory. The way her curves hit the black light positioned over the raised platform, glistening with a soft glow that whispered, "I want to be your sex toy..." just destroyed me. I was ill-experienced for a moment such as this. She gave me the one finger "come hither" motion, and I obliged. I stood awkwardly at the edge of the stage and she took her top off. Her supple breasts couldn't have been bigger than a small B-cup, ideal. This was too much for me to handle, but it didn't stop there. She leaned over and rested her forearms on my shoulders, then leaned into my ear and whispered in English, "If you're not going to fuck me, at least touch me." Seduced to the max, I was putty in her hands. My hands found her hips and as she swayed with them, she bit her lip.

My right hand traced the outline of her thong hugging her hip and moved to inches below her belly button, still teasing the fabric. She raised her ass towards the pole that was by now behind her and out of reach in order to give me full access to her. My hand slipped down between her legs and my fingers found her warmth. She gyrated her wet labia on my open palm and I immediately regretted the brilliance of my "No, thank you" response to her offer. After a moment, she pulled away slowly and returned to the pole. The sheer adrenaline of the moment didn't even allow for the sexual nature of what had just transpired to take hold. It would have been embarrassing to not be in full control of my loins, anyways. Welcome to Mexico, Clifford. I might be able to get use to this.

By the time I returned to the table, Kevin had a beer waiting for me. I wasn't in the mood to drink. "Go ahead," I told him as I slid it his way. I was still trying to process what had just happened. The soft fog of euphoria was still hanging over my brain as we got into the cab, headed back to the Placio Azteca. The cab ride back was in silence as the seven o'clock hour hit. We didn't even go back into the hotel room. Kevin called Olivia from outside the hotel lobby and let her know we were back. Twenty minutes and a couple phone calls later, a car pulled up from the secure parking lot.

"You ready?" Kevin asked. I was starting to have doubts. If this was so easy, why am I driving? If Kevin had been doing this for so long, why do they even need me? I noticed the California license plate, and felt a little uneasy. Plate and ID states did not match. But Olivia said it would be ok, and they have been doing this for what was apparently a certain amount of time. Damn the torpedoes, right? I got in and put the Honda Civic into drive.

Kevin directed me to the border. There was about a 100 car line to get back into the United States and it took us about a half hour to get to where the 4 lanes of traffic branched into ten corrals. With a customs agent at the end of each lane, standing between me and $500, Kevin put his seatbelt on and feigned sleeping. With five cars ahead of me, a drug dog and handler came around our car. Before I could get nervous, they moved on to the next vehicle.

Three cars left.

Two cars.

The yellow signal flashed "Pull Ahead" and I did as instructed, then "STOP." I was next.

I noticed the car ahead of me hand documents to the agent who took them into the booth for a moment and then handed them back and gave them the "move ahead" hand signal. My turn.

Pulling up, I felt the tinge of an adrenaline and anxiety epoxy race over me. The internal struggle of: "Do I try to counter-intelligence the border agent?" or just "Play it cool," which I've very recently failed miserably at.

"Citizenship?" The border agent asked.

"American." I replied.

"Identification." He prompted.

I reached over to Kevin and pretended to wake up my "drunk" friend.

"Kevin, I need your ID." He reached into his back pocket and grabbed his wallet. Fishing out his driver's license, he moaned as if he was about to throw up. "California" was emblazoned at the top of his card. My mind was racing. There is no way this looks legit, I thought. California plates, Arizona driver, California passenger. I concluded my luck was about to change.

"Whose car is this?" The agent asked as he took our ID's. Noticing the license plate cameras when I pulled up, I figured they would scan all plates.

Verbal vomit ensues: "It's mine, I just bought it. I just came from Arizona to buy it." The agent knows I'm sketchy as hell. I've officially blown it.

"Sir, can you pop the trunk?" I look over at Kevin who is still faking sleeping, no direction. I find the trunk release lever and pull. Kevin sits up because he knows we are busted. The agent radios for assistance and comes to me and asks me to take the key out of the ignition and put them on the roof. Out of the back seat passenger window, I see the second Border Agent escorting the two kids from the hotel, out of the trunk and into the main building. The original agent walks us to the secondary inspection area, and the car follows shortly thereafter. We are searched, and the car is heavily inspected. Kevin and I are then taken into the Customs and Border Patrol building. Set up like a bank lobby, there is an array of blue chairs and four teller booths, with computer screens and fingerprint scanners visible from the seating area. Kevin and I sat together.

"Okay, they are going to ask you some questions. Tell them a short Mexican man named 'Juan' asked you to drive the car across. You met him at 'Peanuts & Beer.' He said he would pay you $200. And you didn't know what was in the car," Kevin rapidly explained. It seems like Kevin hadn't been as successful at this venture as he made himself out to be. Getting caught must have been the norm, rather than the exception. Getting caught ensured three things: the car would be impounded, a warrant search would be attempted and you would lose twenty-four hours of your life. That's it. Wasn't my car, didn't care. Dad wasn't back from New Jersey yet to report his car stolen, so I was warrant negative. And as for the twenty-four hours... that's it?

'Smuggling' is a crime, but getting caught illegally transporting an alien, is really little more than an inconvenience. You get a sack lunch and wait for the warrant check to come back. Then they release you, to walk right back into Mexico and try again. I was grateful and relieved that there were no serious ramifications for pulling such a stunt. Olivia, on the other hand, was not too happy.

"Chicken shit," I remember her calling me. In our 24 hours together at customs, Kevin came clean, in a way. He informed me that they had not successfully passed anyone in months and Olivia was $5,000 in debt to the Placio Azteca. This still didn't stop her from spending her days locked in that bathroom smoking methamphetamine like there was no tomorrow. They had spent their last $500 on the now impounded Civic, and he didn't really know what they were going to do.

Out of guilt, I would end up offering my Dad's Ford Escort for another attempt. Same result. I wasn't nervous or anything that time, but was still randomly asked to pop the trunk. A middle-aged man was recovered. Another impound, warrant check, twenty-four hours, and I was back in Mexico, this time, with nothing. The hidden twenty dollars of shoe money was used after Kevin and I got released the first time, for a couple large beers, two packs of smokes, a cab ride, and a little bit of marijuana. The second time we got released, Kevin and I were instructed to walk to Colonio Libertad, a neighborhood a good twenty-minute walk from downtown Tijuana. We met another woman who knew Olivia, her name was Carmen.

I didn't know their exact relationship, be it just friendly, or maybe they were merely two pawns in the human transportation game. Either way, Olivia abandoned me to Carmen, and Kevin stuck with Olivia.

Carmen's organization was truly a family business. She had two children, an eleven year old boy named Angel and a fourteen year old girl named Jasmine. Carmen spoke little English and Angel was the go-between. Carmen immediately made me feel part of the family. She showed me my new living quarters, a small bedroom in a back guest house with a mattress on a bare cement floor, truly no frills, but it was all that I needed. She then gave Angel a 200 Peso bill and asked me to go with him to the Super Taco restaurant down the street to get lunch for us all.

Angel, who preferred to be called Guido, (pronounced 'Wed-o') ordered us each a glass-bottled Coca-Cola and a taco, sustenance for the ten minute walk back. What seemed like thirty seconds later we were both presented with a little paper plate with an open faced corn tortilla taco 'con todo' or 'with everything.' A communal plastic

Tupperware dish was loaded with sliced cucumber, whole red radishes and lime segments and I helped myself to my favorite vegetable.

Lightly salted, cucumbers are hard to beat. The limes were sliced in such a way to maximize juicing and minimize the seed content. It was as if the workers knew a rogue lime seed in a taco would surely ruin the experience, once bitten into. I strategically chose my lime and spritzed the carne taco that was heaping with thinly sliced grilled beef that was chopped up on a wood block, which made the meat morsels glisten. Finely chopped onion, cilantro, and a spoonful of homemade tangy green salsa completed the 11 Peso taco.

Guido looked at my wide eyes in confusion, as if to say, "It's just a taco dude, get over yourself." He placed the larger family order as we finished our appetizer. Guido passed the taco barista the billet and dropped two large bi-metallic coins in the tip jar, labeled "Propenas." He carried the taco bag, and I grabbed the two liter of Coke. We made small talk on the walk back to Carmen's house. I didn't really know what to say to a 5th grader. I gave him the basic rundown that I used to be in the Navy and worked with computers. Then I got married, got out of the Navy for her, and then she left me. He seemed to understand that I was feeling down about the whole scenario, and just offered, "I'm sorry about all of that, but you will like it here. My Mom is good people."

We arrived back at Carmen's and she invited me into the main house where she lived with the kids. The interior was nice. Tile floors and decent furniture, a television and a lot of pictures adorned the west wall. My gaze was immediately drawn to a two foot statue of what looked to be the female version of the Grim Reaper. It looked to be made out of a pale colored plastic or plaster and had many colorful candles surrounding what could only be described as an altar to this scythe carrying hooded woman. She noticed me noticing it.

"Mi Sentissima Muerte." She said. I looked to Guido.

"The Holy Death. She protects us," He informed me as he handed the bag of food to his Mom. She motioned us to the table and we ate during a conversation of 'telephone.' Everything translated through Angel, and every once in a while, Jasmine would help him if he didn't know how to phrase a question properly. She just wanted to know about me and my story. It seemed that business talk would happen after the meal, and it did. Jasmine excused herself as Carmen and I made our way to the couch in the space used as the living room. Guido seemed content standing. Carmen spoke to her son while looking at me.

"Ok, she said tomorrow we will go. All you have to do is drive the car across the border and park at the Subway restaurant right on the other side." He continued to tell me that he will meet me there with someone. We would all eat lunch together and then go to San Diego to drop them off at the safe house. Then we would drive back to Carmen's. I would get $200 per 'head'. She then took me to the car, a Chevy Lumina. It was in decent shape. She showed me the California title and let me know it was in good standing. There was no risk at the border at all for me. What a big change up from my previous employer, I thought. Welcome to the family.

Guido knocked at my door the next morning. Was that a rooster I heard?

"Wakey, wakey." He chimed through the door.

"I'm up." I replied. Surprisingly, I slept like a baby, and was ready to face the day's new adventure.

"We are going to leave in an hour." He stated. Alrighty, then. Dressed in what I was wearing the day before, and the day before that, I needed a cigarette. I had four left. My housemate was named 'Poncho' and wasn't related to Carmen, but acted as a jack of all trades, for her. He also worked at a car wash directly next to Carmen's house.

He was a chunky, happy-looking kid probably no more than seventeen years old. We would bond over food and beer. Language wasn't our strong suit, but we did the best we could. As I walked out and lit my cigarette, I noticed him already working on the engine of an older blue pickup truck. He acknowledged my presence and went back to work.

As the fragrant blue-gray smoke simmered from the tip of my cigarette, I watched him put his oily rag down and make his way to the driver seat and try to start the boxy machine. It wouldn't do more than click. I don't know what that meant, and judging by his hung head, perhaps neither did he, but I was certain he was not about to give up anytime soon. Carmen called me to the black wrought-iron gate that secured the back house from unwanted visitors and handed me two breakfast burritos. One for me, one for Poncho.

"Gracias." I managed. Shortly thereafter, the house started bustling with action. Carmen's Ford Explorer pulled up and a woman and child got out and were ushered into the main house. Another car pulled up with a man simply known as Guymas. Later, I would find out that he was the one who sourced the human cargo from the deep south that were brought up for transport. He would smoke meth out of an altered light bulb in my bedroom, and swore me to secrecy.

Carmen didn't appreciate the potential problems that drugs brought. She was in the business of liberating people for profit, not entrapping them into an addictive mental escape. I appreciated that, so I relegated myself to only smoking weed, and only after 11:00 PM when she was sure to be asleep. Never did I share Guymas' crystalized light bulb, even though I was asked on several occasions. From the moment I saw the contrast of Kevin's ID Photo versus the 130 pound tweaker he became, I swore to myself that I would never touch the stuff. Weed was good enough for me, no point in adding to the narrative of it being a 'gateway drug.' Plus, Poncho always had some on hand.

Carmen gave me a reddish-brown 100 Peso bill for the toll roads. Those roads were quicker and less destroyed. Guido got in the car with me and told me to follow his Mom. They used Boost Mobile phones that acted like walkie-talkies. Until we got to the toll roads, the local roads were for shit. Potholes the size of basketballs forced me to swerve seemingly nonstop, it was like a game of reverse Frogger. I saw the Tecate Beer signage before I saw the city limit signs.

Tecate, Mexico. Tecate beer, one of the staple domestic brews of Mexico, was made there. I followed Carmen to a McDonald's parking lot and pulled up next to her. We went in and she ordered an assortment of food. I didn't ask many questions, but I assumed, with all that food, we would be there for a while.

As I was picking the last remnant of American cheese off of the McMuffin wrapper, I heard the Boost Mobile chirp of Carmen's phone. She responded to it and gave instructions to Guido. He told me to get in line and cross the car.

"Tell the agent you were riding quads with your cousins." He continued, "Wait for me at the Subway." And it *was* that easy.

Carmen had this border crossing on lock. The gig went like this:

First off, the Tecate border is infinitely smaller than that of the San Diego/Tijuana border. Thus, leading to more control for us. There were only two lanes in, to Mexico, and two lanes out, to the United States. The Customs office and foot traffic into the States were situated on the east side of the port of entry. The Mexican side officials were bribed to turn a blind eye and allow Carmen to work her craft. Whenever an eighteen-wheeler would enter Mexico, there was a small window of time when the complete view of border patrol was obstructed. There were no cameras set up at that time on the Mexican owned west side of the port. So, when a semi approached and would obstruct the field officer's view, Guido would lead the 'head' across the border along the passenger side of the semi and immediately enter a Payless Shoes, directly on the other side of the border fence.

The shoe store was so close to the border fence you could hit it with rock, from the Mexican side, with little effort. They would then spend five minutes or so walking around the Payless to make sure there were no approaching agents, then Guido would lead them diagonally across the street to the Subway sandwich shop, sixty yards away, where I was waiting, usually reading the USA Today with a fountain drink. Once the head arrived we would each enjoy a sub, take a bathroom break, and nonchalantly enter into the gassed-up Chevy Lumina.

There were two routes out, each involving a checkpoint. The quicker way was a surefire way to get searched. That checkpoint was less than ten miles from the border, directly west on a back road. I was instructed to NEVER take the left. Heading east, then north, **then** west on the I-10 was where you would have the best luck, being one of thousands that pass through that checkpoint every day.

After my first successful run, it became apparent: if the driver is white, they just pass you through. I didn't even have to roll down my window. On the days it was raining, the checkpoint was closed and it was a free ride the whole way through to San Diego. It was free money for me, and cheap freedom for the head. Not until I hit Alpine, CA, would the cell phone pick up signal and I would radio, "Ama, Ama- PASO! PASO! PASO!"

'Ama' was my way of calling her Mom without impeding on biology. A Viejas Casino sign dotted the landscape and I made a point to remember to go there. Getting into San Diego, I spotted a mall. I was already spending my money, I needed new clothes.

Dropping the alien woman off at the drop house in San Ysidro meant my leg of the journey was done. A twenty-three year old girl named Tiffany, who received the illegals, would drive them north to Los Angeles for another $200 per person. There is one big checkpoint on the I-5 north, but it was more bark than bite the handful of times I made both legs of the journey. Two of those times it was closed because of rain, as well. It struck me. So, the big drug runs move under cover of rain. It is the grand illusion of security, America.

For the next seven months, this was my life. Once or twice a week we repeated the gambit. Always, "Ama, Ama , Ama - PASO! PASO! PASO!" I would slowly build up my room, paint the walls blue, and replace the bare mattress with a new futon. I would buy a PlayStation II with Madden and Grand Theft Auto from the mall in San Diego. I would spend many nights playing poker at Viejas, taking the trolley from San Ysidro all the way to where the casino shuttle would pick up lucky losers. I made stripper friends in downtown Tijuana, but never saw the bombshell from Adilitas ever again. I bought an electric guitar and amp and learned how to play Boyz II Men - 'I'll Make Love to You.' I even wrote a comeback love song for Veronica, although I could never score it with music, I still liked the lyrics. I wasn't yet over her but had accepted it, nonetheless. I picked up conversational Spanish and no longer needed to rely on Guido to interpret for Carmen. I had grown. It was time to get back with the family. It was time for a new beginning.

As I pulled into the Tijuana/San Ysidro border lanes going north for the last time, in the blue Chevy stick-shift truck that Poncho had finally got running, I looked at the sea of brake lights ahead of me. I had lost so much chasing my American Dream, and when it turned to an American Nightmare I fled to the land of the dead. I fled to the land of the forgotten. A land where by sheer necessity, sex is a commodity, while love is primal, yet enduring.

Twenty yards from the agent booth, I was reminded that being born twenty yards south of an enforced imaginary line, you are born into a life of struggle, from cradle to grave with the offshoot exceptions. A land where to legally immigrate to the power to the north, you have to pay over $10,000 and invest up to ten years petitioning or waiting in line for a green card. What deterrent is there, then, for an alien trying his hand at life's slot machine of 'put me in the trunk and try your luck,' or paying Carmen $2,000 cash for a guaranteed cross. Others methods are more expensive, and more dangerous. At the cheapest route, scores die each year trying to cross the uninhabited wilderness, just for a shot at getting a job crawling for miles on their hands and knees picking American cilantro, just to support their families, back home.

With the pickup bed full of my belongings, the border agent rifled through some of it, and waved me through. Welcome to America, the home of the free.

Born twenty yards north of this imaginary line, I am struck with guilt. At what human cost is this inequity of existence justified? Leaving Mexico, I was proud to have done my little good in the world. I had crossed fifty-two souls.

Fifty-two souls: each marked with a penned 'X' on a rat skull I found on a walkabout to Tijuana from Colonio Libertad, in October. In my tenure as a coyote, I saw many families reunited. There were tears. If America is the true beacon of light in the world, how could they allow a neighbor's house to fall into such disrepair, a people into such despair, without an infantry of support standing guard to make sure their teetering abode doesn't collapse?

I exited the I-8 East on the Alpine exit. I pulled as close to the Viejas side entrance as I could, put it in neutral and stepped on the e-brake petal. Walking up to the ashtray, stationed right outside the casino, I placed the marked rat skull on the metallic sand.

"Thanks for the memories." I said aloud to the ether.

The stars shone brightly.

As I pulled away from the land that had changed me, I sensed a smirk come across the face of the two-foot Santa Muerte statue in the bed of the truck, wrapped in the futon mattress.

I hoped I had made her proud.

Chapter VII

13 Rays of the Rising Sun

In full disclosure, leaving Mexico was more of an escape than a mutual separation. Carmen had acquired a new safe house twenty miles from the downtown area, which meant a whole new life that I wasn't keen on taking up. I quite enjoyed walking the mile and a half from Colonio Libertad to downtown TJ. Every night was an adventure. Beers were cheap, and if you bought Mary Jane from the strip club waiters, they would guard the bathroom while you smoked your overpriced, low quality joint, but at least you got protection. I had no say in the matter of moving safe houses. So, before I was to be 'relocated' I made a move of my own and snagged the truck key from Poncho's key ring while he was in the shower, and waited for him to fall asleep before I loaded the blue Chevy stick shift with my belongings.

It would have made too much noise to load the futon frame, so I was relegated to just salvaging the futon mattress, which had enough padding to keep my Santa Muerte statue safe during the long drive home. My clothes, my Sony PlayStation II, my electric guitar, and my TV and DVDs were about enough to justify the other random losses that I would have to leave behind. Being locked behind a seven foot tall gate, I put to use something I saw from the local San Diego FOX TV station.

There had been a story by Pete Fuentes about a string of fitness club locker room robberies, where the villains would use a Phillips head screwdriver inserted into a tube sock (to disguise their intentions) and just snap master locks off lockers by just inserting and twisting the driver against the curved metal of the lock arm. The metal of the screwdriver neck is stronger than the metal of the lock arm so with a little torque... "SNAP!" And just as advertised, impressed that it actually worked, I immediately went into stealth mode.

If the lock recoiling against the gate had produced enough noise to wake up either Poncho or Carmen, an ordeal would certainly have ensued. So, I opened the gate which swung into the quiet, vacant street. Then came the hard part.

Poncho had fixed the running parts of the truck, but the starter was still the problem child. Anyone knowing anything about manual vehicles, though, knows that dead batteries are not that big of a problem, with a bit of a decline in any given road. Just get the vehicle moving, push in the clutch, drop it into second gear, get a little speed, swap the clutch for gas, and you are golden. The decline in the street was there, but I still had to get the truck out of the corral. For a good twenty feet, there was just enough width going to the back courtyard area for the truck to pass through only with both front doors closed. I would not be able to walk it through. I walked the truck as far as I could and straightened out the steering wheel. I would have one good shot at this, if the wheel turned unexpectedly I would certainly hit stucco, and someone would wake. I lifted the handle as I quietly closed the driver's side door. From the level ground of the courtyard, there was a minor incline right before you hit the street, so I had to push, and fast. I still was worried that someone was listening to what was going on or, God forbid, Guido or Jasmine were outside playing past bedtime.

Gripping the side of the truck bed to ensure I wouldn't lose any ground to the incline, I got to the tailgate. Random bits of gravel crunched under my feet. "Don't slip," I told myself.

Getting a rocking start, I made my final push and made it out into the street without incident. Then, I had to do a 'run, open door, jump in and hit brake' before I struck the neighbor's trash cans, situated directly across the narrow, unlit street. The gradual 'decline to freedom' was mere feet away. I didn't even bother closing the gate. I gave myself a two-step, left foot push out the open driver door and was immediately rolling down the hill. I lit it up into second gear, and I was off.

Hours after Alpine, my headlights illuminated the "Welcome to Arizona" sign. Snaking up the Colorado River is Highway 95. I headed north as the gas tank dwindled. Having no cash, I began devising contingency plans for when I would eventually run out of fuel. I wouldn't be able to hock Gant Razors on the side of the highway, this time. My anxiety was alleviated as I spotted city lights on the darkened horizon. Selling a number of DVD's to the McDonald's staff in Quartzite, AZ gave me just enough gas to get back to Lake Havasu City, AKA 'The Black Hole.' As far as running out of gas is concerned, I got lucky to be in an incorporated area of the vast desert. I pleaded my case to the burger flippers that were 75 yards from where my truck came to rest. Between us was a gas station.

"Normally we are not supposed to do this," said a young female shift runner, "but what do you got?"

It was a clear night, and they followed me to the parking lot, out of view of the cameras. I figured I needed just ten dollars to get to Mom's driveway, and with my up-to-date movie collection, it was easy for her and two male coworkers to find a couple selections each. Some were Spanish titled, but I assured them they were the legit

English versions. The only one I was sad to let go of was "La Dia Despues De La Manana" or "The Day After Tomorrow," the apocalyptic climate change movie featuring a mass exodus into Mexico from an uninhabitable America. Something about that scenario stuck. Maybe I was just thirty years ahead of the times? At least if it did happen like that, I'd know ahead of time about Super Taco and to keep the important money in the soul of my shoes. Two things I was proud to have learned about, first hand.

Another stroke of luck was needed as the front passenger wheel was nestled in a large pothole. I tried in vain to push it out but to no avail. Then, as an angel from the night sky, a homeless-looking man approached me.

Noticing the large collection of random things I was hauling he asked point blank, "Hey bud, do you have a bedroll?" Thank you, baby Jesus!

"Yes, I do. If you help me out of this mess, it's yours." Together, with little effort, we were free of the rut, and shortly thereafter, I was parked next to the gas pump I so desperately needed. I gave him my pillow and a rolled blanket and we parted with a handshake and a mutual, "Thank you."

As the dawn broke over Havasu's eastward mountain range, I felt a surprising lack of emotion as I pulled into Mom's gravel driveway. It felt like, "Ok, I failed at my naval career, at my marriage & at my time enduring Dad's narcissism, but I'm still alive with a new found understanding of the abundant economic advantages that were before me. Notwithstanding, tail-between-my-legs, **again**, I was back under Mom's roof. No warrants (thanks for not filing, Dad), but Mom had received and saved a letter from a certain displeased olive rancher asking for his camera back.

"It says that if you return the camera he won't press charges," she let me know, concern on her face. I wasn't worried. They are not going to come after me for a $150 camera, and I don't plan on being back in California for some time. I dismissed this dated threat, wondering where I would be if I hadn't taken that middle of the night b-line for the Mexican border from the ranch. There was nothing in Paso Robles for me anyways, so I squashed that line of thinking. I wasn't ashamed about what I had been through the last nine months. In actuality, I felt blessed to have put myself in the position to enhance my worldview. Even if I had no idea at the time, that that would have been the outcome.

So, I was back in Arizona, with limited prospects. What was one to do? I turned twenty in the Mexican countryside so the best of life was still not available to me. One more year until I would turn twenty-one, then, who knows, Vegas maybe? I had raked in some good pots, and tournament placements at Viejas, who's to say that I couldn't do the same in the big city? I was determined to take it easy, and be ready to move quickly in any direction that life would choose to pull me. I had nothing tying me down.

The next morning, Melody, in a frightful panic, kicked over my Holy Death statuette that was placed at the mouth of the hallway. The ensuing fall broke the globe off of the Deity's plastic hand, and Melody, after being scared shitless that early in the morning, threw her in the garage. I didn't argue. I thought it was funny. She wasn't as amused. I'm still waiting for the negative consequences to graze her life for those actions. Waiting for her karma is on the backburner of my life, but I'm still waiting, nonetheless. Ok, you may feel I'm being a bit harsh, but let us talk about Melody for a moment.

Born Melody Raquel Gant, 371 days after I was brought into this world, she always had the run of life. I became malnourished while breastfeeding because all Mom's biological nutrients were going to the womb. I've seen pictures: I was a fucking 'Skeletor' looking eight-month old. My makers, eventually, and no short of time, had me drinking goat's milk. Looking back, as far as milk is concerned, my choice for initial drink, in order: natural, full-nutrient breast milk, goat milk coming in second, bovine milk a distant 3rd, and empty breast milk absolutely last on the list. If you can't fully wean number one before baking number two, that's just irresponsible. Maybe I should have been more colicky just to make sure that the parents couldn't have sexy time till I finished cutting teeth.

Melody quickly outgrew me, choice nutrients and all, and was always a bit taller than me. She was aggressive, too. She would scratch my back incessantly when we were young. Leaving red marks that would only wound me because by the time I started returning the pain, we would be separated. When we moved to Lake Havasu into the three bedroom duplex at 2776 Arabian Drive it was all three boys in a room, all three girls in a room, and Mom and Dad in a room. Mom and Dad made up for that "slight" by giving Melody the Master Bedroom when we moved to the newer four-bedroom house on Widgeon. She was a staple in sports, which I never got around to exploring. Volleyball, basketball, and softball were her three favorites. Due to an impromptu hand-job in the back of a school bus carrying both male and female basketball players to an out-of-town tournament, she is the reason they don't travel together, anymore.

While I was gearing up to serve my country, and making spending cash at a rate of $5.50 per hour with Arturo, Mom got Melody a job. I mean, it was called a job, but it was more like having a personal ATM machine. Her and Mom tag-teamed, twenty-four hours a day, doing homecare for the widow of a Montana Oil Barron, maybe it was one of the Dakotas, but she had money. Two "Homecare Specialists," even though I doubt either of them knew so much as first-aid, let alone CPR, was the A-Team assigned to offer companionship to this woman.

The woman, Eileen Cannon, was lucid. She bathed herself and handled her own bathroom trips. She lived in a beautiful house on the north end of town. Melody would spend her days sunbathing by Eileen's pool. Making fifteen dollars per hour plus overtime, her and my Mom had quite the racket going on. Mom would commonly leave Eileen home alone and take Eileen's new van around running personal errands, or going to garage sales. Eileen loved to gamble and enjoyed fine dining, always paying for whoever was with her. Christmases were spent at her house.

I remember staying up for three days straight watching Hurricane Katrina footage flowing in from New Orleans, Louisiana on CNN. We, still, didn't have cable at our Widgeon house. I adored Eileen, but felt that she was being taken advantage of, but I'll just chalk that up to jealousy.

Feeling that she was falling behind in life because of her lack of breast development, Melody got implants at a young age, which was likely her pass-key to the societal echelon she felt she was entitled to. Society obliged. She has been to the Playboy Mansion, at one point had a topless photo or two online, and has hobnobbed with some who's-who of entertainers. She has bragged that she shook DJ Tiesto's hand and informed me that Ron Jeremy is a dick in person. So hardcore! Most of that would come later in life, but at this time, she had been out of school for a year and had a new car and had moved into an apartment off of Mill Avenue, in Tempe, Arizona.

When Melody was finished with her visit to Havasu, I decided it might be beneficial to puppy-dog along back to Phoenix with her. I wasn't on the apartment lease, but she let me stay there for a couple weeks to see if I could find a job, which I did, in short time. I went into a Papa John's on the Arizona State University turf of University and Rural Ave. Situated next to a car wash, the unique stand-alone building was not built by corporate. I was hired on the spot, due to A) my pizza experience and B) this store needed extra employees because it was tapped to serve the upcoming Iron Man Triathlon that was normally held in Hawaii, but for whatever reason found itself in the valley of the sun, with the swimming portion to take part at the newly built Tempe Town Lake. Once I suited up and got back in the swing of things, the General Manager, Mark, began to get suspicious.

"Are you from Corporate?" He asked semi-seriously as if I was sent to ensure that standards were being upheld.

"I've just been in pizza for a while." I laughed.

In all my years of 'service to the crust,' I had never seen a three-tiered oven. But there she was, in all her majestic mechanical beauty. As April 9th, 2005 drew near, it became crystal clear that

Mark was going to have his work cut out for him on that cut station. Running at full capacity, cutting and boxing pies is an adrenaline pumping experience for a *double*-stacked oven. I couldn't imagine having <u>THREE</u> layers of pizzas coming at you with not so much as a safety guard. A safety guard is a stainless steel tray coming off the end of the oven that effectively 'catches' the pizzas that would have otherwise just have fallen to the floor. I have recurring nightmares about said scenario, not fun.

After the triathlon, which went off without a hitch, he presented me with the Platinum DVD Edition of Scarface, after he overheard me say I've never seen it, a week earlier. That was really cool to me. Other than Arturo, I'd never really been given anything extra for a job well done, it was more so just how I operated. Being cost-conscious and service-oriented is the only way I allowed myself to work. One of the motivational books I read while at sea said something to the effect of "work like you own the business," so I did. And it showed.

Melody took off for a long trip to California with her girlfriends and I ignorantly sub-let her apartment to a new Hispanic hire at the Papa John's. Pretty much, he paid me more than what I paid Melody for that month, it was a no brainer. I had intended him to be gone before she got back, but that's not exactly what happened. What **did** happen I will never fully know, but I left him at the premises for one week unattended and when I did eventually hear Melody was in town ahead of schedule, the gig was up. All I remember is showing up to the apartment for the first time in a week and she was yelling and crying. The place was a mess.

There were sunflower shells everywhere, the kitchen sink was full of moldy food scraps and there was drug paraphernalia in the bedroom. Meth baggies and trash were everywhere. She was not too happy with me. She had no problem throwing all his belongings in the dumpster: clothes and a number of glass elephant statuettes he referred to as his 'Idols.' Maybe it was even sadistically therapeutic for her to do so. We eventually finished cleaning it up and she turned in her keys to the apartment office. *That* was what I was missing, the one month she rented to me, was her last month of the lease. I was not informed of that. Surprise! Did I go to Havasu that week? Was I on a poker bender? I don't recall my whereabouts at that time, I was just gone.

Driving back to Havasu from Tempe in my Mom's Dodge Intrepid was a somber journey. True, I felt a bit guilty, but I also thought Melody was a being a bit of a drama queen about how it all went down. Oh well. I figured I wouldn't have to deal with her again for some time. That much was certain. It may have been better for my future had she shunned me for life at that moment. But she didn't. We went our separate ways and it was for the better. She had a chip on her shoulder and that was almost as annoying at Dad's narcissism. Dad had to let you know how great he was, Melody just *expected* you to know.

Now what?

The local paper -> The Havasu Herald -> Help Wanted section -> Jackpot.

Across the Colorado River, Lake Havasu City, Arizona's sister city, Havasu Lake, California, boasts a quaint casino on an Indian Reservation, Havasu Landing Resort & Casino. The radio ads end with a jingly, "How lucky can you get?" Well, I was lucky enough to pass a casino clearance and be approved by the, uh, high-priestess? Some woman high in the Tribe had to give me a once over and a head nod, and I was then officially a new line cook at a horrible restaurant.

Not quite Gordon Ramsay's "Kitchen Nightmare," but definitely a disservice to people who paid money to eat. Everything was Sysco frozen. The only thing worth a damn was the Prime Rib, every Friday, and getting an "End Cut" would assure you a hefty chunk of slow cooked greatness. Also worthy was the no frills 100% beef hotdog, which was deep fried. Whatever you do, stay away from the Orange Roughy. Never trust a fancy fish from a dive café. That's like getting Sushi from a gas station. Please, just don't.

The little smoky casino consisted of about 100 slot machines and three blackjack tables. Seven more months and I would be able to hit the floor to waste my money at the stingy machines. Mom and Eileen would play here only as a last resort. The BlueWater Resort & Casino in Parker, Arizona was Eileen's favorite. A thirty-five minute drive, she would bankroll my Mom and try to breach the 'Fort Knox' setup of progressive machines. I can't remember Mom ever coming back a big winner, always with the same mantra though, "We had fun." Yeah. I bet.

Bummer about working at the casino was the 30-minute boat ride on the DREAMCATCHER, a double decker, twin-engine oversized pontoon boat. It was a grind every day, and that trip was on our dime, so the $7.50 per hour California pay was more like six and change if you averaged out the time lost boating to work every day. Plus, management was poor. We did get to listen to low volume music, though, which I danced to while prepping salads, and sang to, while scooping heated vegetables onto burger plates. My coworkers liked my singing, especially in October, when 'Monster Mash' came on the airwaves. I liked doing the 'Frankenstein' for their collective amusement.

April was a thin Native waitress that I was absolutely in longing for. When I realized that even my glorious singing wasn't going to win her eye, I moved on to focusing my energies on the blonde Caucasian waitress, who had been slipping me smiles from where she would pick up her plated orders.

She lived on the reservation with a large female cook who had been at the casino for years. I mean, reservation royalties *plus* rent from an Anglo, would mean that the cook chick, who was in her mid-twenties and super cool, was probably making a decent living. Although their living quarters weren't extravagant by any stretch of the imagination, maybe she was a saver. The blonde brought me into her room after work one day and we drank as we watched the movie, Labyrinth. I don't remember much of the movie, but sex partner number seven was notched in my 'sexcapades belt' that doesn't exist. If you are counting at home, yes you are correct. I have made a glaring error in not reporting number six. Well. In the spirit of the open book theory, I will briefly indulge your curiosity.

Tijuana, Mexico. October, 2004.

I had just finished a full run from Tecate to Los Angeles with whom I deemed to be a sixteen year old female. Being the professional coyote I was, I did my best to make her feel comfortable during the long drive. Making it up to Los Angeles with Carmen giving me directions via my Boost mobile phone, in this rare solo trip without Guido, was different. Usually, he would sit in the front seat and talk to the cargo until we got to the safe house. This trip was almost completely silent, save for the radio. I found my way to our destination and delivered her to her mother and father who were waiting happily. It was a night trip, so I couldn't really see their faces, but I remember her father telling me that if I was ever in town again, to visit. He said they would make a special meal for me out of their sincere gratitude. I thanked them for their kindness. I was really taken aback at what I had just done.

Rarely did I get to experience the reuniting part of my services. It was more like I was just a cog in a bigger wheel. But, shaking his hand that night really let me know that I had just made a lot of anxiety go away, a lot of pain subside, and a lot more heartbeats that night. It truly is an indescribable feeling.

Getting back to Tijuana, I just wanted to relax and get a massage. So I took fifty dollars to a club and told the runner I wanted a massage. It was the weirdest chain of events I have ever experienced.

He was like, "Yeah, massage," and winked at me. I was irritated at that fact and I did not want to engage in commerce that way. I wanted to get naked and have a good, fifty United States Dollars' worth of a non-sexual yet stimulating muscle rub. He brought the first girl. I am not a big breast kind of guy, give me a tight B-cup and I am beyond satisfied. Anything bigger than that, I'll go to K-mart if I need throw pillows. But for some reason that night I was willing to sacrifice for the greater good of not wasting time, and I learned an important life lesson that night. Big Boobs... does not mean... no penis. Aha! You thought you caught me! No-No, my friend, buckle up!

Giving my partner the benefit of the doubt by calling her a 'her,' she deemed it less strenuous to just seduce me into having intercourse, thus not having to *work* for the money, just *slut* for it. 'Slut' being a verb, in this application. Blow job... boring.... Her rubbing herself underneath her lacy outfit... not appealing, but if she is not going to comply with my massage request, what??? Is there a customer service number I can call? "Um, Ma'am, can I please speak to your manager?" Not really going to go over well in the flesh peddling Mecca of Tijuana. So, I was disappointed enough to shelve what I wanted and just decided to bust a nut and say goodbye. Whoop-dee whoop, panties come off, and there it is, in all its glory, Snuffleupagus.

It was dark, and I didn't have a ruler but it was all of two and a half inches long. 'She' was holding it away from what my mind was still processing was *indeed* a vagina. Nothing in me wanted anything more to do with this situation, but I *had* already paid. Was I really about to have sex with a hermaphrodite? I mean, I looked around... Ashton Kutcher, are you there? Am I getting SEX *PUNK'D*? These moments are like three-legged unicorns, how can I pass this shitty situation up? So, I did what I had to do. Fuck you if you judge me! The kicker, though, was walking out of that room, and seeing the runner waiting for me to emerge.

"Tip?" he inquired.

"Yeah, next time don't hook me up with a chick with a dick!" I said without missing a beat.

"She no have dick." He said. "You should really up the vetting process of your merchandise," I thought to tell him, but the logic of that would have been wasted on the Fedora-wearing pimp-in-training. 'That's gonna be one for the books,' I told myself while walking home. I just wanted a shower. Happy you asked? We are not going to talk about this ever again.

Turning twenty-one at Havasu Landing was nothing special. I had already gambled in casinos, just not ever in one this bad. A couple more paychecks lost and I was not intent on continuing to work there much longer. If there had been a poker room at the casino, it would have been a completely different story. Before I put in my two week notice, I took a life inventory and decided what I wanted in my immediate future.

I was sold on the idea that if I had enough money to drink and sing karaoke at the bar every night, I could find happiness once again. The only job I could think of that would allow me that kind of daily cash flow was to branch off from being a pizza maker to pizza delivery driver, and as Carl's Papa John's was out of the question, Domino's was the next best choice. Pizza places are almost always hiring drivers, because if you get hired on part time and are more efficient than someone else on the payroll, they are out and you are in.

I provided proof of insurance and registration. I was given a background and ticket check. I passed everything. Unlike most cities that are set up in grid-like fashion, Lake Havasu is set up like someone threw a plate of spaghetti at a wall. If you work for GrubHub and want a challenge, try delivering in Lake Havasu *without* GPS. I was a better driver than most, and for a while my charted course for happiness was working well. However, my work ethic got the best of me again. I was tapped for management.

I had been delivering pizzas successfully for no more than three weeks when Tony, the General Manager, asked me if I would like to learn how to run shifts. It was to be a bit of a pay cut, but I felt it would open me up to more opportunities in the future, so I agreed. I had been singing three to four times a week at BJ's Tavern, a karaoke dive bar on the main thoroughfare of Lake Havasu, McCulloch Boulevard. The main street was named after the city's founder.

In the 1970's, McCulloch brokered the deal to buy, disassemble, ship and reassemble the sinking London Bridge from England to the middle of the Arizona desert, in what has to be the most expensive puzzle ever devised. To this day, it remains a backdrop for spring breakers and snowbirds who visit the town year round to party or escape the frigid Midwestern winters. At the tail end of my karaoke adventure, I did notch sex partner number eight. She was a girl that completely ignored me in high school.

She and her pox-marked face was part of the popular crowd, growing up. I swore it was a 'Revenge of the Nerds' play. It was a retaliatory hookup for all the boys like me who got ignored in high school. I was a nerd back then, but the Navy had filled me out and, of course, my gleaming smile made me a pretty irresistible catch, if a girl was looking for a good time. I wasn't really into putting a lot of work into hitting on girls at the bar. I didn't have the bank account to pump them full of drinks in hopes I could, what, get lucky and take them to my Mom's house? Not happening. On this lucky night, she took me to *her* parent's house, a very nice two-story near one of the many golf courses in town. My favorite Hollister T-shirt got soiled, cleaning off my glistening seed from her midsection that night, yet her Mom made us breakfast the next morning, it was surreal. I must have not been a rare occurrence. You win some, you lose some. However, my karaoke career had to be put on the backburner for a time while I trained for this management opportunity. Previous spring breaks had led to a strong increase in sales and this spring was going to be no exception.

Training was mostly just learning the Domino's point of sale system. "PULSE" was a lot different than the Papa John's system, which was monochrome and heavily relied on input codes and the keyboard's function keys. The Domino's system, on the other hand, was touch-screen based and a lot easier to learn and manage.

I was being groomed to be an extra night shift manager so I was trained on closing inventory and cash handling procedures. Of the ten stores in Scott Smith's franchise, the Havasu storefront was in the top three in sales. We would run about sixteen to eighteen thousand dollars of product a week, not as high as the Papa John's sales numbers, but we also ran the '5-5-5' deal, which was three, one-topping pizzas for $5 each. It was the low profit-margin special that got people to call in, and it was up to the customer service rep to try to upsell an order of breadsticks or a two-liter of Coke to increase the ticket order total. Papa John's may have made more money, but we pushed more product. Good thing I was pro at the dough station.

It was war every Friday and Saturday night. In the chaos of a $5,000 Friday, if one order got misboxed or one pizza was mismade, there was a literal domino effect that would result in delivery times extended and that would really throw a wrench into what was normally a smooth operating revenue machine. PULSE allowed me to pull up any given business metric at any given time, like up to the minute labor costs, current sales numbers and even average delivery times. If any of those numbers got out of line, like labor creeping above twenty percent, it was the manager's job to take the proper action to 'right the ship', which, in this example, would be sending someone home. I was a quick learner. Then came the opportunity that wasn't even close to being on my radar.

In some sort of dispute, the General Manager of the Kingman, Arizona store walked out and locked the doors at four in the afternoon, in mid-February 2006. All of the staff was sent home. When the District Manager, Sam C.C. Medrano, who was observing operations at the Havasu store that day, began getting calls that the Kingman store was unreachable, he called one of the workers to get the full story. He then recruited me and another insider to go with him to get the store back up and running for the evening rush. It was midweek and Kingman was the worst preforming store of the ten, so I imagined a pretty easy chore. Plus, I'd remain on the clock for the forty-five minute drive to Kingman and another forty-five back to Havasu. It was like a little bonus. Located in a little strip mall off of the I-40, the store was small, with a cellular phone store and Subway sandwich shop, among those sharing the four unit building. We finally arrived around 6:00PM and closed up at 10:00PM with the day's sales totaling less than $1,000. Sam was pacing outside on his cellphone, assumedly with the franchise owner. I went out to smoke. I had ditched smoking menthol and now preferred Camel Wides as my cigarette of choice. Sam put the phone in his pocket.

"I don't know who we're going to get to run the store." He said, visibly worried.

"I will." I said, thinking aloud. Expecting a dismissal of some sort, I was surprised as I saw the wheels turning in his head.

"I mean, I haven't even run an official shift by myself, but I think I could handle it." I said honestly.

"Go help clean up and I'll see what Scott says." I flicked my cigarette butt into the parking lot and headed in. Sam came in soon thereafter.

"Looks like you are it. Scott agreed. I'm sure you'll do a great job." I'm sure he was relieved to give the keys to someone who wasn't going to burn it to the ground. I was twenty-one with my own Domino's store. What was cooler than that?

I showed up the next morning to get myself familiarized with the store and its equipment. It had a large walk in cooler and the oven was in good shape. All mine, I thought. I noticed the ceiling tiles were stained and that would have to be remedied, and the culture at that store was just as drab. Changing that was priority number one.

Over the following two weeks I hired three new part-time high school kids. Two phone girls and one male pizza topper. That changed the vibe instantly. They were eager to learn and proud to be part of a team. I put my book-reading to use and instilled in them that they have just as much power as I had. If there was a problem, they have the full ability to remedy the situation.

"An upset customer is just an opportunity to win a customer for life, if you treat them right." I told them.

We all cleaned the ceiling tiles during a particularly slow Wednesday shift. It got to a point that my employees would show up on their days off to help prep chicken wings or just hang out, off the clock. When my fulltime closing driver, Aaron, and I would close up shop, we would routinely sit on the prep table and smoke a joint while pondering the vastness of the universe. It would have made for a fun reality TV show. In a way, to me it already was, and I was the camera. I genuinely miss those thoughtful, inspiring, careless nights.

I had been at the helm for just over a month when, on an early March afternoon, I heard the door open behind me and as I turned around, I was stunned.

A sundress clad young woman came to the counter and asked one of my phone girls for an application. She was just shorter than me, straight brunette hair and a body that I've seen Roman marble modeled after. I hoped I would see her again, and the next day, I did.

She drove a new Hyundai Tiburon, much more commanding of attention than my Mom's white Dodge Intrepid. Tiburon means 'shark' in Spanish, and I was reminded of one night in Mexico that Carmen took me out and we both had shark fin soup. It had a weird consistency, but I stomached it just to say that I have tried the controversial dish. The girl who drove that jet black car applied to be a delivery driver.

Jennifer Suzanne Gans. She was nineteen years old. I hired her on the spot, mentally, but waited three days for the official interview, to seal the deal. She didn't finish high school, but you don't need to know what years spanned the reign of Attila the Hun to deliver my perfect pizzas to hungry palates. Plus, she was just gorgeous, and that counted for something with me. Her tip average would surely be stellar. Aaron wanted to take a break from the demanding closing hours so I gave those hours to Jennifer. I was a professional and maintained a healthy employer/employee relationship.

I took to sleeping in the store or my car, three or four nights a week, to save the drive time and gas money. Mom's house was forty-five minutes south. Just like at Havasu Landing, I hated the transportation aspect of work. My wage of $10.50 an hour to manage the store didn't last long in Laughlin, Nevada, a shorter thirty minute drive away, twenty-five if I pushed the speed limit. If I wasn't working or hitting on the Chili's waitress, I was in a casino. My gambling was incessant.

The Chili's waitress was reminiscent of a shorty Paris Hilton, complete with her own catch phrase, "That's chill." Instead of saying "That's hot" like the hotel heiress made famous on the reality show, "The Simple Life." She would wind up being lover number nine, after a drunken mountainous accident.

While I was savoring one of my twice daily $12 martinis, she asked me if I wanted to go out after work. "About time," I thought. We went to a dive karaoke bar and after I belted out a decent rendition of a Randy Travis classic, we racked up a game of pool. It was... 'chill'. ☺

After two beers and a shot she whispered to me that we should go to the Hualapai's, a mountain range outside of Kingman that I was not at all familiar with. I agreed because it seemed like she had a plan, and I was cool with that. There was already a blanket and pillow in the backseat of the Intrepid, so why not? All I gathered in my drunken stupor is that she wanted to hook-up in the mountains, and I was totally on board with that. Those martinis were starting to cut into my poker bankroll, which was usually all the money I earned. Conquest challenge accepted, I thought.

She pointed out the winding highway that would take us up the mountainside. Before I knew it, the two-lane paved highway turned into a one-lane dirt road. A fork appeared and to my right was a closed gate, straight ahead was a two-ton boulder, and to the left was the sharp turn I was too inebriated to recognize. I had missed the speed limit sign dropping from forty-five to twenty-five, and that made all the difference.

The dirt rose up from the dimming headlights as the boulder was pushed two feet back from its original position. My head smashed on the steering wheel and her shin clipped the glove compartment. We were ok, but the car was wrecked. I got out to assess the damage. It was bad.

A puddle of liquid started to pool under the car and the hood was bent up accordion-style. I got back in the car and tried to put it in reverse. Very shortly, I realized we weren't going anywhere, and with no cell phone service, we were at the mercy of the night. I turned back the key, shutting off the sputtering engine. We found ourselves in the back seat in no time. I mean, she could have been pissed, or freaking out, but we both took it like champions, and weren't going to let a little car destroying accident get in the way of our "Bow-Chick-A-Wow-Wow" time. We gave Mom's Intrepid a glorious send off into car heaven. In fact, I was even able to coin a term that night.

Fish (noun) — A pre-lubricated anal cavity preformed hours in advance of anticipatory anal sex.

And, although I had ABSOLUTELY no idea what I was doing back there, I did get a whole three minutes of mind altering sensitivity, before she wanted no more. Or, as I like to say, "Her fish died."

We woke to an officer knocking on the back window. We were both naked under the blanket. He told me to put something on and step out.

"I can't prove that you were drinking, but judging by the distance you moved that boulder you were definitely speeding." He assessed the situation and decided to not write me up for anything. "I'll call you a tow."

She and I rode back next to the tow truck operator in silence. The ridiculousness of what happened was soberly setting in. I was grateful that she wasn't hurt and I escaped with only a minor scrape in the middle of my forehead. The driver dropped her off at her house and I never heard from or spoke with her again. Nor have I since stepped foot in a Chili's. But, if YOU ever go, try out the $12 Martini.

Pro-tip: If you drink two... call a cab.

Chapter VIII

Along Came a Kiss

Getting back to the store, I was inundated with questions about my visible injury. I told Aaron, who was vaguely aware of my conquest of the Chili's waitress, that the mission was complete and there was, indeed, life on Mars. I had no time to dilly-dally though, I needed a vehicle. I had very little cash and was three days from payday. I went to the closest used car lot, less than a mile from the store, and informed them of the situation.

"I can come Friday with the $500 deposit, but I need a vehicle *today*." I emphasized. "I'm the General Manager of the Domino's in town."

They put me in a four-door 2002 Saturn SL1 sedan. It was the same shade brown as my '86 Taurus, which immediately invoked memories of Kacy Jacobs and Pat Bennitar. It was a lateral move from the Dodge I had just totaled, but I was grateful to be in something. I signed the contract with little intention of shelling out the down payment that week. But I had a car. I don't even know what the sale price was. I didn't care.

I made the requisite paperwork moves the next day. I paid for and printed proof of insurance from an online source, which I promptly cancelled two days later. The proof was all I needed, not the monthly payment. Also, I submitted my new paperwork to Scott's human resources lady to put my updated info in the computer system. Everything was in line, other than my Mom losing the spare car. She signed over the title to the tow yard realizing there weren't many other options. If she was disappointed in me, she didn't show it in any way.

Jennifer and I got to know each other as the days went on. Sometimes spending time together outside of work at the Humane Society or the local park, and I began to think it would be nice to win her affection. I had begun to feel the proverbial ball was in my court by the way we interacted, but still, I was not the go get 'em type. I waited for them to come to me. Maybe it's the overlooked nerd in me, but when I picture college guys hitting on women, I don't find it pleasant to the senses. I find it highly uncomfortable. You can usually tell if a girl or guy is into you simply by a smile or a look. Or, the soon to be ever-popular pick up line:

"So, do you *own* a...*FISH?*" Maybe not.

Realizing that if the Chili's girl had won me over, Jennifer would have gotten the short end of the stick, she became determined to make her intentions known. I was on the clock one day getting an earful from Sam, the District Manager, over the phone, when she showed up and stood three feet in front of me, out of uniform, looking impatient.

"Yes, Sam, I understand." I cared very little about what he was saying and just wanted him off the phone so I could see what Jennifer wanted. "Ok. Bye."

"Are you done?" She asked.

"Yeah?" I answered quizzically. No sooner did I realize what was happening when, in two steps, she had closed the gap between us and pressed her lips to mine. My eyes closed and everything went white, as if I was ascending (or descending) into a new layer of heaven (or hell) that I had never experienced before. Our lips opened a bit more and we melted into each other. Witchcraft. I couldn't say anything. Our lips parted and she backed up, as I came back to reality. She gave me a bouncy smirk and hopped out to her still running car.

Hit and run. I see what you did there. She didn't give me any time to process what had just happened, and was out the door. Had I just been assaulted? Why did I like it? Another solidifying experience telling me hands off is the way to go with anyone you are trying to attract. Also, playing with puppies at the Humane Society makes you look attractive to the opposite sex, too.

We would start fooling around at work after hours, and in no time it became sexual. Lover number ten, but love number two. I'm not going to lie, girls in fast food uniforms just did it for me. Maybe it was something about the blue Domino's shirt or perhaps it was her skin tight khakis that were against company policy, but Aaron and I weren't about to complain, so I turned a blind eye. Maybe it was getting her wet with the sink sprayer as she tried to finish cleaning the topping dividers or pizza cutters. We were two young lovers in love with being in love. It really bumped up my desire to run the hell out of that store. I did not want to lose a good thing. With my new hires now able to handle most of the day to day actions of running the store, I had a little extra free time to grow our relationship.

She was a bit of a tomboy and liked throwing the football around. We went for walks, still hung out at the animal shelter, and occasionally went out to eat. Working at a pizza place, I tended to keep to a cheese and crust diet, so it was nice to go wherever she wanted to eat, for variety. With the windows cracked in my Saturn, we would sit, smoke cigarettes and talk. I soon noticed some scars on her wrists.

"I use to cut." That much was obvious to me. There were three barely visible parallel scars about two inches up her forearm from her wrists.

"Promise me, if you are feeling a certain type of way that you will talk to me instead of going back to that. Especially if it is something I'm doing. Promise?" She nodded as she ran her fingers over the marks. We closed the store together the next night and afterward she said she wanted to go to the park. Exhausted from a particularly long night, we both fell asleep in her running car without even getting out to sit in the park grass. We woke as the sun came up, car still running.

"Fuck!" She exclaimed, "What time is it?" She had a morning job at Blue Beacon, a truck wash about twenty miles east of Kingman on the I-40. "I'm gonna be late, shit!"

I felt bad, but I didn't like her at that job, anyways. I offered her more hours to quit that job, but she liked being the only female that worked washing trucks. She got something out of doing the hard work that only the boys could do. She was proud of that job, so I stopped trying to convince her to leave it.

"I'll drop you off at your car," she said. Dropping me off at the gas station next to the strip mall was good enough for me. We kissed and I got out.

"I'll see you tonight." I prophesied.

While she was driving home, a Swift truck driver blew a stop sign and crashed into her. I found out, hours later, that she was in the hospital with a broken wrist. I called her cellphone and she said that she was fine, and that she was going to get released the next morning. Her car was totaled. If the impact had been on the driver's side, there is no way she would have made it. Man, bad universal luck in the car department, wouldn't you say? The next morning I showed up at her house with two Starbucks Frappuccino's, her favorites, and a get well card. Her Mom answered the door.

"Are you the one my daughter was with last night?" She asked me like it was a Salem Witch Trial. This was my initial appearance in front of her Mom. First impressions, right?

"Yes, ma'am." She gave me a once over and reluctantly invited me inside. Jennifer was on the couch with a blue cast on her wrist. They were having a spread that her and her Mom occasionally would partake in called a "white-trash picnic". It was probably that much more enjoyable with the pain pills that had Jennifer a little dopey. There were candy wrappers everywhere.

"I'll give you two ten minutes, then she needs to rest." What a bitch, I thought with a side sneer that Jennifer saw and smirked at.

Her Mom disappeared into the kitchen adjacent the living room. I felt a time rush as if I wasn't wanted, but Jennifer kissed me, welcomingly, anyways.

She told me to not worry about her Mom and said that she was happy I was there. For the first time she thanked me for not firing her for kissing me. I countered by telling her I was glad she did. I felt her Mom's presence and I excused myself. She would need some downtime, so I gave her two weeks off.

In the meantime, Sam called to inform me that the last months numbers were in and he wanted to be first to congratulate me on pulling the first bonus out of the Kingman store in over four years. Sales were up marginally, due to a better trained and motivated phone crew, but labor was way down. Ok, so I kinda cheated, and Sam knew.

I ran it like I was the owner. I made sure my staff got their hours and if I had to work a few hours off the clock to ensure that, so be it. Sam once noticed a paycheck of mine under $500 and knew what was up. I built something. I was proud of that. The Kingman store was mine. At that point, I had an understanding that it wasn't much of a sacrifice to short myself a little cash up front to make the numbers work for the greater good of the crew. My $400 bonus that month brought me to just under even for what I should have earned and that was amazing for me.

In three short months I, along with my team, turned the Kingman store around from being worst of the ten stores in the franchise to second best, by numbers. Delivery times fell, food costs were under control, labor costs were contained, and sales were up due to the great salesmanship of my team. But to me, most importantly, everyone was happy working there.

I had built a family, a culture even, where everyone was just as responsible for the success of the store's business as the next. We had each other's backs. That was special. But just as my personal history had taught me until that point, every yin of success carries with it the yang of change, and this scenario was not immune. The yang, this time, came in the form of a promotion offer.

The five 'East Side' store locations were losing money and the District Manager they currently employed had not delivered the results Scott was looking for, even after having been personally trained by Sam, the District Manager of the 'West Side' stores. So one weekend while Sam was acting as my closing driver, he tossed an idea my way.

"Scott wants you to run the East. You really impressed him with what you've done here." He was genuine. The thought stuck with me. Yes, I had achieved some success, but A) it was a team effort and B) I wasn't done. I had plans to have a carwash fundraiser for the local Abused Women's Shelter, where one early afternoon we would all show up and wash cars in our uniforms and I would hand out pizza by the slice and coupons for all those community members that took part in donating to benefit the center. I really wanted to get a foothold in the community and really grow the store. Then, I would have felt successful.

Leaving it behind, in hands other than mine, I felt it would all fall apart. My crew was the glue holding me together and I was the glue holding the store together. Jennifer, back on the job, told me I'd be stupid not to take the offer. It carried a $30,000 base salary plus commission that could be earned on each of the five stores in my area. The team meeting when it was announced that I was leaving, I cried. And that made a couple of my crew cry, too.

The staff bought me a card that featured a Chihuahua and a funny quote. They knew I loved Mexico. I even took a four day vacation back to Tijuana after I got that first Kingman bonus. I couldn't find Carmen, but the original safe house was still there and I saw Guymas chilling with Poncho at the car wash next to Carmen's. I didn't stop the car to say hi. I doubt either noticed me. I ate at Super Taco, still as glorious as I remembered it. Then I did something special. I found a Domino's.

Wearing jeans and another Hollister T-shirt, I passed the lot of branded motorbikes that they used for delivery there, and entered the store. In Spanish, I introduced myself and let the manager know that I worked for Domino's in Arizona and wondered since I had a uniform in my car, if I could suit up and make a few pizzas with them. The manager smiled and told me that was fine. I changed into my khakis, donned my Grey manager polo shirt and came out of the bathroom ready to roll.

"No." The manager said, pointing to his undershirt, "Tu playa blanca." I had forgotten to put on my white Haines tee underneath my branded uniform shirt. Damn, strict with the standards, I liked it. I retrieved mine from the car and redressed. No one spoke English and it was no doubt fun for them to deal with me, the American pizza boy, in my limited but passable Spanish. I took some pictures with my Motorola Razor, at the time the coolest cell phone available. I was able to ask him how much the crew made and was astounded at the answers I got.

The pay scale amounted to seven dollars a day for drivers (plus tips), nine dollars a day for insiders, and thirty dollars a day for the General Manager. Seemed like slave labor to me. Once again, the American guilt set in. What was I doing different in Arizona that commanded almost triple the pay that this man was getting for doing the same job, and for the <u>same</u> company? They didn't ask me how much I made. I don't know what I would have told them.

I processed a few orders. They were impressed with my dough skills, for sure. Upon looking at the menu, I noticed a few differences. The first thing I noticed was a pizza with a hot sauce swirl on top. Mexicans love them some spicy. But the most glaring product discrepancy was something called 'Papitos'. They were potato fries that were akin to "JoJo's" available at any grocery store hot service deli. They came with hot sauce, obviously. I *had* to order them, keeping the unique Papitos box for display in my store back home. Why don't we have these in America! Travesty! I thanked them for their time, took a few selfie pictures with my cellphone, and I was off.

Heading home, I saved just enough money at Viejas to have enough for gas back to Havasu. Well, that and the ten Peso coin that I taped to the Papitos box to let my workers see some foreign coinage.

After I officially left the Kingman store, Sam cited regulations and took the Papitos box down, as the store slowly unraveled. No one respected the newly installed driver-turned-manager, Bill, and many put in their two week notices before the month was over. My woes, however, were just getting started.

General Manager at twenty-one years old is something. **District Manager** at twenty-one is a whole different ballpark. I could control the daily operations of having *one* store under my purview, but having five required a skillset that I hadn't yet mastered. I was expected to run one shift per day per store, do inspections, and ensure standards were being upheld. My inspections, such as cleanliness reports, were directly tied to that General Manager's bonus. I didn't like being the one responsible for the cash going into their pockets, or worse yet, the cash not going into their pockets. Some of these managers had been there for years, while some were newly hired. Yet, I don't know how I would feel if an eighteen year old District Manager came to Kingman telling me what to do while I was in charge, so I felt a bit castrated.

The stores I was put in charge of were; Prescott, Prescott Valley, Cottonwood, Camp Verde and Sedona. Sam cosigned a $1,000 a month luxury apartment with me, in centrally located Prescott Valley. He figured it would be more economical to have a place to stay when he was out my way, rather than having to get a hotel each visit.

One night, soon after moving in, I drank half a bottle of vodka in the empty apartment, and I called Jennifer and asked her to move in with me. I picked her up that night. Meeting her down the street from her house, she had packed all her belongings in two black trash bags. Her Mom was none too happy with me the next morning, but she couldn't have changed Jennifer's mind if she tried. The three bedroom apartment was amazing.

There was Sam's room, our room and an office. I didn't have the credit to furnish it like my marital apartment in Virginia, but Jennifer and I weren't complainers and neither of us minded the air mattress. I had the only car, so she was stuck at home. I'm sure the majority of the time she was bored out of her mind. I eventually sprung for a twenty inch TV/DVD combo but didn't pay to get cable installed. Am I my father's son or what? The gambling trend continued.

Navy money went to online poker. Mexican Coyote money went to live poker at Viejas. Havasu Landing cook money went to, well, Havasu Landing Casino Slots. Kingman Domino's money went to Laughlin Casino's. And Prescott Valley had the quaintest casino twenty minutes from our apartment. Guess where I would be between work and home. She hated that I lost. I hated that she was mad. But I couldn't quit. If I so happened to be at the Camp Verde store, Cliff Castle Casino was just down the road. Imagine how bad it was when I had to take over the Camp Verde store, full-time, while searching for a new General Manager. As I was the opening and closing manager in those days, I would occasionally short the store's daily operating cash down to sometimes lower than $200, to give me a bankroll. Sam showed up unexpectedly one day before I was able to replenish my short, and was furious, but agreed to not tell Scott, as long as I promised not to do it again. I promised, and I honored that promise.

I came home after 2:00AM on an evening I had simultaneously closed two stores and went straight to the bathroom. I had taken to buying two, twenty-four ounce Budweiser's for the thirty or forty minute drive home, depending on the store I was closing that night, and I usually came home with a stinging desire to pee.

She was sleeping as I passed her on my way to the master bathroom and, next to the toilet, I noticed a broken down razor in the trash. God damn it! We fought for the first time the next morning and I stormed out just to return with flowers and a card. I told her I forgave her and promised to work on my shortcomings.

I had been having a hard time with work. Scott was bleeding money and the first thing he was adamant about cutting was advertising. He also wanted me doing more inspections and more reporting from inside the stores.

I countered with, "I can get the stores clean, I can have the staff in pristine uniforms, I can have the best products going out, but if you can't get new people in the door, sales are never going to increase." He didn't see it that way. It had been a month. We were at an impasse. I was feeling unprepared for the job he wanted me to do and I missed the dynamic of what I had in Kingman.

Then, one little plus sign changed everything.

Chapter IX

The Battle of Settling Down

Neither of us were prepared for an addition. We, ourselves, were just figuring out how to manage each other, when in mid-June the future was laid out for us. Apparently the 'pull-out' method was not 99.9% effective, as one might think. She came out of the bathroom visibly shaken.

"I'm pregnant." She said holding the EPT. "Holy shit, I'm pregnant."

I was not freaking out. I was actually calm about the whole scenario. I mean, it wasn't happening to *my* body. Not really knowing what else to do, I held her for a long moment, until a calm came over her and she confidently pulled away. I had always wanted a child, and although I would have preferred to wait until we were a little more situated, the hands of fate would say now was the time.

I had a job that paid well and would get less strenuous in the long run, I thought, as I put more time into it over the short-term. But, after a few weeks this proved to have its own, undesirable side effects. I had cut back my gambling to spend more time with Jennifer, but it still wasn't enough. She came to the realization that she was alone, as far as a support system was concerned, and planted in me the seed that she wanted to move to Las Vegas, where some of her friends and family lived. If I was going to make the move, I needed to make it fast. I mean, Sam had just co-signed the lease with me two months prior, and that would become an un-repairable situation. Once again, I decided to follow the lead of the lady in my life, with soon to be child in tow, to determine how things were going to go. Vegas it was.

Late that August, I wrote an email saying that due to the lack of training and the disconnect that the owner and I didn't seem to find a remedy for, I would be resigning my position effective immediately. Send. Sam met up with me that evening.

"I wish you would have talked to me before sending that email," Sam said. "He was planning on letting you take over the Cottonwood store, as owner, and you would make direct payments to him to buy it." Fuck. Again with these after-the-fact facts. There was no repairing the damage I had just wrought. And even so, Jennifer was carrying my child and she needed to be in a good space, mentally and physically. It was my job to see to that. So packing up the Saturn, we left to Henderson, Nevada.

Not knowing what to expect, we left Bacardi, a puppy that I impulsively acquired for her birthday, at home with my mother. It was by luck of the draw that one of my employees asked if I had gotten Jennifer anything for her birthday, just as another worker was showing pictures of puppies that had just become available for free.

Getting her a puppy fulfilled her desire to have something external to care about, with an internal bundle of joy simultaneously on the way. I thought it would be good for her to learn to care for something that was dependent on her, and maybe take away some of the animosity she held toward me for being gone so much. Better than cable, I thought.

Seeing her Aunt for the second time was interesting. Keri was definitely the hot aunt type, but was seemingly happily married and had two young daughters, so I instantly banished the fantasy thoughts. Showing back up to her house, I was reminded of Keri's warning a few short months ago, before Jennifer's accident, to run away, not walk, because Jennifer was trouble. I didn't see it. I was happy being in a contentious relationship, full of passion, adventure and great sex. Never knowing what to expect was invigorating, and it was a constant state of living 'in-the-moment.'

Living with her Aunt would mean that we had to quit smoking, and at the time, I was not about to give up my stress sticks. Yes, Jennifer had not made the determination to quit, either, and that was her choice. I should have had more of a backbone about the issue, but she was calling the shots, and I was just along for the ride, at that point. If she wasn't pregnant, I would have been just fine calling it quits and moving on. Maybe back to being a delivery driver. Maybe I would have tried to convince Scott to bring me back to the negotiating table. We couldn't stay at Keri's. Next in line was her friend Genevieve. She lived with her boyfriend and an eight month old in a two bedroom apartment off of Stephanie Blvd., in Henderson.

Jennifer would convince them to let us stay there. She then got a short lived job at a Cold Stone Creamery, where she soon found out that her injuries from the accident really hampered her ice-cream mixing skills. The pressure was on again for me to find a living wage. Given that the car had not been paid on for months and the only insurance I had was the printed "Proof of Insurance" but nothing legally valid, I wouldn't be able to drive for anyone, but I could still manage.

I applied for a Papa John's Management position and was hired on after Sam's honest account of my work ethic, as a reference. Even though I needed little training, I was forced to go through the motions as if I had no Papa John's experience. It was an eight-week training program and after completion I was awarded my own store.

The Papa John's I took over was, like Kingman, the worst preforming. But this one was a little different. The employees were robbing the store blind. The office till had no lock. The bad apple employees just had to trigger the mechanism on the back of the drawer to open it and slip a quick ten or twenty dollar bill into their pocket, and finish out their shift. I was astounded at the blatant shenanigans and had only been at the location for an official five days before the next hiccup came.

Genevieve's boyfriend, Marco, lost his job as a forklift operator a couple months prior to us moving in, and was not actively looking for work. They had told Jennifer that they were going to move in with family. Jennifer and I thought that we had time, but that was not the case.

One night, I got off work and Jennifer came to pick me up, as I let her have the car while I was on the clock, in those days. She let me know that she was unable to get ahold of Genevieve. We pulled into the apartment parking lot and saw that their yellow car was there and the lights were on in the apartment, but they were simply not answering the door. In the car, I broke her down.

"Who has been here taking care of you from day one?" I asked, thinking of the next line I was going to throw at her.

"You have," she replied.

"Who has made sure you have not wanted for nothing?" I demanded.

"You have," she started crying.

"Not your friends?" I asked heavy handedly.

"No."

"Not your aunt?" I again pushed.

"No."

"So who is going to be number one? Who are you going to stick with, me or them?" I couldn't help it at this point. If I said that we had sex twice since we moved to Henderson, it would have been an overstatement. I only convinced her one night because I went out and bought the Trojan Vibrating Ring, it wasn't Earth-shattering by any stretch of the imagination, only a long awaited release. I was tired of playing second fiddle in the relationship when I felt that I held all the burden of fiscal responsibility. Living just outside of Vegas, one doesn't need to imagine how those gambling pits ensnared me.

We had no one guiding us in what we were to do with a pregnancy. We had no primary care doctor, she was still smoking, and the one time she complained of pain, I spent eight hours in the Urgent Care waiting room for her to emerge with two Tylenol and ultrasound pictures.

With what little belongings we had in the car, I drove us from the apartment parking lot to the Papa John's store I had just been given the burden of running. Not even one week, Jesus. My salary was $550 per week and I had worked for five days. I took $500 from the safe for my troubles, and left two pennies on the counter, putting in my two cents. This place was a disaster.

Now, I know, there are many different ways in which I could have handled this situation, but this isn't a book on what I should have done, and when, it's a book of disclosure, deal with it.

I was tired of being in a losing town. I was tired of feeling like I had no direction or say in my life and my soon to be child's life. I was tired of putting in the work just to throw it all away on a whim. I **wanted** to settle down. I *wanted* to grow some roots. Between the five hundred I just took and the last paycheck I had, we had a little less than a grand. We stopped at a restaurant and asked the waiter before we paid, "If you had a thousand dollars and could start over anywhere, where would you go?"

"A thousand dollars isn't a lot of money," he replied. No. It wasn't. It was more than enough to get us back to Havasu, though.

Upon returning home, I found out that without bringing the matter to me, Mom had given Bacardi to the Humane Society and I wasn't too happy.

"I had him potty trained and everything. All you had to do was let him out when he waited by the door." I expressed, emotionally defeated, to Mom. Ugh. Mitchell and Mathew couldn't have taken a bit of responsibly while I was busy getting *my* life in order. I tried to get him back but he was already adopted and given a new name, Rumor. I'm still sour about that.

Mom gave us her bedroom for a couple nights, and Jennifer and I went straight to work looking online for a locale that looked promising. If the greater Las Vegas Area was her 'turf,' and Lake Havasu was my 'turf,' we agreed it would be beneficial to find someplace neutral to try settling down at. Looking online at the top 100 places to live in the United States, we somehow came to agree upon Corpus Christi, TX.

Judging by the pictures, it looked the part. But after we arrived on a rainy night, the town looked nothing like the pictures online. Like Kingman, Corpus Christi looks good on paper, and bless those that live there, but it wasn't for us. Plus the stress of hurricane season would have proved to be too much. There **was** a silver lining for our trip out there, though. Well, *two* silver linings. In Texas, I did see and photograph a lovely little place called, the Dairy *King*. Yes. Was there really just one Dairy King to rule all the Dairy Queens? I thought it was hilarious. What a pimp!

Also, Corpus Christi boasted a decommissioned navy ship, the USS Lexington, as a museum. It felt great being back on a ship. The smell of diesel fuel brought back instant memories of being out to sea. Jennifer had heard stories and this was my chance to show her in real life, what one looked like on the inside. The moment was short lived. We were getting short on cash and had no prospects. Deciding that we might have better luck in a bigger city suburb, we headed north to Houston. Then, I found a weekly stay place in the small town of Katy, TX for us to plan our next move.

She would try her shot at getting hired on at a Taco Bell, but being in her second trimester, I don't think they wanted the liability. I tried my shot at getting a shift-runner spot at the local Domino's. Problem was, in Texas, in this particular location, Domino's was run by Corporate, not a franchisee. So to be a manager, you had to have a valid driver's license and valid insurance.

Everything was fine until they did my license check and found out that I had a suspended license from an unpaid ticket from when we were in Prescott Valley.

I had been speeding on the way home, no doubt after I lost at the card table, but was grateful that the officer didn't cite me for the empty Budweiser cans behind the driver seat. So now we were stuck. I tried one Hail-Mary and applied blindly to a door-to-door sales job. Upon showing up for my first day, slacks and a button-up, I found out it was selling vacuum cleaners and I just knew I couldn't put my heart into that. So I fled. Having just enough money to get back to the Black Hole, we made our decision to return.

Sam had spoken to me around Halloween and said that Scott had sold some of his stores and the new owner of the Lake Havasu store, Paul Parker, asked if he knew anyone that would be able to take over as General Manager. Sam threw my name out there. Jennifer knew this, and that helped ease the decision to go back. This didn't stop us from fighting on Thanksgiving Eve, just to pick a fight, but I still went out the next morning and bought a precooked chicken, some instant mashed potatoes and a can of cranberry sauce, to try to have some semblance of a Thanksgiving lunch. We left Texas, days later.

We drove home slowly, over the course of five or six days. It seemed that her bladder had shrunk to the size of an acorn and we had to make frequent stops for that reason. We decided to save cash and usually slept in the car, when we could find a Wal-Mart parking lot.

Getting back to Havasu was a relief. Finally, a nice bed to sleep in and a reprieve from worrying about our dwindling cash supplies. Jennifer was getting bigger and I was just happy to know we were at a safe spot. Mom had found a deal on prenatal vitamins and stocked up for Jennifer. She was happy to present her the collection, when we got home. We took it easy for the weekend.

Dad showed up at the house looking for some tools and didn't even look at Jennifer. He was no doubt disappointed that we were having a child out of wedlock, even though I was the fetus responsible for his shotgun marriage. That stung a little bit. Their marriage ended when I left for the Navy. They were still cordial, though. It was for the better.

Being at home, I was able to locate some MiniDV tapes from my time in the Navy and with Veronica, and was in the boys' room watching video of Veronica and me at the lake, when Jennifer walked in. She got all bothered that I was looking at videos that had my ex-wife in them, like I was reminiscing about better times or whatever. Maybe it was, just, hate to say it, hormones. But her attitude took me to a spot of mania. I took the five cartridges and began pulling out the black tape over the kitchen trashcan. It looked like an overloaded bowl of black spaghetti, or just a three-dimensional map of Lake Havasu City.

"You didn't need to do all that." She shot back.

"Well, you think that all that means more to me than you and now you know. I was just looking at a piece of my past. I can't do that now, anymore." I might have peppered in an 'I'm sorry' just to make her feel guilty. I wouldn't have put it past me, at that moment. Giving it some time to sink in, the next night she came to me.

"Happy early birthday, Clifford." She said in an apologetic tone. I had been quiet with her ever since I took the trash bag containing the bulk of my naval history to the side of the house to await the trash man. "Wanna know what your present is?"

"Do I?" I retorted, still a little upset at yesterday's difficulties. She gave me a 'forgive me' and 'move on' look. I did. "Ok what is it?" I said, instantly smiling.

"On Sunday, you can go out to the casino with your Mom and stay out as looooong as you want and I won't say a peep." We had $180 dollars left in the small digital safe I bought while in Prescott Valley. The wheels in my head started turning. On Sundays, I researched, the Avi Casino outside of Laughlin, Nevada held an evening poker tournament that I would be able to enter for sixty dollars. I was sold.

"You sure?" I asked as if this was some sort of trap. She smiled and kissed me, letting me know her answer. It was these small moments that I tried to gather to counterbalance the pointless arguing. Some moments in life that seem to warrant abundant passion in the moment, in hindsight, fade into the emptiness of things forgotten. A lot of the negative times with Jennifer, have since been erased from my memory. I take full responsibility for not being there as I should have been, or not knowing fully how to demonstrate the affection that I had for her, even after being somewhat aware, at the time, of the same shortcomings in my failed marriage. Reading, <u>What to Expect When Expecting</u>, was no substitute for actually putting in the one-on-one time that was so desperately merited.

Sunday came, December 10th, 2006, and I was showered, dressed and ready to get to the Avi Casino. Mom was a little more lackadaisical. We left late at quarter after five, leaving me mere minutes to register if we **were** to get there on time. We didn't.

Mom has a funny unspoken driving philosophy: thirty-five in a twenty-five and forty-five in a fifty-five. We showed up at 6:07 PM and I was banking on late registration being available, but the tournament had already begun and the poker room manager informed me there was no way for me to buy-in. This meant I would be relegated to playing slot machines. You play the casino, you lose. And my birthday was no exception. However, the $100 I brought did last a bit longer than I thought due to a couple small bonus wins under sixty dollars. I kept playing. Hours later, Mom found me as I was playing my last twelve dollars or so. I was three beers deep and happy that she would be driving home. I finished my machine's slot credits with a few out-of-the-norm bets of three dollars a spin, and my bank was busted.

"You ready to go?" I asked Mom, defeated. I was a little frustrated as we walked by the poker room to see they were down to the last two tables of players. I should have been there.

"Did you have fun?" She automatically shot back. Because that's what matters, right? I determined then, that I **wasn't** done. I was going to be meeting with Sam later that week to set up a meeting with him, Paul and I in regards to running Paul's new Havasu Dominos location and the money would be flowing in no time. I wouldn't tell Mom till we got back to Havasu that I was going to use the car and go back to wager my last eighty dollars. It was my birthday, and I wasn't going to leave any money on the table. The drive back gave me time to sober up enough to convince her that I would be responsible on my return trip. I went into the bedroom to check on Jennifer.

"Hey babe," I said quietly as I climbed onto the far side of the bed and kissed her.

"Hey. How was it?" She asked, almost knowingly.

"I'm going to go back. We were late for the tournament so I didn't get to play cards. I lost $100 on slots." I noticed she was cradling her belly. "You ok?" I asked slightly concerned.

We had yet to get on ACCHS, the Arizona version of health care for the poor, so we were completely blind as to the progress of the pregnancy. She wasn't writhing in pain, so I chalked it up to her body just breaching the third trimester and I assumed there would be some pain involved with the body-morphing final haul of carrying a child to term.

"Could you get me a couple Tylenol?" She asked.

"Be right back." I went to the kitchen and retrieved the bottle from above the stove, where the other supplements and spices were stored. Gathering a half a cup of water from the tap, I was back by her side. Hoping it would alleviate her discomfort, I watched her down the worthless medicine. Tylenol never worked for me, for anything. So, I always regarded it as a placebo. But, at that moment, I hoped I was wrong. I still had a free pass to gamble without restraint and was intent on utilizing this moment to the fullest.

"I'll be back in a few hours." I said, already conceding defeat to the casino.

"I love you." She said, with a tinge of leeriness that let on she would be alone again when she emotionally needed me most. I was oblivious.

"I love you, too." We kissed and I was out the door.

Getting back to the car after leaving the casino, getting less than an hour of entertainment from my eighty dollars, I tried to pump myself up for the ride home. I almost felt sick. It seemed like as I was losing, I was ordering more free drinks, to make it seem like I was at least getting **something**. The last Jack and Coke really did me in, though.

It was a long dark highway back to the California side of the I-40. Once there, I knew I would be ok. "Just stay to the right and keep up adequate speed." Because of my time in Prescott, I had mastered the art of buzzed driving. Not to say that it was ok, but hell, it was my birthday. The last birthday I'd be allowed to be out, running reckless. A soon to be child was near and that would take the self-serving nature right out of me.

Rolling into bed, Jennifer was still up. This time she was visibly in pain. Not keeling over, screaming pain, but the kind of pain that you try hard to tolerate externally, but internally you are being destroyed.

"Something's not right." She confessed. "I think I need to go to the hospital." I was in no mood to roll out of bed and hop back in the car. I was tired, I had just lost, I was still drunk and Havasu cops are notorious for finding me at my worst. I was glad to have gotten home in one piece, without incident. "Do you want to go with me?"

"No." I plainly stated. Remembering the back seat I had to take at the Urgent Care in Vegas, when she was dealing with similar, but less pressing pain, and I had to entertain myself like a cab driver in the waiting room, for hours.

"Can I have the keys?" I fished them from my pocket and placed them in her outstretched hand.

It was 1:15 AM on Monday, December 11th. I was asleep before she left the driveway.

"Clifford, wake up!" My Mom was stretched over Jennifer's side of the bed shaking my shoulder. I opened my eyes.

"Jennifer had the baby. Randy is on his way to pick you up." Randy was my Mom's boyfriend at the time, but I wasn't going to wait for him to drive across town in his Hummer to take me to the hospital. I ran out of the house, hopped on Mitchell's bike and pedaled as fast as I could, mind racing, and dumped the bike two miles down the road at the entrance to the Havasu Memorial Hospital Emergency Room.

What just happened?

What have I done?

I saw the clock as I walked in.

3:22 AM.

Chapter X

XANDER

I had felt the baby kick a distressing kick before Jennifer got the keys from me that night, but I had no idea this would have been the result. I was escorted to her hospital room and found her lying down, dressed in a blue tinted gown.

"I tried to call you before, but I didn't know your phone number. They had to look up Tammy in the phonebook after he was born." She said anxiously. "There was no time." Then I got the rundown of the chaos that had just ensued. I wasn't sober enough for what I was about to hear.

She left the Widgeon driveway in pain she was no longer afraid to display. Hiding her true pain in front of me didn't do either of us any good. She screamed, and cursed my name, as she made her way to the emergency room. Holding her belly as she walked in, they immediately retrieved a wheelchair for her, and in a short amount of time they informed her that she was indeed in labor but they were going to medicate her to stop the delivery. Then the secondary inspection came and the doctors found that she was already ten centimeters dilated and the baby was breached, or upside down. There was no stopping the delivery.

The safest way, the **ONLY** way forward, was to perform an emergency Caesarian Section. At which point, CPR was administered to get the newborn breathing again and he was immediately put on a breathing tube and flown by helicopter to the Phoenix Children's Hospital, in Phoenix, Arizona. The nurse that brought me to where Jennifer was resting explained to me that in all her years of delivering babies, never has she seen a newborn do what mine just did. Namely, not only did he reach out for the mother after being removed from her womb, but he actually *pointed* to her, as he was being ushered out of the birthing room. That struck her as something unique. Was he accusing her of something? I didn't know what to make of it. I would soon find out.

Her mom and stepdad showed up at the hospital the next day after having already made the trip to Phoenix to witness their first grandchild. They came back with an attitude that still makes me cringe.

"It looks like a grown man beat the shit out of him. He is all black and blue and he might never be ok. He will need special attention his whole life, and if you two are unable to handle that, we are willing to adopt him." He scolded us as if this chain of events was somehow plotted behind closed doors.

Why would they be telling their daughter that? Jennifer had no control over the situation, at that moment, and was now just shy of having a mental breakdown, because her parents were flashing horrible images that stuck in the forefront of her mind. I wanted to kick them out, but I just excused myself. They didn't like me from the get go, but this premature birth just sent them soaring off the douchebag ledge. I went outside to smoke and brought a notebook with me, then decided to venture off. It was the night of the twelfth and after walking a little less than a mile to BJ's Tavern, the bartender, Bonnie, noticed me enter.

"Hey hun, haven't seen you around in a while." She was in her fifties and was the staple bartender almost every night, when I would sing Karaoke there. She was country to the max and loved her blue jeans. That made it all the more crowd-pleasing when I sang my rendition of "Baby's Got Her Blue Jeans On" while substituting 'Baby' with 'Bonnie'.

"My son was born yesterday. Fourteen weeks early. He's in Phoenix right now. We're waiting a couple days for his Mom to heal enough from the C-section to make the drive out." I was visibly distressed and she brought me a Budweiser Draft.

"On the house." She offered.

"Thanks Bonnie. Hey, do you have a pen I could have?"

This was supposed to be a celebratory moment, the birth of my firstborn son, firstborn *anything*. But yet, there I was, looking down at the same substance that left me apathetic to caring for what was, at minimum, my shared responsibility. I couldn't drown this pain. I wouldn't. But I nonetheless raised the glass mug to Bonnie out of appreciation and took a heavy pull. I left the bar without finishing the glass.

I hoped Jennifer's parents were gone. I made it to a bench outside the Hospital's main entrance, and placed my cigarettes and lighter on it, next to me. I hadn't let the composition book out of my hand since I slid by her fuming parents forty-five minutes earlier. I opened to a blank page, near the middle, intent on writing something. Looking up at the once again starlit sky, I found Orion.

"Why me? Why me, God?"

I had had a long string of mishaps in life up to that point, but nothing I had done warranted this type of turmoil. Having a child was my way of getting back on track and putting my time, work and love into another human being. That was to straighten me and Jennifer out.

But to have that stripped away from me in such a fashion, or with such a seismic shock, that I couldn't see ever recovering from this if it went south. I decided to banish the thought of fear of failure. I picked up the pen as a stream of consciousness engulfed me. I wrote.

Uninterrupted except for the periodic drag of my cigarette, it was a holy experience. A song. A song of hope. It was a song that would ward off bad energies and lay the spiritual groundwork for a happy ending. I got into the elevator with a renewed determination to get us to Phoenix in the best spirits possible.

To my relief, her parents were gone. I didn't have a moment to tell her about what I had just written because the nurse came in right after me, to change her bandage. As Jennifer was disrobed, over her left shoulder, I noticed three fresh, straight, razorblade cuts. I wanted to scream. I wanted to leave right then and there. What did this mean? Did she do this after I got rid of my tapes of the Navy and Veronica? Or did she do this while I was at the casino, putting *herself* in duress? What was I supposed to do in this situation? All I co*uld* do was focus on my breathing. All I co*uld* do was tell myself that Xander needed me to be there for him and when the immediate issues had been dealt with, I would demand answers from her. I acted as if I saw nothing. Yet, it remains, to this day, one of the most pressing unanswered questions of my life. If she hadn't cut, what would have been Xander's fate? She had one more day left to heal, as per Doctor's orders, and we could head out.

She took a pain pill after we got her situated in the Saturn, that Thursday. One extra pillow to sit on and one pillow to recline onto. Mom told me she had put forty dollars in the ashtray for gas, knowing we literally had nothing. Jennifer had spoken to her father the night before and he sprung for a hotel for our first night in the valley. Her and her dad had barely spoken over the last few years and that gesture meant a lot to her. She slept the whole three hour drive.

Pulling up to the towering hospital with the red and white heart-palmed hand atop what seemed to be thirty stories, nothing could have prepared me for what the next moment had to offer.

Intake paperwork, wristband issuance, and washing of the hands before entering the NICU, or Neo-Natal Intensive Care Unit, was mandatory. We were guided past a handful of occupied incubators until we found our spot off the center walkway, to the right.

"Here you are. I'll leave you two alone for a moment," the NICU nurse informed us. As she pulled away the blanket and disappeared down the walkway, I was awestruck. A child, my child, was there in all his glory. With tubing in his nostrils and mouth, and a pair of foam sunglasses to shade him from the lights that illuminated him, I wasn't freaked out in any way. In fact, I almost felt comforted that there was so much acute attention to detail about this little life to make me feel confident that he was in very capable hands. The lights, the nurse informed us were to help break down the blood from the visibly apparent bruising, attributed to the emergency CPR.

Looking over the sea of plastic cocoons, I tried to keep my composure. Some were adorned with blankets, balloons or the occasional Ty Beanie Baby. There was a quiet room off to the side that mothers would use to privately pump breast milk, the best nutrient for a premature child. It wasn't in use at that moment. There were four couples, at first glance, keeping vigil over their heavily monitored offspring, scattered throughout the floor. I heard a faint crying from a woman behind a curtain blocking off her and her child's incubator. The deep realization came flooding in that not everyone here was going to make it out. Across the aisle, I saw a couple babies that almost looked full term and were fully clothed with minimal medical intervention. Soon, I thought, we would be there.

The nurse arrived with a tote bag.

"Here you go." She offered. The words emblazoned on the black and red bag read, "PROJECT SEAHORSE." It was a gift bag for all those parents who were going through the uncertainty of dealing with a premature infant. It was a lifeline.

Inside, it contained a baby blanket, a couple Beanie Babies, and two books. One of the books was letting new parents know what it would be like in the immediate future having their child in the hospital for an extended NICU stay, and what to expect thereafter. The second book was a child's book, which I promptly thumbed through. Ours ended with the line, "I love you to the moon and back." And wasn't that the truth.

"Do you want to hold his hand?" The nurse asked. I took off my button-up and revealed my "Horn If You're Honky" Hollister T-shirt. We washed our hands again at the hand washing station and the nurse opened up the side access panel for us. I gently touched his shoulder and brought my index finger to his open palm. He squeezed. What a feeling!

"Hey, little guy." I managed to whisper in utter awe of the life I had helped create. He officially weighed in at two pounds two ounces and didn't have a torso much bigger than a Coke can. His diaper was roughly the size of a dollar bill and looked quite oversized for his small frame. They were the smallest diapers they had. Feeling him grip my finger was a lightning bolt moment for me. I closed my eyes and was instantly transported out of time.

I lived a lifetime in that moment. I imagined what it would be like growing up as a father, raising a male child. I had picked out the name Xander Michael Gant even before I joined the Navy. I was determined that if I was to have to take my son to school, giving him a first name at the end of the alphabet would almost certainly guarantee me an extra fifteen seconds of sleep per school day. Roll call in grade school, as I remember it, was done alphabetically. Adam's parents had to be on the ball, Xander's parents could just kind of go with the flow. I imagined learning what he liked and didn't like to eat. How he liked to play, and I wondered if he was going to be smart.

I was under no delusion that he was going to be great at sports, but then neither was I. I would love him, regardless. I imagined how great it was to get my first bike, and no doubt I would get him the most coveted one of his classmates. I would teach him to drive and buy him his first used car. If I could make Kacy Jacobs laugh in a run-down '86 Taurus, he should have no problem getting the girl in anything I decided to put him in. I would teach him the tricks of the pizza trade and by then, perhaps, have my own franchise. Lord knows I've been on the cusp of ownership a couple times.

I would be there for everything he wanted to do, and everything that I never had the chance to. I could live my life vicariously through him, giving him all the advantages of being the sole owner of my attention. I would not continue the cycle of negligent parenting that my Dad subscribed to. Night fell on the first day and we were politely told we could come back in the morning.

Jennifer and I made our way to the hotel room that had been procured for us. It was more like a studio apartment. We made it to the bed where she promptly let me know that she wanted to subdue her emotional distress with some sex. I was hesitant, but proceeded cautiously. It went off without a hitch. It would have been very embarrassing explaining to the doctor how, against orders, we engaged in some activity that busted a stitch. Thankfully, I was skillful.

"Sing me the song?" She asked as I held her in my arms. It had a country twang to it and she liked it. It would become our anthem for the situation. Positive vibes could do no harm. "Sing it again?" I smiled at her request. I whisper sang it the second time and she was sleeping by the time I was finished. Where were we going to sleep tomorrow? I trusted an answer would make itself apparent.

"Have you looked into the Ronald McDonald House?" A social worker asked us the next morning after we finished filling out the ACCHS paperwork. "I'll make a call for you. They help a lot of families that are from out of town."

I never thought just what that Plexiglas container full of spare change and a random few dollars cash translates in real life, but we were about to find out.

From the bottom of my broken heart I want to thank you, Ronald McDonald House Charities, for tending to our needs while we were there. I distinctly remember being shown to a private room with an open diary full of unspeakable truths from patients and parents that had come before us. Every day, a group of people from the community made a big dinner, and outside of that, we were assigned a shared pantry that contained anything that we could have wanted, even though hunger was second on our minds back then. The following days went by as a blur of monitor readouts and nurse scrubs. Jennifer and I kept vigil over his incubator as if doing anything else would have made us bad parents. In the end, though, it just wasn't to be.

We were called into an exam type room off of the main NICU floor. It was about his latest MRI brain scan. The nurse said he had suffered a class IV brain hemorrhage after suffering a survivable class III the day before. The class IV was something you don't come back from. She told us she would get a specialist to look at the images and reaffirm her findings. While we waited the hour or so next to his designated spot, he looked no different than he did any previous day. I didn't know what to think. Maybe he could beat the odds? Maybe I was holding out for a miracle. I didn't want to believe that it was over. The specialist ushered us back into the room with the light up wall device to examine the x-rays.

"I don't see a class IV here. It is definitely a class III which is completely survivable," she gently informed us. Our miracle.

I almost started crying out of sheer relief, and as we made our way out of the review room and out towards the main door to catch something to eat and gather our thoughts, our names get called from twenty-five feet behind us.

We were brought back into the light up room and told excessively apologetically that she had been looking at the scan from the day before, and today's scan definitely showed a class IV hemorrhage. Miracle robbed. This was a death sentence. The death summary is as follows...

PHOENIX CHILDREN'S HOSPITAL
1919 East Thomas Road
Phoenix, Arizona 85016

Account#: _____
MR#: _____
GANS, XANDER
DOB: 12/11/2006
Admitted: 12/11/2006
Discharged: 12/19/2006
Patient Class: IP

DEATH SUMMARY

Parents are Jennifer and Cliff.
Family obstetrician is Dr. ███████ in Lake Havasu.   Primary
pediatrician is Dr. ████, also from Lake Havasu.

FINAL DIAGNOSES:

1. Preterm male infant, appropriate for gestational age
   (AGA) 26-2/7 weeks, now 8 days old 27-3/7 weeks
   corrected gestational age.
2. Status post urgent cesarean section delivery due to
   preterm labor, breech, bulging membranes.
3. Minimal prenatal care.
4. Neonatal depression, coding of the infant for 7 minutes.
5. Respiratory distress syndrome, severe.   Respiratory
   failure.
6. Pulmonary interstitial emphysema, atelectasis.
7. Pulmonary hemorrhage.
8. Patent ductus arteriosus, small.
9. Anemia. Status post multiple blood product transfusions.
10. Neonatal sepsis, suspected, not proven.
11. Interventricular hemorrhage, severe. Grade IV on the
    right side and grade III on the left side.

This most unfortunate preterm male infant was born at 0254
hours on December 11, 2006 at Lake Havasu Hospital and
transferred shortly after birth to Phoenix Children's Hospital for
evaluation and management of prematurity and respiratory
failure.

He had been born to a healthy 19 year old, A positive, serology
negative, hepatitis B negative. Father of the baby is involved
and supportive. The mother had only one prenatal care visit.
She came to hospital in advanced stage of preterm labor with

full dilation, bulging membranes and a 26 weeks baby in breech presentation prompting an urgent cesarean section delivery. This was performed under general anesthesia. The membranes were ruptured at delivery and the fluid was clear. Mother had been given one dose of terbutaline prior to this. The infant was born limp and required full-blown resuscitation for 7 minutes including epinephrine x 3 doses and chest compressions. I do not have a cord pH at hand, but the infant Apgar score were 2 at 1 minute , 4 at 5 minutes and 6 at 10 minutes. The infant was intubated , hand bag ventilated and eventually placed on mechanical ventilator support by the transport team and given one dose of artificial surfactant. Initial blood gasses were appropriate. Umbilical arterial and venous catherters were inserted; sepsis workup had been performed, and infant was given IV fluids and antibiotics. He had an uneventful transfer by the transport team and, on arrival to the nursery, he was placed on mechanical ventilator support.

DEATH SUMMARY

The infant's course was complicated by the following:

RESPITORY: The infant had respiratory failure secondary to respiratory distress syndrome, and received artificial surfactant. It was complicated by pulmonary interstitial emphysema and eventually pulmonary hemorrhage, severe, times two. He was placed on different modalities of ventilation including conventional ventilator, high-frequency oscillator and high-frequency jet ventilator.

The infant developed anemia due to his severe pulmonary hemorrhage and required packed red blood cells x 4 transfusions. Due to abnormal clotting profile, he also received one dose of fresh frozen plasma.

INFECTIOUS DISEASES: The infant's sepsis workup both at Lake Havasu and at out institution turned out to be negative. He was given ampicillin and gentamicin.

RENAL: The infant had normal renal function with highest creatinine level of 0.8. We did not encounter any metabolic problems and specifically the potassium levels were within normal range.

NUTRITION: The infant was maintained on IV fluids and total parental throughout his whole life, and he did manage to get by NG tube a few cc of breast milk of the 5th through the 7th day of life. The infant underwent echocardiograms x2 for a moderate size patient ductus arteriosus requiring no intervention. He was also found to have a small pericardial effusion of no clinical significance.

The infant's blood type is A Rh Positive. He developed hyperbilirubinemia with a maximal level of 4.1 mg%

The infant's major problem was bilateral severe interventricular hemorrhage with grade IV on the right side and grade III on the left side with midline shift and ventrucuomegaly. The cavum pellucidum was compressed because of the mass effect and deviation secondary to the huge hemorrhage on the right side.

He was seen in consultation by Dr. Janet Teodori, Pediatric Neurology.

The infant's clinical course deteriorated. We held two family conferences with the parents and, on the 7th day of life, the family decided for a Do-Not-Resuscitate status. We proceeded to do so and the infant was maintained overnight. The following morning, the infant underwent a religious ceremony at the bedside and the family came forward with the decision to withdraw support. This was done. The infant was given to the mother's arms in a private room and he expired peacefully in her arms.

The time of death was 1310 hours on December 19, 2006.

~

I was then taken into a private room and given a few moments to familiarize myself with the lifeless body of my son. The whole situation reeked of irresponsibility and immaturity and marked an unfathomable low in my life.

XANDER'S SONG

A little boy
Not two days old
Is in a place far from his home
Mom is fine and Dad is just ok
He can fit in the palm of your hand
But the prayers they just won't end
That this little boy will somehow last the week
And the day goes on
And their hopes get strong

Dad is standing right beside her
As they look down at their little fighter
It's been three weeks
But they're taking it day by day
And the weeks go by
For their little guy

Don't ever count him out
Don't ever let fear win
It's God
Whose hands he is in
Don't ever let
Someone say
I don't think he will ever be ok
Because they don't know
How far he will go

They never thought the day would come
That they'd bring their baby home
But there they were at the doorway of their house
They know they got an uphill road
And it's gonna take a while
But when they see him smile it all just fades away
And they years have gone
And he's growing strong

Don't ever count him out
Don't ever let fear win
It's God
Whose hands he is in
Don't ever let
Someone say
I don't think he will ever be ok
Because they don't know
How far he will go

And finally it came around
He was standing with his cap and gown
He threw his hat then he found Mom and Dad
And with a tear in his eye
This is what he said

Don't ever count me out
Don't ever let fear win
Because I know
Whose hands I am in
Don't ever let
Someone say
I don't think he will ever find his way
Because they don't know
How far I will go

Don't ever count me out
Don't ever let fear win
Because I know
Whose hands I am in
Don't ever let
Someone say
I don't think he will ever find his way
Because they don't know
How far I will go

A little boy
Not two days old

125

Chapter XI
The Mourning After

Leaving Phoenix Dec 20th with a black and red tote bag full of baby memorabilia was a bittersweet moment. Getting me through it, in addition to realizing that there was nothing I could do but drive, was the Vince Gill tune in my head, "Go Rest High on That Mountain." Music seemed to come at just the right moment.

Like, before heading back to the Ronald McDonald House, while decompressing the events of day three in the dark of the car, Mariah Carey came on with "You'll Always Be My Baby". And once I recycled the words, I told Jennifer that it was pretty poignant for the moment, probably without using the word "poignant". Sam was aware of the situation and sent his condolences immediately upon receipt of the news, which didn't seem but a 'feeler' phone call to see how soon I could start working for Paul. I agreed to start full time on New Year's Eve, training a new General Manager at the Needles, California location. I can't imagine that I would have participated in Christmas celebrations that year, and if any photos do exist, I will claim Photoshop foul.

I did make it known to Jennifer, timing-be-damned, that I wanted to take a break from our relationship. Right there in the Widgeon driveway, the moment I turned the key back after arriving back from Phoenix. I sighed and turned to her. Too many unanswered questions I wasn't ready to ask or process. I've heard that the statistics aren't that great for couples sticking together after they lose a child. Now, I don't know the sample pool of those couples, but the mathematician in me says odds are far worse for those partners that hold potential blame, not guilt, but *BLAME,* for the instance. I imagine it's really a make or break state of affairs.

Losing a child either solidifies your commitment to each other, or it just shatters the surrounding ethos. I just wanted to be away. I wanted time to not be committed to someone who, only God knows, destroyed or inhibited the proper growth of a life. At that point, once alone, I would attempt the same distancing from myself. I would try to not think about what I was powerless to change. But the inexcusable guilt, blame and shame of watching the doctors pull out his lifelines one by one, knowing I was at least partially responsible for one more corpse at the Reaper's feet, one more statistic of Hades' daily take, had put the validity of my continued existence under the microscope. Also, worthiness thereof.

Of the two deaths I had experienced in life up till that point: my Mom's grandmother, Olga (when I was six or seven) and my Dad's mother, Elizabeth (in 2004), both had lived full and abundant lives. But this life was of my shared creation, my spirit... and thus, in my opinion, timeless. So as to circumvent the vanity of the grieving process, I became committed to the belief that he would be with me for the rest of my travels in life. My shadow. I would show him how to live, anew. His life had eclipsed, but it was as if I was reborn. A New Life. I welcomed it.

Paul was an active owner. He thoroughly enjoyed being in his locations, in his element, participating in his cash-flow machines. We didn't have an official employment contract, but he topped Scott's starting salary by a few bucks per hour, so that was a nice enticement. The chosen General Manager of the Needles store was hard to train because he couldn't understand that I was there to **train** him, I wasn't there to **replace** him. When someone is thinking they are about to get fired at any Arizona Right-to-Work moment, they become more interested in covering their own ass instead of exposing and remedying their shortcomings. He was never going to last. But I did my best.

End-Game was the Lake Havasu store. It was the crown jewel of the newly reorganized franchise. Cash flow was amazing due to the inexpensive rent that hadn't been raised in years. Well, that and being the busiest store of the bunch. What I knew at the time, but was sworn to nondisclosure, was that Paul had been plotting a complete management overhaul for the Havasu location. This was due to two important factors:

1.   Paul was unimpressed with their daily operations and gave them ample warning to change procedures detrimental to Dominos' good name.

2.   And, perhaps more egregious to Paul, the current management's pay was grandfathered. Tony, the man who hired me as a lowly delivery driver a mere year earlier, was earning more than Paul was willing to pay. In fact, the two Assistant Managers, Jill and Darren (a couple) were already making more than what Paul hired me on for. Bonuses for the management team were carried over and, in my view, quite simply, Paul didn't want to pay that.

So, working a shift here and there in Tony's store, I had to look at him, the man who gave me my big break, knowing he was dead to rights. It was just a matter of time. It was soul crushing. It was uncalled for. It was… business. As such was the Navy, I followed orders of those appointed above me, namely, the one writing the checks.

When Paul finally did decide to pull the trigger, chaos ensued. Firing Tony, Jill and Darren simultaneously resulted in eight other employees quitting out of allegiance to the old guard. Four were much needed insider positions. This was not your idle Kingman store.

From the time we opened at 10:00AM until the time we closed, there were orders. Scrubbing the Havasu ceiling tiles, if needed, would have certainly had to have been a 7:00AM chore. Not the concurrent job that was done in Kingman during that weekday shift, a lifetime ago. Same amount of business, with a quarter of the staff gone. Reckless. The new hires that came to my desk were not the choice for the family-style joint I was trying to duplicate. These were kids who just wanted a job. To do as little as possible during their ten to fifteen hours a week, collect their paycheck and call it a day.

I *was* granted a reprieve when Paul sent down an Assistant Manager from another store to help me until the storm was weathered. Frankie Wymbs. Adorable pizza girl. Carl would have approved. With her assuming the reigns, I was able to get somewhat of a break three to four shifts a week, and Sam would cover another two or three shifts, but I was still clocking over sixty hours a week. The overtime pay was not taken for granted, but there had still been no mention of a bonus structure, and, after the first month, I started breaching the subject. To which I consistently got the response, "I'm working on it." It should have amounted to Scott's bonus structure, minus twenty-five percent across the board. I would have been completely satisfied with that. But as another month eclipsed with no mention of bonus structure or any potential bonus back-pay, I was getting impatient.

Frankie was poached from me to manage my old Kingman store, which Paul also bought from Scott, thus further hindering my structural retooling of core store staff. Then, one early March morning as I was gearing up the store for the morning onslaught, the phone rang.

"Hello. My name is Mary with Parks & Rec, is the manager available?" Well, yes.

"Speaking." Relieved it wasn't Paul or Sam checking in on me.

"I'm calling about Teen Break. Last year, you guys donated fifteen pizzas for the three-day event and I was wondering if you would be on board to match that this year?" Really, Tony, I thought. Only fifteen pizzas? For the *children*? What would Nancy Pelosi think? I wanted to test this cold-caller's meddle.

"No, I don't think I can do that, this year." I said despairingly and waited for her response, this was already the highlight of my day. Please, don't hang up.

"Oh?" She responded in utter confusion. Not use to taking a low-balling 'no' this early in the morning? I decided to let her off the hook, before it came to hurt feelings. With Xander watching and all.

"I don't know who you spoke with last year, but I am the new General Manager, and if I'm going to get involved, I'm not going to go halfway with this. What would it take to sponsor the entire event?" I imagined her butthole puckering a little bit as she formulated the words to go for the 'Big Ask.'

"300 pizzas?" Damn woman, who taught you how to ask? I imagine you started your day thinking like this, Diet Coke in hand: "I need 300 pizzas, and Domino's, first on my call list, being a national chain and all, Partner of St. Jude Children's Research Hospital, maybe if they match 'last year's' donation, I'll only have 285 more pies to manifest out of beggarly thin air. Oh, goody gumdrops, what a day I am going to have!" Thank you for making my job easy, Clifford. You're welcome, now up your game, or next year I'm only pitching in a breadstick and you can try to feed 'em like Jesus. Oh, what? God can fuck with my son, but I can't fuck with his?

"Done. What are the dates & times?" At that point I didn't give a flying fuck what Paul would think of this idea... take it out of my bonus, bitch! I called him fifteen minutes later.

"Hey Paul, I just signed us on to donate 300 pies to Teen Break on the 12th through the 14th, and I'd like to get maximum exposure for us, what can we do?"

Do you like how I didn't ask, just casually let him know we were committed and now it's all about positioning. If you are thinking the monetized volume of the task was a lot... think again. Pro-Tip: If you can't make a large pizza for less than two dollars of combined food & labor, you need a new business model. That's how much it costs. Think about that next time you drop $18.99 on a Large Papa John's 'The Works' pizza. But if you got a local joint, cut them some slack... paying for fast food pizza is like playing slots in a casino, you may get a bonus every once in a while, but in the long run, you should be blowing the rape whistle. At least at a local shop, they do the best they can given the leftover foot traffic, but it's as honest as you're going to get, kinda like playing blackjack.

Paul saw, and, as far as I was concerned, was impressed we were 'Fish On' (not that kind of *FISH*...hehe). What a whale of an opportunity to get our name out there for the Havasuvian kids that pull the parents' purse strings of "what's for dinner?"

We went through the Domino's promotional book and ordered branded beach balls and Frisbees. Both were fitting for the lake's beachfront Rotary Park. Also, wanting to leave no question of where we were located during 'The Great Feeding' he sprung for the $500 branded pop-up canopy. Twice!

I don't know how you can fuck up a beach ball or a Frisbee, for that matter, and they didn't. Kudos. But they sure as hell were negligent with the big ticket item. The pop-up part of the pop-up canopy, well, didn't pop up. Bendy metal and twisty garbage is what we uncovered from the box. The branded canopy canvas was fine, no complaints there. Not so much for the framey part, though. So, in a slightly irritated midnight call to the Domino's promo people, I got to hear THE Paul Parker, order a new one with overnight shipping, trust me, it was entertaining.

This secondary box of bullshit, was delivered on the 10th. Crisis averted, we thought... until the Monday wind wreaked havoc and the twisty metal failed to properly expand as we were setting up on day one. We had to man each post with a uniformed employee, for four hours, each of the three consecutive days of the event. It must have been "prayers answered" for the four blasé employees I called in for that task, specifically. Instructions couldn't have been more clear and tuned to their earholes, "Hold Post. Get Paid." That will teach them to strive for the mundane. "Hands getting numb? Shake it off, you lazy premadonnas! I got slices to sling."

Other memorable moments from the '07 Teen Break included a fat kid winning my pizza eating contest, to no one's surprise. I then upped the ante by challenging him to ride the "Twirl & Hurl" which, unfortunately, didn't live up to its namesake. (It wasn't called the Twirl & Hurl, but you pictured the ride it was.) Pro-tip: If you get an opportunity to sing live karaoke to a crowd of 120 tweens, don't sing Garth.

After the last crust was consumed, it was back to business as usual. Another three weeks of somehow making it work, and keeping the tattering store together, I again raised the topic about bonus structure with the owner, Paul. I was dismissed with an all-too-familiar, "I'm working on it." AGAIN. Well, you keep working on that, Paul, I'm going to put in some work, myself.

Sam had closed the store the night of the 5th, and against policy, left that night's bank deposit in the time-delay safe. So closing up that night, to my surprise, was the Thursdays take of a little over $1,000 cash. Not having any intention of making a big deal about it, I counted the till down, and began my nightly routine.

My closing driver was deaf, an awesome hire, and I proceeded to count him out so I could finish my bank deposit. I gave him his cash tips & mileage for the night and he went to the back to finish any straggling dishes. After a short five minutes or so he came back to the office asking if I wanted him to sweep. I knew no sign language save "Thank you," a simple flattened hand to the chin and extension towards the thanked party. We took to writing on scrap paper, short glyphs that got our respective points across. All of a sudden, something snapped in me. I wasn't going to have it. I came to the epiphany that I was, at that point... done.

"Go home, Duane." I verbally told him, knowing he was reading lips. I stood up for what I knew was going to be the last time I'd see him, extended my hand, and gave the most inwardly emotional handshake I've ever given. He had no idea what was about to take place. But in that moment, I knew I wasn't going to stand for Paul's mistreatment anymore. Paul mistreated me, and by proxy, all those that were connected to me.

"I got it," I mouthed while displaying the universal 'OK' sign with my right hand, "Go." He waved his thanks and I locked the door behind him as he made his way to his oversized truck. It was like he was delivering pizzas in the Gravedigger Monster Truck, it was almost comical. Character. He will never be forgotten.

Jennifer was working at the Subway, four units down, and knocked on the front door once her closing procedures were done, shortly before midnight.

"I'm done, Jennifer." I publicized.

"What do you mean?" Knowing by simply looking around there was plenty of work left to do before I would be out of there. It had been about a $4,000 Friday night, and it was APPARENT.

Cornmeal littered the floor and the tables where I had just finished pumping out the day's dough. The make line toppings were yet to be inventoried, uncovered, and mixed lightly with random bits of mozzarella cheese that haphazardly made its way from the catch tray back to the tubs of toppings in a feat of physics that can only be captured in the chaos of a rush. In the aftermath of the day's business, all topping containers were littered with bits of neighboring toppings. Olives found themselves in the pineapple dish, onions peppered the ham bin and about fifteen chunks of Italian sausage and crumbs were remaining in the corner of an almost empty large pepperoni vat.

"I mean, I'm DONE! I'm not taking Paul's shit anymore. Dragging his feet, while I scramble to keep things together, no way. My dignity is worth more than this, not much more, but more, nonetheless." She eyed the two bank deposits, one sealed and one yet unused under a neat pile of roughly $2,600 in cash. The rest of the days take was in credit cards, which were processed as soon as the 'OPEN' sign went dim.

I wondered if getting out of the rat race was our key to rebuilding a shaky relationship. I wondered if I had her alone with no distractions, that we could change the trajectory of our partnership. We were more so 'Friends With Benefits' at that point, which just saved me time and energy finding a new lover. Maybe something way out of our comfort zone would be required.

I looked up at her, "Wanna take a trip?"

Chapter XII
Mazatlan or Bust

Not wanting to be outdone, Jennifer too, who had just received her paycheck for the previous two weeks, wanted her Monday-Friday pay too. I calculated it out to $200 and change. She went back and shorted the Subway safe in that amount. She didn't want to rob the place- she just didn't want to leave any money on the table. It was still theft, in the eyes of the law.

While she was gone, I went to the back and withdrew all the cash from the soda vending machine that Paul had installed for the employees, as to deter thieving of the twenty-ounce bottles of Coke that were for public sale. Plus, it dispensed his coveted Cactus Coolers in twelve-ounce cans. There was over $150 cash in the machine but I left all the change in the hopper, not wanting to weigh myself down. Jennifer returned. I locked the front doors and we both exited, wide eyed, out the back door.

I explained to her that we were going to go back to the house and pack what we could in thirty minutes. Then we would take off. Pulling into my Mom's rental that my Uncle Rick was refurbishing, we went into our bedroom and started stuffing duffels. I grabbed the safe with our important documents. At one point, I had held over $10,000 worth of deposits in that little guy, but not until now, had I felt the urge to make this kind of stand. You can only push an honest man so far. And my limits had just been egregiously breached. Tossing everything in the back of the Saturn, we took off before my Uncle had a chance to wake up.

According to him, SWAT showed up the next day and scared the shit out of him and he had to plead ignorance, saying that he honestly had no idea where we were. He didn't. Nobody did. My brother, Matthew, was crushed. I had hired him on at fifteen years old and he busted his ass daily for me, but this wasn't about him. In the aftermath, Matthew decided to stay on after Jennifer and I's white collar exit, working for Paul. I think quitting may have made him look complicit.

The judge would later accuse me, based on some surveillance video, that I had 'exited through the roof' and I retorted immediately that we merely walked out the back door and that it was no "mission impossible stunt." He didn't take kindly to that answer.

"$3,800 is nothing to laugh at!" He chided. Paul wasn't going to eat any less steak that month. But that comes later.

Now, we have a trunk full of clothes and around $4000 hidden under the removable center console between the driver and passenger seats, in the Saturn. Sleepless, we made our way to San Diego. I wanted to start in Tijuana. Lots of miles for some simple Super Taco, but oh what it would be like to share with my new Partner in Crime. It made her more badass. We were criminals. The feeling of paranoia set in even though I knew nothing would be reported untill the sun came up the next morning and the opening manager would open a store with oven still running, foods exposed & trash everywhere. We stopped at around 6:00 AM at Viejas Casino.

She cashed her check at the cage and we spent a few hours gambling. As far as heist movies are concerned, the system would now know where she was, and thus know where I was. But, it would just be a paper trail. We would be long gone before they looked into what zip code she was in when she cashed her last paycheck. We dropped a quick three or four hundred at the casino, mostly me trying to play big to further the adrenaline that was coursing through my veins, the likes of which I never had felt before, save Jennifer's kiss at the Kingman Dominos.

They were live-filming an episode of 'Deal or No Deal' at Viejas and that would have been fun to attend, but sticking around was not an option. We were back on the road before 9:00 AM, Pacific Time.

Skipping the outlet malls, we headed straight south on the 805 to my old stomping grounds of Tijuana. Just as always, the only barrier was a line of cars and a red and green light. We hit green. Thanks, Mayans. I entered the Mexican highway like I did this every day, pro-style. She decided it would be wise to put her seatbelt on. I twisted our way to the entrance of Colonio Libertad and pulled in front of Carmen's old safe house. Guido was there with Carmen who were just leaving the house.

"Ama, hola!" Like nothing had happened. She didn't seem to hold anything against me and gave me a hug. I'd made that woman so much money, she couldn't possibly have wanted to flag down the nearest cop for the blue Chevy I took, months ago.

"This is my girlfriend, Jennifer." I told Guido, who had visibly gotten older. He gave me a smile, to say that she was cute.

"De donde vas?" Carmen asked. "Where are you going?"

"I don't know," I told her, "maybe Cabo?"

"Undelay, pues." Carmen said, Guido told us that they had to go, but was nice to see us again and to be safe.

Jennifer and I got back in the car and I took her around the corner to Super Taco. I must have eaten three cucumbers worth of salted slices. Jennifer was impressed with the food. Taco breath. I watched her chew as bits of the taco fell to her small plate. I couldn't wait to fuck. Criminals and intercourse just make the act so much more fire. We finished off our glass-bottled, made with real sugar, Coca-Colas, and then I took her downtown.

We found and acquired a hotel to be our point of reference. I paid thirty-five dollars for the room and the accommodations were adequate, nothing special. I wasn't going to keep our money in this rinky-dink room, though. I was blissfully unaware of the attention brought to a gringo and his girl cashing in $3,200 at a casa de cambio, where we received roughly 34,000 Pesos in exchange. Walking around downtown on the first night, we were accosted by the Mexican police.

I tried to tell them that that Jennifer was sick and we were looking for herbal tea. But instead of using the Spanish word for 'sick' meaning "enferma," I used the word for 'annoy'- "molesta." So, I told the cops (that thought we were looking for drugs), that "she was annoying me" instead of saying "she is sick." They frisked both of us and then asked how much money we had on us. I had no idea... "how much is in a fat wad?" I thought. They had me write the number I thought I had, on the side of their dusty van. I should have kept the receipt from the exchange booth. I lowballed, and they stole a 1,000 Peso billet from me, roughly $100. Welcome back, Whitey, 33,000 Pesos left. I just wanted to get somewhere safe. Adilitas. The same bar Kevin took me where I met my biggest regret. But now, I had the sex giver next to me, I wanted to see what she thought about my past life's entertainment venue. After a few girls danced and a few beers each, I nearly spit out a swig when she whispered, "I'd fuck that one!"

@#$#@! What did I just hear? The house music must have been too loud, the beat must have dropped, or did I just hear her throw out a threesome idea with a Mexican stripper? The stripper's music ended and I summoned her over.

"How much?" I asked her.

"Sixty." She replied, in English.

I looked at Jennifer and she smiled. "Just this once." She said. First off, I couldn't believe what was happening. Secondly, fuck that stripper! She went to the back and got a stand in, one that wasn't her, who was intent on just getting me and Jennifer to have sex so she didn't have to do nothing but guide my shaft into Jennifer's criminal twat. I penetrated both of them, but I wasn't happy about it. I remember releasing early, but had to keep my thoughts from letting me go limp, I wasn't going to waste a good sixty dollars on having sex with my own girlfriend. When Jennifer finally let me know that she had had enough of this ridiculous back room rendezvous, it came payment time.

134

"120." She said. I almost laughed out loud.

"She said sixty!"

"Yes, sixty her, sixty you. $120."

"I need to go to the ATM. We will be back."

"NO. You go, she stays with me." She said with some imaginary authority. I had to end this literal 'Mexican standoff.'

"Look, I'm just going to go let the policia know that you are holding my girlfriend ransom because you changed the sex price on us." She knew that would lead to nothing good.

She held out her hand defeated, "Sixty."

That's what I thought, bitch. 32,000 Pesos left. I paid the waste of a woman and we left there thankful that was the end of it. Once again, I felt I had just been snuffluppagus'd or sex bamboozled. We made our way to a main club on Revolution, Animalé.

At this mainstay of Tijuana, the workers come around with a bottle of tequila and whistles and give you a shot straight into your mouth and then shake your reclined head with a towel and by the time you regain your bearings, they are telling you that you owe them twenty bucks for the shot. Pro-Tip: Don't let them run the show!

I've learned fast that 'no' is the proper first response, to anything. Ask for things specifically. "One beer." "One tequila." They speak quickly, and if you say yes to a fast talker, you'll soon wind up with a bucket of eight iced beers and a runner waiting for 200 Pesos, plus a tip, while he is drawing up a line of cocaine for you. You have been so warned.

There **was** a twenty dollar bill well spent, though, when a street artist approached us offering to draw Jennifer and me, on the spot, in the dim light. He made me look like Leonardo DiCaprio, and her, well, the arm candy. She looked nothing like what he drew, but I was spot on. I paid and thanked the man. He rolled the sketch up with a rubber band. The next morning, we would start our adventure, quickly down about $1,000 from the original theft.

Starting down Baja California was nice, ocean view and all, but as I saw high rise hotel after high rise hotel, I got sick to my stomach.

"This is little America," I told Jennifer, brunette hair blowing in the warm, salted air. "I want to see real Mexico, don't you?"

"It's up to you." She trusted me explicitly, especially after the Henderson debacle. I pulled off the road and doubled back to Tijuana. We made it to the gatekeeper of the mainland, Sonora. It was Sunday and the administrative office was closed until Monday at 9:00 AM. We had to camp out in the car for the remainder of the night with nothing in sight to do. Thankfully, I did have my laptop and an FM transmitter, thus turning the Saturn into a movie theater, complete with surround sound. The next morning we got 180-day visas and a placard for the car, allowing it to get past the interior checkpoints. By the time it was all said and done we had an even 30,000 Pesos.

The first day we traveled about four hundred miles to the state of Guymas. It was near the beach. Our visas said we were headed towards Mazatlan, where Scott would have sent us if we achieved the benchmark of running a million dollar store. And yet, here we were, taking the trip, regardless.

I took to always having a beer on the road. Some roads were twisty, mountainous, grand prix-style drives. Others were on paid toll roads. Toll roads were great. They had almost zero cops, like again, paying for protection. As for the winding streets, I would drift with my balding tires, freaking Jennifer out. I could only imagine her terror: beer in one hand, steering wheel in the other, squealing tires feet away from a ledge that drops three hundred unaided feet from the edge of a road that had no barrier. Hang on tight!

Making it to our destination on the third day, I was elated. This is what it was all about... what? Looking at the beach, it again was just one big tourist trap destination. I didn't want that. We walked around. The sands were pristine, and the ambience was indescribable, but again, I wanted to see something real. 1,100 miles from Tijuana and it was like we didn't even leave. Walking around, Jennifer found a pet shop with two caged Doberman Pinschers.

"Baby, can we get one? They're so cute!" She had been getting on my nerves because in any city setting, my neck was breaking, copping looks at all the hot, brown-skinned women. She was completely jealous and didn't like being number two, even though *she* was the one in the passenger seat, not them. So, I sprang for the $100 and bought one, and had the pet shop owner through in two kilos of dog food. We bought a leash and a dog dish, and we were on our way.

"Jack Daniels." I branded.

"I love it! He looks like a Jack!" She would be happy for a moment.

Rooms were tourist priced and we only stayed for one night. I recorded some scenes of the beach with my camcorder. I stopped shortly before we arrived in Mazatlan to document a wild donkey and the clusters of native mango trees that dotted the highway drive.

The mangos just hung off of strings that you would think wouldn't be able to support that kind of weight, but somehow it worked. 166 miles later we would stop in Tepic, the capital of Nayarit State, for food and drinks. The dog had to pee. We were entering uncharted territory, but had enough funds to make it entertaining. In Nayarit, we found an internet café to try to find the next location on our hit list.

Puerto Vallarta was just over a hundred miles away and we decided to press on and make it before nightfall. We had both heard of it, and the pictures online seemed nice. It was smaller than the bustling city of Mazatlan, so I was hoping it would be less touristy. It wasn't.

Going south into the interior of Mexico, they never asked to open my safe at any of the checkpoints. They saw the safe, but never mentioned toward it. Good thing too, below the felt floorboard of the safe, was a bit of hidden weed. But the bulk of our stash was below the center console with the remaining 23,000 Pesos. We spent a few hours at a casino in Mazatlan that killed $300 from our stockpile, but we weren't worried, even though we agreed that money could be better spent outside of gambling. I just wanted to compare the rush, south of the border.

Getting into Puerto Vallarta at night, I found a hotel off of the main drag, and we snuck up Jack in a duffel bag, as pets weren't allowed. The room was cheap, maybe $35 and I got it for two nights. As if it were an ongoing theme, neither of us were satisfied. I think, at that point, road-tripping with the rest of our money was the goal. To just see as much as we could with the money we had left, then just head home to face the music. My music was going to be a lot louder than hers and her piddly $200 theft from Subway. Another five hundred miles and we were in Acapulco, 1,800 miles from Tijuana. 21,000 Pesos left in the console.

Along that stretch of road, there were many villages with signage that declared: "NO TIRE BASURA" or "DON'T THROW TRASH." We obliged. There were many side stands dedicated to the coconut harvest. There were pyramids of coconuts and the roadside stands had everything from coconut milks to sweetened coconut bars to cakes and candies. I was lucky enough to find a flat crate containing fifteen star fruit, I pointed and the lady asked how many, I told her, "All of them, crate included." I paid 120 Pesos and put them in the Saturn, to ripen in the back seat.

A star fruit is a light fruit I would compare to a cross between a yellow grape and a green pear. They are divine. I was blessed to have found them. There were only three left when we hit the Acapulco city lights.

Have you ever been in the middle of an adventure when it all just goes awry, in one fail swoop? Well, keys are important. Putting them in my board short pocket before enjoying the vastness of the ocean, with Jennifer and Jack on the beach, wasn't the smartest move. I laid back and let the waves carry me back to the beach. There was a big rocky out clove that would remind us where to come back to, the next day. It was a nice spot. As we returned to the car, I did that all too familiar 'panic pat down,' and realized that the keys were not in my pocket. Making problems worse, the ocean is big. I should have clipped them to Jack's collar, but I wasn't thinking. At all.

This lapse in judgment resulted in us getting robbed by the first locksmith that told us to pay him and he would be back in the morning with the right tools. Good thing we had gotten a beachfront rental before we got locked out of the Saturn. He never came back. 350 Pesos down.

The next guy, we had to convince that once he opened the car, we could pay him to rekey it, which wasn't a problem. He was a nice enough guy. Problem was, from the time that he rekeyed the car, the alarm icon would constantly flash red. Good thing there wasn't an audible alarm system. I opened the center console stash spot and paid the man a fair price.

The nightlife and food was great in 'Aca,' but I still wanted to go deeper. Money was getting to the point where we had to start being more cognizant of how we were spending. The locksmith debacle set us back a bunch. Back at the internet café, there it was. Twenty mouse clicks into a "Best Mexican Destinations" Google search, we found Puerto Escondido, or, 'Hidden Door'. 16,000 Pesos left.

Arriving there was an immediate sense of calm. It was a small town of about 35,000 people. No high rising hotel towers, or fanny-pack touting tourists. It was perfect. Boasted as one of the top ten surfing spots in the world, it didn't disappoint. There were three main beaches and we explored them all.

Playa Zicatea was the main beach, miles long and had seven-to-ten foot cresting waves, all day long. The two smaller beaches, Playa Manzania and Playa Carrizilo, were more private. I wanted to try my luck in this world-renowned surf. I absolutely had to spend some of what little we had to buy a six foot surfboard and a Puerto Escondido surf shirt. I tried every day, almost drowned, but never gave up. Any teacher would have told me I needed a longboard to learn on. I wanted to be a stud, though. This was where we wanted to spend the rest of our vacation.

We asked around and found an apartment for $200 a month. I paid up front for two months: 5000 Pesos or so, leaving us with just under 10,000 Pesos in cash. That wouldn't last very long. Shopping the markets like we weren't on a budget was fun, and I also lost a bit of cash at the internet café playing online poker trying to supplement our income.

See, if I could load cash onto a debit card, load my poker account and win, or grind out a living, we could stay here for an extended period of time, and that would have been ideal, with prison being the alternative. But it was a bust.

I went on a weed mission one night while Jennifer went for a walkabout. I found some weed. She found a job. I paid ten dollars for three large 'churros' or 'sticks' of budded marijuana. It was like getting it for free, to be honest. I'd never seen so much weed, for such a low price. Twenty-four inches of marijuana. Happy summer.

The dealer girls were wearing bathing suits and belonged in a Venus swimwear catalog. Sitting on each other's laps in the front seat of the Saturn directing me to the buy house, I would not tell Jennifer, but maybe if I just abandoned her? I would close my eyes next time Jenn spread her legs for me, and think of these two goddesses. Go ahead, call me an asshole.

While Jennifer went walking, she somehow discovered the main bar of Puerto Escondido, The Blue Station. Run by two male owners. Names have since escaped me but let's call them Ivan and Miguel. Miguel was the owner while Ivan seemed to have a cut of the profits, and did most of the bartending work. It was a black lit bar with an expensive turn style DJ booth that they let me mess around with. It was slow. Perhaps they thought having a cute American girl behind the bar would bring in business. They agreed to pay her 200 Pesos per day, which was nice, but nothing compared to the money we were spending, at an alarming rate. Two weeks into the first month of rent we were down to about 5,000 Pesos. I started crunching the numbers, it would take 2,500 Pesos flat to get us home, just for gas. That is with not so much as drinking a Pepsi or eating a Twinkie, the whole way home.

Ivan did take kindly to me, presenting me with a large jug of mescal tequila sweetened with pomegranate and it had about fifteen baby scorpions floating in it, provided by the lady who brought them their oranges. With a simple twirl, the baby scorpions would spin around the vortex, and you thought "Sharknado" was a panic ensuing idea! Scorpnado has a bit more 'sting' to it. Epic.

"When you are here, you drink from this for free!" Well, alrighty then! He also presented me with a kraft paper sack but told me not to open it until I got home, but to go 'straight home.' A staircase and a block away from the bar, our apartment rested. Imagine my surprise opening the package. There must have been a pound of weed in that bag. Jack, Jennifer and I were high for days. That obviously raised the food bill, due to the omnipresent munchies. We couldn't win.

One particular Friday night, after they had me do a 'reverse tequila shot', I got officially plastered for the first time there. A reverse shot consists of shooting a shot of Patron, then snorting a line of salt, finishing by squeezing the lime into your eye. The six bar patrons couldn't stop laughing. One bought me a Tecate, afterwards. One was a uniformed cop. Another was a man named 'Jam' from some eastern European country. Belgium or maybe one of the Slavic nations, who knows. Point was, I got so wasted on that pomegranate mescal, 'Jam' took my keys and drove me home, then walked back to the bar. I woke up the next morning alone. Jack had tipped over my surfboard and chipped the tip off, also somehow started chewing up the Tijuana Animalé portrait, chewing off Jennifer's face but leaving my half of the drawing alone.

"Yeah, bud, I feel the same way." I told him, trying to get my bearings.

Walking down the cement stairway I veered left to find The Blue Station, locked up. I knocked. I heard movement and from behind the locked mesh door I saw Jennifer's face appear on the other side.

"I just wanted to make sure you were still alive." I flatly said. Then I turned around and walked straight back home. Slut. I could hear her calling behind me as she was fumbling with the door lock. I was gone. 1,200 Pesos left.

She got home minutes later. "We just watched movies and hung out, I promise!" Truth came out later from her friend in America that she got coked up and fucked him all night, but we were long over at that point. If I knew then, I just might have left her ass right there or sold her to the cartel. I'm not fucking around. Oh, I didn't tell you about getting **into** Puerto Escondido?

On our first day there, I found the surf shop that had an array of surfboards for sale. I strategically picked one that I thought would do the trick. It fit nicely in the backseat of the car, a quarter of it poking out the rear passenger side window. We found a decent hotel and I parked out front.

We took a walk and began getting on each other's nerves somehow, someway, and we went back to the hotel. I proceeded to get drunk and shortly thereafter, fell asleep.

I awoke to find my car gone, my board in the hotel lobby, and 1,000 Pesos in the nightstand. *She* tried to abandon *me*! But she didn't know the first thing about how to get the fuck out of Mexico, so she had to come back. My wad of cash in her hand and all. Ohhhh…. I was over it. She was just a high maintenance vagina at that point. But thing was, I could have scored better quality, for much less than I was having to shell out for her upkeep. Whatever. Go ahead, pretend you know what I was capable of. "Clifford, how could you say that?" Listen, ever since this bitch sliced up and short-circuited her easy bake oven, potentially killing my kid, I have no restraint in telling it like it is, especially when it comes to Jennifer Suzanne Gans.

I told my landlord that my Mom got in a car accident and I asked for the second months' rent back. He said ok, but the last week of the first month he couldn't refund, I knew that.

Saturday, May 12th was our last day there. Thanks for the accommodations, Puerto Escondido. Pinching pennies, I returned my surfboard to the surf shop who only gave me a little over half of what I paid due to the damaged board, ala Jack. We returned to our rented room to pack the car up with every belonging, except for Jack. I didn't think that animals were allowed past the border and I didn't want to have problems on reentry with the very real possibility of me getting taken away, with Jenn left to fend for herself. So, the decision to leave Jack behind with my landlord's guard dogs made a certain amount of sense. To me, anyways.

"Tu Perro?" The landlord asked. I replied that we were just going to get something to eat and would be back. Blatant lie.

"Do you want to go say goodbye to Ivan and Miguel?" I asked Jennifer.

"I don't want to go back there." She replied, head down.

Wonder why.

3,000 Pesos left, around 2,000 miles, and I'm having a strong feeling I'm sitting next to a cum dumpster.

Just like in Spain, I had multiple opportunities to get some action on the side, but I remained faithful, in deed anyways.

So, that afternoon, leaving paradise in the rear view, we embarked on the long return journey.

I was suspicious.

She was beyond guilty.

Open Hell.

Chapter XIII

Music? What Music?

On the way back home, we avoided toll roads if we could, to save what little money we had. We stopped at roadside taco stands once or twice a day and kept a gallon of water behind the passenger seat, for if we got thirsty. Regardless of the suspicion that she had cheated on me, she was my responsibility to get to safety, and I would see to that.

Getting back to the states, I figured since it was my first felony, my first *real* crime, I would get something like one year in jail, and I was prepared for that end. But, instead of driving straight to Mom's house, Jennifer pleaded with me to take her back up to Vegas for her to stay with her other friend, Jenna, to ride out the impending separation. Jenna lived with her parents and made money by modeling for car shows. They were friends during Jennifer's last days of high school and it seemed like a good place for her to settle for the time being. It wasn't like Jennifer's parents were waiting to take her back anytime soon.

I pawned my laptop for the extra gas money to get her to Vegas and me back to Lake Havasu. Once I got a cell signal, on my way back to Lake Havasu from dropping her off, I called Paul and asked how he wanted to handle the situation. He told me to call the investigator assigned to the case, Sgt. Thomas, with the LHCPD and gave me his number. The line went dead.

I called the investigator, but it went to voicemail. I let him know I was the one wanted for questioning about the theft from Domino's in April and gave him my phone number. Two days, no call. One week, no call. Apparently, I wasn't as wanted as I thought.

When we crossed the border in Yuma, Arizona, Customs inspected the car thoroughly but never opened the hidden compartment under the center console, which was lucky because there was still about two ounces of weed from the poundage that Ivan had presented me weeks earlier, in the original paper bag. After the fact, I would realize that I had, indeed, just successfully smuggled drugs into the United States. I felt like even more a gangster. The agent informed me that I had a warrant out of Mohave County but they didn't want to extradite me, at that time. They also informed me that my license was suspended, and that Jennifer would have to drive. Good thing I didn't sell her ass to Guymas.

She knew the way to Jenna's house and we were there about six hours later. I didn't even bother getting out of the car, Jenna didn't like me and I didn't care. Girls will gossip. It was pointless to try to defend myself after an onslaught of negative propaganda. Go lean on some foreign cars in scant clothing, collect your paycheck and buy some self-respect, I thought. Maybe they needed each other.

Back in Havasu, I would wait (and wait) to face the proverbial music. Nothing. I saw an ad in the White Sheet, a local free classifieds bazaar that came out every Wednesday, which informed me Pilot Travel Centers were hiring for a maintenance person. They wanted someone to wash the showers after the truckers had busted off some knuckle children, and also collect the trash from the sprawling grounds and to clean up the rare diesel spill. Pro-tip: Kitty litter does the trick.

They were impressed, early on, with my work ethic and tried to press me to get into management, which I thought was a joke, considering any day I would be convicted of felony theft.

"No, thanks. I just like being the guy low on the totem pole. Maybe one day, though." I lead them to believe there was a chance.

Before I had received my first paycheck, I was flagged down from collecting trash in the golf cart and was told I had a phone call. I answered, not knowing who the hell would be calling me.

"How much did you take from Paul?" The caller demanded. It was Darren, one of the management crew that got fired so I could be installed, and he wasn't very happy. Apparently he and Jill had seen me working outside while filling up on gas or while ordering a frosty from the Wendy's drive thru and were giddy they had found the henchman who fucked up their world. For the record, **THEY** fucked up their world. **THEY** continued the practice of pre-making breadstick orders, to the tune of about twenty to thirty a night, so when an order came in they could just throw them in the oven and be done. This created a not so fresh product and Paul knew that, and gave them ample time to remedy their actions. They didn't. Not my fault.

I told my boss I had an emergency and had to go. Nothing would have been worse for optics than having a LHCPD squad car arresting a uniformed Pilot employee on their grounds. I decided to get home, fast. Mom called during the ride into town from the Pilot Gas station off of the I-40.

"The cops were just here looking for you." She said with no tone to her voice.

"What did you tell them?" I asked.

"I said you were at work and you would be home around five." She wouldn't lie to the police.

"Ok, I'll be home soon." I responded.

Once I had secured that job, I got it in me to ask Jennifer, who was having a hard time adjusting to Jenna's lifestyle, if she wanted to stay back in Havasu, instead of Vegas. We pulled a midnight sneak out, again, just like we did with her parents, black trash bag and all. The only thing that was missing was her favorite hairdryer, and although she was sour about that, she didn't want to chance going back inside to get it. She had been doing very little at the house, and was happy to have a chance to leave.

Mom was gone when I pulled into the Widgeon driveway and Jennifer greeted me with a hug.

"What are you going to do?" She asked. I had like $2.76 in my pocket and asked her if she wanted to go get some Carl's Jr. fries, kind of a shitty last meal scenario. She agreed, but I did most of the eating. We returned home.

"Do you want to fuck real quick?" I asked. Look, I was going to go to jail for the first time. I had prepared myself for possibly a year behind bars and wanted a little quickie before I paid the price of OUR vacation, which would have lasted seasons longer had I been solo.

"No." She replied to my irritation. Cum dumpster full? God-damnit!

"Well, will you take me to the station?" I asked reluctantly.

"You ready?" No, I was not ready, my dick was parched and I've heard stories of rapey jails, I hoped this wasn't one of them. The three minute drive to the Police Station off McCulloch Boulevard, was in silence. We pulled up and I opened the door.

Four words. She gave me four words that I was happy to hear at the moment, but in hindsight seem so empty. "I'm Proud of You." Dad never told me those words, so I held on to them like they meant something. June 11th, 2007, I walked into the police station, knowing I wouldn't walk out.

I found my way to the receptionist and let her know that there was just an officer at my house looking for me. Shortly thereafter, a uniformed detective escorted me to an interview room and asked me a series of kindergarten cop questions.

Miranda rights, then, "Yes, I took the money." "No, I didn't have any left." "I spent it all in Mexico." "Yes, I know taking the money was wrong." "No, Jennifer had nothing to do with my actions." "Yes, I know I'll be taken into custody now."

Ten days later the Grand Jury came back with "A True Bill."

A stipulated Guilty plea was agreed to on August 3rd and signed by me at the next court appearance on August 7th. I would get no additional jail time, have the Class 4 felony dropped to a lesser Class 6 and be sentenced to three years supervised probation.

Let me get this straight:

I steal $4,000 and go on an epic adventure and my punishment is 57 days of waiting to be let go? My time was spent watching TV and playing cards with the other 100 jailed subjects at the Mohave County Jail annex building, and this is my punishment? They called it Camp Snoopy. Wait, I'm still not understanding. A free vacation, and now I just have to be on good behavior for three years? If I could turn back time, I would have waited to bounce till that Monday, with $10,000 and NEVER came back. 57 days' time served and probation. Where do I sign?

Sentencing in Superior Court, the next month, was a little intimidating. The judge, the Honorable Robert Moon, Division 5, presided over my case and fate. He didn't appreciate the "this wasn't a mission impossible stunt" and he let me know that my restitution payments would start in one month. Ha, good luck. I ain't paying shit.

I was freed on a Friday and went home. Where was Jennifer?

From June 11th till Sept 7th, 2007, a sum of 88 days, I received a total of one letter and one visit from Jennifer. She told me that she had gotten a job at Sterilite, a plastics company in town. Gritty, factory shift work. She let me know that she had a group of guys she would hang out with after work playing 'hit for hit' or going to Denny's after their twelve-hour shifts. I would have rather not been told any of that.

I had spoken to Mom a few times while I was in jail, but she was always quiet when it came to talking about Jennifer. Turns out, Mom knew Jennifer was fooling around behind my back. To make matters worse she didn't tell me because she 'didn't want me suffering any more than necessary,' while I was in jail. Well, cat's out of the bag now, bitches! Where the fuck is my ride?

Matthew told me where she usually hung out when she wasn't working, and I biked according to his directions. Sure as shit, there she was, my Saturn SL1 just parked in someone else's driveway. Let's give it a little looksee, I thought.

Next to the odometer, was a Polaroid picture of her holding Xander. Awe, how adorable, it almost made her look like a fit mother. I opened the glove box... jackpot! There was a cash wad of at least $300 there, well that's for renting my car, slut, and oh, what's this? The Polaroid of *me* holding Xander with my 'Horn if you're Honky' T-shirt, let's just switch those. At least she will know who paid her the visit.

I biked down to the lake and spent the money at Havasu Landing Resort & Casino, without remorse. I was waiting for her when she pulled back into the Widgeon driveway.

"I don't know anything about your missing money!" I replied to her interrogation in such a way that she knew I did it.

"Why was the picture switched then, I know it was you!"

"Oh yes, I did switch the picture but there was nothing in the glove box but the owner's manual and a bunch of random shit. You know the insurance is expired, right?" I said, trying to hold in my devious laughter. I was trying to destroy her. "Look," I told her, "I need the car now. I have some errands to do." After all it *was* my car.

"Well, I have work at seven o'clock, will you be back?" she asked, trying to mask her concern.

"Of course," I said. There was no way in hell I was coming back for her ass... she can ride Mitchell's bike to work for all I care. You are not getting anything out of me, anymore. I can't kick you out of my Mom's house because, well, it's not mine, but I sure as hell can make you wish you were <u>anywhere</u> else.

One weekend, she got dropped off at the house and told me, in passing, trying to crush me, "I just got fucked in the ass on Rocky's boat. Never doing that again." She found another place to live, shortly thereafter.

The joke was on her, I got a job two days later. Sterilite. The first day, the foreman put her and I on the same stamping machine until I chimed in, "That's my ex-girlfriend." And they promptly separated us. I soon found a studio apartment, walking distance from work, but I still kept the car.

I saved up to buy a new laptop and had a nice couch and TV setup, it was livable. The landlord was the owner of the same tile getup that Dad had worked at for years, and rent was a reasonable $350 a month, utilities included. I would get back to my karaoke grind. I was still making the trips to Parker to gamble, sometime with Mom, sometimes without. Sam came over once.

I should have turned the laptop camera on. He wasn't too happy. After all, he was responsible for one of the bank deposits I took, not to mention the broken lease of the $1,000 apartment in Prescott that was just becoming a red mark on his credit. Pro-tip: Never co-sign, for ANYTHING, <u>EVER</u>.

I thought It was just going to be a 'Hi, sorry, how you been' type thing, but he mounted me on the floor, a 245 lb. city councilman, and told me he wanted me to cry, because that's what he did, when he found out I just took the money and ran. He started punching my chest. It hurt. Tears fell.

"There, are you happy?" I managed. He got off of me. "I'm going to be late." And I **was** five minutes late punching the time clock, my second strike. The third would result in termination. Glad I wouldn't have to deal with Sam Christopher-Cruz Medrano again. 'I want to see you cry.' Petty.

I had been paying the minimum fifty dollar, payments to the court (probation fees) now that I had a job, but hadn't paid a dime towards restitution. December rolled around and I began getting stressed out about the one year anniversary of Xander's birth. I didn't want to be in the same town where that entire trauma took place. I was working a shift during the official one year mark, but decided to play a 10:00 AM tourney at Harrah's, in Laughlin, the next morning.

If I won, or made it to the final table, I would be late for work and it would be my third strike, but I would have a big payout coming my way. There were roughly forty people, at sixty bucks a pop, first place would have gotten over $1,000 and that would have been worth it. I made it to the 'bubble,' which is to say, right before the payouts began.

I had spent three hours and drank about five beers, confident that if I just stayed out of pots I didn't belong in, the crowd would wean itself down so I could get a payout. But it didn't happen like that. I busted out.

Leaving the casino in a rush, I had forty minutes till my shift started, and I would have to make up ten minutes by speeding. Taking the California side, I was convinced, would be quicker because it was all desert. The Bullhead City, Arizona drive was full of traffic lights and it would have stressed me out. Three miles down the road, I was tagged by DPS.

"You didn't see me flash my lights at you, as a warning?"

He was oncoming traffic and I had a BAC, and wasn't paying attention.

"No, sir."

"Where you coming from?" He asked.

"Harrah's. I busted out of the poker tourney, I'm heading back to Havasu for work now." I told him.

"Been drinking?" He knew.

"I had a couple over two hours." I fibbed.

"Well let me get your license, registration and insurance and we will get you on your way."

"Oh," I fished out a business card from my wallet, "I'm on probation." He came back to collect the number.

It took forever for him to come back, and looked like he was just going to write me a ticket from the metal-backed ticket tray he was holding.

"Your probation officer didn't answer." What luck, I thought. "I'm just going to need you to come out and sign this for me." I came out like nothing was going on, and approached the hood of the squad car, where he held the ticket book.

"Put your hands behind your back, you are under arrest." WHAT THE FUCK!!! Poor form, officer, you could have just told me outright, didn't have to get my hopes up. That was unnecessary.

"For what?" I was genuinely confused. I wasn't combative.

"You have a warrant for a theft out of Clark County." Papa John's. Damnit.

I had to wait a day at the substation for CCDC to come pick me up. I got fingerprinted and sent to a bay holding about fifty inmates, on December 15th 2007. Intake was easy enough, and a film crew from the "American Jail" series was there filming someone in a full floor restraint. Most episodes were geared toward getting footage of prostitutes and combative mental cases, but I just sat patiently, watching the free entertainment.

For my $500 'theft', I signed at the first opportunity for unsupervised probation and restitution. Restitution came to almost $1,000, I don't know how they calculated that, but I had no plans of paying anything, anyways. I wanted to go home and was willing to say or sign anything to achieve that end. My Mom, on a phone call, said that if I did sign, my Probation Officer would make sure that I was out of Havasu jail by Christmas, and my Probation officer was true to her word.

Soon after getting released from Clark County Detention Center, I had a meeting with my lawyer assigned to my Domino's case, Alex Bolobonoff. I explained to him that I wasn't trying to run amok or party hard in Laughlin, it was simply because my son had died a year earlier, and I just wanted to get out of town. He told me that in light of that, he would argue to get me reinstated on probation and we would continue with the status quo. The status quo. That bothered me.

I had lost my job, my apartment and my car, all in one fail swoop, and wasn't keen on keeping up the 'status quo'. I wanted something more. I needed Mexico, or perhaps they needed me, as I would find out.

CRAIGSLIST- Jobs
Mexico – Baja California – Tijuana
Looking for an English speaking I.T.
        phone sales professional
$1000/mo. + commission
Must live in Mexico

Jackpot.

Chapter XIV

Johnny 'Epic' Walker

After quick emails were exchanged, the craigslist poster and I scheduled a phone interview. It was merely a craigslist ad, so I didn't feel the normal pressure of an in-person job interview. Plus, I was hundreds of miles away from Mexico, it really was just a shot in the dark, but we connected.

The owner of the company, OSI Datatech, based in Del Mar, California, wanted to hire a phone rep to cold call Southern California businesses, pitching a cost-effective managed services offering. Basically, the company took the stress of running an I.T. department out of the incapable hands of people wanting to run a growing business.

I.T. was a necessary evil that if implemented incorrectly, could ruin everything one had worked for, in one simple outage. We were insurance. My job, explained the owner, Karl Tschauner (pronounced Shauwner), would be to cold call these businesses and discover the need for either a managed service solution, or a backup and disaster recovery solution. He was a great salesman in his own right and taught me that we weren't *selling* anything, we were solution providers. If you had a problem regarding anything computer related, we could come up with a solution for you that will save time, money and heartache, when compared to the alternative of getting caught ill-prepared for a natural disaster, i.e. earthquake, or power surge, or, simply an incompetent I.T. guy who isn't doing his job. We were the heroes. We would save you.

The brainchild behind our digital services was Gabriel De La Pena, a dual-citizen, who resided on the Mexican side of the border with his wife, Joenna and two sons under the age of seven. OSI Datatech held the managed services contract with LifeForce, a Multi-Level Marketing powerhouse, which gave us the foundational cash flow to try to grow OSI from the ground up. Karl said that we would keep in touch and that they would make their decision within the month.

At that time, I had met again with my lawyer in the Domino's case. He was confident that he would get me reinstated on probation, with my apologies to the court, for my unapproved out-of-state adventure and subsequent arrest. I wasn't about to start all over in Havasu, again. I didn't have the stamina or the desire. This time, back at Mom's, I didn't even have a car to start with, or a girl to lean on. But the opportunity to restart in Mexico, with a steady paying job, sounded like the best of both worlds. Female comfort was just a strip club away and I would be making enough to cover my living expenses, plus the occasional luxury. They called me back.

Karl and Gabe said that they would be ready for me in March, well past my new court date of Feb 19th, but I had no plans on waiting. I explained the situation to Melissa and her boyfriend, Travis, and they agreed to drive me down to Tijuana, on the first week of February. I didn't pack for the biting cold.

I was so excited to show them the town, that when we finally found a hotel room for the night, I let Melissa go up the stairs, alone, to pay, while her boyfriend and I hung out at street level, taking in the night scene. A man in a cowboy hat walked calmly down the stairs and Melissa appeared shortly thereafter. The hotel keeper didn't have change for Melissa's $100 bill and a random Mexican told her that he would go get change for her. She gave him the $100 bill, never to see him, or the money, again. I felt so guilty. She started to cry like she did something wrong. Fuck, I hate these border town tourist rapists.

We went to get change at a 'casa de cambio' and ended up getting the room, anyway. That experience took the fun out of the night. $100 in downtown TJ would have made a great night. Now, she just had a little more than gas money home. I didn't have much, if any money at all, and was amazingly shocked when she slid $150 in my hand as we parted ways the next morning. In the bumper to bumper traffic of cars waiting to enter the US, I pulled my heavy sea bag from the trunk and slung it over my shoulder. She got out for hugs and a picture as traffic inched onward. I was not expecting anything from her but a heartfelt goodbye. But that little wad of money, full of random Mexican and American bills, squeezing every cent out of her budget just to make sure I had the best start, meant so much. It still chokes me up to this day. The woman is a saint.

There I was. A bustling morning with cash in hand and a sea bag that held everything I owned of importance. I needed to find a place to wait for work. Surely something was available in the Tetris style downtown area. I needed direction, I needed a cigarette, I needed a friend. Enter, Nacho.

An unassuming Brownskin in dirty slacks and a polo shirt made eye contact with me, the white boy with the green bag, walking down the same littered sidewalk.

"Hola, senior." I managed, Spanish a bit rusty but I was sure it would come back to me in no time.

"Hola, como estas?" he replied.

I had to ask, "Tu hablo Engles?"

To my relief, he did, and just like that I had found my guide. The trick is with any new guide in a foreign land, ask a little, have them deliver, than tip a little. This establishes a rapport. And never let them handle the provisional cash. Pay them their tips as they earn them. First things first:

"I need some cigarettes." I offered as chore #1.

"Venga." He turned with a 'follow me' motion of his hand. I did as instructed. A half block later, we came to a narrow opening that boasted an interior cooler loaded with Coca-Cola and a large selection of cigarettes. The man behind the counter looked up at me.

"Un caja de Marlboro Rojos, por favor." I offered. Then I turned to Nacho, "Do you smoke?"

"Yes." he said anticipatorily.

"Go ahead, get yourself a pack." I replied.

"Un caja de Delacados, sin filtro," he told the shopkeeper. I grabbed two lighters from the display and held them up to the light to make sure they weren't half used and placed them on the counter. You can never be too careful. The black lighter wasn't translucent so a simple shake satisfied my curiosity of value. I gladly paid the 65 Pesos and wasn't two steps onto the street before I was packing my Marlboro Reds. Nacho and I both pulled out a stick and lit up. A nice needed breather. What next?

I asked Nacho if he knew of any places to stay weekly. Was there anything better than a nice morning cigarette in the chill Mexican February air followed by a mission to find a safe house? I think not.

We weaseled through some back alleyways, which contained a variety of street dogs rustling through the remnants of yesterday's taco stand garbage. I'm sure they knew there would be some worthy gristle if they put in the work. We emerged at a corner that instantly brought back memories. F. Martinez & 2da Street.

I craned my neck and found the very 'palletta' store that I had parked Dad's Ford Escort in front of that fateful night almost four years earlier. Nacho tapped my shoulder and pointed to a black gate.

"Hold on, I know the owner, I'll see if she has a room for you." I pulled out another cigarette as he rattled the gate then let himself pass. Fucking F. Martinez. What are the odds? He came back a few moments later with a woman who dared only poke her aged face out from the acutely opened gate.

"She said thirty-five a week, American. It's a room, an electrical outlet, one light, a bed and a lock. No shower and a group of outhouses. Also, no drugs." All of that seemed fine by me. I could go a week without a shower. Hopefully I could convince OSI to take me on early, since I was there anyways.

I paid her from the cash Melissa left with me, and she gave me the key. Room seven. Now, if you consider a room, a space to sleep with walls of wavy plastic and aluminum siding that keep neither heat in nor cold out, have I got the exotic foreign rental unit for you! The key was utterly unnecessary. Anyone who wanted in could just have removed the six by eight foot green plastic chunk of siding that I could have imagined was useful only in keeping the roosters out of the units. Yes, there were roosters.

Every morning, for the three days I could handle, this little red and black fucker announced to the whole neighborhood that it was indeed I, the gringo, who left the fresh steamy floater in the port-a-potty, pre-dawn. Every morning he would wait for me to venture out from my rickety dwelling, and I wager he won the bet with his other rooster friends saying that I wouldn't last the week. He won.

Nacho would meet up with me daily during those horrid days, to see if there was anything else I needed help in acquiring. I told him after day three, I needed new digs. The neighborhood was sketchy and no matter how many sweatshirts I would layer on, I was still cold sweating all throughout the night. The damp sweatshirts made the brisk mornings all the more unbearable. When we met late morning on the third day, I noticed he had upgraded clothes. He was visibly in great spirits when we met up for breakfast burritos at the stand twenty feet from the 'Puerto Negro De La Slums.' I gave him 200 Pesos for helping me find the place and instead of wasting it, he found and bought a new pair of black slacks, some newer, used shoes and two button up shirts, one still in the bag.

"Look what I got last night, from you!" He said gratefully. I quickly corrected him.

"That was all you Nacho, for all your help. I'd be sleeping with the perros if it weren't for you. You earned that. Now, new mission... I have to get out of here!" We both laughed and I packed my soggy sweatshirts into my sea bag.

"I know a place but it's a little more expensive." He let me know. A three minute walk ensued and we were in front of another large black gate. "Hold on," he told me, which was my queue to light up another Red. The gate opened and he went behind. I had just flicked my filter into the already littered street, when Nacho appeared with the new rundown. "OK, bathroom, shower, bed, electricity, seventy dollars a week." Oh, Nacho! You had me at 'shower'.

I paid the woman a mix of American and Mexican currency and she was fine with the exchange and gave me the key. The room was up the stairs and three rooms down, key tag read 23. I familiarized myself with the lock which was a two-part locking mechanism. Turn the key once counter-clockwise, the deadbolt extended 1/2 inch, another turn and it extended the full inch. I paid little attention to the 1/4 inch gap between the steel frame of the door and the deadbolt locking mechanism. Details, Clifford, details.

I had little cash left in reserves, but made it a point to find a street vendor selling a computer monitor, on the cheap. Nacho did the negotiating. I had brought with me my Acer Aspire laptop, a great piece of machinery, and although I had removed the cracked LCD screen before leaving Arizona, I was grateful it had a port for an external monitor. I had illegally downloaded a vast array of movies from LimeWire, and that was going to be my entertainment during my downtime, to help me save up when getting my feet wet with OSI Datatech.

With the last of my disposable income of 500 Pesos or so, I decided to spend a 200 Peso bill at Caliente, the casino on the main drag in Tijuana. Gambling in Mexico is far different than in the states. There are no table games and I think that their respect for tarot is a main reason cards are not played. No cards. Just machines. Legally, they are all 'bingo' games. The screen visual of reels is just a secondary action to a random bingo card and balls drawn almost instantly after you push the bet button.

A little screen akin to the players card interface in American casinos shows a little bingo card and when you make your bet, twenty to twenty-five random numbers are generated and if that results in your bingo card getting a line straight or diagonal, the reels will display a winning combination. It's like a three-second head start for you to know, before the reels stop, if you won or you lost. Winning is fun because one bingo line win could mean three pirates in a row (paying barely anything), or it could mean five knights on a paid line, which I hit for $300.

I had won on slots in the states before: $1,000 on a 'Price Is Right' nickel machine in Parker, AZ, and another $1,000 hit on the 'Frog Princess', in Lemoore, CA , where I hit the bonus betting the three dollar max bet and kissed the frog revealing the Prince and the top prize. In that game you get three kisses in the bonus and can keep whatever credits are associated with the character you reveal, but I got the Prince on the first kiss, and that was rare. This was the same Taichi Casino where I met the olive rancher. But neither of those times did I garner the attention that these five knights did.

I had about fifteen Mexicans standing around, looking at me like I was the oracle. I simply printed out my cash out ticket and took it to the cage for payment. With my winnings I treated myself to a guitar that I paid seventy-five dollars for, from a vendor that had an assortment of around twenty-five or so. Many had plastic strings, I needed the metallic ones. It was just my luck that it came in black. Then, even that changed. A blast from the past, from my Colonio

Libertad days living as a coyote, 'Wicked' came walking down the street.

Now, there are many characters that occupy many streets in a vast array of cities around the world, but this character I would never forget. He was a skinny tweaker Mexican kid, probably no older than twenty-five, and a scammer. I knew it, but he was the first recognizable face this time around and he had never done me wrong so I gave him the benefit of the proverbial doubt. It wasn't a cheap error in judgment, but it did get me to work sooner.

After hanging out at the casino, where I asked him to get change for a 500 Peso bill for us to split, he came back empty handed after playing the entire 500. This should have been my first hint of the bad to come, but I was oblivious. I was wise to put the rest of my Bingo winnings in my shoe. He asked if he could crash at my place, which I let him do, for one night only. The next night he tried the same tactic and I politely told him, "I need the room to myself", and he left, disappointed no doubt.

That night, I went out for a random adventure and came back to find my room ransacked. In my hurry to leave, I only twisted the deadbolt once, making for one solid pull to breach the security of a deadbolt arm extended a mere quarter inch into its housing. My laptop, my precious MySpace account, 'NothingWorthFightingFor', my collection of pirated movies, my guitar, and my toolkit were all gone. He left the monitor though, too bulky to carry out, I'm sure. Everything else would be sold for meth money. I called Gabe the next morning.

"Hello?" He answered.

"Dude, Gabe, I just got robbed, my laptop and my guitar got stolen from my room last night." I was pissed and exposed to say the least. I loved my MySpace. My password was auto saved, so you know what that meant.

I spent hours at an internet café, after calling Gabe, emailing customer support at MySpace and kept getting asked to send a picture of me holding my username and a two-finger peace sign. I tried for a good part of the day but they weren't impressed with the shoddy, low quality pictures from a five Peso per hour computer portal, and I was forced to chalk it up to a loss.

By that time, Gabe had found me a rental apartment in the Costa Azul neighborhood of Playas de Tijuana. From the third floor window I had an ocean view, which was a short five minute walk to the sands adjacent the cool, rolling waves of the Pacific.

The room itself was nothing special. A small four burner stand-alone gas stove, with a propane tank underneath, a bathroom with shower, a small main living area, and one adequate bedroom, with built in closet. All of those amenities were secured for a total of $200 per month. Not bad. It took two days to get the electricity and internet set up at the place. In the meantime, I spent my mornings getting taken out alongside Marco, Gabriel's father, who was an ex-Mexican CIA operative. I thought that was cool, but I never breached the topic with him.

We would go out to breakfast a block away from my apartment at a place called 'La Gruta' or 'The Cave'. Imagine a Denny's with production quality. There was a wavy brown foam ceiling and waterfall, giving the actual ambiance of being in a legit cave. A cave that had a fresh fruit juice bar and served my go-to order of a "Grand Slam," every morning. A tall glass of freshly squeezed orange juice, and I was ready to take on the day.

Our regular waitress, Mayra, always came to keep our coffee cups topped off. She always said, "con permisso" which just means 'excuse me,' but it seemed such a subservient remark when spoken in Spanish. She would never make eye contact, but I was instantly in love. It would take a number of more visits before I would ask her if I could take her for a walk.

Once, weeks later, I brought her flowers, trying to win her affection, but we know that I am the standoffish type and she never made any move after that, so I figured it wasn't to be. I did briefly meet her family though, on a night we agreed to go see the movie "La Misma Luna." However, when it came time for me to pick her up she was sleeping on the living room floor while I sat on the couch next to her brothers and sisters just looking at me like I was supposed to wake her up. But I wasn't going to wake up a Mexicana dreaming with the Mayans, I figured it just wasn't my time.

She left La Gruta a couple months later, I didn't know if she got fired or quit, but I still kept eating there. She would have been a catch, though. I would have needed to really brush up on my Spanish with the quickness, if that was ever going to work. Gruta trips lasted only forty-five morning minutes, after that, it was time to work.

While my apartment was still being outfitted to handle a VoIP Vonage phone with a (619) San Diego area code, I was ushered into OSI Datatech's operations trailer, if we can agree to call it that. It was Boiler Room meets Breaking Bad. There were three VoIP terminals and in front of me on my first day, a script. I hate scripts. I knew nothing of the offerings, our products, our prices, or our play. They just wanted me to qualify people for managed services. OSI would charge a company a monthly rate and then for an hour or so a day Gabe would remotely log on to their network to ensure smooth operations and improve any security flaws or schedule a digital backup of that day's work. My first call was a nightmare.

"Hello?"

"Hello. This is Cliff from OSI Datatech, how are you doing today?"

"Ok, what's this about?" The man responded.

"Well, we are a local IT Solutions Provider and I was wondering if you would be interested in saving money on your managed services?"

"No, we use freeware." I didn't understand, was freeware a brand?

"Yes, but we can save you money on that."

"How, it's free!?"

"Oh, well, great for you, have a good day."

I looked to Karl, who wasn't paying attention to my call and I wanted to rip the script up immediately.

"Karl, I don't know about this. This script sucks." I told him honestly. "Shouldn't we be finding out if they are having any issues with their current situation before pitching a money saving measure?"

"If you think you can handle that, hotshot." It was really a learning experience for both of us on how to deal with each other as boss/employee, respectfully. I was his only phone rep and he wanted me engaged. Couldn't I just have some Brewer tickets to sling door-to-door instead of fishing for people's problems? Most I.T. professionals are understandably reluctant to admit any pitfalls in their system, especially to a stranger calling on the phone. The trailer training lasted only two days with me mostly pretending to dial numbers and hanging up to dial tones. God, that script was horrible.

Once, in the comfort of my own apartment, with my own captain's chair and headset, I got rolling. The window was always open and the breeze of March air made a pristine ambiance for calling Fortune 500's from SoCal. Helping the pipeline was IBM.

We had a computer portal that informed us about companies that had asked for further help in purchasing or qualifying a purchase for their respective business or school. Some inquiries were for small 'GoVaults' that were less than $300 each, others may have been looking for a new LTO-4 Tape backup solution, that could run around $12,000, with a $240 commission for me for selling something like that. Using a business tracking platform, called ACT, loaded with listed businesses from Dunn & Bradstreet, I would begin qualifying business for any potential help we could offer. But five times a day, like clockwork, along came the propane man.

"SEIS-OCHENTA-UNO-SINQUENTA-UNO-SINQUENTA-UNO!" Accompanied with loud mariachi music. There is nothing like being in a qualifying call with an IT manager with fifteen servers under his direction, and hearing this Mexican Siren Street Song that you can hear from football fields away just rattling in the background of the call. Whenever I heard them approaching, I took a moment to light up another Red and enjoy the slow melodic tunes of the Gas Man's phone number, repeated over, and OVER, again.

156

"SEIS-OCHENTA-UNO-SINQUENTA-UNO-SINQUENTA-UNO!"

After the third week, I took to taking my lunch breaks around the noon hour, when the gasman would be most active in the area. I would go to the beach and enjoy the sunshine, wondering what more I needed in life. Once, my landlord and his child-toting daughter came with me to the beach. They had the other third floor room, while the other room on the floor remained vacant. It was a little bigger than mine but didn't have an ocean view, which is the reason I passed on it. Come to think of it, I may have gained a view, but I lost a refrigerator. All I had was a foam cooler, half full of ice. Bread could stand the elements, and canned goods could be cupboarded, but the cheap lunchmeat had to be on ice. But the beach!

It wasn't Mazatlán, but it was as good as mine. There were probably only twenty-five people that used that stretch of beach, so it was very intimate. We all found our own spots and one particular outing, from the parking area that led to the sand, a man appeared with a mutt of a puppy.

"$30! Hey wanna buy a perro? $30!" I had like two dollars on me, but a dog didn't seem like a bad idea at the time. I just looked down the long line of potential customers lining the oceanfront and figured he would surely find a buyer. Brown and black on its face, with two dark dimples, the puppy was adorable. Even if the man did just pick it up off the side of the street on his way to the beach, everyone's got a hustle in México. He started down the long line of sunbathers and boogie boarders. I looked back at my landlord.

"Tiennes dinero?" I asked him

"Four dollars," he replied, just about as broke as me. Who needs money when you got the beach and a beer in hand? The dog man returned about thirty minutes later.

"Oye" I caught his attention.

"I'll give you six."

"Ten," he bumped.

"Six, it's all I got." Not bad for a thirty minute walk with a street stray.

"Fine." I grabbed the four dollars from Amado, and fished the 25 Pesos from my pocket.

"Here you go," and handed it to the man. He handed me the puppy and left. I was on cloud nine. I brought it up to show Maria's kid immediately. The three year old boy just grabbed at my new companion. I hoped he wasn't a biter. He wasn't. I took the beast to the tide to see his reaction to water and he didn't seem to be amused. Ok, dog doesn't like water. Got it!

"Lunchmeat today, payday tomorrow and I'll get you some perro food, ok?" I told him. Now, I thought, what the hell am I going to name this little fucker. Think of the lineage, Clifford. Bacardi, Jack Daniels..... AHA! Johnny Walker. Johnny Walker it is. Now, are those ticks?

I took him home where he immediately decided that he liked my box spring mattress as his potty pad. Great instincts, pup. Featuring planets and spaceships, Karl and Gabe spared no expense on a bed that would have made a six year olds Christmas wishes come true. It was good enough for me, as long as I didn't break out of the fetal position. Johnny sat next to me on the floor nearest the window and leaned against the white painted wall as I browsed YouTube for anything worthwhile.

As I looked down for the first time after watching an Ari Galper, "Unleash The Game" video on sales techniques, I noticed these little black spots on the white wall and started crushing them with the backside on my fingernails. Little splats of blood. Ticks. Fucking Ticks.

Ok buddy, YouTube is going to have to wait. You are done being the host of these fuckers. And, for two hours, I sat on the linoleum floor, which was peeling in some areas, and de-ticked him. Many were on his head, around his ears, more than enough on his belly and also randomly scattered around his doghood. I made sure to get the tip of them even though I didn't have any rubbing alcohol, he squirmed a few times but I think he discovered quickly that I was doing him a really solid favor.

"We are going to meet the vet, tomorrow." I told him. I must have nail-squashed or picked-off a good forty of those black blood suckers. Karl came the next morning to pay me. He usually gave me the option of Pesos or American. I usually chose American, and I would exchange them, as needed. It was a Saturday and we parted ways with minimal small talk. He liked the dog, figured it would keep me from making the semi-dangerous trips to the TJ strip clubs, so that was less liability for the business. I got paid twice a month, but liked to get rent out of the way before I spent anything. I took $200 of the $500 and paid my neighbor landlord. I pocketed the $300 remaining and made our way down the street, to the vet.

The vet started a new chart and gave him three shots, one for worms and two that were reserved for awesome life companion dogs...☺ I have no idea what the other two were for, but I paid. It was pretty inexpensive, like thirty-five dollars. Three days later, there was a dead tapeworm in the middle of the kitchen that was the length of a Trident bubble-gum pack, like three and a half inches long. Gnarly. And, boy, did Johnny have energy after that!

I kept plugging away at work, qualifying people for our services and YouTubing at night. I found a funny newsy guy, SXEPhil. I liked his quick delivery even if it was chopped up like a Dexter victim. He let the world know that he was going to have a live show on a site called BlogTV, and I wanted to see what he was like off script. I never even made it to his show.

BlogTV was everything I never knew existed. You could turn your webcam on from anywhere in the world and run your own show, with viewers, cohosts, and topics of your choice. You could interact with the chat room and make new friends, ask and answer questions, and boy, what a better use of my time, watching live shows rather than looking at videos that already had millions of views. I could be original here, I thought. So, I registered using my email I set up in Oaxaca while I was hoping for an online poker career, mybrotherinmexico.

I registered that because I had a vision of one of my brothers, Matthew or Mitchell being at the library sending me an email, and someone no doubt would ask them nonchalantly, "Who are you emailing?" To which they would respond, "mybrotherinmexico", of course. So it just kind of stuck. It was my brand.

I named my show after one of the most hilarious Dr. House one-liners, I can't recall the actual quote now, but the punch line had to do with "Sunshine and Puppies." Like, "Yeah, Thirteen, lupus is not bad at all, it's all SUNSHINE AND PUPPIES!" My blog show was born. What made it even cooler was that I actually had a puppy! Anytime someone would join the show I would give my tag line, "Welcome to the Sunshine and Puppies Show, I am your host, and I live in Mexico." To which most people would ask why would I want to live in Mexico and I would reply simply, "I'm just ahead of the times. Rent is cheaper, most food is cheaper, the laws are more relaxed, and I can see the ocean from my house."

"When the US fails, and it will, you will wish you would have come over with me."

I would get drunk on Costania, the cheapest alcohol you could find in Mexico. Gabe gave me a quarter bottle of Patron when he found out that I was drinking the little half-liter beehive-looking amber drink. He told me it was like drinking mouthwash and would probably cause minor brain damage. I didn't care. For less than four bucks you could score a bottle of Costania and a two-liter of Coca-Cola. Totally, my style. The Patron lasted less than a day.

I would get high on marijuana, and engage with my Blog audience, which grew and grew. Once, I had a show to pick Johnny's middle name. My viewership voted for it to be 'Epic' making his initials J.E.W. We all got a good laugh about that.

Months followed and my viewership plateaued.

Then came the MUMM-RA's.

Chapter XV

You're Not in Kansas Anymore

In BlogTV world, there existed a secret Skype chat. Full of the major entertainers, it was a who's who of BlogTV broadcasters. You had to have your show vetted by the group and discussed about behind your back, if you were going to be let into the 'cool kid's club'. A girl with the handle of 'QuestionableKisses' brought my show to the group and thought I was funny, with my tagline, and nostalgic 90s music shows, and even the naked coffee pot chef show. That one was a riot.

"One coffee pot, one meal." Corn where the coffee should be, hotdogs in the pot, pour the water in and let it brew. The dripping water heats the corn, and cooks the dogs at the same time. Then, you take out the dogs from the water and add instant mashed potatoes to the leftover water, and voila! A three course dinner, with ½ a frankfurter for Johnny, of course. I was deemed bankable material and was extended an offer to join the group.

We usually shared websites we stumbled across, or found clever ways to Rick-Roll each other. Occasionally, we would find someone under eighteen broadcasting on blog and flood the show before we let the moderators know they had to shut it down. We would take screen caps, though.

For the previous month, I had usually twenty-five to fifty unique visitors at my show at any given moment, which was on the higher end, but then there were the Mumm-Ra's. They came in floods, usually twenty at a time, which made my viewership stats go through the roof, and then the site algorithm would be triggered to display "You're Popular" on the bottom of my screen and the site would record a five minute clip.

BlogTV, which was based in Jerusalem, now operates in America under the name YouNow, with the same basic concept. A lot younger crowd, though. Blogging was a great work escape. A girl in the Skype chat, MiniTacos, eventually let me know that she was the 'Mumm-Ra's.' I had her attention.

It was August and business had started to slow. There was chatter on the web about a potential financial crisis looming dealing with bad mortgages, but I was in Mexico. I didn't think that bad NINJA loans were going to affect me in any way. I had a crib, I had a dog, I had a guaranteed income and the random times I would stumble upon a legit customer, I'd get extra Caliente or stripper money. Not a bad set up.

It had been five months, and my little pad was getting smaller every day, and more uric. I didn't even care I was sleeping on a forty-gallon pee pad. Many were living with worse, and I wasn't one to complain. But, I needed a change. Like, a **real** apartment, with more bandwidth. Broadcasting on BlogTV, the audience would joke that 'donkeys were carrying my internet across the desert', as my picture would only refresh every five seconds or so, often with me holding some odd contortion of my face. I guess that made the show even more entertaining. Back to craigslist. Immediately, I found gold.

It was a two bedroom, one bath, house in Rosarito, Mexico. The same town they filmed the movie Titanic in, you can still see the movie silos near the beach, it's neat. This house boasted a breakfast nook and bay windows, gated, and had an orange and banana tree out front, as well as a variety of flowers. Morning glories, roses, and birds of paradise adorned the gated entrance of the house. $375 a month.

It was located next to a new Ford car dealership, in the Lucio Blanco territory of Rosarito, translated meaning, "white lights." There was a taco stand twenty yards from my house and an OXXO, Mexico's version of Circle K or an AM/PM, twenty yards in the opposite direction.

Karl lived in Rosarito and was head of the HOA of a community on the beach there, and he drove me to inspect the house in question. We put down the first month's payment, on the spot. It was perfect. He agreed to get me better bandwidth, and a new grill as a housewarming present. The foliage provided an amazing ambiance as a relaxing hangout. But Karl, Gabe and I were three dudes, I needed a female companion. Anyone. And so I put it out to the Skype Universe.

Mybrotherinmexico: Hey guys, there are some sick opportunities out here with the electric company effectively paying qualified companies to consolidate their servers to more energy-efficient IBM Blade Centers and I need help qualifying these companies. I can't guarantee pay, but you have room and board in Mexico with me, a ten minute walk to the beach and a mall and movie theater right across the street, anyone game?
CAzKid: Sounds Fun, Cliff.

I waited five minutes with Caz being my own reply. He had a job, and wasn't going to be in the running but there weren't many users on, so I went about my daily business. After work, I logged on and had an instant message from MiniTacos, a heartland queen whose smile would melt your soul, and the Skype Chat was buzzing. I had been to her show once or twice. She was way out of my league.

One time, I won two $25 gift cards from a long forgotten show, and sent her the codes. Only one of them ended up working, but she bought a new webcam with it, and sent me two pictures. One, with her smiling holding a page that had 'Cliff' smack in the middle of a hand drawn heart and the second had her dolled up with, like, twelve small plastic barrettes in her hair like some kind of over-accessorized doll. She was my Venus.

She was interested in my offer. After telling her, "It's either going to be a money-making summer, or you get a free vacation for a few months and get to gain a cool experience. She saw nothing holding her back. We scheduled a time for me to talk with her father, Austin, who instantly bonded with me. We were both Navy boys. He had been a Nuke, the job I wanted when I first joined the Navy. He told me to be happy I wasn't, they were a weird bunch.

I gave him my pitch and he just asked me to do what I could to take care of his daughter. I promised I would. She would show up two weeks later, in September, to an empty house, save Johnny's pee pad, AKA, **my** bed. She flew in to San Diego and we had a mutual friend, Muzzel619, pick her up and take her to the TJ side of the border, where I was waiting for them. After passing each other in the airport, not recognizing each other, they circled around and met each other in real life, for the first time. Then, he helped load her bags into his truck, and they were on their way.

I'll never forget seeing that truck pull off the side of the road to scoop me up, right past the red light inspection area. Amber was in the cab's backseat wearing a Jonas Brothers hat and I just started laughing, I thought it was just part of her shtick, but maybe she really did like them, or maybe she was still in character. Time would tell.

Mikey hadn't been to Mexico for a couple months since he last came to visit me at my old place, which was embarrassing. Not only was the pee smell unbearable, I was at the end of my paycheck period, and he had to spot for pizza. I promised next time, I would buy. Arriving at the new empty house, 2333 Guillermo Troncoso, with the house number spray-painted directly on the grey stucco, Dos Equis beers would have to suffice as a 'Welcome to Mexico' toast.

We started a blog show while she unpacked and everyone from our Skype chat wanted to see. Two internet personalities together, not knowing what the future was going to hold, was definitely something to pay attention to. How long could two arguably sexy, hilarious, icons live under the same roof without it becoming sensual? I was just happy to have a friend. It was almost over before it started.

Muzzel left before it got dark because he hated driving in Mexico during the *day*, it was un-attemptable at night, for him. So there we were, Amber Dawn Haya and Clifford Frederick Gant. MiniTacos and MyBrotherInMexico, seems like a match made in heaven, I mean tacos belong in Mexico. The first night almost broke her. She noticed that there were a few dishes in the sink and began washing. Living alone with her Grandma in Topeka, Kansas, she was used to doing things the American single way. Washing by running water over the dishes and scrubbing? That was a waste of water, in Mexico. Nothing I made was ever caked on to the point of needing more than a quick wipe with soapy water. So, I showed her how it's easier to just fill the sink with hot water, and let them soak for a minute and wash, rinse and set them in the dish rack. (Which was made by Sterilite. ☺) She started crying. What! What did I do? Did I just break her?

"Hey, hey it's ok. Don't cry." What was happening? I mean, I understand that moving out of the COUNTRY, to another person's house in the middle of MEXICO might stress someone out, especially when the person you moved in with had known you for a total of seventeen hours of online chat. But the waterworks, already? This one is fragile. I gave her a hug until she calmed down. "It's going to be ok, I promise. K?"

Killing the mood to get drunk on the first night, she looked around the empty, newly acquired, house and I'm sure wondered, "Where am I supposed to sleep?" I felt that question. And, me, being Mr. Chivalry, came to the rescue with a pile of thick blankets. Not giving a shit about appearances, I spread out the blankets on the living room floor and that let her know. If she did catch a glimpse of the spaceship bed in the bedroom adjacent the kitchen, when she was doing dishes, and thought I was being greedy, I was really just protecting my secret of canine pee sleeping. No amount of blanket would have killed that smell and tile floor or not, "You are sleeping there tonight," I said without words. And she did. She tapped out the next morning.

"I'm not sure this is going to work." And there it was. The crossroads. Time to break out the big guns. I recited my Navy story and Xander story to her, and she was as good as mine. I wasn't going to let this beauty leave me thinking I'm just a face and an online tagline. I have substance. I have depth. And I wanted to know hers.

"I have Scoliosis and need a bed, first off." First the dishes, now her back. Ok, grow up Cliff, find the solution. I wasn't getting paid for ten days. Gotta keep this one engaged.

"Well, I just literally got this place, you know, I told you it was empty, but I don't have any cash coming in for ten days. What do you want to do?" She had brought $500 cash and had a FUCKING

AMERICAN EXPRESS UNLIMITED CARD. She just had to pay it off monthly. Charge $10K, pay $10k, or else! How does that happen? I can't get a box of saltine crackers on credit and this video rental employee gets an all-access black card? I am in way over my head.

I went to the back office and told my landlord, Sal, that we needed to find a bed ASAP. He knew just the Ruka. He took us to a building where there were piles and piles of beds, frames, and mattresses. It was like an episode of Hoarders, Sleeper Cell. We found a bomb-ass wooden headboard and frame that had sliding compartments on his and her sides, with an open middle area for more accessible storage and we had to have it.

"$150." The woman told Sal. Amber couldn't count the bills fast enough. The woman even had her staff uncover it and load it in their delivery flatbed and followed Sal and us home to install it in what was now OUR bedroom. There was a little 'V' shaped closet/storage area in the bedroom that I maneuvered the space bed into. The wooden frame was HER bed. I wasn't going to just invite myself in. I just needed to be sure to be the first in the shower every morning before the gig was up and she catches me smelling like a dog-park fire hydrant. Hard to break that stigma, once discovered.

Johnny now had an outside area and a tree to pee on. We let him out all the time. Amber's favorite flower turned out to be 'Birds-of-Paradise' and that gave me baller status. There were four on the property. Oranges would be ready in December, and the bananas had already been harvested for the summer. We went to the Super Wal-Mart across the highway to get some bedding. On sale was a king comforter set with watermelons on it. I think they were overstock items because the words were reversed on it. Like, you would have to hold it to a mirror if you wanted to read what it was supposed to say, we didn't care, for 239 Pesos, like twenty-two bucks, it was a no-brainer. We hid it in a corner of the store because we wanted to hit up the movie theater, without lugging a bed set inside.

After the movie, we were lucky to find the bundle where we hid it. The remaining fifteen sets that were on sale, were all gone, leaving just an empty crate. Good deal, indeed. Good thing we stashed it. We went home. She made the bed while I made dinner.

Our food staples were Arturo's style pastas, always with a big salad. I made and seasoned my own pasta sauce with tomato sauce, paste, and Italian seasonings that looked like the grocery store just collected all the random leaves from the curbside and jarred them. But, I would take a little in my palm and crush it between my fingers and call Amber over to smell. It was magic.

Barilla pasta, mostly ziti, was my go-to meal and she ate it all, always. It was great cooking for someone else, especially when she would watch me wide-eyed. She would ask questions about my life and what led me to Mexico. I withheld that there was probably a warrant for my arrest for failure to appear in a felony theft case, but I'm living in Mexico, the thought had to have crossed her mind. The stars seemed to shine brighter, the second night.

"You don't have to sleep down there if you don't want to." She called to me. My heart was pounding. She was porcelain. I didn't want to do anything that would lead her to feel was an obligation. I had yet to know, save Katie, what it felt like to be wanted. This had vulnerable undertones, and I didn't want to feel that I was taking advantage of the situation.

I took a deep breath, trusting her decision, and made my way up to the wall side of the bed. She inched toward me. We looked at each other as if we were sizing up each other's souls, her eyes fell to my lips and we both felt it before our lips even touched. Like a Beauty and the Beast sample, 'both a little scared, neither one prepared, Beauty and the Beast.' We held each other until sunrise.

"TOCINO, HUEVOS, y PAN!" I called to her, while she was in the shower. She emerged, minutes later, like a beauty straight off the silver screen. I couldn't believe what was happening. After all the bad that I had just been through, all the positive life trajectory that I felt was robbed from me, am I really making it happen with a girl that makes me question if my existence deserves her? Is this real? How long do I have before life tries to take *her* away from me, too? She entered the kitchen and hugged me like a six year old would hug a new stuffed animal, 100% unadulterated love. Karl and Gabe saw her as a distraction. She saw perfection. I saw the state of global affairs as having the potential to destroy us.

I would spend the following days working on pushing the $120,000 worth of potential deals further down the OSI pipeline. I would try to gather information on when budgets were going to get finalized, or maybe re-quoting a schematic change for a customer, and the truth soon became apparent. No one knew what was happening in the financial world.

No one, not even UCLA Neuroscience Division, was going to spend a penny on even a drastically needed upgrade, in this business environment. If the banks were having liquidity problems, why would any business put themselves in the same position by acquiring expenditures, prematurely? It was all chatter and speculation, at that point, anyways. People were just erring on the side of caution. Right now, cold calling was pointless.

Amber and I took to watching The Daily Show and The Colbert Report on Hulu, every night it was available, often coupled with a dose of 'inspiration,' as she called it. She liked to smoke all the time. I could only partake in the evenings and only if there was something interesting to watch. I had acquired a dealer in downtown Tijuana from my days in Playas that always was holding.

His boss, an older female, owned a huge storefront downtown, and he would take me to the second level to make our transaction, usually with Amber's money, she was the heavy smoker, I just knew the guy. Ivan was a rock star. He was low key, but a wealth of information. After a deal, I once spent forty dollars on a piece of framed Mexican abstract art for the house.

I wanted to fancy our house up a bit, the exposed wood beam ceilings were rustic enough, but to add a little art, always added to the livability of a space. As long as there was someone home to enjoy it, after all.

Amber had two major trips planned in October. One was a trip home for two weeks to celebrate her birthday with local friends and family in Topeka. Second, immediately after that, was a group trip to Universal Studios in California with some of her online friends from a non-BlogTV platform. She assured me it was with purely platonic friends. I had no reason to distrust that. Karl and Gabe were happy for this break and thought that they would get a lot of work out of me.

I took her to the border's pedestrian bridge, and we parted ways with a long kiss and tight hug. She had already scheduled a shuttle service to pick her up and take her to the airport. I was missing her already but I had a new work project to help keep me occupied.

Spearheading the San Diego Gas & Electric, or SDG&E, Server Consolidation Incentive, I had qualified about fifteen companies that could benefit from this energy and cost saving offering. Karl decided to get IBM directly involved. IBM hired a call center for $5,000 to secure extra reservations for an IBM BladeCenter seminar Q&A at Donovan's Steakhouse in Los Angeles. The call center boasted that they got twenty 'RSVP's' for that $5,000. I was proud of my seventeen, picking up two at the last minute, for a grand total of **ZERO** extra dollars.

When we were brainstorming the event, Karl and Gabe both foresaw me joining the festivities. At which point, I had to inform them of my legal problems. They took it in stride and in fact informed me that if this event went well, with the extra funds raised they would get me a lawyer and get it taken care of. I was thankful they had my back, in words, anyway. At that time, I finally felt that I had justified the salary they were paying me. I mean, I probably sourced $100,000 worth of sales in my first six months, nothing special, but given the business environment, not entirely 'Loserville'. Coupled with a successful Donovan's presentation, our flowchart would have a bunch of fresh meat for the grinding. I remember that night. Gabe and Karl were unreachable, as they were setting up in the conference room for the meal. It was to start at 7:00 PM. The matre'd had two lists of RSVP's, mine and IBM's. I called at 6:30 PM to see how things were shaping up.

"One from IBM, and two from OSI," the director informed me and I quickly thanked him and hung up after letting him know I'd be calling back shortly to get another status update.

I was in my office, alone, wishing I could do more, knowing what was at stake, and hoping that my personality on the phone and my weeks' long relationship-building would pull through. I got a beer from the fridge.

Yes. This house had a full size fridge and freezer. A washer & dryer out back was rare for most Mexican abodes. Most rare was the tiled bathtub which Amber and I made the most out of.

7:10 PM, final count.

"Donovan's Steakhouse." The representative answered.

"Hello this is Cliff from OSI Datatech, looking to get the final tally for the IBM Presentation."

"Hold, Please." I heard some papers rustling and the receiver move. Here goes: "Two from IBM, thirteen from OSI Datatech, it's a packed house, you did a good job." My voice cracked as I thanked him and put the Vonage phone back on its cradle. I did it!

Against $5,000 and a call center, I got eleven more professionals there eating steak. All while calling from a $375 a month crib in Mexico. I couldn't help but cry, alone. Out of accomplishment? Out of loneliness? I couldn't determine. All I know is it really validated the way I was operating my prospects. Developing relationships with whoever was on the other side of the phone, and not just pressing the customer for a purchase order, proved in this instance to be the secret sauce behind my phone skills. Even life survival skills, for that matter.

Karl called me at around 9:30 that night, beside himself. "IBM says there is more than $250,000 worth of potential deals out of this! You did an amazing job here, Cliff. Thank you."

"Better than IBM did." I replied, teeth clinched, wishing I saw a cut of that $5,000, wasted.

"I'll talk to Kim and see if we can't get something extra for you. See you Monday." Nothing ever came my way from IBM. Couldn't even spring for a stressball? Fuck. Whatever, I rock and my girl is going to be back soon. "Goodnight."

I told her on the phone, I told her in the Skype chat, "When you walk back into Mexico, stay STRAIGHT! The path curves and a majority of the people follow the curve, I'll wait for you, just WALK STRAIGHT!" I should have made her get a tattoo. It was night out, early night, maybe six o'clock when she arrived with a sea of other foot traffic.

I showed up early and waited patiently, but as the designated time for her arrival elapsed, she was nowhere to be found. I didn't have a Mexican cellphone, just the Vonage at home, thirty miles away, so I RAN. I RAN to where the masses exited the United States into a smorgasbord of food stands and taxi cabs, the exact area I was trying for us to avoid. I told her to go straight, but she followed the crowd. God. Damn. It.

There she was, standing by the roadside with a pair of wheeled suitcases, crying like a girl who just lost her ice cream cone. Breathing heavily, I held her.

"I thought you forgot." Yes. I'm just going to leave you to get wise in a country you don't speak the language of, because that's the kind of person I've been since day one, haven't I? No time to be petty, Clifford, the girl is delicate. I gave her the "Are you serious?" look.

"Ok," I said cautiously trying to change the subject, "How was the flight?" I asked comically.

She laughed through her tears and hit me in the arm, "Shut up and get us a cab." She said brandishing that dead to rights smile. I got us a Taxi Libre and we were off. And when we got home... man, I love this woman!

"OK, PRESENTS!!!!!!" She exclaimed as she threw her suitcases on the breakfast nook table.

"Oh Boy, Oh Boy, let me guess!!! Let me guess!!! Ummm ... a ... Deprovera shot!" She rolled her eyes, apparently that wasn't very funny, but yes, there would be no baby making in Mexico, just A LOT of practicing. "OK, lemme guess again... a troll doll!" That's all I could muster, I have no idea what this chick is capable of. Then, I heard it... the heavy gauge plastic of a goody container... not one, but *two*, five-pound bags of gummy bears! Oh my God, I think my penis just moved a little.

I love gummy bears, and not just any gummy bears, although all will do in a pinch, but these were the extra firm Habaro gummies. The top of the line, cavity cracking, madness in a pouch! I gave her the over the top hugs and kisses that she deserved. She let me know that she even had to pay more at the airport, because they made her suitcase overweight, and there was more.

"Close your eyes." She asked.

Now, I have gotten a gift or two from my female cohorts in the past. Jennifer knew I loved Steve Nash of the Phoenix Suns, and bought me an autographed card as well as a jersey card of the man repping number thirteen, for Arizona. Katie, in anticipation of my backpacking journey, bought me a fifth of Jack and a flask. Great gift, practical, tasty, timely. Veronica… Ummm… she gave me… divorce paperwork?

I opened my hands, not knowing what in the world to expect… and seconds later, felt a hard rectangular object. "Open." She prompted.

Now, for the audience still reading, maybe you have never been given a book by your lover. Maybe you have never had that opportunity. Maybe it started a fight, like "Here, Honey. Look! <u>How to Improve Your Life in 30 Days Guaranteed!</u>"

"Thanks, bitch."

No, not from my Amber, not from the truest love I've ever known, and the love that will be the measure of any future love. She bought me, "<u>The Ayatollah Begs to Differ.</u>"

The idea gelled after one comment I thought I made under my breath while the book and author were being interviewed by Stephen Colbert, on the Colbert Report.

"I'd like to read that." Tears well up thinking of that moment because when you have someone, ANYONE, who is in tune with you to the point of taking a whispered comment in the middle of a comedy show, and manifesting that desire for you, weeks later, un-guided, un-reminded, *that* is someone you should **NEVER** let go of. But we know my life. We know greatness burns at the foundation of effort. And boy did we put it in.

Amber, if you are somehow reading this, I wrote you a shitty song after we split, (don't worry reader, the details are coming) and I'd like to just throw it out in the book, now. Most humans won't get it, but we loved like aliens, so maybe Lil' Wayne might lend an ear to interpret. For all those who have lost as we have, I have no choice but to document the fall.

My Secondhand Serenade 'Fall For You' rendition probably has a better chance at bringing back a smile of remembrance. So, I'm sorry in advance. But this was, and is, your song…

Amber's Song

I'll buy you medicine for your tummy
I'll protect you from Zombies
I'll be the one who shares your pillow
While we're watching the Report

I'll take you places you've never been to
Trying foods you never thought to
And all the while
Behind the smile
I'm lost in your kiss

I never thought it'd end up
Quite like this
But since the day you left girl
There's so many things about you I miss

Like being your two inch extension
Torrent racer, not to mention
Never have I met or seen
A girl who knows how to 'cuddle extreme'

Getting our dig tools out at sunset
Trying our best to not get wet
Just feel the sand beneath our toes
Where the time goes, no one knows

So I'm standing here before you
Took a song for me to ask you
Amber, Will you Marry Me?

Sucks, don't it?

Chapter XVI
Words No Lover Ever Want's To Hear

November 2008

Getting back from Universal Studios in the beginning of November, she was clearly exhausted. She had spent more of her money than she had planned because her friends didn't plan as well ahead as she did, so Amber ended up footing the bill for a lot more things than necessary. I somehow told her before the trip, in passing, that she wasn't going to like the trip as much as she thought she would and, when she finished unpacking, she asked me how I knew that.

I was like, "Babe, you left me just two weeks ago to spend time with friends and family in Kansas, then went right into hanging out with internet friends in California with no down time. I just thought it was an exhausting itinerary. Plus, you were bound to miss me sooner or later!" I was right, but I wasn't keeping score. Then the next domino fell. Her Mom and Aunt were set to drive to Mexico to visit us November 13-17th, 2008. We were going to celebrate an early Thanksgiving, and they would get to meet me and see how I was treating her in real-time. I was excited. They were going to leave Amber's car with us, so we would have transportation, and then were going to fly back.

We kept the house cleaned up pretty consistently, she was an amazing cleaner. It was like we both loved our duties serving each other. Something about cooking a good meal and watching her joke with me with sudsy hands, doing dishes the Mexico way, was just another shade of love. It wasn't a chore, it was an honor. We liked it that way.

I told Karl I would have to take off mid-week till the following Monday while her family was in town and he reluctantly agreed. The drumbeat of potential serious economic pain was now hitting the mainstream news nightly, and the Auto Industry and the Bank Bailouts, or almost lack thereof, were cause for great concern. I started frequenting the Huffington Post and Daily Mail and was convinced that this might be the end of our current system of money governance. I told Karl I wanted to stock up on some supplies, just in case. He met me at my house and took me to a bulk store, akin to a small Costco.

I bought a twenty-five pound bag of rice and beans, cooking oil, instant coffee, and water, and had about $100 worth of things in the cart when Karl said, "That's enough." I wanted to pre-spend my entire paycheck that I would be getting the following week, on pure storage food. He thought I was over-reacting. I took Amber out later that night and we used her AmEx to buy eight cartons of L&M Cigarettes, she had started smoking lights, the blues, and I kept to chain smoking full flavor reds. She bought us four of each. When I did get the remainder of my paycheck, I went out to buy a store of chocolate and eight bottles of Bacardi White Rum.

I was satisfied with our new reserves, stored where the spaceship bed used to be, in the 'V' closet-like addition to the master bedroom. The spaceship bed however, made it to the trash three days after Amber let me know my place was next to her in bed. I also bought us a folding chessboard, about half the size of the one I smuggled back to base in boot camp, along with two decks of Hoyle Playing Cards. I put them in my side of the sliding headboard and forgot about them. If the end of the world came, I could teach her chess and then play some strip poker.

The bug-out collection went a long way at calming my nerves. Then before I knew it, we met her Mom and Aunt in the same fashion Amber and Mikey Muzzel originally entered my world. The direct curb on the right, the moment you pass the green and red lights, entering Mexico.

We did somewhat of a Chinese fire drill and I hopped in the driver's seat and her Mom got in the back with Amber. Her Aunt stayed put on the passenger side. We gave short introductions as I wildly got into the flow of traffic. Twenty-five minutes later, we were at the Ford dealership and took the left circling off ramp to my neighborhood. We pulled in front of the house and I opened the black gate and pulled the car in and locked the gate with a master lock, behind us. The house was underwhelming to look at from the outside, but the flowers and trees compensated for the lack of house paint. I helped them with their belongings and we entered the house. Immediate spiritual warmth.

A couch, a loveseat, a glass and wood coffee table, and a lovely piece of abstract art hanging from the west wall on an oversized nail that was there when I got the place. (I figured that was the only spot for the art.) Tiled. Clean. Open floor plan. They were definitely impressed.

I was a little nervous about having to be in the power position of keeping my guests entertained. I think it was more like anxiety of having to balance out two new personalities for a little while, but they were very easy going. Hell, if I could entertain a BlogTV show full of friends and random viewers, surely I could keep these two entertained for the balance of their stay. And I was sure if I ever did need to tap out for a little bit, Amber would pick up where I left off.

I showed them to our room and there was a little disagreement about where they would sleep, but I insisted that Amber and I could handle the couches, while the women took over the bed. It was the least I could do. This was the first possible future in-law visit that I was hosting in my life. I felt proud to have built this from nothing but a little bit of Amber's love and phone call sweet-talk salesmanship. Jennifer and I had our 'Luxury' apartment in Prescott Valley which was more than double what this rented for, but didn't have a tenth of the charm. I was loving life. I grilled out for our first meal.

When you buy fresh tortillas in Mexico, they come in like two-pound wrapped brown paper packages. There are so many warm flour (or corn) tortillas in a pack that you wouldn't be able to use all of them if you tried. So, one drunken night I made Amber spit out her Dos Equis, our beer of choice, when I told her to "use them as napkins then throw them to Johnny! He surely won't mind." So, she repeated the story to her Mom and Aunt while the meat was grilling on Karl's housewarming gift.

I heard them laughing over the pot of simmering beans. I was inside with my food processor blending cooked pinto beans, two de-seeded serrano peppers, and one square of American cheese, to make the perfect refried bean mixture for the carne asada tacos. I chopped onions and put green Herndez salsa in a black plastic salsa dish. I brought in the meat and chopped it up with my serrated nine-inch grey-handled blade and called them in for dinner.

We didn't pray or anything, but I was praying on the inside that they were satisfied. It was perfect. Tomorrow, I would have to handle Thanksgiving dinner, with a little chicken recipe Karl taught me. The pressure was on. I'd only attempted it one other time, and he was there to guide me. It was all about continuously basting it in its own juices. I was in my element in the kitchen. Still am. Night fell and we all went to sleep. I had never seen Amber so happy before. I mean, even our BlogTV friends told me, in secret, that they have known her for years and never had they seen her as happy as she was, with me. Looking back, in this moment, I had never been happier than I was back then, either. I thoroughly enjoyed my hosting duties.

We woke the next day on a mission to add to her Mom's bell collection back home. She wanted one that had 'TIJUANA' written on it, but I didn't know the word for 'bell' and Ivan was nowhere to be found. We did end up finding a small collection of ringers on Revolution but none inscribed. The shopkeeper said he could take a Sharpie and write Tijuana on it, but that didn't interest her Mom. I felt like the adventure was a dud. It was getting later in the afternoon and I still had to do the shopping for that evening's meal, so I tried to politely guide us all back to the car and home. I went shopping by myself.

A pack of two whole chickens, potatoes, carrots, celery, vanilla ice cream, a few Bartlett pears (I had an idea for dessert), a bottle of Merlot, and some rolls that were baked to crinkle perfection, were placed in the cart. I also had to get cranberry sauce, and a dry packet or two of poultry gravy. I would get to work while the women smoked outside and gossiped about me, which I was fine with. I was sure Amber would fill me in later. She came in while I was cooking.

"Hey babe, a friend of mine wants to know if I could go to Corpus Christi for a Dance-Dance Revolution Tournament, complete sponsorship, they would pay for everything. Can I go?"

GRRR. Too little info for such a big move. I know that the true love of her life was Dance-Dance Revolution, and that is the only part of being her boyfriend that I failed at, when we gamed at Peter Piper Pizza. I was completely uncoordinated, maybe I should have at least TRIED taking up skateboarding in my school days. This is when I would have used that skill. She was an ultimate expert, only thing missing was a Pikachu tank top, to really Japanimation the look.

"Can we talk about it after your Mom leaves?" I countered.

"Yeah, sure!" She bounced off, back to her Mom. Corpus Christi, I thought, ugh, fuck my past. Corpus Christi was a dump, and who was this friend? Time to re-baste the chicken.

It's a lot more involved when you are baking with a gas oven, than an electric, 'set and forget' type meal. The veggies were cooking in the chicken grease, it was salted and peppered to perfection, and was crisping nicely. I had prepped the pears for caramelizing to reduce time from the end of dinner to the beginning of an on-the-fly dessert. I would serve the dessert in these cute little clear rose teacups we bought from the market, for cheap. They were really just for look, neither of us drank tea. We did kill pots of coffee a day, though, a nice Oaxacan blend. Maybe one day I would take Amber on the same trip to Puerto Escondido. Then, those highways would be repaved with good memories, other than the trail of deceit from Guatemala to America that still exists to this day.

The only words uttered during dinner, which we did offer thanks for, before we broke in, were from her Mom.

"Does he cook like this for you **every** day?" And Amber gave her mom an 'as a matter-of-fact, yes,' nod. As they were finishing their veggies, Amber's Mom was beside herself that I got Amber to eat her carrots, which never happened in Kansas. I started on my dessert idea, all in view of them eating on the nook.

White sugar, a little brown sugar, and some butter were added to a frying pan, over heat. The concoction melted up nicely, then I dumped in the chopped pears. Over low heat, I caramelized the shit out of those pears. Scooping out four balls of vanilla ice cream, each in its own rose dish, true Beauty and the Beast fashion, I doled out the hot pear topping and sprinkled a dash of nutmeg on each. Adding a spoon to each teacup and bam! Mic drop! Best Thanksgiving of all time, in the bag!

After the meal was done, I played some Ron Paul YouTube videos for our guests. The passion and universal message of individual liberty and honest money made me cry every time. I held it together in front of her ladies, though. Obama had already won the election, so it was kind of a moot point.

I always found it interesting, though, how Obama's slogan was: "Yes We Can," which *could* translate to "We Are Able" and he was running against, and won, against 'McCAIN.' It struck me as a pre-destined karmic win. Cain got Abel in the garden, and now Abel bested Cain in the 2008 election. Not quite an internet conspiracy, just me thinking. I wish it stopped there, but it didn't.

Her Mom asked me to take us to an electronic store, noticing that we had an entertainment center, but no TV. She bought us a floor model flat screen for $300, saying that this was Christmas for both of us because she wasn't coming back for a while. Amber's Mom brought her PlayStation II from Topeka, the model with the 'pop top', which was a big deal to Amber; I was like, "whatever." I guess they are hard to find.

We pulled back to the house and as the TV got unloaded, in went their luggage. We went online and arranged for a shuttle to pick them up at the Jack In The Box in San Ysidro, walking distance from the pedestrian crossing bridge. Karl was going to show up at noon, and we were supposed to close a deal with the Bureau of Reclamation Montana for about $16,000, a $300 commission for me, so I had to drop them off as close to the border as I could, then hurry back. There is a back frontage type road that bypasses all the traffic waiting to enter the states, and that's where we parted. I made sure not to dilly-dally in getting back home with Amber.

Montana didn't answer, but we had a conference call talking about the Donovan's prospects and how to add them to my ACT accountability program. I was just waiting for Karl to leave, so was Amber. She was dying to re-ask about Corpus Christi. Karl always found a way to be long winded, but he finally left, and Amber popped her head in the office as soon as she heard his engine fade down the street.

Sparing the theatrics, she let me know it was her ex-boyfriend who wanted her to go, and it was only one week away, she was just gone for two weeks, and I just now had us alone, since the third week in October. I didn't want to be alone again, just so she could play some tappy-tap game, with her ex. This marked my first official 'Dick

175

Move' of the relationship, there were tears on her part, but nonetheless she came into the office hugging me saying that she would stay. I wanted that win, but I would have rather had her fight for it, if she really wanted to go. Not that I didn't trust her, I did implicitly. I just didn't know him.

Things were getting stressful, even more so globally, and I needed someone to lean on. Johnny was only good for belly rubs and comforting kisses. Being alone, I was at the mercy of the internet, while doom-scrolling. And I was already gripped by the gravity of the rabbit hole I had started exploring. If I got any more involved, I didn't know if even she would be able to pull me out to safety.

Karl showed up the next morning while I was still in bed with Amber. The pounding on the door woke me up instantly, in a fright. In the eight months I had worked for OSI, I had never needed an alarm clock and was never late to start the coffee pot. This was a first. I opened the door completely disheveled, and he got irate.

"What the fuck! We have to be ready for a call in ten minutes, you haven't even showered!" He saw the marijuana baggie on the coffee table. "You are a fucking child!" And that was the last straw, although I didn't let him know it. My girl was sleeping and you come into *my* house to yell at me. Nope, never again. "Go take a shower, and I'll put on the coffee," he prompted. I did as I was told and came out fifteen minutes later with him already on a managed service call that I knew wasn't going to yield a customer.

Afterward, I did get a hold of Nancy at the Bureau of Reclamation and we put her order through. That calmed Karl down a bit. I just wanted him out. I cold called to hang-ups for the next four hours and he decided to call it quits for the day. I apologized and reminded him that this had never been an issue before. I was just recently under a lot of stress. "We are all under a lot of stress," he replied. Ok, brick wall, I got it. He left. I went to Amber, still hiding out in the bedroom.

"I think I'm going to quit. They are talking about me having to hit calling quotas and I'm not down for that given the current business environment. I think that if I told him I'd drop the salary for a higher commission rate, that way if I don't sell, I don't eat, he might go for it. He loses nothing if I want to take the day off, plus, I'll be highly motivated to get the deals in our pipeline completed. What do you think?"

What could she think? She hated how they seemed to slave me. And, if I saw this as an opportunity to really make it or break it, she would be there to support me as much as she could. I sent the email that night.

The next morning, Gabe called me telling me that Karl was on his way to pick up the computer, he didn't want me poaching potential customers, as if I was the type. Karl's SUV was there five minutes after Gabe's call. I thought Karl was going to kick my ass, so I called my landlord from his back office to witness. I gave him the computer, he loaded it and the monitor into the back of his green Escape, and we shook hands.

"I'm sorry we weren't a good fit." I said, apologetically.

Without a word, he was gone. I saw Amber watching from the bay window, and just hung my head. What was I going to do? He did just pay me the day before, $800 total, practically made me beg for it, given my tardiness that morning. Rent wasn't due till the fifteenth, so I figured there was time for him to calm down and come to his senses.

Amber wanted me to use the money for Mexican car Insurance. I, on the other hand, knew silver was the wisest choice. The next night, I went to the Banco Azteca where people cashed their paychecks or exchanged currencies, but they also offered the sale of silver Libertads, the one-ounce Mexican silver coins. I bought a fresh roll of twenty. At 160 Pesos a piece that meant that one purchase ran about $300, maybe a little more. We went downtown to get an ounce of Lemon-drop weed from Ivan, and came back home. I took command of her Toshiba Satellite laptop and that was the beginning of the end.

One conspiracy theory website led to another. And I took each information drop with a grain of salt, trying to find the one silky shred of truth in all the chatter. I had open spiral notebooks and was writing down generic equations about the value of human life over time vs. the perceived value of money over the same time period. In my equation, humanity didn't stand a chance. Try to understand, Clifford, why is this happening? You are smart. You can figure this out.

The banks gave homes to those that couldn't afford them, purposefully. Commercials ran "get a home with no money down," and, "we will teach you how to get started in real estate using other people's money," then every other commercial, once the crisis became widespread, was "cash for gold now!" Why were the powers that be stripping the proletariat of what little hard assets they had, who would this benefit, other than the banking cartels? Think bigger, Clifford. What about money in general? What is it and what does it represent? What has it evolved from, historically? Where does the shell game have the value hidden now? Interesting, I might be on to something here, I thought.

Amber saw me losing grip and tried to get me back.

"What is going on?" She asked fearfully.

"I don't know, but I think it's something big. Bigger than us, bigger than the governments."

"How can I help?" She asked, honestly wanting to be close to me. More aggressively now, "Explain it to me!"

I replied harshly, "I don't even understand it yet, what do you know about **math**!" It came off as an insult, and that hurt her. I felt it. But from the last three days of not sleeping and rolling over the numbers and energy flows of the global banking escapades, and upon taking a step back, I told her what I felt was happening inside of me. Somehow I saw the balance, I just didn't understand the scales.

"I think I might be the Second Coming." I outed.

I sent Ron Paul's campaign an email saying that I thought I knew the inherent value of Gold and Silver, and would like to talk to anyone. I was afraid for my life. An earth altering financial transaction was about to take place that would seal the fate of the world, saving it for the time being, but marking its days, once enacted.

She tried to bring me back again, "Come fuck me," she demanded, thinking that would distract me. The sex was short, the numbers in my head were vibrant, and I dismounted her mumbling, "If silver is $400, then gold is $8000. Holy shit!" I didn't get it then, I just knew it had me and it wasn't letting go.

The next morning I took her computer and pile of Pesos and silver and was intent on talking to the Mexican Government about my findings. I left her a note.

It read: "Don't worry, you will be taken care of." I didn't realize that this note could be interpreted many different ways, but I foresaw President Calderon wanting to meet me and then I would tell them the whereabouts of Amber. I imagined they would acquire her and bring her to Mexico City, with me. Surely, on the helicopter, she would realize that I had indeed done something big. None of that happened. I blame my presentation.

I asked the two guards who were guarding the Government building, in Spanish, if they had any children and gave each guard a silver Libertad per child and made sure to tell them not to sell it. They let me pass to the government offices. I made it to perhaps the Mayor's office, and I poured the coins on his desk to his dismay.

I tried to explain my case in Spanish that the Pesos minted since 1992 represented silver. 1992 being the same year the monetary rules were rewritten with the Maschrist Treaty, setting up the stage for the new Euro currency, under the leadership of King Juan Carlos, of Spain.

In 1992, the Pesos were minted with 'N$' representing the New Peso. Perhaps, like an abacus. One worthless bead, slid right or left, representing a unit of value or commodity. One New Peso minted perhaps accounted for one ounce of silver belonging to the Mexican treasury. Or, estimated to be in the silver mines of Mexico that are all owned by the Banco De Mexico. It was a hunch. Banks have always liked playing shell games. But riddle me this, and Wikipedia is omittant on this fact... there does exist a one centavo Mexican coin. They *mint* them, mint mark and all. Ask yourself why? Why would you waste the mold and metal to stamp out a miniscule coin that is worth, at 20:1 exchange rate, 1/20th of one US Penny? 2,000 of them would be needed to buy a single taco. But, what if minting it represents $4 worth of treasury silver or gold? I was asked to leave. I came home to an irate Amber.

"I thought you stole my computer and abandoned me!" Ugh.

"Yeah, just give me some silver and a computer and I'm going to leave all this for nothing," I thought.

"I called my Mom and told her you yelled at me and said you were Jesus." What the fuck, Amber? You are a shitty scribe! I said nothing of the sort! I could see that this was well out of control and there was no contact from Gabriel or Karl yet. I couldn't keep her like this.

"Can't you just read a book and be happy for a minute while I try to figure this all out?" I pleaded.

"No! There is nothing to figure out, Clifford you are going crazy!" I didn't know how to explain it, but I knew I wasn't losing it, just deviating from society's norm of 'keeping calm and carrying on'.

"The world is changing, it's like you are today's Mary Magdalene and I'm like Jesus." She relished the thought for a moment, but then the smile disappeared. Thinking of the breaking of the arbitrary laws that bind society, I told her somehow that she is going to *want* me to be with other women, and she really didn't want to hear that!

"WHAT!" Ok, now she was explosive. "That's it!"

And nonchalantly, not thinking of the ramifications that this statement would have for me going forward, I uttered the words, "Then I will just go after Taylor Swift." If Amber didn't want to be my muse, I picked the then relatively unknown "Master Muser" to unknowingly be my guiding light.

Taylor Swift was nothing back then, just a house fly in Faith Hill's chardonnay. Taylor walked into a recording office before her breasts had grown in and demanded (and got) a recording contract. I had just walked into a government office and demanded global societal liberation and got an eye roll. Note to self: work on sex appeal.

My whole operating mode was that if the world ended, Amber and I would end, and I would move heaven and earth to make sure that didn't happen, even if that meant putting her on the backburner for a moment. But Amber, I never took you off the stove.

"What if you go back with your family in Kansas and we meet back up when all this passes?" She said that she would call her Mom, who had just driven all the way to Rosarito and had just flown back, days earlier. I was thinking of the money involved and felt guilty, but apparently it wasn't that big of an issue for them.

We got in line to cross her car the night of Dec 3rd. There was an abnormal amount of traffic and we sat in silence as the car idled. A street vendor came up asking if we wanted a plate of fruit, coconut and honey. I gave him a silver ounce. He was shocked, asked me if I was serious and then made the transaction. I felt rich. Paying the equivalent of fifteen dollars for a bowl of fruit, he came up two minutes later asking if he could give me another one for free, but Amber didn't want one, so I politely declined. The silver was supposed to be car insurance, so she was a little bitter.

A girl in a plaid schoolgirl uniform came up on the passenger side, asking for donations and I gave Amber a silver coin to put in the can. She tried, but the slot wasn't big enough, so it just kind of sat there, until the girl took it in her hand and ran off to her guardian.

"How did that feel?" I wanted her to feel that donating real money to the less fortunate should make you feel something positive.

"It felt like I just gave away twenty bucks." She was still not happy. I would have to be happy for both of us. We pulled up to the line. I hadn't even thought about my legal status in Arizona. Too late to turn back now.

"Citizenship" The booth keeper said.

"American" We replied in unison.

"Identification?" We both got out our driver's licenses and handed them over.

"Whose car is this?"

Amber replied that it was hers and pulled the title out of the glove box.

"You know it is missing its plates?" Amber freaked, again.

"Who stole the plates! I have to drive to Kansas without plates! What the hell, Cliff?" She replied.

Well first off, I didn't steal them as a 'memento,' and second off, "If you get pulled over, just tell them the truth. They got stolen in Mexico, hand the cop the title and say you will get new ones when you get home." She wasn't the best troubleshooter.

She calmed down enough and the booth attendant gave me a look like, "Good luck with that one," with a wink and passed us through. American soil. For the first time since February I was on American Soil. The nostalgia was short lived as we had to get to the Jack In The Box, where her mother was waiting.

There was a fleeting thought that I would go with them, but it was instantly decided not to be the best idea. I gave her mom a hug, surprised that she wasn't furious at me. If she hadn't have just experienced Thanksgiving, maybe she would have had less character attributes to judge me against and would be more likely to display the warranted fury.

"I love your daughter." I told her Mom as my arms didn't want to let go.

"I know." She replied with a tinge of loss in her voice.

Amber and I shared our last kiss and before I knew it they were gone. I had ten ounces of silver in my pocket and, what? No!

I did the emergency pat down. FUCK! I put my wallet and ID in the car's dash cubby right below the radio while we were getting waived into America. I couldn't do anything without an ID. I wanted to go to Viejas. It was night and no pawn shops were available to get me come American cash, so I was forced to take the walk back to Mexico. I stayed straight and got in the expensive yellow cabs.

"Donde Vas?" The cabbie asked.

"Rosarito." Surely he thought this would be a lucrative trip, but he pulled forward ten feet and I flashed him an ounce of silver, and he told me to get out. Ok, yellow cabs don't understand value… enjoy waiting four hours for your next customer, loser. I took the walk downtown to where the van shuttle to Rosarito departed.

Amber and I frequented this bus line and enjoyed it, to the max. It only cost us like two dollars per person for the thirty minute drive, usually done just to make a weed run. But the scenic drive was worth the price of admission, itself. There was no one else around, and being the only one waiting, the requisite five minutes lapsed and I gave the driver a Libertad and told him it was all his. He told me to close the doors. This was a special trip. I was with the spirit.

I told the driver many things on that drive. I spoke to him about labor, and how his work came from his heart, mind, and hands and could never be properly valued by another man, but by God only. I told him how he works every day to keep his family and life above water, but many in America get incentivized to do nothing, or expunge zero effort, and are taken complete care of.

"Un Vida es un Vida." A life is a life. I spoke to him about opportunity, and how if it isn't available to everyone, it isn't opportunity, it's a racket. I spoke many things to him, all in Spanish I hadn't perfected, but there was so much passion in what I was saying that this cab driver, this random working grown-ass Mexican man, started crying.

Not just tear, tear, wipe. It was more like pour, pour, sniffle. It was like he had lived a life of such integrity and honesty and finally heard the words of a universal truth that instantly broke down the façade of the hard working role he was playing in society.

"Todas tiennes sueñeos grandes, un dia, senior, un dia, me promitias." We all have big dreams sir, one day, one day, I promise.

I turned my head as he passed the normal drop off spot, and he asked me where I lived. We took the left-circling exit ramp to Lucio Blanco that was thirty-five yards ahead of us, and he dropped me off in front of my house.

"Gracias senior, en serio." Thank you sir, seriously.

"No, Angel, gracias tu, y Buenos notches."

The checkered van pulled away with a double honk, and I faced my locked gate.

A couple more days and I'll eat all of those oranges. They were ready, but I was going to let them live out a few more days of the good life. For the last three months, I didn't pee inside- I peed on the tree, and was anxious to see how Mother Nature converted that.

I opened the gate and made my way inside.

"Hey, Johnny. It's just us now."

I had work to do. But I needed to sleep.

It had been four days.

Chapter XVII

7 Days

With no laptop or phone to utilize, I was stuck with the composition books full of generic charts, graphs and equations regarding human population over time and chicken-scratch charts concerning the way our money has changed mediums all while trying to look similar to the original Ponzi scheme. Then something happened that I had never experienced before and instead of being shocked or intimidated by it, I simply complied nonchalantly. An audible voice in my head directed me to, "Go Get The Cards."

I was equally excited, equally relieved that somehow, someone or some*thing* was getting the message, or trying to get the message to me.

Two days earlier, Amber and I had been camped out in the bathroom after flushing her weed and breaking up her glass bubbler pipe for my fear that we were going to get raided at any minute, because the philosophical ideas/realms that I was exploring weren't meant for people to think about. She was in the bathtub, the safest place to be in case of a tornado (basic Midwest knowledge) or a bombing, due to the heavy piping in the walls, I sat next to the toilet. She despised me for that scenario.

"Why do we have to stay in the bathroom, and why am I in the bathtub?" She asked.

"Because if they bomb us, the bathtub is the safest place." I'm sure she didn't see it that way. She thought I had officially gone off my rocker or was sneaking more illicit drugs than her marijuana, which I wasn't. I deleted my Facebook and BlogTV accounts, thinking that I was going to get tracked somehow, it was 100% bug out time. She stayed compliant for two hours before she had enough and said she was getting out, and I figured the danger had passed, but the weed was flushed so she didn't have much to do but tell the Skype chat that I had lost it.

I don't blame her for being angry or afraid. Fear kills anything it touches. But once she was gone, so was the fear. If they killed me, so what? But if they killed the love of my life, I could never live with myself knowing that I was supposed to protect her. And if they managed to get both of us, our story would never be told. Alas, here we are.

December 4, 2008. 8:00PM, I broke the seal on the first deck of Hoyle Playing Cards, a brand of Bicycle® Cards, and immediately pulled out the face cards. It popped instantly. I noticed that the faces of the cards were people involved in my life. Like not in a way to say 'they spiritually resemble' or 'this represents that.' This was: the queen of spades has Ambers face!

The three remaining queens have my sisters' faces! The King of Hearts and diamonds are Matthew and Mitchell, respectfully. The King of Spades was my boss Karl, and the Jack of Clubs was my other boss, Gabriel. Other faces I didn't recognize, but to have nine out of twelve cards resemble not just my family or newly departed associates, the Jack of Spades was ME!

I didn't need pictures to compare them all, I have lived a lifetime with these people and knew all their angles. This was a conspiracy of the highest order. I had played over 10,000 hands of live poker at that point and NEVER, not once, had I ever thought that playing cards had anything other to do with me than to win a hand or to rake a pot. NEVER have I had some forced feeling of "Wouldn't it be cool if these cards looked like me or my family?" There must be a mistake. I opened the second deck. Same result. Four of the twelve court cards are facing to the right, their left, K-Spade, Q-Spade J-Spade & J-Club, those are the four that had been my circle of influence during my tenure with OSI Datatech. The rest of the family fit in to their respective suits, spiritually.

Hearts are love based souls, engaged with food, music and fun. Clubs are of the earth, nurturing, caring, always there when you need them. Diamonds, well, Melody is the Queen of Diamonds, and she likes money, money as a symbol of power. Extrapolate as you wish. Even in 'Desperado' the songwriter says "Don't draw the Queen of Diamonds boy, she'll beat you if she's able, you know the Queen of Hearts is always your best bet." And I can count on Jessica, the Queen of Hearts for anything, anytime. She is a successful restaurant manager in the Phoenix Metro Area. Got to love what you are doing if you are willing to put up with the stress of running a high octane storefront. I know a thing or two about that.

I didn't get too hung up on the missing faces, but to have been led here, on a path I would have never thought to take, had it not been for the audible instruction, I would have never made it to those cards. I needed to get to a church, ASAP.

Johnny was particularly excited as if he sensed some kind of breakthrough. I got on my knees and let him kiss my face. This might sound weird, but fuck you, I opened my mouth. Not to tongue kiss my dog, it was at his insistence. Later, I would find out that in pack life, the lower echelon canines will clean the mouth of the Alpha as a sign of respect. So yeah, it kind of made me feel a little weird back then, but came full circle when I learned of the "Alpha Code."

By now, it was close to 10:00 PM, maybe a bit later, and I went out in the darkness with no direction, and had no idea where a church would be, or if anyone was going to be there, or what I was going to say. I mean, I just found characters of my life emblazoned on brand name, widely available, decks of playing cards. Perhaps the church knew, and was waiting for me, somehow. Before the cards, I was entering some field of energy and knowledge that I had no business or certified aptitude to pursue. But yet there I was, discovering, what I thought to be the base inherent value of Gold and Silver, and the detriment of the manipulation thereof.

Before Amber left, and I was alone in thought and study, I DID NOT say that I was "Jesus Christ," rather I questioned, "I *think* I *might* be the Second Coming." That wasn't a catalytic moment begetting delusions of grandeur. That was me being scared shitless, if I *was* somehow a major character in this grand play. If I somehow discovered the blueprint for a global metal backed currency, the question became, why me? If I was to somehow be the center of all of this, who was there to challenge or validate my proof? No one. But nothing is hidden from God. So, I went to find sanctuary in his house.

Lucio Blanco, 'white lights,' which was exclusively what my mind was flashing at that moment, had always been a quiet area. Houses lined dirt streets that branched from the main paved road that went east to west, from the Highway to the OXXO roughly a mile in distance. Then it met the north-south main thoroughfare that brought you into the business district. I headed towards that mile stretch of paved road, seventy-five yards from 2333, when I noticed a man walking behind me.

"Oye, donde estas la Iglesia, por favor?" I turned to ask. He answered in broken English and gave some vague description that my mind couldn't handle, with all I had just been through.

"Can you take me there?" I asked.

"I can't, I'm really hungry." Well, it's your fucking lucky night, man who doesn't live on my street and is walking randomly at my need's greatest hour.

"C'mon, I got tons of food." I brought him to the house and introduced him to Johnny and gave him the basic rundown of the kitchen. Pasta, rice, sandwiches, I wasn't about to cook for him, I had playing cards scattered over the breakfast nook table, with upside down Budweiser caps to signify the royal ones, my bloodline. Giving the display a second glance, I was amazed at how natural and simple the order of things were. No sibling was missing, just three unidentified characters, it was like I was in a Scooby-Doo mystery episode.

I paid no attention to what he was doing in the kitchen or his consistent ramblings but when he left after the first night, I couldn't find any of the four lighters I had placed around the house. Thief. Oh well, I had matches in the plastic change bowl.

Amber and I would use the constantly filling Peso change bowl to pay for doughnuts delivered via a thirteen year old boy on bicycle every Sunday morning, or to exchange our five-gallon water jug with a full jug of Sparkletts, they would drive by blasting advertising from a bullhorn three or four times a week in our neighborhood. No ice cream truck, just a water truck and a propane truck and occasionally a flatbed just carrying random junk of all sorts, for sale. Everyone in Mexico has a hustle.

I opened a fresh red pack of L&M's and lit the match that had a face of a German Shepard on the striker side. No church tonight. But I had a big bed with watermelon blankets and a couple of Amber's quarter-cut sleeping pills under the bed I stashed, just in case I wanted to shut down early. A quarter of a pill knocked my ass out. I love it when pills do what they claim. I had a little cash left, but only four Silver Libertads till I would be dead broke, and rent was still due on the 15th. I was certain some sort of negotiations would have to be had once we approached that date. Maybe I'd have to sell the furniture? I was all-in on saving the fate of the world and $375 for rent was not even a blip on my radar screen. More beer was, though. A lone Dos Equis was the final holdout in the fridge, and I grabbed it.

I slept until 4:00 PM the next afternoon, Dec 5th, and went to the Commercial Mexicana down the street. The Taxi Libre charged less than twenty-five Pesos for the ride, and I was there in no time. Amber and I called it the Pelican store, due to the huge Pelican mascot weaved into the store labeling. It was a bustling store, comparable to Wal-Mart with only 'Made In Mexico' offerings. There was a man pushing a cart, and upon seeing me head to the cervesa area quipped:

"Modelo makes this special elemental twelve-pack only available during this time of year, if you are smart, you'll pick one up." Thank you random gringo! I will take your tip. I bought two cases without inspection.

Pro-tip: If you are in a foreign country and someone speaks your native tongue and recommends something, you listen, hesitation only kills the moment.

I bought some sliced turkey and a huge jar of McDonald's style pickle slices. 'Chips,' if you're into kitchen lingo. Another twenty-five Peso ride back and I was down to pocket change, leaving the cab driver two ounces of silver. One for each of his two daughters. Good thing all my food commodities were stocked. I got home and put one twelve-pack in the freezer, and the other in the V shaped closet off the main bedroom. As I set it down I admired the offering. Three bottles of each element. Earth, fire, air, water. Twelve total. They were each brewed with different ingredients, and at different temperatures if I recall, not to mention the bottle designs were pretty cool. Add to that, four Dan Brown DaVinci Code illuminati references. Nothing surprised me anymore, and that put me in a very vulnerable position. To trust blindly.

I cracked open a warm 'Fire' not intent on waiting for those in the freezer to chill. Not having a partner to release sexual tension, began to wear on me. So, as I took another swig of my warm 'Fire' brew, which was almost the perfect temperature for the taste, even though I would have rather had the bubbles a little more crisp, I would nurse it till the other eleven in the freezer were ready, I swiped the six-ounce container of Extra Virgin Olive Oil above the gas stove. I needed something slippery. I put it on the headboard and determined I would wait until I got drunk, then take full advantage of myself.

I hovered above the playing card spread, still wondering who the missing three were. Was the Jack of Diamonds Obama? Hours passed in what seemed to be minutes and then there was a knock at the door. It was damn near midnight. What time zone are these fuckers on?

An older white gentleman, whom I had met briefly two months prior, asked if he could come in. I obliged. He was a little taller than me and older by at least forty years, wearing a Georgia Bulldog hat that simply displayed the wide set 'G.' He had stopped by the first time to see if Sal, the landlord, would rent the house back to him, as he was an old tenant. He then asked *me,* if he could move in, to which I said, 'no.' I had a girl and a business to run. No room to take care of a random sixty-four year old 'wish-I-would-have-stayed.' Nevertheless, he wrote a note in letters that I didn't recognize as being English or Spanish but I wasn't really rubbernecking that hard. He folded the letter and asked that I get it to Sal. Once he departed, I was reminded of the weird timing of this man, who, when first introduced, told me he was from Appleton, Wisconsin. Cable commercial, anyone? What the fuck are the odds of that, Vegas? Appleton, Wisconsin…is this a joke? It wasn't a joke two months ago, that was before the cards and just a cool coincidence, now it was a slap in the face. I jammed the note in the swirly door design of Sal's back office, it was secure. As a government trained courier, I did not read the message. But I touched it. Two pill chunks left. I took them both. I wasn't in the mood to rub one off after that, tomorrow would be a new day. Let's sleep.

Dec 6th. I woke up at 12:00 noon and headed outside to smoke my morning Red in the fresh Mayan air, and have myself an orange. The first fruit of the harvest. Sal told me the tree would yield

300, but I stopped counting at fifty realizing there is no way there's more than a hundred fireballs on this stump. I open my front door and there he was, the hungry talker man, cleaning up my yard, and tending to my flowers. Awkward.

"Hey there." I said trying to understand how he thought this would be kosher, just hanging out cleaning a random good Samaritan's front porch. I was in no way mad, just confused a bit. I got over it fast and he asked me for a cigarette. I tossed him one and watched him light it with my green lighter. Well, that's communism, I guess. I ain't mad. If you need something bad enough to steal, your government is failing at providing opportunity. If you own a propane stove, you are never out of a light. So, I justified his motives. Good for him.

"Want some lunch?" I offered. Content on letting time pass, I think I was still under the assumption that Karl, in realizing he overreacted, would show up and negotiate a way forward. But that was not to be. I made pasta, and poured a glass of Bacardi for each of us. I asked him what his name was, and he told me. I then corrected my inquiry.

"What is your family name?" I asked.

"SILVA" he replied. So, let us get this straight, I have my family in the cards, I blueprinted what could only be described as a new silver standard, and this random getting-to-a-church distraction is brandishing the last name Silva. I have two Silver Libertads in my pocket and maybe five dollars in loose change. I told him after lunch he would have to leave, but thanked him for cleaning up my porch, and I gave him a couple oranges to go. Best oranges I have ever, EVER tasted. If I could wrap and overnight one to then King Juan Carlos of Spain, I would have. Maybe then he could entertain the idea of decriminalizing urinating in public, as long as it benefited his trees. (He has since abdicated to his son, now King Philippe of Spain. Boy, what I wouldn't do to get a peek at the royal libraries.) Silva wasn't gone long. The next night, he showed up with a woman in tow.

December 7th. Knock. Knock. Knock. The fucking strip clubs downtown don't get this amount of foot traffic at 11:00 PM, what am I, an all-night soup kitchen now?

Silva was beaming as I opened the door.

"Remember the lost girlfriend I told you about? This is her! I was walking and I saw her, it's been like seven years!" She didn't seem as excited. I was cooking a pot of pasta and having this interruption caused the scorching of the pot, as I was distracted trying to figure out what these two could possibly be wanting at my house. I was trying to act like I remembered his story yesterday, but I listened to nothing he ever said. He was a drone, a witness, and now there were two. Next to him was an overweight Mexican woman with a fucking NAVY hat on. The cosmos *IS* fucking with me! Then smelling the burning pasta, I went to throw out the scorched pasta and she stopped me.

"NO NO NO, Mira," she told me, and then spoke to Silva in Spanish, and he said she was going to fix it. She did, and I ate. It was the first thing I had eaten since the oranges, the morning before. It was really good. I broke out my guitar and played a little to pass the time. They left soon thereafter.

Back to the proofs, the theories. I divvied out the whole world to the family where they would best serve, in my eyes. I had some reasons for the continents I assigned each of us. Based on their lifestyles, based on their spirits, I thought that any new world would have to have a Gant at the helm of each of the land masses of the world:

Clifford	ASIA
Melody	SOUTH AMERICA
Jessica	AFRICA
Melissa	NORTH AMERICA
Matthew	AUSTRAILIA
Mitchell	EUROPE

I wrote the world capital to be ALEXANDRIA. Country or state, unknown. I wrote that the earths export to the universe would be Cannabis.

I wrote the trust resources that could be available to every human to be $31,557,600 or $1 per second for a year. I think that is a fair valuation of what every human deserves to have access to, in tiers, of course. Don't confuse this with how much a human is worth. That is for their respective life decisions to appraise. But with that fund, there is no opportunity ever out of reach. All I'd ask if put in the position of distribution: plan, account, execute. Just how the government gives grants.

At the conclusion of that page, I was granted one final directive. "You have to make a sacrifice." Which, based on the gravity of the spiritual paradigm shift that was taking place in and around my ether, it was not a request. It was a command. *They* (God) showed me the cards, *They* (God) will walk me through this. I had to keep reminding myself that God was watching. Johnny Walker. Johnny Walker.

I had never sacrificed anything before, I mean the worst thing that I had ever done to nature up until that point was when I caught a carp at the millpond in Waupun, and poked its eyes out with my Leatherman tool. You don't really need eyes to bottom feed. I still feel uneasy about doing that though, maybe it was just to impress the group I was fishing with, I was young.

The best way to kill a breathing being, in my mind, would be to put it in a choke hold and squeeze as hard as one could. If you recall the dog killing scene in 'I AM LEGEND' you understand what I attempted. That scene is far too real life for me.

I took Johnny outside between the orange tree and the rosebush and I laid down on the small patch of dirt and grass and started squeezing my forearm and bicep together with his neck in between. There was labored breathing. God, it would suck to suffocate. I just wanted to stop blood flow to his brain and hold it until he breathed his last. The six dollar puppy I bought on the beach with a four dollar loan from my landlord, would soon leave me companionless.

I didn't need a leash with that dog. He was loyal to a fault. One time, he chewed up Ambers shoes and I took us all to the park, five miles away, and as he darted off to inspect a horse and rider, Amber and I jumped back in the car and took off. The next morning, as I emerged from the house to have my morning coffee and Red, he was sitting patiently at the locked gate, waiting to be let in.

I loved this animal, this relationship, this loyalty, and now was under command to snuff it out. I squeezed harder and he was gasping for air, but I didn't relent. Through my cries and tears I saw out from the carport gate there was the neighbor kid all of seven years old, doing figure eights on a bicycle in the middle of the dirt street, at the darkest hour of the night. 'What the fuck?' I thought.

No matter how hard I squeezed, Johnny kept getting air, so after a three minute ordeal, I released and wiped the tears from my eyes. Silence. God is watching. This wasn't an Abrahamic Punk'd episode, where he was commanded to take his son up on the mountain to sacrifice him, and at the last minute, God said, 'Just kidding. I just wanted to see if you were willing to do it.' No such panic button for me.

Johnny laid lifeless, snout facing the rosebush. And I escalated the method by going to the kitchen and retrieving my plastic-handled serrated blade. The same knife I made our first carne asada with for Amber's Mom and Aunt.

I approached him. He was completely limp. But a command is a command, especially given the content and context of its delivery. I grabbed the scruff of his neck and counted to three. The knife didn't make it a quarter of an inch in, and Johnny yelped. I dropped the knife. I can't do it, I thought. Not with a knife. Looking around at the tools I had, my eyes were drawn to the stone basin of the birdbath.

Weighing at about thirty-five pounds I thought for sure if I slammed it down on his head with all my might, it might just finish the job. I walked the eight feet from where the knife was and lifted up the circular stone. Waddling back to Johnny's still oxygen deprived body, I raised the stone tablet over my head and slammed it down with all I could muster. The unthinkable happened.

The stone broke into two symmetrical pieces, half-moon shaped, and, robotic-like, Johnny sat up, walked to the black carport gate, and sat down. Something was not natural about that. I had to process it. What was happening? I turned my back and took two steps toward the house, looked back, and he was gone. He disappeared.

The front patio door had iron bars spaced three inches apart with chicken wire rising to the deadbolt lock which was about three feet from the ground. The carport bars were the same three inches apart and was locked. The entire patio was dimly lit, and had a surface area of 200 square feet. He was gone. I was unsurprised, and resolved to head in, turn the heat up and enjoy some of the elemental Modelo beer that had been migrated to the refrigerator recently. Nothing made sense and I accepted that. I headed in.

Every time I opened the fridge I couldn't resist the Costco size jar of pickle chips, and I pinched off five or six, every trip. Then I went to the room. I lied naked on the bed and invoked DaVinci's Vitruvian Man. It was like I was doing a naked snow angel on the bed sheets. I may have used a little of the tin of oil, but I don't remember. Energy was vibrating all around me and I finally found sleep at 2:00AM on Dec 8th, with beer still left in the 'Earth' bottle on the headboard.

I woke up around 11:00AM, put a pot of coffee on, and reached for a new pack of L&M's. No sooner do I pour a cup from the middle of the brew process, spilling a few drops on the coffee pot hot plate, do I go outside to pick an orange and from the OXXO side of the street, the main east-west paved road, came Silva and his NAVY hat girl, *with* Johnny walking right beside them. What the actual fuck!

I unlocked the gate and let them in, confused to the state of numbness. There was no small talk and we entered my house and they went for the couch, I rolled out the wheeled chair from what was left of the office.

"You can't kill him, he's Jesus." She said matter-of-factly. Ok, I'll bite. My family is displayed in poker cards so, sure, why not have a dog be Jesus.

Then I asked her a question with my mind, "Should I give him a bath?" She responded only with a head nod in the affirmative. So, I took Johnny to the bathroom. I had a mop bucket that I filled with a two gallon jug of Ciel water, and also for whatever anointing reason, I urinated in the bucket, too. I inspected where the knife punctured him, there was a little matting of blood on his fur where I broke skin, but there was no cut mark. I couldn't believe it, I rinsed the area expecting to reveal a cut mark, but his skin was flawless. Wound mysteriously healed on a dog who disappeared into thin air to only be brought back by two vagabonds claiming that he is 'Jesus' and, thus, not able to be killed. What was I to do?

At that point, I was handed a blanket from the couch and was told to go to the bathroom and undress, coming out wearing nothing but the blanket, for a covering. I did as I was told, not judging the angels in disguise these must have been. I stripped and came out wearing the blanket. I sat on my office chair. Then they asked me to drop the blanket, to reveal myself to them, it wasn't a sexual thing, it was as if they were inspecting my body. After a minute, they told me I could cover up or put clothes back on, whatever my preference was. She offered me some crystal in a pipe. I declined. The only intoxicant I wanted to allow to enhance this crazy chain of events was beer, because I could control that.

I told them I had an errand to run after they had helped themselves to my kitchen, again. I didn't care, at least someone was eating. It was dusk and the stars would soon be out. Eighteen Pesos for the bus ride to Tijuana, so I can talk to someone in the American Chain of Command. TARP was a financial terrorist attack and I was going to try to show my country why. I had forty-four Pesos left in my pocket and two ounces of silver.

The pedestrian bridge line at the border was abnormally long and I was in a hurry, seconds mattered to me. I asked a badged line-keeper, "What do I do if I have information on a terrorist attack?" He told me to run to the front of the line. Cool, maybe we will get farther than we did at the Rosarito City Council. I got to a twenty-one year old entitled brat of a customs agent and told him before he asked for citizenship, "I need to report a terrorist attack."

"Are you high?" Really? That's the million dollar question? Am I High? Why yes, I make it common practice to get blitzed out of my skull and then come into a building full of law enforcement telling tales of impending doom, all the while being at risk of losing everything I own if Mohave County placed a BOLO or warrant for my arrest for the Domino's theft. Yes, that sounds responsible. And what the fuck should it matter if I **WAS** skull-fucked halfway to Nibiru? If I went and smoked two grams of meth while listening to a pissed-off street level Mexican Mafia foot soldier talking about how he's going to spray down the pedestrian line at 9:00 PM with his newly acquired AR-15 and here we are at 8:08 PM and you are holding me up because you want to give me a urinalysis diagnoses, fuck you, that kid!

He eventually passed me to the boss on duty, having a gold oak leaf on his collar, a Commander in Navy insignias, and he calmly sat me down to take notes. I was talking so fast he asked me to slow down. But then understood that a lot of what I was saying was abstract and mathematic at the same time.

He said, "It's kind of like A Beautiful Mind, huh?" And I felt that finally I was being understood, even if this info is above his level of comprehension. He asked me another qualifying question that made me think I was making some semblance of logic. "Who do you need to prove it?" He asked.

Without thinking, I replied instantly, "Paul Krugman."

Paul was a sometimes controversial economist that Steven Colbert liked to jest about. The commander wrote it all down, along with my Mexican address. After he put his pen down, I tossed my beloved Ed Hardy eagle cap in the wastebasket. It was the last item Amber and I bought together.

"Why would you do that?" he asked.

"Sacrifice of the moment, I guess." I said.

He continued, "Our Intel team is in Washington D.C. until Thursday..."

"Perfect, call them," I interrupted. My thinking was that if they have bodies there already, and if these findings hold weight, action can be taken at the Capital, to pause or reverse the $787B shakedown of the American worker that I was referring to as the terrorist attack.

"I can't." He looked at the floor. I know and he knew he could, but he wouldn't. Chances were high that this was just a crazy person rambling. I was just some crackpot who should be directed to call George Noorey from Coast to Coast. To call D.C. on my account would be embarrassing for a man that high up at that command post.

"Do you need directions?" I asked, deflated.

"We will find you." He promised. Start the clock. Thursday the 11th was only three days away. I just had to find a way to keep busy. I thanked him and started walking out the way I came in, and was redirected to enter the United States of America, unchallenged.

It wasn't anything special, I noticed an American girl crying at the border and made me think of Amber, spiritually. Crying because she left me, crying because I was right and no one could understand. I took out one of my silvers and offered it to her. She thanked me but declined, while still crying. Having no money and no ID, America is pretty boring.

I picked up trash for an hour outside the Jack in the Box: straw wrappers, plastic cups, cigarette butts, broken glass of every color, and the occasional napkin. Someone noticed my work and bought me a large Coke, which was definitely a come-up. The sun was down and I was getting tired, it would be a thirty-five minute voyage back to

Rosarito if I kept a good walking pace to the van/bus line. An hour, if my timing was off. Three days was all the time that mattered.

I got home in one piece and there were no extra characters loitering there, so I was comfortable to finish the last six Modelos until I got a bit frisky with myself. Overdue.

The next day, Tuesday the 9th, the witnesses came back as the sun went down. I passed the time during the day by eating all of the reachable oranges, and there was only a dozen or so that were out of reach. The ones I was able to pick were amazingly good, perhaps the 'tree of life?' If that is considered blasphemy, is the 'Tree of **THE** Life' trademarked yet?

Sal had taken notice that others were coming to my house and he didn't approve. Somehow knowing drugs were being used, the cops were called. I was in a state of nirvana but aware when the police came asking me for my sister, Melissa's, phone number. The police asked if they could have some oranges and I told them they could keep whatever they could pick. The police were nice enough, not there to start trouble. Had I known that Sal planned to call her to ask her to come pick me up, I would have been very, very stationary.

Silva and his girl prophesized that the police were going to come, and asked me to tell them that I was alone. Which I did. The police came and left, but something was weird. Silva kept pulling on his groin area, and **she** said she wanted to have sex. I said they should hook up then. I don't know what kind of Geronimo field exercise this was, but to interact this way with a being, reborn, should be against some celestial law. I couldn't get a grip on what was happening.

Eventually, I bedded the NAVY cap wearing tweaker chick, who was on her period, and went at it for a short time before I got a little too passionate and pulled her hair gently, and I was rebuked. The radio was playing Bob Marley's, "I Shot the Sherriff." She stopped me before I could climax, what a waste.

Next, she left and Silva came in. Look, if I had to take one for the spiritual team than so be it, but with all the content and context of the last six days mingled with the spiritual awakening that occurred in the last weeks with Amber, I was not in a position to say no to anything, thinking it was a rite of passage. A test administered, after having already seen the answer laid out plainly in the cards. I was getting spiritually raped, from every direction. I had no idea.

Silva came in and I prostrated, like I knew what was about to happen. He asked for lube, and I handed him the olive oil. It wasn't a sexual act, it was a power play. I was scared. So was the alien spirit within me. Nonetheless, I reached my arms around to spread my cheeks and he grabbed my right wrist and flung it forward as if to say, "I don't need your help, this isn't for you to GIVE, this is for me to

TAKE!" He got his urethra to penetrate barely past my o-ring, and I cried out. As if that was the mission, just like that, he was done.

"Don't worry about it," he said as he walked out of the room.

They left, apparently accomplishing what they had set out to accomplish. I cranked the little floor heater to full blast, and was content running it on high until the gas ran out. The water bill of thirty dollars had yet to be paid, so water was off. I still had twenty-eight two-gallon bottles of Ciel branded water, so I was good. I saw the doughnut kid on his bike. A different bike and rider than was out during my, "I Am Legend" scene, with Johnny. He didn't have doughnuts, it was not Sunday, but I gave him my last ounce of silver, and made him promise to not sell it. He agreed.

It was my 24th birthday, but with no one to remind me, it was just another day. Tomorrow, the Intel team will be back, I kept telling myself. A lot of fucked up spiritual shit just went down in that house and I wanted out. I slept during the day and went to the OXXO at around 8:00 PM on the 10th.

I got two glass bottles of Coca-Cola and gave them to the shopkeeper behind the counter. He gave me a total, and I told him I didn't have money, at which time he told me to put them back. I did. But, for some reason, before leaving the store, I looked down at the red laser scanning portal, and it scanned my eye and 'beeped.' The shop keep was busy doing inventory and was paying me no attention. Did OXXO just BUY ME? It would be a cool gig, I suppose.

Cops were outside the OXXO and told me to run home, they were watching me, apparently waiting for the arrival of my sister, whom I still didn't know was on her way. Passing my house, out of sight of the police, I took a stroll. I rarely explored the rest of my street.

The five main places of interest for Amber and I were, the mall, the house, the OXXO, the taco stand, and the beach. Other than that we really didn't explore what wasn't necessary. My neighbor, three doors down, had a van and a 1989 Camaro Z28 in his driveway and I wasn't shy about inspecting them. After all, I **was** the king of the world, even if no one recognized or accepted it yet. The keys were in the ignition. What a setup.

I went home to wait. I wasn't going to take a car that wasn't mine, regardless of the importance, at least not with three squad trucks chilling at the OXXO. I would change my mind an hour later. After compiling all my evidence, I figured I had to get to the border, and being completely out of money, I was limited in my way to get there. There was no way they were going to come for me, Commander 'Beautiful Mind' was just talking down a manic kid. It wasn't part of his job description, but he did an amazing job. I had to see them again. Looking out of my front porch, the cop trucks were gone, and I determined, so was I. I didn't even bother shutting my front door. I jogged to the epic car that had a huge stuffed Tasmanian Devil in the back seat. I turned the key and I was off.

Dirt road to paved road, making a squealing right turn, and a mile down the paved road it meets the highway and I took it towards Tijuana. I thought I would be back in an hour, no harm no foul. The world's future hung in the balance.

The highway traffic was intense that late at night, and everyone seemed to have blue lights on their tailgates. Was this a Mexican Christmas thing, decorating your truck with lights? I followed the blue lights like an autism awareness grand prix. Off to the right of the highway, there were these ditches that made me think was a dug out racetrack. Getting the car in would have ground level be a foot above the top of the car. Complete with jumps, the image was too good to pass up. I decided to divert, I was God.

I wanted to jump this Camaro. I pulled off the side of the highway to inspect the feasibility of accomplishing that goal. It wasn't going to happen. There was no entrance to the dugout track, and if I tried to skid into it, the car would surely end up on its side, stuck. But two feet in front of the hood where I stopped to inspect the track, was a six foot high pile of gravel. I inched closer until the hood of the Classic Chevy scraped into the rocks. A mini avalanche resulted in rocks rolling over on the hood. I looked in the rearview. I looked at all the highway traffic. I closed my eyes and floored it.

The tires slipped and began to smoke, the speedometer read 78 MPH, but I wasn't moving. The smoke billowed into the night sky. After a long six seconds there was the loud boom of the rear passenger tire blowing, followed three seconds later by the rear driver side tire blowing. As I looked out the windshield and saw the billowing of smoke, longer than the length of a football field, rising to the stars.

"The new Pope has just been elected." I whispered aloud. No one cared. I saw one car pull over on the southbound side of the highway and attempt to make contact with me, asking if I needed help, I just waved them off and they drove away. I sat in the car, looking at the owners work ID lanyard hanging from the rearview. Not having anything else to do, I sat and reflected. Ten minutes later, my neighbor's secondary vehicle, a minivan, pulled up next to me.

I had never met this man before, but he sure made an entrance. He was the Hulk, some 300-pound Paisa who yelled at the driver window for me to get out, which I did. Immediately he wound back and gave me the biggest left hook I have ever experienced. I didn't pass out, but I did fall to the ground, and looking up, said simply:

"Calmate, dile la policia" or "calm down, call the police." We waited twenty minutes for a cop truck to show up, with my neighbor's foot on my back the whole time like he was claiming a prize. They handcuffed me behind my back in the freezing December air and threw me in the back of the truck. Driving with excessive speed and paying no mind to the safety of the person riding in the bed, turns were sharp and fast. We eventually made it to the holding cell, no telling where I was.

After the first hour, the State Department showed up and gave me two Power Bars. Thanks, America. Two hours later, Melissa walked in, balling. Crying nonstop, she knew that there was nothing that she could do to get me out of this predicament. I squeezed my hands through the bars and held her head and whispered, "Be happy, Melissa, it's ok. I'm God." That was an impossible pill to swallow. What can I say, a lie is a lie even if everyone believes it. The truth is the truth, even if no one does. They let her see me for a few more moments, told her it was time to leave, and she was off to my Rosarito house to salvage what she could.

Happy 24th, Clifford.

Welcome to prison.

Abroad.

Chapter XVIII

The Cabbage Patch

Having only a base cursory knowledge of the wrong side of a jail cell from my short stay at Camp Snoopy, I was relegated to following instructions blindly. I was un-cuffed and sat in a chair next to a data entry person who spoke English. He read me the police report and asked for my personal information.

"Happy Birthday," he said.

I chuckled and was sure he understood the irony, "What time is it?" I asked.

He stopped typing to check his watch. "2:04 AM." Well, for that matter Happy Birthday, Xander. I have a sneaking suspicion I'm going to need a guardian angel while I'm here. I was instantly sobered. God is watching.

I was wearing my favorite Hollister jeans with holes in the knees, which my Mom hated, and an unremarkable T-shirt. I had left the house without putting on actual shoes, and was wishing I had something warmer than the pair of Amber's house slippers I chose to sport that night. After he completed his part of the intake, I was escorted to another room that was bare other than a computer terminal with a large Mexican woman operating it, and a pile of clothes that must have been three feet tall and eight feet in diameter.

"Tu ropas," she demanded, and pointed to the pile. I got the charade, everyone coming in would have to strip and their clothes would end up in the pile. It looked like this was the end of the road for me and my holy jeans. It had been a good run. Mom would surely express her condolences to my face upon hearing the news, while feeling unadulterated relief, and perhaps even joy, in her soul. She hated those jeans. I stripped down and tossed the clothes on the pile. Another one bites the dust, I thought.

Just like the American intake process, I had to do the 'turn around', 'bend over and spread cheeks', 'lift scrotum', and then squat. The squatting part was new, but it assured the security personnel that no one was carrying in a knife or syringe in their prison wallet. Safety first, right? I was then handed my prison issue.

Grey sweatpants and a grey T-shirt. At least I matched. Donning the new garb, she had me positioned in front of a webcam to take my intake photograph. The right side of my face was severely swollen, from the punch. I must get my indigent supplies at the next station, I thought. Wondering what kind of toothpaste they give the prisoners in Mexico, I was tapped on the shoulder and the man pointed to the exit. My handler escorted me to a holding cell where there were about ten inmates sitting around, some still in street clothes, some in greys.

Occasionally someone would stop in front of our jail cell, in street clothes, offering to sell a pair of Jordan's or other coveted footwear. The shoe game was alive and well in prison intake in Mexico. As outside, so inside: everyone had a hustle.

I found an abandoned pack of cigarettes, Delacados ovalados. They were filterless oval shaped cigarettes that came eighteen to a pack and featured the bust of some Roman or Greek Goddess, to me it was Amber. I smoked two while the others in the cell looked at me like I was about to get my ass handed to me. Then, the owner of said pack was let back in the room.

He looked at me smoking his cigarette and to everyone's surprise, said nothing to me. He angrily asked the troupe something I understood to translate as "who the fuck told him he could have my cigarettes?" To which they replied with hands up, exaggerating their innocence, "No one did. He just took them!"

The right side of my face was swollen to the point of being half of a volleyball, so I assume he figured I'd suffered enough for one night and just took the cigarettes and German Shepard match pack and put them in his jean pocket. Would I be here for a night, or a few days? I had no idea. Would I have a bond? Would Melissa try to bail me out? All my questions would be answered in the following hour.

No, to all of the above. A guard with keys came up and shouted my last name. I got up from my perch on the second tier bunk bed, and followed him out. I started looking around as we approached a large building, housing prisoners. I'm getting the sneaking suspicion that this grey outfit was all I was going to get from my stay here. There were three tiers of building five, or 'edificio cinco'. Surrounding the entire prison, were forty-foot concrete walls. Not like the chain link and razor wire surrounding the outside area of the Kingman Jail Annex. This was Prison prison. You didn't even get to *look* at freedom. Just sky.

As we made our way up the first flight of stairs, the long corridor looked like a scene from a max security prison in San Quentin, say. Just a long line of tiered prison cells, one or two men per cell. "Ok," I thought, "I hope I get a good cellmate." My only other experience was dorm style jail living, I had never been confined to an actual cell before, but that was jail and this was prison, I accepted my fate.   Three steps down the hall my worst nightmare began to develop.

As I passed the first cell, prisoners were packed in a standing room only environment. I didn't have time to process their living conditions, when the first barred cell became obstructed and into view came the second cell, 211. This room had been modified to add a somehow constructed fourth bed on top of a shower area, and was strung up and secured with some two-by-fours and rope attached to the ceiling. It was about 4:00 AM and everyone was for the most part sleeping but, passing cell 212, I realized they were roughly all the same.

Two metal bunk beds adorned opposite walls of cell 213 with two prisoners in each bed, sleeping foot to face. The metal beds were three tiered, with three feet between tiers, not even enough room to sit erect.   So, two bunk beds, three tiered, two prisoners per, totaling twelve prisoners in beds. Between the beds, prisoners were on the blanketed floor lined up like sardines, foot to face, six deep, right up to the one stone sink that was centered on the far wall of the cell. There was a concrete toilet to the right of the sink and to the left was a three-by-three foot area with eleven, white, five-gallon buckets full of water, a floor drain and a curtain to add a certain level of showering privacy. The interior walls were painted a mossy green and as I carefully stepped over a sea of bodies, I leaned back against the sink, facing the cell door, to take it all in. A couple guys took a quick look and went back to bed. Surely, we would introduce each other in the light of morning, a couple short hours away.

I couldn't sleep, I was wired, America was coming for me, they had to.   The Intel team was getting back to CBP that day from Washington D.C. and when they read the report they are going to have to find me. The helicopters would show up in no time. I would stay vigilant.

Dawn began to break over my new reality. Literally and figuratively. I heard the banging of metal, and something scraping along the floor coming in my direction. It seemed to be making stops at each cell. I heard movement and light chatter in the other cells. Slowly, one by one, the prisoners in cell 213 began to wake up, some seeing this gringo for the first time, two others, who woke when I was brought in, couldn't go back to sleep and just stared at me convinced I just snorted a Scarface pile of cocaine. Soon the cell was awake and buzzing.

The prisoners sleeping on the floor all got up and rolled their blankets to the base of the bottom bunks, in Little Debbie Swiss Roll fashion. During the day, the rolled up bedding was then used as seating for everyone who slept on the floor. One of the twenty-two gave me a wide plastic microwaveable Tupperware dish. Breakfast was being served. A trustee, or runner, walked by the cell door and handed who I would find out to be the 'Head' of the cell, Shrek, a stack of warm tortillas wrapped in brown paper, and he tossed the package on his bed. I heard a double tap of metal on metal and then the dragging sound again.

Dragging up to our door was a 2 ½ foot tall, forty quart metal pot containing brown water and beans. Another, flatter pot, was brought up shortly after the tall one, containing nothing but scrambled eggs. The cell started lining up. There was a permanent opening in the old-fashioned, iron-barred door and, one by one, everyone in line would reach out their unique bowl and receive one ladle of eggs and one ladle scoop of beans. That was breakfast. Every morning. I started thinking that if this is the staple breakfast diet, what are the daily farting protocols? It's breakfast in a foreign country's prison, Clifford, just observe and do as the Romans do. When in Rome, right?

I was last in line and extended my dish out of the opening. The cook extended a verbal greeting, knowing I wasn't there yesterday, and gave me an extra half scoop of eggs. His name was Cirilo. I noticed he was missing his right ring finger when he reached out his hand for me to shake. I wondered how that happened? I'd be sure to get the story in the future.

"That's the cook." Shrek informed me. He then divvied out three tortillas to each of us, and we started eating. Many used the tortillas to scoop up a mound of beans and eggs in a low-key attempt of making a breakfast burrito. Some just rolled them tight and ate them like an empty taquito, a flat, corn based, appetizer. I would mimic the latter. As I finished my plate, I was surprised at how full I was, and was really impressed at the flavor of the beans. They tasted lightly salted and had a whisper of pig fat, maybe a small amount of bacon made its way to the giant pot every day. But it wasn't bad at all.

One by one, everyone got in line with their empty dishes and lined up in the center of the cell, facing toward the sink. There was a bag of 'jabon de polvo,' or powered soap, that was communal, every dish would get a little sprinkle. Everyone washed their own dish, unless someone volunteered to wash multiples at a time. I wasn't about to ask anyone for any favors this early in my prison career, so I washed my own when it was my turn, and placed my dish with all the others hanging in a knit bag that contained the other twenty-two mismatched bowls. With breakfast out of the way, it was interrogation time.

Shrek, a 36-year old bulky Mexican, started off. Shirtless, his "DURANGO" tattoo proudly stretched across his upper chest, he was one of the two keeping a close eye on me from the moment I arrived, earlier that morning. He would ask me questions as the others looked on, and periodically he would relay the information to the Spanish speaking majority. It seemed like an hour of questioning. Name. Crime. What happened? Why are you in Mexico? Did you bring in any drugs? Why didn't you sleep last night? Where are you from in the states? Did the police do that to you? (Referring to my swollen face.) They all laughed when I told them how that happened.

Satisfied with my answers, we changed topics. We went around the room and everyone gave me their names. Pildero, Valin, Shrek, Cebollia, Raton, Chunky, Soy, Bruha, Paisa, Zecchas, Tabo, Teto, Little One, Chiapas, Bebo, Oso, Panchito, Cattorra, Victor, Nero, one old man called himself Indio, one who got released later that day, and now me, totaling twenty-two. Twenty-two souls in a twelve-by-eighteen foot cell, ponder that!

Shrek gave me an opening to ask my questions, and I had a few.

"When do we get supplies?" I inquired, naïvely. He laughed.

"What you have now, is all you are going to get. There is a general store, that the runners will go to and buy you what you need, but this isn't like the states." Shrek would know about the prison system up north of the border. He had done prison time in California, and during a prison riot, got his face smashed in with the hard yellow plastic of the wringing mechanism from a mop bucket, leaving the left side of his face permanently disfigured. Upon hearing that story, I could see why he called himself "Shrek," even if it was a little self-deprecating.

"Shrek, I mean like a toothbrush, toothpaste, toilet paper, soap... we don't get provided any of those basics?" I asked dumbfounded.

He motioned for me to scoot over, moved a bedroll blocking the small storage area under the bottom bunk, and pulled out a stuffed sweatshirt. He untied the rope knot and displayed to me a stash of cut up T-shirts, all in two inch squares.

"We call it Charmin. But only under emergencies. I have a store and can get you things on credit, but not until your first family visit." This was him, insuring that he would get paid in the future if I bought items from him, but didn't have the cash on hand. When a family visit happened, which was two hours every Friday afternoon, they could put money on your books. Then, once a week, the "banker" would set up a table at the end of each run and anyone who had funds can get these little duckets with Peso denominations on them. Yes, like monopoly money. The max you could take out was 500 Pesos a week, or roughly fifty dollars, which was a lot of money, given the setting. It acted like currency, and facilitated bartering and trading.

The prison had its own economy. Those that had money, bought, and those that didn't, would hustle, labor or create. The general store had just about anything you could want, two-liter Cokes, candy bars, chips, cigarettes, matches, phone cards (for the payphones on the yard) and hygiene supplies including razors. The runners had access to just about anything else you could want, a cellphone to use, a syringe, heroin, chronic, speed, even a tattoo gun was available, which I got to see in use once, when a guard was paid off to let Pildero get a tattoo from an artist from the third tier. If family was not able or willing to physically come to visit, the secondary cash market was in prepaid cellphone reload packs from TELCEL, the unofficial phone service of Mexico, run by one of the world's richest men, Carlos Slim.

You could have your family or friends buy, for example, a $20 TELCEL top-up phone card, scratch off the back, and have them give you the access code. You could then sell the code at a small discount to the Prison Guards in exchange for Valles, the name of the prison cash. For one card code you could usually get fifteen dollars' worth of Valles out of the guards. Not to mention, developing a rapport with your keepers.

Every Tuesday, each tier would get an hour of recreation time outside. Every other Thursday, we would get an additional hour, for a total of six hours a month. Once on the yard, you could use the chipped phone cards they sold at the general store to call anywhere in Mexico, or the even states if you dialed the additional numbers for the United States country code. Those calls weren't cheap and I usually limited them to two minutes or under. You could then talk to your contact on the payphone and get the TELCEL phone card number, write it down, and it was as good as cash. Among the prisoners that had cellphones, they would give you dollar for dollar for the codes. Twenty for twenty. But they were usually pretty good at keeping up with their phone accounts, and rarely advertised their need for codes. Valles could also be used to buy drugs.

The big three were available for the asking. 50 Pesos bought a 'gallo', pronounced 'guy-o', of Chronic. It was enough to make two decent joints. I called it white lightning, because if you struck it twice, you were beyond high. There were about five daily heroin users in our room. One, Raton, never getting into debt, would be high all day, every day. He shot up into his neck, which always made me queasy. I have had a phobia of needles since a blood draw went horribly wrong when I was six years old. Another heroin connoisseur, Oso, on a number of occasions, fell while climbing to the top bunk after shooting up. Before he could reach his destination, he nodded off in a drug induced sleep. He would always come-to minutes later, and try the journey again. He never fell twice in a row. He, also, shot up in his neck, then filled the syringe with water and squirted the contents into his mouth, just to be sure not a bit of black went to waste. Opposite Raton's regimen, Oso got deep into drug debt. Crystal meth was discouraged among the prison population but was still available, however, no one in our cell used it. In contrast, everyone would enjoy weed when it came our way.

With Charmin as my emergency toilet paper that I was ashamed to ask for, durring the first three weeks, I reused the clean areas of used toilet paper, collected in the five-gallon bucket next to the toilet. Mexican plumbing can't handle the paper waste. The other bucket was full of water with a small round Tupperware bowl floating on top. This commode, in particular, couldn't handle much of anything.

My virgin dump, was met with disgruntled cellmates telling me to 'pour water on it.' This kept down the stench. Upon clearing my bowels, I was then in panic looking for the flush mechanism that didn't exist.

"Uh, Shrek?! What do I do now?" I asked for all to hear.

"See that Valentino salsa bottle?" He was going to love this.

"Yeah." It was against the back wall in a smaller, one gallon, orange, plastic, ice cream container.

He laughed out loud and advised me, "Get plunging!"

Now, you know that I was far from being considered 'white privilege,' although **they** might have thought I was. I did flash an amazing smile due to five years of braces, but this tested me. As I plunged, it broke the form of the excrement and released a potent newer, woodsier, smell.

A chorus of, "AGUA! AGUA!" came from the prisoners, one coughed and offered up a "Dios Mio!" So, I poured more water on. After a small time, embarrassed, but accomplished, I slid the privacy curtain open, and everyone was looking at me.

They were either holding their noses or hiding their heads under blankets. Shrek chimed in.

"Next time be quicker and don't be afraid to use the water."

"Got it! Lo siento, dos-trece!" I announced, to their laughter.

Next order of business was my 'gang' affiliation. Shrek called me over.

"So you have three options to choose right now. In the cell, everyone is expected to get along, but on the yard, anything can happen and you need to have a group to align with." Oh boy! My very first prison gang! I wonder if I'll have to 'blood-in?'

"Your three choices are the Sur 13's, or 'Chicanos', the Paisa's, who are Mexican Nationals, or the Diez y Ochos, a small 'click.' Each has their different rules but the Paisa's run the yard. There was not one white prison representative in the 5,000 souls that were within those tall walls. I was the sole gringo. Decision time.

"Well, if the Paisa's run the yard, I choose them." For my first legit prison experience, yes, I would prefer to be in the majority. Strength in numbers. Informed consent, and such. I felt so gangster, and hadn't even been out of the cell yet. Shrek told me that on Tuesday I would meet the Head of the Paisa's, 'El Diablo', I couldn't wait.

Shrek needed to come up with a cool gang name for me, and would eventually dub me "Pelos de Oro." (Literally 'Hair of gold', or, maybe derogatorily, 'Goldilocks.') I didn't mind either way. But I like the name I came up with more, "El Mexicano Blanco." Roughly translated as 'The White Mexican.' With all that out of the way, I sang for them, I told them of my adventures throughout Mexico. I told them I was in the Navy, "You know, marinas con los barcos" or "sailors with the ships." I told them about my days as a Coyote. It was a really cool moment, like my own fifteen minutes of fame, but it lasted for weeks. I had everyone's attention.

I was a foreigner, who tried to speak their language as much as I could, I could sing, I wasn't in for an immoral crime, and I had seen more of Mexico than most of *them*. I was like a new TV/radio combo that shits out mustard gas. I was the token white guy. I heard scraping and banging, was it dinner time already? Food times were twice a day, 7:00 AM and 4:00 PM, with a bread roll and a rotation of hot cider, tea, milk or oatmeal water at 8:00 PM, right before roll call.

Dinners would be a little more varying than breakfasts. Rice was the staple. Every dinner came with a ladle full of rice from the short wide pot, and a scoop of a random protein from the forty-quart tall pot. Of the meals I can recall, only the seafood rice dish was disappointing, I would always sell it for a cigarette or two. But it was probably a two-week rotating dinner menu. Posole, menudo, mole, a chicken drumstick, lamb cutlings, beef stew, chicken soup, and really random concoctions that they came up with on the fly in the kitchen that could never be duplicated. Every day was a culinary journey. It wasn't always that way.

In September or November of 2008 there was a prison riot at the Otay prison 'La Mesa', my prison. The prisoners weren't getting fed enough. Only if you paid, would you get enough to be full. The video may still be online, showing prisoners on the top of the wall at the lookout point, waving their grey T-shirts over their heads. A couple prison guards got burned alive, as I was told. The men broke into the general store, and emptied it completely, the woman's side was also breached and it became a consensual fuckfest.

Eventually the Mexican National Guard had to come in to return the prison to normalcy. No punishments were given, they were already locked down basically 24/7, what could you take away? Those that stockpiled goods from the general store, were allowed to keep their loot. Thereafter, the food started to flow. That's how that story went. Shrek assured me I showed up at a good time.

On that Tuesday, I had the honor of meeting El Diablo. He was the tallest Mexican I had ever seen, at least pushing six foot four, and was also the whitest Mexican, save me, I had also ever seen. He reminded me, in all respect, of a white cockroach. Shrek talked to him privately and then waved me over. We exchanged greetings and he shook my hand. Shrek gave him the basic rundown of everything he had learned about me in the few days prior and then informed me of the three main Paisa rules:

1.   Every time we hit the yard we would all line up and work out for 30 minutes, no exceptions. Old, young, overweight, EVERYONE worked out. Bebo, who would become my best friend in the cell, bellowed out the cadence for everyone when we worked out. He was a statue of physique, who always wore a black cross pendant with a downward facing white dove in the center. He never was without it. For some reason the pendant made me think of Jennifer. Bebo was there serving life for a murder he swore he didn't do. I believed him.

Policing in Mexico is notoriously lawless. Every cop has a side hustle as a shakedown artist, or of orchestrating mass arrests for simply standing on the wrong street corner. I felt sorry for Bebo, but he had accepted his fate and was in high standing with the Paisa's. Dwelling on things that he couldn't change, he would tell me, just puts you in a mental prison. He was as free on the inside as one could be. His leadership was unparalleled and he just had an aura about him that screamed respect. The workouts he led would consist of pushups, sit-ups, jumping jacks, and a ten-minute circular jog that would complete our workout. The leftover thirty minutes was for everyone to mingle or make phone calls. Sometimes, like that day, we used the last thirty to work out, and went in right after the jog. But to see over 100 prisoners working out in unison was something special. It reminded me of my Navy workouts. Oh, nostalgia, go away.

2.   When you get a visit and receive goods, a tax is to be paid to the tier runner, who would deliver it to El Diablo. This would subsidize the organization and ensure continuation of 'Paisa perks'. Namely, once a month you get a Gallo of your drug of choice. For Free. Enter song : "It's the first of the monthhhhhhh!" ☺. They never taxed your money, just the goods, so if I brought up a bag of ten dollars' worth of things, giving them a single Snickers bar would satisfy the tax requirement. It was nothing close to a shakedown, it was just paying respect.

3.   Don't get into debt. Not talking like four or five dollars' debt, we are talking like digging yourself a hole you can't get out of, i.e. hundreds.

El Diablo dismissed me, and then spoke to a huddled thirty-member group of Paisa's informing them of the new white boy that had aligned with the group. After my fifth solo lap around the fenced yard, he caught my eye.
    "Oye, Cliff," pronounced by every Mexican I've ever met, as 'KLEV', "Cien Porciento PAISA?" Diablo asked.
    I got the message and hollered back strongly and proudly, "CIEN PORCIENTO PAISA!" (100% Paisa.) The thirty that were sitting started yelping and cheering. I was definitely now the cool new kid. Someone came up to me from the group and said that they would find me some shoes because it was an eyesore to see me in Amber's house slippers. One of those Paisa perks, I guess. They took care of their own, and I appreciated that. Before I knew it, the hour was up and we all headed back to the dungeon. The front door of our cell was secured only with a Master Lock. Anyone got a screwdriver? Pro-tip: If you've never busted a Master Lock with a Phillips Head, you haven't lived.
    Melissa would show up three weeks later, around New Year's, buying a bag full of goodies from the general store before we met on the yard that was adored with folding picnic tables and plastic chairs. The hug was long and overdue. She was a little nervous looking around at the twenty or so guards all brandishing loaded AK-47s. I told her it was normal. We flagged down a runner and I asked Melissa to order me a pack of Marlboro Reds and two books of matches. The cell was so frugal that when we lit a cigarette, we split the match in two, to not waste an extra light. Waste not, want not, type lifestyle. Oh, the first Red in a month.
    Up until that point I had no credit with Shrek, but would now. She told me that she put $300 on my books. That was a lifesaver. She told me how she tried to pay my neighbor to not press charges, but he wouldn't take $1,000 and that was all she could gather, with help from Jessica, too. She told me that her and Travis Charles, who I then began realizing was the King of Clubs, got as much as they could from the Rosarito house. She didn't think to take the artwork hanging, and I had to hide my disappointment. But she got all my notebooks, and most of my clothes. She said that she also paid the thirty dollar water bill to Sal, my landlord. She told me how she was so sad that she missed me by less than two hours. I let her know that if I knew she was coming, I would have stayed home. There were more tears.
    We ordered some food from the grill and ate in silence. She showed up a little late, and with maybe fifteen minutes left of the visit,

she asked if there was anything else I needed. She was so good. One of the guards hollered the five minute warning, and I asked her to go to the general store and get me another pack of cigarettes, as I wouldn't be able to access the new money for a few days, at least. She did as I asked, and we hugged again. Exchanging 'I love yous' she found the nearest guard and let him lead her out the way she came. She said she'd be back as soon as she could. She told me to stay strong. And then she disappeared into a sea of other bodies, and a guard hurried me along to take me back to 213.

Walking back, every prisoner on my tier had their hands out, looking for offerings. I hurried past them and got to my cell, where everyone was waiting to hear the story. From the top bunk, Cattorra had watched the whole visit. From the right angle you could see about 35% of the yard, and I guess we picked a good location for him.

"Red hair, you sister beautiful." He managed. I thanked him for his compliment.

The runner was outside the door immediately asking to see what was in my bag. A pouch of Doritos, three Snickers, two packs of Marlboros, three packs of Delacados, a liter of Coca-Cola, a toothbrush, toothpaste, three rolls of toilet paper and a handful of matchbooks. It was prison Christmas. The runner said to just give him a Snickers, and Shrek nodded in agreement. Well, that was easy. I went to Valin and asked if I could buy my blanket back.

See, on day three, I ended up selling my sole possession, a blanket that I got from a Catholic Sister that just so happened to be walking by the cell, my second night in the prison. The cell inhabitants uniformly called to her saying I was new and needed a blanket, and she handed me one through the food trap. I sold it for cigarettes, the next morning. Shrek got mad at the transaction saying that I got ripped off, and I told him I could handle, or so I thought, being cold. I explained to him I could NOT handle being without cigarettes. So he allowed the transaction to complete. I gave Valin, who looked like a tall, Mexican 'Where's Waldo,' a pack of Delacados and he gave me my blanket back, doubling his initial ½ pack purchase.

I opened another pack of Delacados and tossed two to whoever asked. I gave Shrek three books of matches for safekeeping. I had no personal storage area, save the plastic bag I brought everything back in. Survival was no longer a pressing issue. All I had to do now was to wait and allow the Mexican legal process to slowly grind into gear. No lawyer, no appearances in front of a judge, just waiting. If this was the system in America, I thought, no one would want to come back. But money in prison makes you more a king than a prisoner, and it felt great.

Paisa was a large man, built like a retired linebacker, and tried to teach me some Spanish Cancions, or songs, really operatic style. He really wanted me to sing from the gut with gusto. There was one time I hit the line he wanted me to and was so proud of my vibrato he presented me with his cigarette pipe he fashioned from a hollowed out chicken bone. Those Paisa's are so industrious.

It was an epic pipe, about an inch in length and resin-coated from months of cigarette smoking. During the first three weeks, when I had nothing, he would always let me have the last two hits of his cigarette. Raton, as well, would let me collect all the cigarette butts from his aspirin bottle ashtray, and I loved rerolling them. They hit hard. Shrek told me I would get TB if I kept it up, but I wasn't going to be deterred. For rolling paper, as well as for joints, we would peel the foil off of the Delacado's inner packaging to reveal a smoke-able paper material.

Paisa and Pildero slept next to each other on the shower side of the cell, right next to me in the sardine line. Their feet and bodies would be under the first bunk, lengthwise, exposing only their heads and chests. Every once in a while Paisa would have a midnight cigarette and wake me up to share with him, probably the only perk of being the last sardine in line. Valin and Chunky would sleep next to each other under the bunks on the opposite side of the cell. There was a 4½ foot brick wall that sufficed as their respective headboards. I slept flush against the step that separated the living area from the shower, sink and toilet level. This meant that every night, I would awaken to people stepping over me to get to the toilet to take a leak. Three out of ten would step on me, accidentally, and offer whispered apologies. I eventually got desensitized to the disturbances and would sleep the whole night through.

Once I got my first Valle withdraw, Shrek told me that him and Tabo would sleep on the floor if I wanted to buy the "Presidential Suite" for two weeks, for a sum of twenty bucks. It was an insta-deal. He told me I had to pick a bunkmate, and looking at the remaining sardines, I picked Bebo. In return, Bebo offered to wash my clothes, get my dinner so I wouldn't have to wait in line, and wash my plate afterwards. He was a great soul. Every time I started singing, he would request Celine Dion, "My Heart Will Go On." He must have had a lot of turmoil in that heart of his if he keeps asking for "Titanic," I thought. But not one of the other twenty complained. Fond du Lac, WI and Kira Kempfer were remembered. Then Pildero's family made all of our lives complete.

His family bought and gave the cell, upon passing inspection, a 13" TV/Radio combo. What a home upgrade! Novellas ruled! Shrek even put on English subtitles so I could watch along with them. We watched scantily clad women dance on the beach for hours with 'DESCONTROL'. Every day we watched the national Mexican Dating game '12 CORAZONES'. We were addicted to the cartel thriller, 'EL

CARTEL'. Following that, the TV played 'SIN SENOS NO HAY PARISIO,' and 'The Summer of Love' or 'VERANO DEL AMOR.' The Simpsons and The Smurfs in Spanish were the most entertaining thing to watch when stuck in a bolt of white lightning. Do you know what they call the "Smurfs" in Mexico? PANTUFLAS! Fucking PANTUFLAS! Epic.

The radio went on midday and stayed on at low volume all night, and played the top fifteen Spanish jams on repeat, on the borderline of stroking insanity. One of the novellas introduced me to Genesis Rodriguez, a natural beauty, and the music video hour introduced me to Fanny Lou and Paulina Rubio, both super-hot, and mega-talented. Congrats on the baby, Paulina.

"Que Tu No Eras Para Me," featured Wilber Valderamma being messed with by Fanny Lou's voodoo and was a joy to watch. Paulina Rubio's "Causa y Effecto," is one of my favorite music videos of all time, put on your Yeezy's and Kick Rocks, Kayne! Bey is still cool, though, but "Single Ladies" doesn't make my top 100. Anyways, the entertainment had shifted from me to the television. I enjoyed the respite. It made the cadence of the days more tolerable than trying to just get max sleep.

Melissa visited again in March with another $300, and said that she and Amber were in contact and she was trying to schedule a conjugal visit. It sounded promising, but it never developed. In April, I was promised a visit from Mom, Jessica, **and** Melissa. However, it was thwarted on many fronts.

First, Mom was wearing what they deemed as "Gang Colors" and had to quickly find a used clothing shop to buy a plain white shirt. Jessica had forgotten her birth certificate, so they wouldn't let her in, but she did give Melissa the book, "Big Sur" by the famous beatnik author, Jack Kerouac, as a much welcome gift. The only other English book in the cell was Shrek's English Bible. (Which I read, twice.)

I read Kerouac through three times before stowing it under the bunks. I loved the "Raton Canyon Bridge" reference, but decided against telling Raton he had a bridge named after him in California. A couple pictures of the family, a picture of Amber and me on our Rosarito couch taken by her mother, a blue felt blanket and two composition books rounded out the care package of April. Melissa kissed me on the lips when she left that time. I felt something. It threw my equilibrium off, but banishing the thought, I headed back to 213. Zecchas immediately saw the composition books and asked if he could have one. He worked in the kitchen and would always come home with extra food for sale, so I figured hooking him up would be rewarded, eventually. I spent the following month journaling.

I documented the fall of Oso, who called his mother begging for money, as he was deep in drug debt. His pleas were heartfelt, but that's what addicts do, I guess. Two days later, a guard let three prisoners into our cell, locked the door and walked away. They proceeded to beat the shit out of Oso, who didn't even attempt to mount a proper defense. He just lied on the floor and took the punches and kicks. Days later, he was removed from the cell never to be heard from again. Shrek told me he went to another prison under protective custody. Oso was Chicano, a Paisa would have been cut off long before it became a problem. I documented the meals, every day, describing what we were served.

I wrote poetry.

For your enjoyment:

CRICKETS

> Even the crickets are thirsty
> As they sing their singsong
> From rusty cars hanging off dusty wheels
> In the backstreets of a brickyard
> In a small town square not far from here
> It ain't easy for a Brownback with a rucksack
> Just 'a travellin' the mighty ocean's shores
> At least not while the summer's yours
> You just sit back and try to turn your tears to tans
> You get riper as you get rotten
> In this cabbage patch
> This time-snatch
> That snuck in and lit a match
> Under your watermelon hammock space cloud
> And all the movies watched and popcorns popped
> All the kisses made and love displayed
> All the tacos cornered and water bills paid
> Is all there, stored
> In my pendulum stringed rucksack
> That swings from the hardest most rock bottomest part of
>   my heart
> And everything unremembered will never be forgot
> The crickets rise the tears
> Thirst is laid to rest
> Overlearned and under taught
> Yet, I passed the test.

Cebollia had the top bunk on the toilet side of the cell. He got approved to go to drug rehab and I got to take his spot in May,

Chiapas was my bedmate. I received my sentence from the Judge later that month. For 'Robo Un Caro,' I received a sentence of two years in prison. There were three options in my sentencing. I could serve the two years. I could pay a fine of $600 and be on Mexican probation, which meant I'd have to return to the prison to sign my name once a month. Or, pay the greater fine of $2000 and have the crime forgiven, and wiped from my record. The family opted for option two. Melissa, upon finding out I had been finally given a sentence, said she would be down to pay it as soon as she was able to get the funds. I was as good as sprung.

I still had $200 on my books and promised the cell a pizza party before I left. The runners could order us hot food from the food visits on Fridays, and that's what I was planning to do. Everyone opted for a Gallo each, instead. Convincing the banker to give me $100 wasn't a hard sell, I told him I wanted to have a pizza party for the cell, because I would be gone within weeks. He counted out the Valles and handed them to me.

"Baller, shot-caller, twenty-inch blades on the Impala."

That weekend was pure Pantuflas pandemonium. I called Melissa via cellphone on June 7th, 2009 and she told me they were coming on that Tuesday, two days away. I stayed awake for the last 72 hours I was there.

At night, the radio would go open air, and the Spanish top fifteen were replaced with random English songs. "Happy Trails" and Rosie and the Originals "Angel Baby" played almost on repeat. I took it as a message from 'The Watchers' that I had fulfilled my duty to Mexico and would soon be free to go.

Tuesday night at around 6:00 PM, a guard came to the door with a paper and called my name, unlocked the door, and hugs and handshakes were hastily doled out.

"Don't forget about us." Shrek implored.

"I won't," I replied. "I promise."

There were a number of security protocols that I had to pass. Literally it was a quiz on my own life.

"What's your birthday?"

"What's your mother's name?"

"What's your social security number?"

The quizmaster had a decal on his radio of a cow jumping over the moon, and that was suiting for the moment. That's how I felt. Over the moon. Two gates later, I was street side somewhere in Mexico. Jessica was waiting in the Chevy Cobalt she bought from Melody. I saw her waving to get my attention, but there were so many homeless people around she didn't want to get out of the car, but as I approached her car she did roll down the window to give a food plate to someone who came asking her for something to eat.

After I got in the passenger seat, I opened my stupid mouth. Just like boot camp graduation, asking Grandpa and Grandma, "Where's Randy?" The first words out of my mouth were not that of greetings or hallelujahs, it was "Where is Melissa?" That hurt, I'm sure, and I'm sorry for it, Jess. Open mouth, insert foot. We all have our moments.

"Where do you want to eat?" She asked as if I had been eating gruel for the last six months.

"Anywhere," I replied. We found a random sandwich shop and she ordered me a club sandwich to go, as we had a long drive ahead of us.

"You're going to love it!" She said overly hopeful. I ate half, it tasted like cardboard. Then the drink spilt on my composition book on the floorboard of the passenger seat, rendering my writings ink-smeared and unreadable. I didn't react. She drove two hours and asked if I could drive the rest of the way. Fuck yeah, I want to drive! There was nothing like the open road to cure six months of being locked down.

"Can we buy a pack of cigarettes?" I asked her, she smiled. Jessica, Jessica, Jessica. She surprised the hell out of me when she said she actually had a pack in the trunk, so I pulled over. She was in restaurant hospitality and when work would get particularly stressful, she would light one up. They were Marlboro lights, and came in a 24-pack and I was like, "Where the fuck did you pick these up at?"

"A friend at work gave them to me." Wait a minute, I'm gone for six months and America just changes the cigarette pack count on me, what else is different? Did they discover that the blood of the Loch Ness Monster cures cancer? Oh, what a world! I finished the cigarette as cars whizzed by and she was sleeping as I pulled off the shoulder, homeward bound.

I woke her up as we approached Phoenix and she directed me to the Lofts at Rio Solado in Tempe, off Washington. She brought me up to room 420, and I was amazed at the quality of the place. But, before I could look around, she gave me a blanket and told me to take a nap on the couch. I told her early in the drive I hadn't slept since talking to Melissa that Sunday.

She told me she had to go to work, and Melody would be home that night. She gave me twenty dollars and left me her spare apartment key, just in case I wanted to go for a walk or get something to eat, as their fridge was empty, save for a can or two of Coors Light.

I hugged her and thanked her for all she had done. It was uncomfortable. It was like going from being homeless to occupying the White House. Like, being abused naïvely, to being loved unconditionally. It took a moment for me to get my bearings. The bathroom was upstairs and, after she left, I looked in a mirror for the first time in a long while. I turned around and flushed the toilet.

I cried.

Chapter XIX
Check Yes or No

I woke to Melody's arrival and gave her a hug. She gave me the tour of the grounds and showed me one of the two pools that 'The Lofts' boasted. Their loft was more visually appealing when compared to something that had a practical living use. A show house. An entertainment venue. Jessica was waitressing at the time and I believe that Melody was moonlighting at Victoria's Secret at the Tempe Marketplace, while going to school to become a nurse's assistant.

She introduced me to her new 2008 Volkswagen Jetta that had astronomical monthly payments and the insurance was almost more than the car payment. This infuriated me. I believed strongly in living at or below your means, and she was living the opposite. Flashy. 'Look at me and my perfect life,' she exuded. Yet, she would call my Mom on occasion asking for grocery money. Melody was the kind of girl that would buy an expensive dress and wear it out twice, then return it, tag attached. From all the experience I had had up until that point, I had learned or been forced to accept, that everything can be taken from you in a moment's notice, and if you have no backup or contingency plan or resources, you are at the mercy of the wind. A simple chain of events could leave you exposed, vulnerable, and in no position to say "no" to a deviant act or behavior. But that fact alone wasn't the tipping point. That came later.

Waiting for me at the apartment was a package from Amber, who had been in contact with my sister, Melissa. She had a few decorated pictures and my Skin wallet I had left in her car the day we parted. The silver coin was not among the items. I called Melissa to get Amber's phone number, and called immediately to see how she was and where we stood. She wanted to see me. I then contemplated getting a Greyhound to Kansas, but having no cash... I concluded I'd just have to find a way. She informed me that she kept the silver coin. The first one I acquired that had three deep scratches on the face, the one that started my investigation into the true value of a 'thing'. She kept it as a 'memento,' she told me. I would call it a theft. But LAW would laugh at me if I wanted to pursue it. It was only $16 of metal to the world, but it held infinite intrinsic value to me. The world doesn't see a 'thing' that way, now does it?

Have you ever had anything force removed from your life that had an incalculable value to you, but was a simple line item to the taker? Was there recourse for justice then? Of course not. Not in America's America. It then became a true modern silver platter containing the head of John the Baptist. The platter in question never held a bundle of grapes, but it held my minds paradigm shift, or at least marked the moment I became inspired to wonder about it.

Provenance means everything in determining the market value of something. Where did a thing come from? Who had it touched? Where had it been? At auction, which would command a steeper premium? A $5 silver bangle (bracelet) from Wal-Mart, or the same sized wrist-piece made out of an E-string cut from Taylor Swift's guitar during a live show? Upon first glance with no history, the Wal-Mart offering would look to satisfy most, due to its uniform appearance and professional clasping mechanism. The E-string offering would look like the counterfeit, which might appeal to your more earthy types, looking more chic-cheap-unique. But without the whole story, you would be flying blind to try to price one. Continuing down this tangent, thank you for amusing me, what if the Wal-Mart bangle was purchased by Michelle Obama from her Becoming royalties and would be hand delivered to the auction winner? Now, we might have a true bidding war. What if proceeds were to go to digging wells in African villages? Or Taylors E-string hitch-up would raise money to buy hand warmers for the winter-bound homeless in Savahanna, Tennessee or Pittsburgh, Pennsylvania? Pro-tip...Think about it.

Amber kept talking and I responded to her blunt admission by sending her the YouTube link to "You should have said NO" — By my Tay. The live awards version, where Swift starts off in a dark hoodie, tears it off then gets rained on. What a feeling that must have been, Taylor. Amber said her hookup didn't "mean anything." Well, it did to me. You can try to call me a hypocrite, but I caution you.

I'm not against open relationships on the male OR female roles, but a side discussion of the possibilities beforehand is paramount. An after-the-fact admission is a slap to the face of the one who was banking on trust and, at the minimum, honesty. I was over it, she didn't want to apologize, and I didn't want to waste my time chasing a girl who had never had an orgasm. The ancients would say she had a curse. It was like fucking a mirror. She was the girl version of me. But without her orgasm, sex was pointless, and so encapsulated the end of our relationship. She posted pictures online of her Mexican adventure, covered over my face with opaque silver from Microsoft Paint, and went on living her life.

I found out from the Skype chat that while I was in prison, she told the masses that I was caught stealing a car with the "biggest meth dealer in the area," so unless the stuffed Tasmanian Devil was the 'plug' of Lucio Blanco, I call slander. Libel, even because she typed it in chat. I decline to press charges, statute of limitations and all. She also said I sold her beloved PlayStation II to the neighbor boy for meth... I couldn't even defend myself against her tirade of lies. My words written did come to fruition though. Remember when I promised her she would 'be taken care of?' She now has at least one child with her second husband, a military G.I. She looked happy in the few Facebook pictures I saw of her stone-stepping over a bobbling brook. Long live!

I spent a week in Havasu upon returning to the states, where I met Dad and his new help-mate, or life partner, Penny, for the first time. Dad gave me the biggest hug I can remember him ever giving me, and quipped in my ear, "Water under the bridge, son. Water under the bridge."

After stealing his car, he was forced to bike to his destinations in Paso Robles, and on one occasion fell and broke his collarbone. That made my theft of his Escort emotionally unjustifiable and just as spiritually burdensome. But it did take him out of the running of being the Messiah, so I could then temper his sermons on how to live a life, with, "You're not God, and just guessing at this point, Dad." That put a loving smile on my face, just now. I returned to the Lofts.

In her upper echelon of social networking, Melody had made her way to the Playboy Mansion somehow, and unrelatedly had made a friend or two from the XXX solo girl porn outfit, VIVID. (I hope they power washed the Bunny Pool if she went swimming. Just saying.) So the plan was for Melody and her pornstar friend to meet up and party in San Diego for the weekend. Now, I'm sorry, but I still have the Foreign Prison Pheromones, and to have just been released from an emotionally torturous six months, you'd think a sister worth a fuck would have at least given me the opportunity to **shake** a pornstar's hand. I was in great shape. She might have seen something in me and given me a contact outside her niche market. I had no intention or false ideas about hooking up with this girl, but, just to meet one in real life, would have really taken the edge off. Alas, no.

Melody told me to stay in the apartment and she, with cellphone in hand, told her friend, "I'll meet you in the parking lot. I will be there in thirty seconds." **Tipping point.**

Do you blame me? In certain decks of cards, unless you are looking at the court set of flamingos or the opiate enhanced kingdom, some will have Melody, the Queen of Diamonds, with a flower covering the very bottom of the red diamond pip in the upper left corner. This was that moment. When she told me to stay in the fancy dungeon and let the potential opportunity of a lifetime, drive off with her in the passenger seat, thinking that Melody was the best option out there. I mean she *did* shake Tiesto's hand, my God, give the woman a scepter. What garbage! Jessica took me to Melissa's house to stay for a day and collect my belongings.

At Melissa's house, a quite lived in townhouse in the Phoenix-area, were her and her boyfriend Travis Charles and their Min-Pin's, Diamond and Duke. They bred them and sold the purebred puppies for a pretty steady supplemental income. Melissa was always there for the deliveries and took great care in helping Diamond through the births.

I was told a story during my Havasu trip from Mom, that in a recent litter where one was born still in the sac, Melissa bit through it and put the liberated puppy at Diamonds head for cleaning and inspection. I would expect nothing less than a pure Earth spirit like that from the Queen of Clubs. She gave me two duffel bags full of my clothing she had retrieved from 2333 in Mexico that fateful night, and also picked up some things that I didn't know were stored there, namely my birth certificate.

She had it saved in a plastic accordion-style filing unit, and when she remembered, she pulled out the aged tri-fold document and presented it to me. As she walked out of the office area where the computer was, where Travis Charles made side income on FullTilt, I was immoveable.

In the lower left corner, written in red, inside the circular seal, was my birth certificate number, screaming at me. 6.6.6.1.8.4. The number of my name, after everything that had just transpired in Mexico, the inexplicable miracles, the spiritual conspiracies seemingly against ME at every angle, here it was on Bona Fide Stock Certificate Paper... 666.

Now I know, logic says that there are 999 others with that prefix, and if anyone of those would like a proper sit down debate to see who is likely the true Vicar, bring it!

Keeping my calm, no need to freak everyone out, or to have them banish me to the nuthouse, I spent the following few days just vegging out to the TV and playing a couple freerolls on Travis's poker account. Then it was time to get back to Melody's and figure out my next move.

There was a bench warrant for me out of Mohave County for failure to appear in my re-sentencing for the Domino's case. My lawyer asked for as many continuances as he could, but the judge had had enough sometime in June 2008, and put the heat on. A warrant. The loose plan was to enjoy freedom a little bit longer and surrender to face the fire. It was June 24th, I had been in the states for 15 days. Then, everything changed with a dream.

Infinite black, in all directions. There was me, a roulette wheel, and the dealer. Truly an Einsteinian moment for those who catch the reference to his thoughts of God. Off to the right of my vision, a wooden door appears with a rounded copper knob. The door opens to two men dressed in suits, packing heat. Calmly, the first agent addresses me:

"We were sent here to kill you." At which point I calmly grabbed the barrel of the gun in my right hand, pressed the muzzle to my right temple and said, "Don't miss."

Click

My mind and body went into surge mode, trying to attain stimuli to computate my biological status. Was I dead? Is this a dream? Am I in the afterlife? White points of light began piercing the black darkness, like when Jennifer kissed me for the first time.

I was still at the roulette table, white ball still waiting on gravity and depreciating centrifugal motion to depart the groove and find a home. I'll say my money was on Black 13, but that would just be a wishful shout-out to Taylor Swift. The agent with the gun looked at his partner, back at me, still surging with stimuli, gathering awareness, and he fired again.

I woke up.

With Melody and Jessica sleeping in the downstairs master bedroom with the double doors closed, I began the imparted mission. I began not-intelligibly or knowingly, for that matter, removing the apartment's smoke detectors and batteries thereof.

This was some government, 'Operation Bluebeam', or 'Project Monarch,' type shit. Just like when I slammed the birdbath on Johnny's head, this mission was just as automatic. Like how Johnny went from being in a comatose state to robotically sitting up and walking 15 feet to the carport gate, unaided, after having a 35-pound cement stone bash his head in. I went full Bourne Identity. I went upstairs and unwound a roll of toilet paper making a thread line from around the base of the toilet to the closet, weaving in and out of empty multi-colored hangars and left the remaining half-roll on the bed.

In the downstairs bathroom, I filled the sink with water and submerged the girls' hair curler and admired the fine underwater smoke that resulted. Making my way to the kitchen, all seven detectors were stacked on the kitchen island, with a pile of Duracell's neighboring them. Three bottles of wine were on display next to the coil element stove. I was surprised a place of this quality didn't use natural gas stoves. Oh well, beside the point.

I took and opened the bottle of "Crossroads" with Brittney Spears in mind. Fuck you if you judge me! That was a great role, Britt. But if you don't think I can go hard, I'll direct you to send your complaints to Bone-Thugs & Harmony. Ohhhh!! Now, shut up and listen.

There were two other bottles. 'Middle Sister,' and why would I want to harm Jessica? I wouldn't. So, I left it there. The third bottle, name unremembered, would be the weakest link. It was a red.

I turned on the right-front burner to high and placed the bottle horizontally on the side of the counter that was flush with the stove. With the unopened stem (the bottle was still corked and sealed) directly over the center of the now red coil. I grabbed my cigarettes from the couch, a glass vanilla candle from the coffee table, Melody's keys off the island, and was out the front door in one fluid motion.

Getting down to her car I noticed that Melody's old Cobalt, Jessica's current car, was parked right next to the Jetta, so I opened Melody's trunk and took all the junk and put it all in Jessica's unlocked Chevy. I closed the trunk and opened the driver's side door, candle in one hand and the now opened bottle of "Crossroads" in the other. I took a swig and looked back... "This is for a Vivid mistake, Melody." I didn't say it out loud, but it did float from my mind. I was sure they would wake up soon and shut the stove off, right? I mean, someone always has to wake up to pee, right?

I lit the candle and it fit snugly in the multi sized cup holder. I was impressed at the pristine interior of the vehicle. Wow, I thought, as I looked up. It even had a sunroof, so I opened it. I checked the lit up dashboard, ¾ tank... perrrrrfect. I framed the mission parameters.

MISSION POSSIBLE- TO BRING THIS AMERICAN FLAME INTO MEXICO, WITHOUT INCIDENT

I have no paperwork informing me at what time the All-Points Bulletin left the Precinct, but I somehow avoided being discovered...for a time.

After getting out of the city lights, moon roof open, and flame doing its thing (flaming), I finished the bottle of Crossroads and being the only car on the I-10 in eyesight, I threw the bottle straight up in the air and heard it shatter on the highway behind me. Closing the moon roof, it was "Go" time. New car... lets test your meddle.

I, for the first time in my life, put the proverbial "pedal to the metal," with no intent on letting up. 100. 110. 115. 120. She was humming along like the finely tuned German machine she was. I was on the fucking Autobahn. 85 yards ahead, I see it, and hesitate for a split second. Object detected in the median. Object Identified. It was the FUZZ. Was he clocking me? Did he already gun zap me? The rush was inextinguishable. I think I bent the floorboard a little as I pressed even harder on the gas. "Let's do this!" I mentally challenged the cop. Jetta Vs. Crown Victoria. 3...2...1... GO!

It must have taken him a good four seconds to wipe the coffee from his crotch and swallow the last crumbs of his powdered jelly, but I saw the cherries and berries coming for me out the rearview. It was still dark and there was light to moderate pre-dawn traffic, so I began to drive like I would in Mexico, like a mackerel. Weaving through traffic, heavy long haulers speckled the slow lane but I was able to find easy lines to not endanger anyone. Keeping steady at 115-120 MPH there was a bottleneck up ahead of me. I had no option but to leave someone with a story for the grandkids.

Passing a six year old white sedan on the left, between the cement barrier and the fast lane, I sideswiped the innocent vehicle and it was left without the driver's side mirror. Escaping that relatively smoothly, I wasn't looking back, but was thinking, if he gets me, he earned it. My 'swimming' was impeccable. Paul Walker tips his cap to the reading audience, but he ain't giving me any credit until I do it again, with a manual.

C'mon man, I **was** Fast and Furious, at Melody, but I wasn't thinking about that just then. A line of four cars in a row were socially distanced in the fast lane, I had no play there. The slow lane had a Covenant shipping truck keeping pace. Once again, my hands were tied.

I backed off the gas a millimeter and hit the gravel shoulder opting to rip the band aid off fast, rather than take the weak, ease it in slowly approach. All four tires were shooting gravel. Now I was in rally mode...in a Jetta! I've always believed in my limited but thorough research that a Subaru WRX is one of the best rally cars on the market. I personally would play that as my backup, to a custom Suzuki Aero with a roll cage, because that shit would probably tip, but this Jetta definitely held its own.

I passed the semi-truck. It took a few extra feet, due to the slowage of slipping tires, but I did it. Then I gave him the old double flick of the headlights, to say thanks. I choose to remember him flashing me a "nice pass, asshole" type high-beam, in return.

The car was pushing on fumes, and I slowed to the next exit, Prince Blvd, in Tucson and parked in the Chevron/Wendy's parking lot. It was still dark. No police. Looking behind me, there weren't even cop lights coming. I just outran the law. After watching all those cop chase videos, I assumed that the perp rarely got away, but I did. However now, I was thwarted on another front. Fuel. I had no gas, and was wanted. (The bad way, not the Hunter Hayes kind of 'wanted.') I blew out the candle thinking of Elton John and Princess Dianna.

<u>MISSION ABORTED</u>

Here's the Juice from the Release Questionnaire:

The Arresting Officer
W. Vanek
Serial Number
11450
Tempe P.D.
(480) 858-6342
Case number
09-105337
Charge & Class
13-1814 A1 Class 3 Felony
Date
7/20/09
PROBABLE CAUSE STATEMENT

"On 6/25/09 between 0030 and 0700 hours (S) Clifford Frederick Gant removed the car keys from the kitchen counter belonging to his sister (V) Melody Gant and drove away in her vehicle from their residence, without her permission. Melody indicated that Clifford was the only person that had access to her keys that is now missing along with her vehicle. Melody indicated Clifford has been experiencing severe mental issues, along with some possible drug issues.

On 6/25/09 approximately 0700 hours, Clifford was located and arrested by Tucson Police for two outstanding warrants while he was walking along I-10 near Tucson.

On 6/26/09 approximately 0530 hours, Melody's vehicle was recovered by Tucson Police in Tucson. The exterior of the vehicle had numerous scratches and the interior seats had pictures drawn on them. Melody stated, the pictures drawn on the interior of her vehicle reflects Clifford's mental state. Melody will aid with prosecution.

(initials) (Handwritten) On 08/04/09 Clifford was interviewed by telephone and admitted to taking Melody's listed vehicle without her permission. Clifford said he takes full responsibility for taking the vehicle and causing the damage. (initials) 8/10/09"

Now, in the sixteen days that I had lived in America since my departure from the Cabbage Patch, I had smoked only cigarettes. So, let us just say that I would have had a clean UA. But if THAT slanderous/libelous 'indication' from Melody to the reporting officer had been even remotely possible, a drug screen should have been warranted, at the minimum, and an immediate mental health examination administered, if those words were to be used in the processing of charges brought. Not in America's America, though.

Plus, those interior 'pictures' were not indeed pictures, but a message to my muse:

(In pen, connecting the perforated dots in the leather passenger seat, I made a constellation of a message)

DEAR TAY,
WILL YOU GO
TO VEGAS
WITH ME?

CHECK
YES OR NO

Progressive Insurance should have the evidence photos. I still don't know how an enforcer of law can report a clear and concise **message** as being "PICTURES", like I drew 3rd grade shapes and animals. He reported 'scratches' and 'pictures drawn' but Progressive Insurance Company claimed $9,977.29 of damage was done to her car that had a reported value of $20,000. If over $10,000 worth of damage had been done, it was Progressives Policy to replace the car entirely.

$22.71 stood between the insurance appraiser's estimate of the damage, and doing the righteous thing of giving her a new car replacement. $22.71! Seems that I can't do anything right. Break a window, couple hundred more in damages. Break the LCD screen on the radio, another hundred dollars. Break off the glove compartment door, that's got to be worth at least $65 in replacement parts. If 1/10 of one percent of the MSRP of said car would have been officially damaged or in need of repair, I would have WON her a new car. Instead, the adjuster did what was best for the company, and Melody was forced to wait for a car cursed with Farrah Faucett's death. While I was fucking 'drawing pictures,' I had the radio on and that's how I heard that bit of news. I found out Michael Jackson died when I got to the Jail Intake. What was happening?

Progressive... do you think that claim was justifiably for the benefit of your premium payer, or just for Progressives bottom line, and 'fuck the customer?'

If I wouldn't have failed in creating $30 more damage, Melody probably would have thanked me, and chosen a new Jetta with a different color. She would have learned her lesson about the importance of being humble and not braggart about the life God has provided her. But with what you know about me at this point, you know I'm usually always one chip behind breaking even.

On June 25th, 2009, I was arrested after being interrogated by a female police officer about just why I was walking down the I-10, barefoot. I was cuffed when she radioed my name in and found me to have an outstanding warrant out of Lake Havasu City. I spent about two weeks waiting at the Pima County Jail, in Tucson, for extradition. To my surprise, the van didn't take me to the off ramp to the highway for the long haul to Lake Havasu City, but took another subject and me to an airport where there was a single engine Cessna with a Pima County Sheriff logo emblazoned on it.

"No fucking way," I thought. "I get a plane ride out of this! This is awesome! It's going to be like Con Air!" The Hispanic kid next to me was visibly nervous and I told him not to worry and to just think that he is on a boat. They secured our body chains to the floor of the plane and we took off. I tried to make conversation with the pilot but he wasn't in a talkative mood. We were cargo, not passengers.

Getting back to Havasu, it took the standard two months to sentence me. On September 15th of 2009, I was sentenced to the Department of Corrections for a grand total of nine months, with credit for 130 days' time served. Of course, ordered to pay $3,856.93 in restitution to Domino's, which was never going to happen. But the kicker was that with the way they calculate prison time I didn't even make it to a real prison yard.

I was held in Phoenix, at Alhambra, which struck me instantly as a palindrome for Abraham L. But regardless, I was there for a grand total of 25 days, followed by two months of unsupervised probation.

The food there was leaps and bounds above county fare. We even got a salt and pepper packet with our meals. Even if the quantity of the food was just enough to keep you satiated, but never full, it beat county, hands down. I didn't have to endure much for very long. I was still waiting for the other shoe to drop in Melody's case. Nonetheless, they released me without incident on October 16th, 2009. Travis Charles picked me up and bought me a pack of cigarettes from the nearest Circle K. Oh, Marlboro, how I missed thee.

The rest of that month was spent in an RV with my Mom, Randy and my brother Mitchell. Randy use to be a multi-million dollar real estate producer in town but fell upon hard times during and after the real estate meltdown, and now, they were living the RV life at Campbell Cove RV Park, in Lake Havasu. The RV Park had a hot tub and internet access, so I wasn't going to complain. I would help Randy do side jobs and find other ways to pass the time. But come

November, I was informed by Mom that there was a warrant out of Phoenix for me.

Having no way to drive out there, I called myself into the local police, who showed up, four squad cars deep, thinking it was going to be an ambush of some sort. Once cuffed and in the back of the officer's car, he told me that not a lot of people just turn themselves in like that. I just told him that I was saving the gas money and time of having someone drive me out to Phoenix.

Another two weeks of waiting at the condemned Kingman jail, I was extradited. Once in front of the Phoenix judge, to both of our astonishments, the reason for the miscommunication with the court was made apparent. My court mail was being sent to Melody's house. So, needless to say, I gave the court a proper address and he released me, right then. What the fuck? Now, I have to find a ride back to Havasu.

Travis and Melissa would pick me up from jail and drive me back to Havasu, for the second time in a month, a few days later.

Between getting back to Havasu and my sentencing in the car theft case, was nothing but a few random hookups, most originating from BJ's Tavern. I stopped counting sexual partners when I made my official roster, topping 30 partners, while I was bored at the jail. My bunkmate didn't believe my count because I couldn't recall a lot of their names. Most of the listed referred to what kind of encounter it was. My list consisted of: 'The girl who liked to be choked,' or 'girl from Ken's Pizza & Pasta,' or simply 'The Earth.'

'The Earth' was a woman who was pushing 285 pounds, who bought me drinks at the Havasu bar, Kokomo's, and after taking me back to her house, had like six casserole dishes of food for me to pick from, once we left the bedroom. She wasn't a glutton, though. Her bodily form was due to the aftermath of a hysterectomy she had years prior. She told me that it had been over seven years since she had sex. I felt that that was terrible. She wanted to continue meeting, but I was a legal mess, and didn't want to trouble her. If I saw her today, I would strip her down again, no questions asked.

During the daytime, Randy would leave me lengthy lists of things to do while he was at work. It definitely had a slave labor feel to it. I was finally sentenced to 15 months in prison for stealing Melody's car. With 57 days credit for back time. I signed the plea agreement for 12 months but the judge, Judge Anderson, decided that I had to "learn a lesson," and gave me an extra three months.

"Oh no, judge, not another three months out of life, whatever will I do?" What a joke, I thought.

On June 18th 2011, I 'killed my number' (another way of saying I did 100% of my time) and was a free man.

Chapter XX

The Unintended Consequences

Of Bearing False Witness

After spending what little money I had from a job hookup I had been at for four weeks, I spent a lot of time homeless on the Vee Quiva Indian Reservation in Laveen, Arizona. After running out of cash, and almost breaking my ankle jumping into a polluted canal after executing an ill-advised cannonball. (I thought the water was deep and planned to clean out the unsightly, floating trash.) Only after, did I find out that it was only eight inches deep. I painfully climbed out of it, after completing the task.

Melissa picked me up at a public Phoenix park, took me to the emergency room, where I found out that my right foot was only sprained, not broken, and then drove me home to Lake Havasu, a few days after that.

Two days after my return, I was walking the Havasu streets and came across an abandoned lot that used to sell ATV's. I arranged some items I had found during my walkabout on the sidewalk, and sat down on a raised cement plateau where, previously, a car or ATV would have been displayed for sale. I was there for less than ten minutes when three squad cars pulled up. This was during morning rush hour traffic and at a main intersection in Lake Havasu.

The policemen began questioning me about a pole that looked like it had been removed from its fitting. That was me. It was disconnected when I found it and I moved it five feet down the gradient mesa to see broken wires exposed. They explained to me that they received a complaint that there was someone standing at the corner yelling at passing cars and exposing himself to street traffic while also pulling up metal conduits from the ground. Well, I was the guy on the corner, but none of those things, save trying to fix the electric capabilities of a broken something, were true.

I like fixing things, especially when no one knows or complains about them being broken in the first place. With my rapid speech telling the officers I was just headed two blocks away so I could see Randy at his place of employment to borrow some cash to get some more tobacco and a Polar Pop. They felt there was enough evidence to arrest me.

My Mom cried to the judge and I was released. With an initial hearing scheduled for three weeks later. I was steadfast in wanting a trial. I wanted to see this ONE man in all morning traffic get on the stand and repeat under oath what he had reported to the police that fateful morning. Disorderly conduct and criminal damage were the charges. The owner of the property refused to prosecute or ask for restitution, which was obvious because that shit was broke before I got there. But this meant an open court case, and one that I was not going to be bullied into taking a plea offer.

Back in 2012, I fought my own case after I had sent some ill-advised text messages to Annette. Blast from the past, right? "Threats and Intimidation via Telephone," was the charge.

She and I had been hooking up regularly at that time and, well, she wound up pregnant. This was a shocker to me, as I knew her to be on birth control. As it was told to me after-the-fact, she claimed she "lost it at a party." I don't know why any woman is whipping out her birth control pills at a party but you should let the dude know, "Hey um, don't cum inside me," at least as a simple, common, courtesy. That wasn't the kicker though.... She couldn't even tell me if I was the father! Her ex-husband, whom she had a restraining order against, hooked up with her the night after I did, after selling her some ecstasy pills.

So there I was... do I play the soon to be father role again, and find out the kid is not mine, or do I ignore the slut and the kid **does** turn out to be mine and then I'm just a shitty Dad. Talk about bringing on a mental firestorm. I think there should be some sort of laws about non-consensual conception. I was content with the child I lost.

Getting arrested for this "crime" kept me in jail for 180 days. As I chose to represent myself, I had no warning as to when the court date was and wasn't given so much as a pencil during my time in isolation. The documents I got had a text message deleted from the original conversation of Annette asking me if "I was drunk?", which would have went to show she wasn't as devastated or scared with the text I sent, reading to the point of "It was I who killed the unborn Kennedy," that's what she had chosen to name the unborn, but as I was typing I was thinking of the death of President Kennedy, not killing a fetus. It was a rough time emotionally and mentally.

At trial, I was completely blindsided by the date which was never passed on to me and I was never given access to the law library. I asked the judge for a lawyer at the onset of the gorilla court and he replied that it was "too late for that."

One of the arresting police officers spoke and then Annette took the stand. I asked her basic questions about my demeanor toward her. Have I ever been violent? She couldn't remember if I had ever babysat her two current children, which blew my mind. I had babysat them both weeks earlier and we all pitched in to make her dinner. See, at that time I **wanted** to be the father figure, I **wanted** to have a four year old son to help raise, I had a lot of paternal emotion to deliver and I thought that it could have worked out for everyone's benefit. I then asked her who the father of the child was, to which she replied she didn't know. Then, I asked, with a quick objection from the prosecutor, who the other father might be.

"Irrelevant," the prosecutor claimed. And I didn't know how to proceed. The third line of my notes that I had written, in the four minutes the jailer let me have his pen, did say, "expect objection.' I think it would have definitely mattered.

She had a long standing restraining order against her ex-husband, who had once sodomized her with a loaded gun, that she was "gravely afraid of" and what she thought "he was capable of." Well, if that was the case, why is she allowing him to enter her home, for a drug deal and some sex?

The police are not her personal drama coaches, to enforce law only when she deems fit. I closed my argument knowing there was no point. Having doctored evidence against you and no way to fight it out in legalese, I just gave up. The 2x180 day sentences were run concurrent and I was out of solitary around April 20th of 2013.

I wanted the same experience with this Brian Chinnarin character, but with a lawyer this time. I wanted to have him lie on the stand under oath and I would gladly do the petty time, if found guilty, attributable to disorderly conduct and criminal damage. One glaring decision standing in the way was my cousin Chanel's wedding in Wisconsin.

It was going to be an open ended kind of trip to see the family up north, and when Mom asked me if I wanted to go with Randy and her I explained "no" because I had a case and didn't want to have to keep asking for continuances. It's like, who wants to go to a class reunion when you have fucked up every angle of your life and are effectively on the streets? I didn't want to show my face. So I decided to stay. The wedding wasn't going to happen until August, anyways. I had time to change my mind, if I had a change of heart.

After walking off the job of putting on another coat of paint of a failed rental property, Randy had become somewhat of a slumlord, but did dig himself out of the RV Park when I found a FSBO home with a pool on the north side of town, within his price range. He would leave notes of things for me to do while he was off selling boats and RVs. Cleaning the pool was a bitch of a chore. But in July, I was done, for the last time.

228

I was tired of the never ending string of shitty tenants, who left me with the job of cleaning up their messes. I walked across town and took the casino shuttle to Parker, AZ and started walking around. I found a food kitchen and ate a nice meal using the fake name of Davy Jones in the registry. I slept under a flagpole on a bench for two days. (Reminder- I had no money.)

One night, a truck with two male occupants asked if I wanted a Sparks. It's like a Red Bull, with alcohol content. They're great. Anyways, the driver, Shawn, who reminded me a bit of Freddie Mercury, saw me the next day and brought me a bag of newer South Pole clothes. It was very nice. He lived in an RV on his parent's property, in Bouse, AZ. Bouse was a very small town. He made a living doing home repairs and mechanical work on all sorts of vehicles. I stayed with him for a couple weeks, met his parents and they approved of me staying there. His dad didn't like having a gay son, but I did my best to explain to him that his son had a good heart and it's a shame that so many have taken advantage of his kindness.

I was not one of those looking to gain anything from him, maybe just a friend and a place to sleep. Not like Mexico where I felt something was taken from me, Shawn only wanted to give pleasure. That didn't bother me. I consider myself A-sexual. If an act doesn't spiritually take from either party and provides pleasure, I do not judge what the act may look like, from any other perspective.

We hung around each other for a couple weeks and then I went back to Havasu to stay at Mom and Randy's house while they got ready to take off for the family wedding, in Wisconsin. Shawn & I would keep a conversation going on Facebook. He came to Havasu to meet Mom once, and even met Dad and Penny, on one occasion.

As Mom and Randy packed the small trailer that attached to their Prius, like that was a normal thing, I was getting more and more excited to finally have the house to myself.

Randy had been supplementing his income by buying model helicopters and drones from China and selling them for triple the price at the weekly swap meet in the shadow of the London Bridge. It was early morning work and I hated most of it. He paid me about $50-$100 a day depending on what we sold, so that was the one redeeming factor I won't take away from him. We didn't often see eye to eye regarding the living situation, though.

Shawn was in a very compromising position. He was going in for back surgery which was going to leave him with a 60/40 chance of not being able to walk again, due to a work accident years ago, at a major retailer in Arizona. Before the operation, he wanted someone to spend some time with him, if only to watch a movie. I told him I didn't have a ride, and his van was acting up, but I told him I'd see what I could do.

This is the transcript of what ensued according to reports, my response will follow.

The Arresting Officer
J. Wilson & K. Mitchell
Serial Number
#184 & #84
Lake Havasu City P.D.
(928) 855-1171
Case number
CR-2014-1069
Charge & Class
13-1814 A1 F3
Date
08/07/14

PROBABLE CAUSE STATEMENT

"ON 08/07/14 AT APPROX. 1205 HOURS CLIFFORD GANT WAS ARRESTED AT 1770 N. McCULLOCH BLVD. (LIBRARY) FOR THEFT OF MEANS OF TRANSPORTATION AFTER HE WAS CONTACTED DURRING FOLLOW UP INVESTIGATION AND HE ADMITTED TO TAKING THE VICTIMS VEHICLE WITHOUT THEIR KNOWLEDGE OR PERMISSION. CLIFFORD ADMITTED THAT THE VEHICLE IS IMPOUNDED IN MEXICO WHERE HE DROVE THE STOLEN VEHICLE."

INCIDENT REPORT

SOMETIME BETWEEN 08-01-2014 AT APPROXIMATELY 2200 HOURS AND 08-02-2014 AT APPROXIMATELY 0730 HOURS, CLIFFORD GANT COMMITTED THEFT OF MEANS OF TRANSPORTATION AT 3389 SHIEK DRIVE AFTER HE TOOK HIS STEP-FATHERS TRUCK WITHOUT HIS PERMISSION OR KNOWLEDGE AND DEPARTED THE RESIDENCE.

ON 08-02-2014 AT APPROXIMATELY 0731 HOURS, I MADE CONTACT WITH RANDALL SHARMAN VIA TELEPHONE. THE FOLLOWING AS A SUMMARY OF SHARMANS STATEMENTS:

--HE IS RANDALL SHARMAN.
--HE RESIDES AT 3389 SHIEK DRIVE WITH TAMMY GANT (WIFE) AND STEP SON (CLIFFORD GANT)
--CLIFFORD SUFFERS FROM SEVERE MENAL DISORDERS AND HAS NOT BEEN TAKING HIS MEDICATION.
--HE AND TAMMY ARE CURRENTLY IN WISCONSIN AND WILL NOT BE IN THE LAKE HAVASU CITY AREA FOR A FEW MORE WEEEKS.

--PRIOR TO LEAVING THE LAKE HAVASU CITY AREA THEY TOLD CLIFFORD HE IS NOT ALLOWED TO DRIVE ANY OF THEIR VEHICLES WHILE THEY ARE GONE.
--THE KEYS TO THE TRUCK IN QUESTION WERE IN A NIGHT STAND INSIDE THEIR MASTER BEDROOM.
--PRIOR TO LEAVING THE LAKE HAVASU CITY AREA THEY LOCKED THEIR BEDROOM DOOR.
--DUE TO HAVING TO LEAVE THEIR PETS BEHIND AND CLIFFORDS MENTAL STATE, A FRIEND (WILLIAM HORVAT) IS STAYING AT THEIR RESIDENCE TO TEND TO THE PETS AND CLIFFORD.
--HORVAT CONTACTED RANDALL VIA TELEPHONE AND ADVISED HIM CLIFFORD TOOK OFF IN HIS DODGE TRUCK.
--AT THIS POINT HE CONTACTED THE LAKE HAVASU CITY POLICE DEPARTMENT.
--HE DOES DESIRE PROSECUTION ON CLIFFORD.
--HE HAD NOTHING FURTHER TO ADD AT THIS TIME.

AT APPROXIMATELY 0900 HOURS, I MADE CONTACT WITH WILLIAM HORVAT VIA TELEPHONE. THE FOLLOWING IS A SUMMARY OF HORVAT'S STATEMENTS:

--HE IS WILLIAM HORVAT.
--HE IS CURRENTLY RESIDING AT 3389 SHIEK DRIVE AND "BABYSITTING" RANDALL'S PETS AND CLIFFORD.
--LAST NIGHT (08-01-2014) AT APPROXIMATELY 2200 HOURS, CLIFFORD RETURNED HOME AND WENT TO HIS BEDROOM.
--THIS MORNING (08-02-2014) AT APPROXIMETALY 0730 HOURS, HE WENT OUTSIDE AND NOTICED RANDALL'S BLUE DODGE TRUCK WAS GONE AND CLIFFORD WAS ALSO GONE.
--HE IMMEDIATELY NOTIFIED RANDALL OF THE SITUATION.
--HE HAD NOTHING FURTHER TO ADD AT THIS TIME.

OFFICER ACTIONS:

--DUE TO RANDALL BEING OUT OF STATE HE WAS READ THE LAKE HAVASU CITY POLICE DEPARTMENTS STOLEN VEHICLE AFFIDAVIT VERBATIM.
 --RANDALL STATED, "YES" HE UNDERSTOOD THE AFFIDAVIT WHEN ASKED
--RANDALL WAS MAILED A VICTIMS RIGHTS FORM
--DISPATCH CONDUCTED AN RNQ CHECK FOR VEHICLES WITH RANDALL BEING THE REGISTERED OWNER DUE TO RANDALL NOT KNOWING ANY INFORMATION REGUARDING HIS TRUCK (LICENSE PLATE NUMBER AND VIN NUMBER)

--DISPATCH WAS ABLE TO LOCATE A 2002 DODGE TRUCK REGISTERED TO RANDALL
--THE VEHICLE WAS ENTERED IN NCIC AND THE NIC NUMBER IS V136914245.
--AN ATTEMPT TO LOCATE WAS SENT OUT TO ALL SURROUNDING AGENCIES IN THE LAKE HAVASU CITY AREA
--DISPATCH RECEIVED A TELETYPE STATING SAN LUIS BORDER PATROL HAD RUN THE PLATE SOMETIME THROUGHOUT THE NIGHT OF (08-01-2014) OR IN THE MORNING HOURS OF (08-02-2014)
--AT APPROXIMATELY 1000 HOURS, I MAKE CONTACT WITH AGENT TAPIA FROM THE UNITED STATES BORDER AND CUSTOMS SAN LUIS STATION.
--AGENT TAPIA ADVISED RANDALL'S VEHICLE PROCEEDED THROUGH THE BORDER CHECK AND INTO MEXICO AT APPROXIMATELY 0644 HOURS THIS MORNING (08-02-2014).
--AGENT TAPIA ADVISED THE CAMERA SYSTEM WAS ABLE TO OBTAIN A PHOTOGRAPH OF THE LICENSE PLATE.
--AGENT TAPIA WAS ALSO ABLE TO LOCATE A PHOTOGRAPH OF THE DRIVER FROM WHEN THE VEHICLE WENT THROUGH THE BORDER.
--AGENT TAPIA ADVISED A REQUEST THROGUHT THE TUCSON OFFICE WILL NEED TO SENT IN ORDER TO BE ABLE TO OBTAIN THE PHOTOGRAPH OF THE DRIVER
--AGENT TAPIA DID ADVISE THE DRIVER IS A MALE AND HE HAS HIS FINGERS IN FRONT OF HIS FACE DOING A "PEACE" SIGN.
--A REQUEST TO THE TUCSON BORDER AND CUSTOME OFFICE WILL BE SENT TO BE ABLE TO OBTAIN A PHOTOGRAPH OF THE MALE DRIVER
--THERE IS NOTHING FURTHER TO ADD AT THIS TIME
CASE STATUS: ACTIVE

THIS SUPPLEMENTAL REPORT IS IN REFERENCE TO A VEHICLE THEFT CASE TAKEN BY THIS AGENCY ON 08-02-2014
ON 08-03-2014 AT APPOXIMATELY 0800 HOURS, I MADE CONTACT WITH UNITED STATES BORDER PATROL AND CUSTOMS AGENT MARIA GARCIA. GARCIA WAS ABLE TO E-MAIL A PICTURE OF THE MALE DRIVER BELIEVED TO BE CLIFFORD GANT. THE FOLLOWING IS A DESCRIPTION OF THE MALE DRIVER:

--THE MALE SUBJECT HAS A GOATEE, WITH SEVERAL BRACELETS ON HIS LEFT WRIST.
--IT APPEARS AS IF THE MALE HAS SPIKEY HAIR.
--OFFICER DAILEY #260 RECENTLY HAD CONTACT WITH CLIFFORD GANT ON 08-01-2014.

--DURRING THE CONTACT WITH OFFICER DAILEY, GANT HAD SEVERAL BRACELETS ON HIS LEFT WRIST SIMILAR TO THE ONES HE IS WEARING IN THE PHOTOGRAPH AND "SPIKEY" HAIR.

--SERGEANT GRAY AND I VIEWED OFFICER DAILEY'S AXON VIDEO (DR #14-10879) AND WERE ABLE TO POSITIVELY IDENTIFY THE MALE DRIVER TO BE GANT

--OFFICER DAILEY #260 AND I WERE ALSO ABLE TO POSITIVELY IDENTIFY THE MALE DRIVER AS CLIFFORD GANT FROM PRIOR POLICE CONTACTS.

--THE PHOTOGRAPH WAS BOOKED INTO THE LAKE HAVASU CITY POLICE DEPARTMENT'S EVIDENCE ROOM AS EVIDENCE

--AT THE TIME OF THIS SUPPLIMENTAL REPORT, IT IS BELIEVED GANT HAS NOT YET RETURNED TO THE UNITED STATES OF AMERICA FROM MEXICO.

CASE STATUS: ACTIVE

THIS IS A SUPPLIMENTAL REPORT OF A REPORT OF VEHICLE THEFT TAKEN BY THIS AGENCY DR14-10929

ON 08-04-14 AT APPROX. 1322 HOURS RANDY SHARMAN CONTACTED THE POLICE BY PHONE AND STATED THE FOLLOWING:

--CLIFFORD CALLED HIM AND SAID HE WAS IN SAN LUIS, MEXICO*

--CLIFFORD SAID THE TRUCK WAS TAKEN BY THE SAN LUIS POLICE

--HE HAD NOTHING FURTHER

CASE STATUS: ACTIVE

*THE "CLIFFORD" REFERRED TO WAS MY FATHER, CLIFFORD

AXON EVENT

ON 08/07/14 AT APPROX. 1205 HOURS, CLIFFORD FREDERICK GANT WAS ARRESTED AT 1770 MCCULLOCH BLVD. N. FOR THEFT OF MEANS OF TRANSPORTATION AFTTER A FOLLOW UP INVESTIGATION REVEALED HE UNLAWFULLY TOOK THE VICTIM'S VEHICLE FROM THEIR RESIDENCE AND DROVE IT TO MEXICO WITHOUT THEIR KNOWLEDGE OR CONSENT.

ON 08/07/14 AT APPROX. 1150 HOURS, I CONTACED RANDY SHARMAN BY TELEPHONE AND THE FOLLOWING IS A SUMMARY OF WHAT HE TOLD ME:

--HE REPORTED HIS TRUCK STOLEN BY CLIFFORD GANT ON 08/02/14.

--CLIFFORD APPARENTLY TOOK THE TRUCK TO MEXICO AND HE HAS NOT BEEN HEARD FROM SINCE TODAY.

--HE (RANDY) JUST RECEIVED A PHONE CALL FROM CLIFFORD'S FATHER STATING THAT CLIFFORD CONTACTED HIM AND STATED HE WAS IN LAKE HAVASU AT THE LIBRARY.

I RESPONDED TO THE MOHAVE COUNTY LIBRARY AT 1770 MCCULLOCH BLVD. N. WITH OFFICER MITCHELL #84
ON ARRIVAL I OBSERVED THE FOLLOWING:

--A WHITE MALE, LATER IDENTIFIED AS CLIFFORD FREDERICK GANT (S) BY HIS ARIZONA IDENTIFICATION CARD, STANDING NEAR THE FRONT DOORS TO THE LIBRARY.
--CLIFFORD WAS WEARING A DARK COLORED BASEBALL HAT, A LIGHT BLUE BUTTON UP SHIRT, BLUE JEAN PANTS AND BLACK SHOES.
--CLIFFORD SAW ME APPROACHING HIM FROM THE SOUTH EAST CORNER OF THE BUILDING AND PROCEEDED TO WALK EAST INTO THE PARKING LOT.
--OFFICER MITCHELL CONTACTED CLIFFORD IN THE PARKING LOT.
--OFFICER MITCHELL AND CLIFFORD WALKED OVER TOWARDS A SHADED PATIO AREA AT THE FRONT OF THE LIBRARY ENTRANCE
--I CONTACTED CLIFFORD AND THE FOLLOWING IS A SUMARY OF WHAT HE TOLD ME:

--HIS NAME IS CLIFFORD GANT.
--HE USED TO LIVE AT 3389 SHIEK DRIVE BUT HE DOES NOT WANT TO GO THERE NOW.
--HIS MOM'S HUSBAND, RANDY SHARMAN, IS PROBABLY WAITING FOR HIM TO COME HOME SO HE CAN REPORT HIS TRUCK STOLEN
--HE DID TAKE RANDY'S TRUCK LAST WEEK.
--HE TOOK THE TRUCK IN THE MIDDLE OF THE NIGHT TO DRIVE TO BOUSE, AZ TO VISIT A FRIEND OF HIS.
--HE THINKS THAT HE MADE A WRONG TURN WHEN DRIVING TO BOUSE THAT NIGHT BECAUSE HE ENDED UP JUST 20 MILES AWAY FROM YUMA, AZ.
--HE DIDN'T HAVE ANY MONEY SO HE DECIDED TO JUST GO TO MEXICO FOR A COUPLE OF DAYS.
--HE DROVE THE TRUCK INTO MEIXCO AND HE ENDED UP WORKING WITH SOME LADIES AT THEIR SWAP MEET BOOTH.
--HE WAS HAVING A GOOD TIME HELPING THE LADIES SELL PRODUCTS.
--THE ENDED UP MEETING A GUY AND LETTING THE GUY DRIVE THE TRUCK.
--HE THOUGHT HE WAS DOING SOMETHING REALLY NICE BY LETTING THE GUY DRIVE THE TRUCK BECAUSE A LOT OF PEOPLE DON'T HAVE NICE THINGS DOWN THERE IN MEXICO.
--THE GUY WAS BACKING THE TRUCK UP IN A PARKING LOT AND HE HIT A PARKED CAR.
--THE OWNER OF THE CAR WANTED $300 FOR THE DAMAGE AND NEITHER ONE OF THEM HAD THE MONEY.

--SOMEHOW THE POLICE WERE CALLED.
--WHEN THE POLICE ARRIVED, THE GUY DROVE OFF IN THE TRUCK WITH HIM INSIDE.
--THERE WAS A CHASE BEFORE THE POLICE FINALLY CAUGHT THEM.
--THEY BOTH WENT TO JAIL AND THE CAR WAS IMPOUNDED BY THE MEXICAN POLICE.
--HE WAS ABLE TO HAVE HIS FRIEND (IN BOUSE) WESTERN UNION HIM MONEY TO GET OUT OF JAIL.
--HE WENT TO GET THE TRUCK FROM THE IMPOUND YARD BUT THEY WOULD NOT LET HIM HAVE THE TRUCK UNTIL HE PAID THE $300 TO THE VICTIM OF THE ACCIDENT AND HE HAD TO HAVE RANDY COME GET THE TRUCK BECAUSE HE IS THE REGISTERED OWNER.
--HE WAS JUST GOING TO COME UP WITH $2000 IN THE NEXT TWO WEEKS AND GO BACK DOWN TO MEXICO AND OFFER THEM THE MONEY TO GET THE TRUCK.
--HE ENDED UP CROSSING BACK INTO THE UNITED STATES IN SAN LUIS.
--HE WAS ABLE TO HITCH A RIDE BACK TO HAVASU FROM THERE.
--HE DID NOT GET RANDYS PERMISSION TO TAKE HIS TRUCK.
CLIFFORD WAS PLACED UNDER ARREST AND TRANSPORTED TO THE LHCPD JAIL.
CLIFFORED WAS BOOKED INTO THE LHCPD JAIL AND HELD TO SEE THE JUDGE
I CONTACTED RANDY BY TELEPHONE AND ADVISED HIM OF CLIFFORD'S ARREST AND COURT DATE.
THE VEHICLE IS STILL ENTERED INTO NCIC DUE TO ITS UNKNOWN WHEREABLOUTS.

<u>END OF INCIDENT REPORT</u>

MY TURN:

First off, I had exclusive access to using Randy's vehicles in the past. I would mostly be alone in the 4:30 AM chill of the morning, driving his loaded 2002 Dodge Ram to the swap meet to set up. Secondly, they left me no money and I had no cell phone at the time, even if after-the-fact they said there was a $100 bill on the nightstand for me. Well, if the door was locked than how was I to acquire it? The door was NOT locked, there was NO money, and my "Babysitter" watched me enter their room from his view from the living room couch, twelve feet away from the door entrance.

Months earlier, Randy had stated how Melody shouldn't have pressed charges on me for stealing her car, because that was a family matter, but yet here he was, pulling a Mitch McConnell. Secondly, if I was not to drive 'ANY' of their vehicles, why leave the keys behind at all? The tank was ¾ full and I knew that getting to Bouse that night to watch a movie and come back would do minimal damage, all for a friend in need. Randy decided to press charges the moment he knew his truck was gone, and didn't even give me a chance to make it right, or be a little more understanding of my "Mental State."

Never having driven to Shawn's residence before from Lake Havasu meant I was kind of going off of memory. There are not many intersecting highways and back streets between Havasu and anywhere. There is, however, one stoplight in the middle of nowhere, and instead of continuing easterly, I took the right and went south, and didn't stop until I saw signage declaring "20 miles to Yuma." At this point, I figured I hadn't been in Mexico since Jessica bailed me out, so why not. I had planned to get to an internet café and ask Shawn to Western Union me some gas money, so I could get back. But I wasn't going to just dip in and out. I wanted to explore a little.

Reports were correct when I found a few swap meet ladies selling clothes and made quick allegiances. I sold her some of my Hollister shirts and got some food. The reason I befriended the local, is because I didn't know the layout of the city and didn't feel like getting lost, not because 'Mexicans don't have nice things.' My new chauffeur was really just using me to run errands for himself and I was cool with that because I had little else to do, maybe I'd find a female who thought I was cute enough to fuck.

But, backing out of driveway one late afternoon he hit another vehicle, a van, and the owner wasn't too happy. There wasn't a lot of damage, just a little dent in a 20 year old minivan, but hey, he had a rightful claim. With cell phone in hand, the victim was threatening to call the cops if he didn't get paid. I told my driver to stay put and I showed the angry man Randy's insurance card, like that mattered in Mexico. The cops were there in what seemed like ninety seconds, and the driver of the Ram just floored it, with me in the passenger seat. The back streets of San Luis are not paved and there was a huge cloud of dust that followed us. The cop was only two car lengths away but this did not disturb the driver at all. He instructed me:

"Jump out when we get to my Tia's house, the cops can't come in and get us." Some kind of unspoken law down there, like, 'your home is your safe house.' If you open the door for the police, they can proceed, but they are not trained to force entry into a home. He pulled up to the gate, threw it in park and bolted. I got out of the passenger seat and touched the sky. The driver hopped the fence, as planned, and went into the back of the house. The two officers walked over and arrested me.

I told them, in Spanish, that I told the driver to stop, yet I was still taken to the San Luis Jail. The officer spoke to the judge and then shined a light in my eyes to check for drug use, of which I was clean.

They offered the following: If I came back the next day with $100 they would release the truck to me. I was then walked out of the station, with maybe 30 Pesos jingling in my pocket. I went to the nearest internet café and logged in. Telling Dad what had just happened, hoping he might have some support to offer, the green dot next to Shawn's name popped up.

I told Shawn how the night before, I tried to make it to his house and got turned around and now the truck is impounded and I need a bill to get it out. Without any further questioning, he sent $150 the next morning. I showed up to the police precinct and tossed the cash on the counter, like I slammed down Mediterranean and Baltic Avenues, at McDonalds in Waupun, boss as hell. Then, the supervisor came. The rules changed.

Not only was the impound fee $100, I needed a signed statement from the victim saying I made amends, and I would need the "titelo" or title, and registered owner, to get the car out. Well, FUCK! None of that was going to happen. The only thing I thought of, at that moment, was if I got back to Havasu, I could call upon my Facebook acquaintances to let me do some side work so I could come up with a decent bribe before Mom and Randy got back. It was the working plan.

Shawn drove down to Yuma, AZ in his newly acquired car. He was over-the-top excited about it and he reminded me of a conversation we had about a medical payout he was expecting and hoping that this particular mint condition car was still going to be available, when the time came. He told me that I had somehow prophesized that he would get both the settlement and car, within a short period of time. I don't remember anything as aggressive, but it would completely be in my character to offer positive reinforcements or affirmations.

Shawn brought me back to Lake Havasu and we ate at Golden Corral. The macaroni and cheese sucked. He dropped me off at the public library on McCulloch Boulevard, so I could use the internet. We parted with a hug and he started crying, asking, if not begging me, to stay with him to help him recover from the impending surgery, offering to pay me $1,000 a month until he got back on his feet. If I agreed, the cops would just get me at his house, I reasoned. I had to get this truck back. Into the library I went.

Getting a guest pass pin code, I logged onto Facebook and made a post saying if anyone has ANY work, I need to get quick cash or I'm going to prison again. Before I posted that message, Dad logged on with the instant message:

"If I send someone to San Luis to pick you up, will you go?" He asked.

"Dad, I'm already in Havasu at the library, could you come pick me up and take me to the tobacco shop? Some guy saw me digging for cigarette butts outside K-Mart and just gave me seven dollars."

No response.

I posted my only hope to rectify the situation. I figured I had a month until Mom and Randy got back. (It turned out to be **two** months.) I watched an Avril Lavigne music video and logged off. As I walked out the doors, thirty yards away I saw two officers approaching.

Thanks, Dad. He snitched. On his own son, to the man who is loving on his ex-wife. Real classy, Dad.

I didn't even have a chance to fix the mistake.

Randy may never have given me permission to use his truck, but he explicitly didn't tell me I *wasn't* allowed to.

Eighteen months in prison. To this day he is still driving that truck. Missing cousin Chanel's Wisconsin wedding meant that my chance to see my Aunt Patty for the last time also was forfeited. She beat stage IV breast cancer, but it spread to her brain, seasons later, and there was no fixing that. She passed away mid-way through my prison sentence. I missed the birth of my only nephew, Jax, Melissa's son, as well.

With a class 5 felony guaranteeing the state a conviction, the prosecutor in the disorderly conduct and criminal damage case immediately took their plea offer off the table and the entire case was dismissed, due to me getting sentenced to prison for 1½ years, over the family truck. I never got my day in court to see the man who falsely accused me on that busy morning intersection, thwarting Wisconsin, initiating the current criminal case of "borrowing transportation", and opening the eventuality of me meeting Kathleen Lorraine Huffer.

Where does there exist a rectifying motion for an unfortunate chain of events that is seeded in a liar's police report?

There doesn't. And even if there was, how would you quantify damages? In currency? In pain? Eye for and eye? Lie for a lie?

You decide.

PART 3: MURDER

Chapter XXI

Dear Senators: From ASH

A Harbinger

(written 11/2019)

Las Vegas, NV early 2014

As I was walking down Las Vegas Boulevard, homeless, penniless and loving it, a slightly intoxicated young man in a tie-dyed T-shirt with a red bandanna wrapped around his shoulder length hair, stumbled toward me walking in the opposite direction.

"Hey, man... Do you know where New York, New York is...? I want to play some Blackjack." Having nothing else to do, I offered to escort him to his destination. We talked during the quarter-mile walk as if we were kindred spirits. The feeling is hard to explain, but maybe, in your respective lives, you've felt it once or twice. He let me know if I wanted to play, he would spot me. At that time, I was not one to pass up any opportunity that would take me away from my cigarette "butt hunt" that had so far, impressively, lasted over two weeks. So I was pretty thrilled at my luck.

My food stamp card and the Walgreens on the strip, sufficed to keep me fed, and the casinos kept me swiping abandoned ½ full drinks and lipstick stained cigarette butts that were left hastily in glass ashtrays next to slot machines or at casino entrances. It was nice to take a breather.

We played cards for about an hour, not losing, but not winning much either. We ended up getting 86'd because I recommended Johnny Walker Reds with Marciano Cherries for the both of us, to keep the buzz going, and he ended up falling off the high-backed barstool that adorned the Blackjack table, after the third round.

On the long walk back to the opposite end of the strip where they were staying at a hotel/casino that has since shut down, James let me know that he was there with his girlfriend and buddies from Phoenix, and if I wanted, I would be welcome to come back with them and have a place to stay and maybe start a new life. He just had to clear it with his crew, who all lived in a five bedroom house in the Garfield neighborhood, near downtown Phoenix. I met his clan and although his girlfriend wasn't happy about him befriending a "homeless person" and offering their pad to a total stranger, she was outvoted. We all left, two days later.

I showed up in downtown Phoenix late at night, and was ushered into a house at 1021 E. Garfield. I can still remember the giant pyramid of assorted beer cans that adorned the entire wall of the interior's left side. There was a little tag next to it, "Beeramid: Multimedia" and the date it was constructed. "Artists," I thought, this was different from anything I had been around my whole life and it reassured me that maybe with this new group of people, I might find out something more about myself, being with them, than I had in the stringent life of military service and restaurant management that had brought me to that point in life.

On day three, never having really explored Phoenix, I decided to check out the city at night. I had never really lived on a "grid" before. You know, straight streets, city blocks, very squared off. I thought it was amazing. Beautiful, even. Maybe it's the math nerd in me... but it felt perfectly divided.

As I walked toward the buildings that had me mesmerized, I heard music. I followed it in the dark, and shortly, I came to see three people playing instruments on a front porch. I approached slowly, wearing my black leather "Monster Energy" cap, and walked up in awe of the moment, and casually dropped my last $5 bill into the open guitar case, resting three stairs up from the sidewalk.

"You don't have to do that," one of the singers told me. But to me, in that moment, I valued that experience. I was completely floored by the raw talent, discovered in the wild, in its natural habitat. So, yes, I left the bill right where it was and I was invited up. If I remember correctly, I was even offered a beer, and as I sat on the railing of the porch nearest the street, you played.

To me, it was a private concert. A message from the divine that I was on the right path and a reward for taking the leap of faith that somehow brought me literally to **_your_** doorstep. You played "Belly of the Beast" for me. The moment I needed something to believe in, teetering on the edge of "content with the life I've lived", "tired of the pain that never goes away", and "contemplating this existence and my place in it," we found each other. It was a defining moment in my life, even if you never have given it a second thought. As we parted, I wanted to stay longer, but didn't want to wear out my welcome. I just remember, as I walked down the stairs, pointing to that $5 bill and saying, "That is the moment you just got signed!"

I skipped the self-guided downtown tour that night and went straight back to Garfield. I immediately hopped online using the community laptop, and went to Facebook. I am a Taylor Swift fan boy, so I did a little research to find her record label and president.

"If my Tay is represented by this guy, he has got to know what talent is and sounds like." I was thinking.

"Jimmy Harnen, Republic Nashville." I aspiringly pressed the "Send Friend Request" tab, and hoped for the best. Two days later, I received the notification that Jimmy had indeed gotten, and to my amazement ACCEPTED, my friend request. He had 2,000 friends at that time and for a man that powerful to include me into his circle, meant a lot. Still does. In the following days, I would keep a keen eye on my Facebook Instant Messenger, hoping to see that little green dot next to Mr. Harnen's name where I could fire off a quick message to him live and in real-time. I finally got my chance.

Now, since my son died in Dec. 2006, I have tried to get a song I wrote some attention. But I knew that that wasn't the time. You guys had put something truly unique together, and deserved, in my eye, to be seen and heard. Green dot. I sprung to action.

"Mr. Harnen, I just moved to Phoenix and the talent down here is disgusting. If I find someone worthwhile, how do I get them in front of you or any of your people? I will not waste your time." The 'Jimmy Harnen is typing' message came up and my heart started pounding. Quick and to the point, as I would expect nothing less from a man in his position, "Send me the website of a band you think is special." I posted the link.

You guys played a free show that weekend and I invited the whole Garfield house. I remember being a little nervous about how they would like it, not to say that your music isn't good, but their tastes may have been tainted. They all showed up, all seven of them, and they loved it. They were right up front watching and periodically looked back at me with a smile or a thumbs-up, as if to say, "Thanks for not letting us miss this!" I felt proud. After the show, I went up to your lead singer, Jesse Teer, and shook his hand. I told him that I talked to the president of Republic Nashville about the band, and hoped it would amount to something. As my friends left, I remember sticking with you guys as you were packing up the amps and whatnot.

Jessie, you asked me, "Why would you do something like that for us?" And I was grateful to be recognized for my attempt to promote, and if I didn't say it then, I will say it now, "If we all started looking out for each other's best interest, instead of our own vain attempts at shameless self-promotion, there would always be someone in a position to offer you a hand up, if needed, instead of the negative forces associated with trying to climb any metaphorical ladder, where mathematically, someone has to fall, or be pulled down, to make room for those rising."

Months later, I was back in Lake Havasu City and saw a commercial: a concert from the American Idol winner, Phillip Phillips, at Chase Field. Opening for them, brandished on my television screen, was <u>The Senators</u> logo. Was it true? Was it coincidence? Did my actions have any part in that? I don't know, I don't need to know. But when I saw that, I was so proud of you guys. I was so excited for you. If you all get to where you deserve to be, then my dream for you will have been fulfilled. And I can get a certain amount of solace from that.

So, here I am, years later, at the Arizona State Hospital. A forensic mental hospital for those the courts have deemed "GEI", or "Guilty, Except Insane." I received a life sentence under the Psychiatric Securities Review Board, which means for the rest of my life there is a governing body to oversee my actions and treatment. My tenure at this facility will be close to ten years or so, where I will be conditionally released, once deemed 'stable.' This was my lawyers doing, as at my first court appearance I wanted to plead guilty, but apparently in Arizona, you have to fight a murder charge, no matter what. Please consider carefully what I am about to ask you.

What would it take for The Senators to put on a set here at the Arizona State Hospital? We have a decent sized gymnasium, where we have 'Music Studio' three times a week with pianos and guitars, and there are many good musicians here. There are 100 patients that are housed here, and never before has something like this been attempted. I really don't want to 'sell' you on the idea. You either see the opportunity, or you don't. But nonetheless, I want to throw a couple reasons out there for it.

1. Johnny Cash @ San Quentin Prison (Historic? YES! Epic? Undeniably.)
2. It's press and precedent. How awesome do you think it would be for a bunch of societal castaways to get a top-notch performance, possibly paving the way for future events, maybe once a month, where live music gets to be brought into our lives? And new startups could get a captive audience? Everyone here has at least one MP3 player and music is the only constant that I have seen here that touches everyone's lives, as it does in society as a whole. I can see the headline now: "The Senators to play for State Hospital."
3. I really don't want to sensationalize what I think would be a great messaging opportunity, from many different angles, and I also don't want you to feel like you owe me something. Because you don't. I am not calling in a favor, or seeking a return on my $5 investment, shit, I still feel like I am indebted to you! All I can say for certain is it would help a lot of people cope, even if it was never to happen again. But with the potential to turn into something bigger, know that YOU ... THE SENATORS... were the catalyst all those years ago, for

the unique path that inspired me to look beyond my own self-interest and give credit to a deserving voice, and you could renew that spirit, by being the trailblazers of this scenario.

I remember you, Jessie, telling me weeks after we met, that you were going through a particularly hard time the night we met, and when I showed up out of nowhere it 'picked you up' somehow. Is it wrong, or a character flaw of me to ask the band to consider 'paying it forward'? Knowing many of the patients here, what a feeling it would be to see any successful professionals deliver that kind of inspiration to a collective that society has efficiently swept under the rug. I can't say enough about how much it would mean to us.

4. If you need compensation, I will find a way to cover it, I get only $30 a week for my work here, and after saving up all 2019 was finally able to buy my family quality Christmas presents, for the first time ever. (I was never in a position to repay them for all they have done for me, so I made it a point to not let that cycle continue. I spent $800 on them this year.) I have roughly $300 cash left and I know it's not a lot, but at the minimum it should cover most of your expenses, I imagine.

In the years since we parted ways, I've seen some prison time, for 'stealing' my step-fathers truck while he was out of town. I ended up in Tucson for my parole following an 18-month prison sentence. Unfortunately, my parole officer was on vacation when my request to parole out of Phoenix was made. My family was living in Phoenix at the time and my Mom had found me a decent halfway house, but once I was released and the paperwork said 'Report to the Tucson Parole Office', I did. At that time, my parole officer pretty much said, "Too bad, now you are stuck with me." Three months and a violation later, my number was 'killed.' This meant I was free.

I had met a woman on Craigslist for a hookup six weeks earlier, and we ended up complimenting each other to the point of her eventually asking me to stay with her while I planned this adventure I dubbed, "FromTucsonToTennessee."

It was to be my journey of tribulation, to record myself walking the 1,600 miles or so, talking to a Go-Pro about life, love, politics, or anything that came to mind that I thought would gain me some notoriety, so when I got to my destination, I would have developed an online following, that could have influenced any record label to help me record the song I wrote, and distribute it, free of charge, to Neo-Natal Centers at Hospitals across the United States. (My son was 14 weeks premature and only lived for eight days, before suffering a massive brain hemorrhage that he would never have recovered from, so we made the decision to take him off of life support.)

Kathleen listened to my story, believed me, believed IN me, and wanted to be a part of it. I was 30, she was 52.

Kathleen was ill. She told me that she had a disease that destroyed her body from within. She was constantly medicated with liquid morphine, hydrocodone, and never was without her blue marijuana vaporizer, and still, couldn't sleep through the night.

She would come back from her monthly hospital visits and they would have had her cut open to remove the remnants of the disease. The way she helped me understand it was that it was a disease that tunnels through her body, grows hair, and becomes infected, and then they have to cut her open to remove the 'debris,' for lack of a better term. She would employ me to insert ribbon gauze into the open wound that, most recently, was below her right breast, two inches wide. She would remove the soiled gauze the next day and I would fill it again with new. No matter how careful or gentle I was, to see her wince as I cared for her, just crushed me, but who else was there to do it?

I was with her for a couple months when she came to me. She conveyed to me that she didn't think she was going to make it out of the hospital 'this time', and she had taken the action of adding me to her will, stating that if something were to happen to her, that I would be allowed to stay at her residence for a period of time, while I got my footing, or set off on my adventure. She didn't want her sister throwing me out, as they didn't like me from the get-go, and at one point told her, "It's him or the family." She chose me, to their dismay. To see someone you care for, be in constant pain, where you can look them in the eye and see that they are hurting, not just physically, but spiritually and emotionally, it wears on you. And one day...well...

Kathleen had just gotten back from Beyond Bread where her and her sister had had lunch. I was in the shower in the master bedroom. The night before, we had dyed our hair, highlights of green. It was fun. As I opened the shower door to grab a towel, she opened the bathroom door, took one step inside, and slammed down a black box-cutter on the vanity and walked out. I looked at it as if the rest of my life was hanging in the balance.

She had never displayed erratic behavior in the past and this was well out of character. With the talk of life and death that we shared the night before while mixing the emerald 'Splat' hair dye coming back to me, the idea became more solidified in my mind. This was a distress call. She wanted out. Suicide might just land you in hell, and asking someone verbally to take your life, is suicide-by-proxy and that might be just as bad. Slamming down a weapon like that, left just enough leeway, should the afterlife exist, to clear her of

245

any wrongdoing. Sending me a clear message like that was telling me that if I didn't take action, she would never ask me again. But if I did, she would be relieved of the turmoil she suffered daily with no respite in sight. I got dressed, and went to the living room.

"Do you want to be tied up?" I asked her, never having previously experimented in that area, with the thinking that if I was to act, natural instinctive defensive measures may cause undue pain and suffering.

"Yes." she said.

I then went to the computer room, "What kind of music do you want?" She was a Nickelback and Warren Zevon junkie, so when I got no reply I offered, "Megadeth?" Which we had NEVER come close to listening to before, but in asking that, I was really asking her the fate-sealing question, "Do you want to die?" She replied in the affirmative. I knew what I had to do, I knew the ramifications of what would happen when I did, and not once did I think what I was doing was wrong in any way. I left the music off. What was the point?

We went into the bedroom and she undressed, I grabbed the nylon rope from the closet as she lied face down on the bed. I tied her hands behind her back, then brought her ankles up and tied them to her wrists. The gravity of what was to take place had set in. She had no way to defend herself. I told her I was going to the kitchen for some water, stood over the kitchen sink, closed my eyes and took a breath. This was it. I knelt near the entrance to the room and asked God to let me know if there was any way for this not to happen. Silence.

Hammer in hand, I entered the room, straddled her body and completed the task at hand. It was quick, she did not suffer. I thought to myself that I'll be killed in prison within the next two years for sure, and if the afterlife exists, I'll have a question or two for the big man before he sends me away. And if the afterlife doesn't exist, well, then everything is for nothing. But I have to believe that, at the very least, she would be waiting for me, knowing, caring, no explanation necessary, because she's been watching every step I've taken since that day.

There have been news stories that the ASH forensic patients are the worst of the worst, the criminally insane. Well, I have been here for 2½ years and I beg to differ. Yes, there are some people here you wouldn't want to have a dinner party with or let them babysit your kids, but we are all not the scum of society that we are made out to be. If you remember me, you know me of a man of honor, integrity, appreciation and respect. My story is just one example of how we are all just one decision or moment away from having our lives turned completely upside down. No one is immune. There are a lot of things that are wrong with this hospital, but now is not the place or time for me to try to change policies or regulations. After all, the administrators are the 'highly skilled', 'moderately paid' Doctors, and we are the, well, 'mental patients.' Can't have the proverbial mental patients running the asylums, now can we? Maybe the future will usher in the winds of change, but I don't plan on forcing the idea.

Even if you decide it to be worth it, there may be some barriers yet to overcome. As I said, nothing like this, to my knowledge, has been attempted here before. But if we can work to make something like this a reality, it would give me great footing to make other lasting improvements to the establishment and the life I will have here for the next 7-10 or beyond. And I can't put a price on that.

Sincerely, Clifford Gant

Legit.
Biggest.
Fan.
Ever.

XXII

The Official Reports

There were about 20 officials involved with the crime scene at 3060 Richey Blvd in Tucson, Arizona on 08/30/2016 and I will not hide the identities of those involved with the following narratives. With the 100's of pages associated with this report and investigation, I have decided to relay as much as I can that holds pertinent information that will allow the reader to see the scene from the law's point of view. My truths have been laid out in the previous chapters. However, any glaring errors I will address immediately by adding "{" and "}" indicators. I will also use "..." to indicate that there was more written but not important to the investigation. The following are not *my* words, but transcribed directly from police reports.

OFFICIAL REPORT
Case Number: 1608300515

--HALL, IAN (100756)
On 08/30/2016 at approximately 1935 hours I was dispatched to the listed location; the caller stated she had found her sister, Kathleen Huffer, tied up and deceased on her bed. While I was in route dispatch advised the caller, Kelly Spivack, had stated the victim's vehicle was missing and that the victim had a friend named "Cliff" who was not there. Dispatch later advised Coplink showed a Clifford Gant as having been associated with Kathleen. Ofc. Hecht advised over the radio that he had been flagged down by Kelly and was out at the location.

When I arrived Ofc. Hecht, Ofc. Guinee, and myself entered the residence to make sure no one, but the victim was in the residence. Inside there was a small dog and a cat, both alive and appeared to be well taken care of. Other than the animals and the body there was no one in the residence. In the doorway to the southeast bedroom there was a piece of paper on the floor with a handwritten note on it. In the bedroom there was a body face down on the bed, with its hands tied behind its back with and unknown material, a blanket covering its head and various objects placed on or around the body.

I touched the body with a gloved hand, it was cold to the touch all over and I could feel rigor mortis had set in everywhere I touched. The blanket covering the head appeared to be stuck to it with dried blood. I pulled back the blanket enough to see the victim's eyes appeared to be covered with some kind of sleeping mask and there was what appeared to be a hold in the skull at least two inches in diameter. There was a hammer lying partially on top of the blanket that covered the head.

The house was messy but did not appear to have been rifled through. Ofc. Guinee stayed at the front door and Ofc. Hecht took responsibility for the Crime Scene Log... This concludes my involvement at this time. NFI

--HANSON, FRANK (40737)
On 8/30/16 at approximately 2000 hours Sgt. Borboa called me at home and asked me to respond to the incident location to assist in a homicide investigation. Upon arrival I met with other detectives from the Homicide Unit, Aggravated Assault Unit and Night Detectives. I then attended an investigative briefing.
Synopsis:

Officers responded to a death call. Upon arrival they met with Kelly and Mark Spivack. Kelly had been trying to contact her sister, Kathleen Huffer, for an extended amount of time. Kelly told officers that Huffer was not answering her phone and no one in the family could get in contact with her. Kelly has a key to Huffer's house and she and Mark drove to the incident location. Upon their arrival they found that Huffer's vehicle was missing and the lock on the front gate was positioned on the outside of the fence. Kelly unlocked the gate and went inside the yard. Kelly and Mark knocked on the door to the house but got no answer. Kelly opened the door to the house with her key and both Mark and Kelly entered the house. Kelly found Huffer deceased on the bed in the master bedroom. Huffer's hands and feet were bound and she had head trauma. Kelly and Mark left the house and called 911. Ofc Hall, Ofc Brown and Ofc Guinee entered the house. Officers found the victim deceased on the bed in the master bedroom. The victim was bound and various items were placed on her body. The victim had trauma to her head and a hammer was located on the bed near her head. A triangular shaped piece of concrete, a glass pipe, and a container were located on the front steps along with a business card placed in the door frame. A subject by the name of Cliff had been living with and hanging out at Huffer's house. Cliff was identified through past calls to police at the house as Clifford Gant 12/10/1984.

...

I noted a Queen of Spades playing card tacked or stuck to the west side of the residence. At the front door I noted that there was a large triangular piece of concrete sitting on the steps in front of the main entry door to the residence. Also on the steps was a glass smoking pipe {weed pipe I dropped} and a plastic container of what appeared to be marijuana or tobacco {funny how an officer can't tell the difference between marijuana and tobacco}. There was a business card stuck on the west side of the door frame approximately six feet off the ground. The card had the Jack of Spades printed on it and "Invoke Greatness", "FromTucsonToTennessee" on the card. The air conditioning was on in the house. Upon entry I could smell the odor of decomposition emanating from the residence. The residence was a 3 bedroom, two bathroom residence. The main entrance led into the living room. The house was unkempt. The kitchen appeared as if it had not been cleaned in several months. There was a computer in one of the bedrooms on the west side of the house along with a white board with notes written in dry erase marker. The other bedroom had men's shoes and clothing strewn on the floor along with other belongings. In the living room I noted that there was a DVD under the television and polished rocks on top of the DVD.

Just outside the master bedroom door was a credit card with Kathleen Huffer's name on it and a note with what appeared to be a spade and a note that had "Barack...Mission Complete", "Behold!!! The uprooting of modern speech", "AZBC #666184" and "Tennessee Titans" and '322' under a skull and crossbones in one corner.

... {Evidence collected from bedroom listed 48 items of interest}

All of the items were marked with placards and photographed prior to collection. The items were collected and placed into bags. Det Cheek transported the property to EPIC. I entered the items of evidence into the Beast evidence management system. Det Cheek packaged the items and signed the seals. Det Szelewski signed the labels. The evidence was placed into the evidence binds and secured. Det Cheek obtained photographs of Clifford Gant crossing the United States/Mexico border at San Luis, AZ on 8/29/16 at 0336 hours. {Kathleen's truer time of death was closer to 08/28/16 before sundown at around 1630 hours, if it matters.}
...obtained warrant for 1st Degree Murder and Auto Theft...

On 9/1/16 Det Cheek contacted me and advised me that Clifford Gant had been arrested at the san Ysidro port of entry just south of San Diego, California. On the evening of 9/1/16 Det Cheek and I drove to the San Ysidro Port of Entry where we interviewed Clifford Gant. Gant was sleeping in a holding cell when we arrived. Gant woke up and agreed to speak with us. Gant seemed to be expecting us.

The interview with Gant was video and audio recorded and took place in an interview room at the port of entry in the CBP area. The following is a short summary of the interview. For exact quotes and details refer to the taped statement.

Interview with Clifford Gant:
Gant made the following statement post Miranda.
Gant has been staying with his Fiancée Kathleen at 3060 N Richey since approximately February 2016.
Gant tied Kathleen up in a sexual manner and they played around a little bit.
Gant put a blanket over Kathleen's head and then told her that he was going to get a drink of water.
Gant went and picked up a hammer instead of water.
Kathleen was face down on the bed and Gant straddled her buttocks.
Gant then hit Kathleen in the head with the hammer approximately 18 to 20 times.
Gant took a break after the first 8 to 10 strikes. {I gave the spirit time to de-attach itself from the dying body}
Kathleen's breath left her body and Gant knew she was dead at this point. {When I took my 'break' there was heavy labored breathing, the breath of life had not yet been extinguished}
Gant hit Kathleen in the head 10 to 12 more times until blood splatter hit Gant in the face.
Gant said that he filmed the murder on his laptop.
After the murder Gant looked into the camera with blood on his face.
Gant transferred the video to a thumbdrive that is in the vehicle in Mexico.
Gant then placed items on Kathleen.
Gant said that after he was finished he was disgusted by the reason for the crime.
Gant blamed this incident on the government saying that if they would have listened to him this would not have happened.
Gant went on to say that he had been in the Navy and had reported that people were selling laptops with secrets to the enemy. Gant was discharged from the Navy.

Gant was wearing a 'Twilight shirt' {Breaking Dawn} that is now in Kathleen's car.

Gant described where he had parked the vehicle in Mexico

Gant told us that he had sold the laptop to a taxi driver

Kathleen's car ran out of gas in Mexico.

Gants calling card was the whole scene. Gant wanted the reaction of the person who walked up to the scene to be "Holy Fuck!"

Gant left his business card in the door frame of Kathleen's house.

Gant held the hammer in his right hand.

The Jack of Spades represents Gant.

The Queen of Spades represents a person named Amber Dawn Haya/Beatty/Ramos who lives in Radcliffe, KY and then 8 years later came as Kathleen Loman. {who willingly took on the persona of the Ace of Spades}

The King of Spades represents Gant's brother Matthew Gant. {Never. Matthew has always been the King of Hearts}

Clifford Gant said to look at the picture of those playing cards and you can see the facial recognition of all three people.

Gant advised that he did not kill Kathleen, gravity killed her. {as in the gravity of the situation}

Gant also advised that no one made him do it and that he did not need to explain anything.

Gant talked about conspiracy theories that he had from his time in the navy and also when he was working as a computer analyst.

Gant had dyed green stripes in his hair. Gant also had his pants tucked into his socks when we contacted him. Gant was eager to talk to us and tell his story.

...placed into holding and then transferred to San Diego County Jail...

On 9/16/16 Det Cheek, CSS Brauer and I went to the DPS Impound lot in Yuma, Arizona to process Huffer's Vehicle.

...{It was recovered in Mexico stripped down, even the battery was stolen. All of my defending evidence, gone.}

This ends my involvement in this case at this point.

--SZELEWSKI (49282)

...

At 2136 hours, Det. Pike #35801 conducted an interview with the victim's mother Gale Cassidy. I sat in on this interview. Gale provided the following information:

-Kathleen Huffer is her biological daughter

-Kathleen suffered a mental breakdown in 2009 possibly caused by several sources of stress (father's death, house repairs, going to college, and stress at work)

-Kathleen is no longer employed at the University of Arizona and receives social security as well as long term disability

-Kathleen's sister Kelly delivers anxiety and depression medication to Kathleen twice a week

-Gale talks to her daughter six days a week via telephone and spends time with her once a week, usually on Thursdays

-Gale last knew her daughter to be alive on Saturday when she spent time with her other sister Eileen Rioux

-Gale did not speak with Kathleen on Sunday and Monday but thought nothing of it

-Gale called Kathleen three times without success on Tuesday. At which point she became concerned because they have never gone 48 hours in between talking to one another

-Gale sent a message to her grandson Daniel Rioux inquiring about Kathleen, but Daniel had not heard from her

-Gale sent a text message to Eileen, but received no response

-Gale contacted Kelly and asked her to check on Kathleen

-Kelly informed Gale Kathleen's vehicle was gone and the exterior gate was locked

-Gale asked Kelly to let herself into the residence at which point Kelly discovered the body

-Gale could not provide a description of Kathleen's vehicle

...

-Kathleen's current roommate is Cliff LNU. She described their relationship as being friends with benefits. Cliff is described as Caucasian 5'7" average build and 32 years of age. Clifford also suffers from mental illness possibly schizophrenia. Cliff has no money and does not contribute to paying bills {except my food stamp $200 monthly allotment}

-She last saw Cliff 10 days ago

-Gale believes Cliff killed his pet chicken {as a spirit pet for a previous murder on the Richey corner, I mean, I entombed it in a 'Rothschild's' Cigar box, so that had to mean something, right?}

-A prior police report was filed because Kathleen tapped Cliff on the head {it was domestic violence against me and the cop did nothing but ask if I wanted to be mentally evaluated}

-Cliff has never been physical with Kathleen nor has she heard him say anything bad toward her

-Gale does not know Kathleen to have ever traveled to Mexico {just the beginning of what they didn't know about Kathleen}

-Cliff does not drive but has been incarcerated in Mexico for unlawfully using vehicles and taking them to Mexico

-Gale does not know Kathleen to have problems with anybody
-Kathleen was known to have a couple of sexual hook-ups of whom she met online
-Kathleen has a medical marijuana card and only obtains her marijuana from dispensaries
...

At 2306 hours Det Pike then interviewed Eileen Elizabeth Loman Rioux and I sat in on this interview. Eileen provided the following information:
-On Saturday 8/27/16 Eileen picked up Kathleen from her residence at 1030 hours to go to yoga class. Cliff Gant was at the residence as well as Kathleen's vehicle.
-After yoga class, they went to lunch at Beyond Bread. Eileen dropped Kathleen off at her residence at 1330 hours and hasn't seen her since
-Cliff was forced by his father to have sex with his sister when he was 10 or 12 years old {I reverse engineered sex at the age of 6 with Melody being 5, I had a '1' and she had a '0', they obviously were meant to go together. Punishment ensued, therapy ensued. But this was the most libelous statement of this book. I don't think that Kathleen said this maliciously, maybe trying to get some family sympathy in my favor, we will never know}
-Cliff lives with Kathleen because she does not like to live alone. They are not romantic together. {really?}
...
-Her son Daniel Rioux lived with Kathleen and Cliff over the summer
-Daniel and Cliff Bought a Chicken, but the chicken died. Cliff made a shrine for the chicken
...
-Kathleen would hook up with people online for sex
...
-Kathleen used methamphetamine in the 1990s
-Her sister Kelly drives Kathleen to counseling once a week
-Daniel and Cliff are friends, but haven't seen each other in two weeks
...
...telephonic warrant was issued and evidence was collected...
This ends my involvement in this case at this point.

--MILLER, TRINA L (52897)
...
...items of interest collected {with my commentary}

Item 34E: a white and green rope type of material located around the decedent's left ankle area
{A white and green shamrock charmed hemp ankle bracelet I made for her}

Item 34I: An apparent incense container with possible burned incense on it located on the decedent's left buttock area.
{I had one cone of "jasmine" incense that I used to release the spirit to the heavens at the highest point of the body, which was her buttock}

Item 34k: A red colored apparent beverage can stay tab located on the decedent's left buttock area
{A Monster tab with 'claw' logo representing the Hebrew digits "666"}

Item 34L: An apparent "Icicles hand blown glass massager"... located on the decedent's buttocks
{A glass dildo vertically adorned the crack of her posterior, she was a sexual woman and displaying that was homage to her sexual nature}

Item 34M: A bag containing various items located on or near the decedent's right hand
{A mesh gift bag containing items that I believed would help in transition to the next world}

Item 34N: A "Redbox" case located on the posterior side of the decedent's torso

Item 34O: A DVD of "The Man Who Knew Infinity" located on the posterior side of the decedent's torso
{THE MAN WHO KNEW INFINITY... It wasn't 'Friday After Next' or a 'Saw' series DVD. That item and placement was important to me at the time}
...
This ends my involvement in this case at this point.

--CHEEK, JOSH (41238)

...

Officer Hall indicated there were strange notes left inside the residence, as well as objects placed on the victim's body. He said there was a Freemason symbol hand drawn on the victim's foot.

...

Sergeant Borboa then gave assignments. He assigned me as the case detective, and assigned Detective Hanson 40737 as the secondary investigator. He assigned detective Dowling and Detective Lockwood with obtaining a telephonic search warrant for the residence.

I met with Kelly Spivack, who was waiting in the street near a vehicle with other family members. I introduced myself to her and asked her if she would talk to me. She said she would, and I walked her to Detective Hanson's vehicle to conduct a recorded interview with her at approximately 2126 hours. Below is a brief synopsis of the interview. See the transcript for exact wording and for further details. She relayed the following information to us:

...

She has met Cliff 5 times, doesn't like him, and has tried to stay away from him.

She described him as being very strange.

He would speak in a very anxious way, and Kathleen told Kelly he was bipolar.

...

Kelly doesn't believe Cliff used Kathleen's Impala and he did not have permission to drive it without her.

She doesn't believe that Cliff was receiving any mental health treatment.

He would talk incessantly about politics, and how the government alienated people.

Kathleen took a large quantity of medications for a number of ailments including hidradenitis, which involved outbreaks of boils.

...

Her sister had frontal lobe issues and had a hard time remembering things.

She had a traumatic work incident 12 years ago that Kelly described as a nervous breakdown as a result of emotional trauma.

...

Kathleen previously told Kelly Cliff had been in prison, and that he had some kind of physical altercation while in the military.

Cliff reportedly did something violent to be kicked out of the military.

Kathleen never said she was scared or threatened by Cliff and never mentioned physical abuse.

...

There was a strange triangular brick on the front step, face up, with a glass pipe next to it.

Kelly moved the rock, and her husband moved the pipe.

...

Kathleen's bedroom door was closed and there was some kind of note posted on the door.

...

Kelly went to the far side (east side) of the bed, and tried to move the blanket that was over the female's head.

Kelly said it didn't look like Kathleen.

Kelly walked out of the house and called 911.

The inside of the house normally looks like it does now.

Her sister took pain medications, as well as medications for anxiety, allergies, and Alzheimer's disease (for her frontal lobe issues).

Kelly claimed Cliff previously told her that he was not Kathleen's boyfriend, and Kelly doubts they had a sexual relationship.

Cliff told Kelly and Kathleen's mother he didn't want a sexual relationship with Kathleen and claimed he had no sexual feelings toward Kathleen. {'mature for younger'... yup... not interested in fucking}

Cliff's family lives in Lake Havasu, and he was previously arrested there.

He had a weird vision that he was going to walk across America.

...

He had a good relationship with her 17-year-old nephew Daniel Chance Rioux.

...

Kelly didn't approve of this relationship.

Daniel was close to Kathleen, and was at the house often.

...

She doesn't believe that Cliff had a phone

At one point, they had a chicken at the residence they were taking care of.

Cliff would often talk about how the presidential candidates were fighting with each other, and talked about how we were perceived by other countries.

He posted something on Facebook that led to Kelly unfriending her sister Kathleen.

Cliff said something to the effect of, "I'm a Jew, not from Israel, but a different kind of Jew."

It sounded racist to Kelly.

...

Kelly's mother told her that Kathleen would go onto Craigslist to hook up with people.

She used her name and cell phone number.

This is how Kelly suspects Kathleen met Cliff.

Kathleen responded to ads on Craigslist, but Kelly doesn't think that she placed ads herself for others to respond to. {again, 'Mature for Younger'}

After the interview, we walked her back to the rest of her family. We then met with Mark Spivack, Kelly's husband. I asked him if we could talk to him, and he said we could. We conducted a recorded interview with him in Detective Hanson's vehicle. Below is a brief synopsis of the interview. See the recording and the transcript for exact wording and for further details. He relayed the following information to us:

His wife Kelly manages her sister Kathleen's medicines, delivering 3-4 days of medicine at a time.

Kathleen has had a lot of problems with drug use her whole life.

...

She also has pain issues.

...

There was a male staying with Kathleen whose name started with a "C."

Mark has never met him, but Danny hung out with him a lot.

Mark believes this male had his own mental problems.

The male has confronted Kelly a couple times at the house, asking why she doesn't like him.

He posted comments on Facebook that mark described as being sort of anti-Semitic.

Kathleen reportedly 'liked' the post with these comments, which caused problems between her and Kelly.

...

(they came to the house)

...

Kathleen's bedroom door was closed, and there was what appeared to be a note and a credit card somehow attached to it.

When they opened the door, it appeared both fell to the ground.

...

Mark saw the leg and the buttocks of an individual lying on the bed.

The person was partially covered in a bed sheet.

There was 'Satanic Stuff" wrapped around the body and the body was bound up.

...

He thought there was a note on the body that he initially thought might be a suicide note.

He moved the sheets and touched her leg and buttocks.

He doesn't believe the body was clothed.

It didn't seem real to him.

...

The police reportedly came out recently and had contact with Cliff after he called 911.

The issue involved an incident when Kathleen touched Cliff on the shoulder {struck me on the head} and Cliff told her "don't ever touch me again"

The police came out but no one was arrested. {funny, domestic calls 99.9% result in one party going to jail for the night, not this one though}

Kathleen used Craigslist to meet up with people.

After the interview I walked Mark back to the vehicle in the street where the rest of the family was waiting.

(Serving the search warrant)

...There was a queen of spades card nailed to the west side of the exterior portion of the house. There was a large paver in the shape of a triangle placed on the top step leading up to the open door. There were several smaller rocks off to the right of the triangular rock. There was a glass pipe on a plastic container next to the smaller rocks. Over the door frame outside the residence there was a business card that said "Invoke Greatness," "FromTucsonToTennessee," "www.whosonfire.com," and "COMMING SOON." Also on the card was a jack of spades, along with a flower and a dragonfly. The name Clifford Gant was on the back of the card.

Aside from the open door, all doors and windows to the residence were secure.

...the note had an image of a spade, and had "Barack...Mission Complete," and "Tennessee Titans" with inverted exclamation marks before it and regular exclamation marks after it (in the style of Spanish writing) written on it among other things. ... There was what appeared to be a Freemasonry symbol drawn on the decedent's right heel with the "G" in the middle. A pen was stuck between the decedent's right toes.

There was a stuffed animal posed face-up between the decedent's knees. There was a note placed on the upper back portion of the decedent's thighs, just below the buttocks. On the note, the word "Infidel" was written, among other things. There was a picture frame with a photo of a young male {Daniel} in it resting against the decedent's right buttocks. On the glass of the frame, the words Jesus

Christ had been written in toothpaste. The eyes of the young male had been whited out with toothpaste. {let me be clear, death=Jesus Christ=infidel} {although they were not attached together, they were most definitely connected.} ... There was a glass sex toy on the decedent's buttocks. On the decedent's left buttock there was a pop top from an aluminum can {monster}, a polished stone, and a metal tin with what appeared to be ashes from incense on it. {I took postmortem spiritual care of this person, it wasn't just a careless wonton Murder.}

...

I conducted a recorded interview with Daniel at approximately 1129 hrs on 083116. It should be noted that, during the interview, Daniel was visibly trembling, and he appeared to be terrified. Below is a brief synopsis of the interview. See the recording and the transcript for exact wording and for further details. He relayed the following information to me:

The male who had been staying with Kathleen was named Clifford Gant.

Daniel gave me what he described as Gant's "business card."

It appeared to be the same card that was placed over the front door of the residence.

Gant wanted to go on a political journey and to bring awareness to certain issues.

He planned to walk from Tucson to Tennessee and to make video blogs that he would post on social media while he walked.

...

Daniel described Gant as having a "God complex."

Gant believes that he is a higher power and can be everyone at once. He thought the TV was talking to him.

He liked to dip his cigarettes in PCP and smoke them. {In Laveen, AZ I did this once}

He believed that he would be scooped up by the CIA and would make the USA Great again

He claimed he had been discharged from the Navy after he discovered a conspiracy in which Naval Members were selling classified laptops.

Gant believed he could help Donald Trump.

He thought Taylor Swift was his destined lover, and would pick him up anytime.

Gant believed the jack of spades represented the god of war. And he felt a connection to it for this   reason. {King of Spades is god of war, Jack is Peace}

He identified with the number 666, claiming his social security number started with it. {birth certificate}

He talked about the antichrist when talking about reforming the government.

He would talk about world order, and believed that there was a conspiracy of elites controlling the world.

Rosarito is the only place Daniel would know Gant to go.

...

Kathleen described him as having periods of hyperactivity, followed by periods of sleeping.

Gant was supposed to take antipsychotic medications, but didn't. {Kathleen said they made me sexually unresponsive}

Kathleen told Daniel that Clifford had schizophrenia.

Kathleen was worried that Clifford would hurt himself due to his reckless behavior.

Gant had a stillborn son, and Kathleen's theory was that when that happened, Gant went crazy.

Gant is from Wisconsin, but has also spent time in Lake Havasu.

He went to prison for stealing his step-fathers car.

Kathleen met Cliff through Craigslist for a "Sexual hook-up"

Gant claimed to be a communications specialist in the US Navy, and said he spent time near the Strait of Gibraltar.

...

Gant felt he was associated with the CIA.

...

Gant wanted to travel to Nashville, Tennessee to become a country music sensation. {hardly}

Daniel believes Gant liked Tennessee simply because it started with the letter "T."

WhosOnFire is a domain name on GoDaddy that Gant created.

Gant took issues with Hillary Clinton and other public figures.

...

He carried around a partially burned jack of spades card, but Daniel never saw any cards posted around the house.

...

After the interview, I met with Sergeant Borboa and informed him of what I had learned. I reviewed images of Kathleen's vehicle crossing the Mexican border. One crossing occurred on 081316 at approximately 0406 hrs. at the Nogales port of entry. There was a photo of a male driving the vehicle and a female front passenger. The vehicle re-entered the United States at approximately 0749hrs on 081316, and officials with Customs and Border Patrol conducted a secondary inspection of the vehicle. The occupants were identified as Clifford Gant and Kathleen Huffer. The vehicle also crossed the border into Mexico at the San Luis Port of Entry on 082916 at approximately 0336 hrs. The same male who drove the vehicle on 081316 was driving the vehicle on 082916.

...
On 090116 We conducted a recorded interview with Gant at approximately 0451 hrs at Customs and Border Patrol Custody in San Ysidro, California. {I was read my rights and answered that I understood.}

He relayed the following information to us:

He has no phone.

He was last staying at 3060 N. Richey with Kathleen Loman. {she preferred her maiden name}

He described Kathleen as his fiancée and said he had been staying with her since February. (since he was released from prison)

I asked him to talk about what happened and he said, "We already know that I'm guilty" and referred to his calling card.

I asked him if he was referring to his business card.

He said he was referring to the capstone on the front doorstep.

I told him I wanted to hear his side of what happened, and he asked me if I had seen the video.

He said, "the whole thing was recorded."

He initially crossed into the U.S. using his brother's name (Mitchell) but claimed the official at the border told him to "have a good day Clifford."

He then went back into Mexico to retrieve the USB Chip with "everything on it."

He said he told officials at the border to contact the consulate in Mexico to locate the car with the evidence inside.

He asked if I saw the house, and if I had been to "the scene of the crime."

He also asked if I was there "with the remains."

I asked if he was talking about Kathleen's body, and he said yes.

He stood up to show us what happened, and described the layout of the house.

He said Kathleen "knew what was about to go down."

Gant said he was trying to find a way to bypass it.

He said he and Kathleen had never explored the "BDSM kind of stuff."

He said he tied her up in a sexual manner, saying he tied her feet separate from her hands.

He demonstrated with his hands behind his back.

He said they had a little playing around, but said he was "so pissed."

He said it felt like a waste of something that was "beautiful and pure."

He said he got the blanket, then told her that he was going to get some water and winked at me in an exaggerated matter.

He said he went to get the hammer instead.

He said the hammer was moving him, and he was getting closer and closer.

He said he approached her, "Mjolnir in hand"
It should be noted that Mjolnir is the name of Thor's hammer from marvel comics.
He "kneeled over her ass"
He gave her shoulder a little squeeze, "Like I love you" {as if to say}
Then he motioned with his right hand bringing something down.
The said the first "tink" elicited a soft noise from Kathleen, like she didn't know what was happening.
He guessed there were 18-20 strikes but he stopped after 8-9 to take a break {misreported}
He said he had the video camera in the laptop positioned facing the bed.
He said that the video of the incident was in the car down in Mexico and said someone would "have a snuff film down there."
He said what he did wasn't malicious, and said it wasn't because he wanted the $300 in her checking   account.
After the 8 strikes, he said he heard her making noises, and he demonstrated by making labored breathing sounds.
He said this was not the first scenario of death he's had to deal with.
He described a 20-30 second break, then got back up and "went to town" wanting it to be done.
At one point there was blood splatter that came up on his face, and he decided that he was done.
He placed the hammer down ...
He went to the master bathroom and saw the blood splatter on his face.
Then he looked at the camera and said "happy now guy's?" before closing it up. {I said "Are you happy now?" talking to Kathleen, who I imagined would be viewing spiritually somehow.}
He sold the laptop to a taxi driver down in Playas to get gas money.
He said this wasn't a "murder and flee" situation.
The USB Sticks in the car have the video of the murder.
The said this wasn't a crime of passion and said he didn't even want to call it a crime
I asked him about the items he placed on Kathleen afterward.
He said he wrote "Infidel" on her.
He said he had a "call to Allah" on one of his YouTube videos.
He said he put an ace of spades on the door.
He said there could be a facial recognition comparison between the ace of spades and Kathleen.
He referred to his family as a deck of cards.
He said after he finished his task, he was disgusted as to why he had to do it in the first place.
I asked what the reason was, and he said it would be my job to figure it out.

He said by killing Kathleen, he sent someone to the other side to see the kind of power Gant can yield.

He asked us to give him the needle as fast as we could because he wanted to go over with the one he   loves that he sent over first.

He said he had fulfilled the hit he didn't want to do and said it was too late to turn back now.

He said he wouldn't turn back now if he could.

He was wearing a black Twilight shirt during the murder, and the shirt should have blood splatter on it.

The shirt should be in the vehicle.

He parked the car on Playas in Mexico near an "M" arch near the Torro bullfighting ring, near the compass rose. {The same arch Amber, her Mom, aunt, and I were photographed under in '08}

The car keys were on the dashboard of the vehicle.

He described the car as a 2400 Lb. shrine to the Santa Muerte and said it was a sight to see as he currently left it.

He said that anyone who saw it parked with the windows down and tried to take something would probably think twice.

He said there were a bunch of lanyards inside, and described it as an eclectic piece of art.

The laptop is a purple HP laptop.

The picture in the frame on the bed was Kathleen's nephew Daniel.

He wrote "Jesus Christ" on the photo in toothpaste.

He burned a cone of incense on a piece of metal he described as an upside down Monopoly hat.

He described a murder that occurred on the same block as their house possibly 3 weeks to a month prior as well as a memorial at a nearby telephone pole.

He thinks items from the bag came from the shrine.

He described the bag as being a silver mesh material, and said there was a plastic room key, a pepper shaker, and other items inside he placed in Kathleen's hand.

These were things to assist Kathleen when she got to where she was going.

He thinks he may have left the Rothschild cigar box back at the shrine.

It should be noted that there was a homicide on 062816 just north of 3060 Richey ...unrelated to this investigation.

I asked if he drew anything on Kathleen and initially he couldn't remember.

He said it would have been prudent of him to draw a pentagram on her.

I told him it appeared to be a symbol.

He asked if I brought any photos to show him.

We described the symbol as similar to an upside down 'V' or 2 'V's' on top of each other.

264

He said this was a Freemasons symbol, and he remembered drawing it on her.

He said he wrote "mission complete Obama" on the note on Kathleen's bedroom door.

He mentioned that the ace of spades was placed "in every dead Viet Cong gook's mouth."

He then went back to the symbol he drew on Kathleen and said the G was for Gant.

I asked him about his business card outside the house, and he said that it was the Invoke Greatness card.

I asked if this was what he was referring to when he referred to leaving his calling card.

He said "The whole scene" was the calling card.

He said the Earth was slated for complete annihilation, but now that he has one in the bag he is fine with it.

He said he is never going to die, and he and Katy Perry will be young forever. {LMAO}

He is ambidextrous but prefers his right hand and he used his right hand to hit Kathleen with the hammer.

He said he put a stuffed animal in Kathleen's "crackish" area.

He doesn't remember for sure but thinks it's possible he got the stuffed animal from the shrine from the previous homicide up the street.

He asked me if the autopsy had been completed yet.

I asked why he left instead of staying at the house.

He asked me if I would want to be in an area that was full of so much emotion of disgust for the land that I was in.

He clarified that the back of Kathleen's head was already concave when her body "expired itself of breath" and it wasn't like she was struggling to survive.

I asked him about his statement that this wasn't his first scenario of death he's had to deal with, and asked if there were others before Kathleen.

He said there were other spirits, but not other people.

He also said he tried to kill a dog he had in Mexico because he was told he had to make a sacrifice.

He talked about pictures from the scene that may have been released.

I asked him if he took pictures, and he said, "I can neither confirm nor deny," and smiled.

He did the same thing when I asked if pictures of the scene had been posted.

He went back to the dog in Mexico and said he tried to kill it by choking it.

This didn't work so he got a kitchen knife and tried to stab it, but he couldn't do that either.

He then picked up a stone tablet from a bird feeder and dropped it on the dog. {Slammed is more accurate}

The dog popped up like a robot, walked over to a gate, and disappeared.

Then days later, 2 people dressed in sackcloth arrived and told Gant he couldn't kill the dog because the dog was Jesus.

Gant said that gravity was more responsible for the death of Kathleen than he was, and said he didn't see what he did as killing or murdering anything because energy cannot be added or subtracted only transferred.

Detective Hanson asked Gant about the queen of spades card posted outside the trailer.

He said the Queen of Spades is Amber Dawn Haya.

Her married name was Beatty at one point, but later remarried and changed to Ramos.

She lived in Radcliffe, KY.

Gant said he once told her the thought he was the Second Coming.

She was once a girlfriend of his, but she tried to distract him from trying to free the world.

He said the other half of her came around in the form of Kathleen Loman.

There are 4 or 5 thumb drives in the car, one of which is a Lexar purple 32 gig with Facebook posts on it.

He wanted to leave on 080816 from "A" Mountain and walk to Tennessee.

He talked about going to the scene where he left Amber, who he said is still sitting on a silver dollar belonging to Gant.

He told her that she could go back to be with her family in Kansas {during Dec. 08}

He drove her across the border, met her mother at the Jack In the Box and dropped her off.

At the end of the interview he told me to enjoy the investigation.

He also talked about wanting to terminate the "savior of the world" as soon as possible

He said he was referring to himself.

{the interview terminated and officer Cheek informed them that I had made suicidal statements}

CONTINUING

On 090616, Jessica Gant called the Tucson police station asking to speak to a detective about her case. I conducted a recorded phone interview with her at approx. 1012 hrs. Below is a brief synopsis of the interview. See the recording and the transcript for exact wording and for further details. She relayed the following information to me:

She is Clifford's sister, but she knew Kathleen also.

She described Clifford as being schizophrenic, and very ill.

She just saw two of them a couple weeks ago.

Kathleen would text Jessica and would keep track of Clifford's "cycles."

Most recently, Jessica said that it was obvious that Clifford was not in the right state of mind.

He was in the US Navy but was discharged because he thought there was treason going on.

She believes that is where his mental health issues began.

He was married and divorced, and had a child who only lived 9 days and then died.

This was approximately 8 years ago, and Clifford's state of mind got really bad after that

His most recent diagnosis was schizophrenia with psychotic features.

He had a romantic relationship with Kathleen and talked about marrying her.

The relationship started as a Craigslist hookup when Clifford got out of jail.

Clifford has been arrested numerous times and has fled to Mexico numerous times.

Clifford would say that he was going to the white house, or that the Mayor {a Rothschild} was coming to pick him up.

He would often post his GPS coordinates with the understanding that the government was tracking him.

She believes that he would go to Mexico because once he was out of the country, the US Government couldn't track him.

For that reason, she said Mexico was his escape when he couldn't handle things.

He recently told her that she was going to walk from Tucson to El Paso. She took Clifford to Wal-Mart to go shopping for the trip approximately 3-4 weeks ago.

Clifford was in a scattered state of mind.

Among the supplies Jessica bought for Clifford, she bought chap stick for Kathleen.

When it was time for Clifford to give the chap stick to Kathleen, he had a hard time remembering what they had bought for her.

Clifford was very emotional and nervous giving Kathleen the chap stick.

Recently, Kathleen told Jessica that she (Kathleen) was either the angel that saved Clifford's life or the devil.

Clifford believes that he is God or Allah.

He had a fixation with playing cards for years.

He would see people's faces in the face cards and would say that different people represented certain playing cards.

It seemed to her that he wanted to talk about this very much, but he refrained from talking about it because he didn't want it to seem like he was crazy.

Clifford was with Kathleen pretty much since he got out of prison.

They picked him up from the prison in Tucson and checked him into a halfway house.

Clifford said that he couldn't stay there after a short period of time.

She believes he found it too restricting. {multiple people had propositioned me to take their court mandated Urinalysis tests for cash, and in saying no, they ostracized me}

He moved in with Kathleen soon after leaving the halfway house.

She only found out about his arrest after seeing news stories online.

Kathleen had experience with mental illness because of her father and ex-husband, who both reportedly committed suicide.

She was seeing a counselor.

She seemed normal and stable to Jessica.

Jessica said it would take a very special person to love her brother Clifford for how he was.

Kathleen told Jessica the nephew Daniel had Asperger's Syndrome, and Jessica described it as "cute" the way Clifford and Daniel interacted with each other. {Seemed like a normal kid to me}

She described them as being "close" to one another.

Kathleen told Jessica a service called CMS would come out regularly to check on Clifford, evaluate him, and adjust his prescription medications. {um, LIE}

Clifford didn't like to take his medications. {also, at Kathleen's bequest}

Recently, his pharmacist called the doctor because the pharmacist was alarmed at the dosage of Clifford's prescribed medications, but the doctor confirmed the dosage was correct. {I am unaware of this scenario}

Clifford either fell asleep or blacked out driving Kathleen's previous car, and he crashed and totaled it.

Officers reportedly said that they couldn't believe he walked away from an accident so severe.

She has never met or seen Daniel.

She has never been inside Kathleen's bedroom.

Clifford kept his belongings in the office in the house but there is no bed in there.

She gave me the contact information for Clifford's mother Tammy, and said Tammy wanted to speak to me as well.

Jessica expressed an interest in going to a memorial service for Kathleen.

268

She asked me to give her phone number to Kathleen's family.
Jessica said she had text and Facebook communications from Clifford and from Kathleen that she wanted to send me, so I sent her my email address.

--end of interview—

CONTINUING

On 090616 at approximately 1531 hrs, I called Tammy Gant and conducted a recorded phone interview with her. Below is a brief synopsis of the interview. See the recording and the transcript for exact wording and for further details. She relayed the following information to me:

She also uses the name Tammy Sharman
She said that Clifford hadn't been acting right, and she believed him to be a danger to himself.
In Lake Havasu police found Clifford at approximately 0300 hrs in the lake, in the water. {illegal?}
She briefly described a disturbing incident involving Clifford's sisters, but then changed the subject. {The Volkswagen/Vivid incident}
She said at one point he was in the back of her truck, dancing, as she drove down the highway, so she took him to the hospital to commit him. When he got out, he took one of the family's trucks and drove it to Mexico. {big timeline error, there}
He was arrested for this and went to prison.
She begged the prosecutor to get Clifford help.
Clifford's mental illness would get worse every time he got out of prison.
He was diagnosed as being bi-polar with psychotic features.
Clifford believes he is God and Satan at the same time.
At one point he was seeing a woman named Annette Wooldridge.
She got pregnant, but wasn't sure if the baby was Clifford's and he became very angry at her.
He sent her threatening messages that really scared her.
I asked her again about the incident involving his sisters.
She was upset and crying throughout the entire phone conversation, but became more upset when discussing this case.
His sister picked him up from being in prison in Mexico a few years ago.
They took him to stay with them in their house in Phoenix.
Clifford was acting very strangely, and talking about the FBI, the government, and things he needed to do.

He told them he was Jesus {which I adamantly deny} and told them this would be their last supper.

They went to sleep and woke up smelling smoke.

Clifford had put a bottle of wine on the stove and turned the stove on.

He had placed strange objects all over the room, including a number of items he stuffed into a guitar.

He laid out lines of toilet paper on the floor in patterns.

He wasn't in the house anywhere.

Police later found him walking barefoot on the freeway and arrested him.

In prison in Mexico, he always had playing cards, and he would talk about how each member of the family was represented in different suits. {not once did I have a deck of playing cards in Mexico prison}

He previously worked for a private company in Mexico near San Diego, working on computers.

One day, his boss called his sister and asked her to come pick Clifford up.

Clifford was acting strange, but she didn't know any further specifics.

He would tell people a spirit entered him at a very specific date and time he always remembered.

He lost a baby approximately 8 or 9 years ago, and this was very hard on him.

When his boss fired him {I quit} Clifford lived with a girl from Idaho {Kansas} for a period of time in Mexico.

She reportedly came back to the U.S. but Clifford stayed behind.

He stole a vehicle in Mexico, but the vehicle broke down and the owner caught up with him.

The owner severely beat him and put him in the hospital, and he was subsequently sent to prison in Mexico for over a year. {one hit, no hospital, and 6 months in prison, you all know this story}

Kathleen and Clifford thought they were soul mates.

She last talked to Kathleen on 8/19 or 8/20.

Kathleen told her they were making adjustments to Clifford's medications.

She didn't know who he was receiving treatment through.

In the Navy, Clifford was a cryptologist, and he worked on secret codes.

She described him as being very intelligent, and said he received grants in High School at a young age. {a Navy bonus we all know I never got to actualize}

After he entered the Navy, something wasn't right.

His wife at the time said something was wrong with him, and wrote a letter to the Navy {my Captain} telling them he shouldn't be there.

Clifford heard voices and had a constant high pitched tune in his head for about 7 years.

Tammy said, "His eyes can change, I've seen it."
She has gone before a judge, written letters and called police trying to get him help but nothing has worked.
He once had a driver's license on which he signed his name as "SATAN."
He thought he had 666 on his birth certificate. {666184 on the original, in red ink}
Recently, he talked about wanting to walk to Tennessee to get a song published about his baby that died.
He was working on dominating the world.
He posted comments saying that he should be president.
His relationship with Kathleen was a romantic relationship.
She was a wonderful woman for all that she had accomplished.
Her father and ex-husband both had bi-polar disorder, and they both committed suicide.
Kathleen's mother said that there was an incident one day at work when suddenly Kathleen lost the ability to recognize anyone around her.
Shortly after that, she stopped being able to make decisions for herself.
Kathleen and Clifford both mentioned getting married, and Kathleen told Tammy that Kathleen's family adored Clifford. {Especially with all the anti-Semitic comments and all}
She said Clifford got along really well with Kathleen's nephew.
Clifford constantly wrote in notebooks.
...
At one point, Kathleen and Clifford had a chicken on their property, but Clifford recently told Tammy the   mayor had the chicken. {The mayor's namesake cigar box, at least}
He has tried to kill himself on 2 prior occasions once in prison {suicide watch, never an attempt} and once in Tammy's house {large dosage of the sleeping pill DOXE-PIN, was never going to kill me}.
She emphasized that he is very intelligent, and can carry on about world events.
He has talked himself out of past attempts to have him committed.

--End of Interview--
--PIKE, KELLY G. (35801)
...
After the briefing concluded Sergeant Borboa asked that I make contact with the victim's mother Gale Cassidy and conduct a digitally recorded interview with her. Detective Szelewski #49282 and I conducted the interview in my unmarked vehicle. Cassidy's interview is summarized/paraphrased below.

-Kathleen Huffer is one of her three daughters. Kelly Spivack and Eileen Loman-Rioux are her other daughters.

-Kathleen suffered a nervous/mental breakdown in 2009 (father's death, pressures at work; U of A Fine Arts Dept., and attending school) and has been unemployed (long-term disability) since that time.

-Kathleen suffers from Neuropathy, Anxiety, Depression and Hydranitits, sees a variety of Doctors, and takes numerous medications.

-Kelly helps oversee Kathleen's medication regimen/management.

-Kathleen also smokes marijuana on a regular basis (holds a medical marijuana card).

...

-Kathleen met Cliff on-line possibly through craigslist, they were friends with benefits

-Cliff is mentally ill and might suffer from Schizophrenia

-Kathleen's monthly income is $2000 per month (SSI Disability and LTD) but Cliff does not financially contribute to the household.

-Kathleen has a couple of men whom she sees strictly for sex. One of those men is a guy named Casey.

...

-She is not aware of any physical violence between Kathleen and Cliff.

-Cliff is not supposed to drive Kathleen's car (doesn't have driver's license) {yes, I did}

-Cliff has supposedly spent time in a jail in Mexico.

---end of interview—

CONTINUED

After completing our interview with Mrs. Cassidy Det Szelewski and I made contact with Eileen Loman-Rioux and conducted a digitally recorded interview with her inside my vehicle. Loman-Rioux' interview is summarized/paraphrased below.

...

-While they were out Kathleen told her that she recently found out that Cliff was sexually abused around the age of ten (10) or twelve (12)

-Cliff's dad allegedly made him have sex with his sister. {libel and slander}

-Cliff has been living on and off for a couple months, but to her knowledge they are not romantically involved.

-Kathleen had a habit of taking in strays (men) and a history of hooking up with younger men who she meets online.

...

-Kathleen suffers from Anxiety and has trouble sleeping (sleeps 2 hours at a time).

...

-Cliff was like a mentor/friend to Daniel (related on same level, teaching him how to drive, discussing life issues).
-Daniel has not seen Cliff in about two weeks
...
---end of interview---

Chapter XXIII
The Séance

"Are you happy now?" I asked the laptop camera that was positioned on the dresser facing her final moments, with a tinge of irritation. In the moment, I was thinking that in the immediate time following her last breath she would be able to watch the digital recording live as it was being recorded. I maneuvered the mouse pad and stopped the recording. A vertical splatter of light pink blood had, seconds earlier, just hit my face and that signaled the end of the act. After stopping the recording and closing the laptop face, I went to the bathroom. Surprisingly, I didn't find it hard to look at my reflection. After all, this was better. I imagine had I killed someone out of anger or rage I might have been some kind of nervous, or felt some kind of immediate regret, but I didn't.

I turned on the faucet and splashed the warm water on my face. Watching the blood-tinged water disappear down the drain, I was thinking about what was going to happen next. I had cellphone video that I was sure would come up at trial that would show us, the night before, naked in bed and talking about death and her thoughts about what comes next. It was almost like a pre-death interview. The big takeaway for me was that as much as her bubbly personality was concerned, she loved life, but was physically and emotionally spent. I put my hand on her thigh. It was already cold.

A mantra she developed weeks before her transition was, "It is the job of the Ace of Spades (the image to which I assigned her), to do whatever it takes to see that the Jack of Spades has the best start," and it would take a truly messed up soul to see how this was what she meant, but I was there, you weren't. I imagined a long drawn out trial, akin to the Jodi Arias trial. I guess only when *both* people are sexually appealing does the drama of the high court come begging for a narrative. I resolved that everything would play out in just the way it was meant to and I got to the task of tending to the body.

I went to the home office and printed off six full page copies of the Ace of Spades, and took two. One, I placed on the body, and the other I wrote on and closed in the door to seal the room, once I was finished. Before that, I adorned the body with items my understanding thought would help her in the immediate afterlife. It was an artistic collective of meaning, which only I understood in the heat of the moment.

I know what you may be thinking, and you would be only half right. There **was** drug use involved in my time with Kathleen. But her marijuana had very little effect on me. Synthetic marijuana, also known as 'Spice,' was my drug of choice. It was available at certain smoke shops as an under-the-table type transaction. Usually purchased in $5 baggies, all you would need is one or two small hits to get the desired effect. Namely, a 20-30 minute 'trip' usually leading to a zombie-like state, or sleep. I would have visions, all subliminal, and once I awoke, would be back to business as usual. Marijuana would leave me sleepy and hungry, and would drag on for sometimes hours. I could usually spend $5 and have the contents of the small bag of spice last the better part of a week. Kathleen would supervise me, when I wasn't smoking outside, at a bus stop or at one of the many public parks in Tucson.

Up until my time in Tucson, I never was a big drug buyer. If the moment presented the opportunity to smoke some free weed, I was usually ok with it, given the situation. In my mid-to-late 20s, I would smoke spice with my brother, Mitchell, when he was around. He was almost constantly high. When I was working for Randy at the swap meet selling helicopters, the first $10 of my earnings for the weekend would go for a black bag of unlabeled spice. That would last the full week, back then. When I was in Phoenix, with the artist collective on Garfield, I tried cocaine for the first time, and deemed it too expensive for the rush. Closer to the end of my time there, I tried methamphetamine for the first time.

I had many preconceived notions as to what 'speed' did or the 'high' one might expect to receive. Nothing prepared me for what it really felt like, though. I took two hits, with a stranger that didn't like to smoke alone. I felt ten pounds lighter and like I was a being of light. It is hard to describe. I remembered Kevin in Mexico, and most of the characters that I would see passing me in downtown Tijuana. I resolved to not get hooked. It was just experimentation.

In July 2016, Tucson came down hard to eradicate the spice epidemic. In a span of three days, you couldn't find a single seller of my drug of choice. Look, you may say that I was a spice-head, and that is your right. But to have gone through what I had been through, namely losing a child and the 2008 Mexico incident, if smoking some Chinese chemicals spritzed on some marshmallow plant kept me from jumping in front of a bus, then so be it.

The 2016 Presidential Election was in 3½ months and I should have been half way to Nashville by then. There was a certain amount of depression creeping in about not having succeeded in my fund-raising campaign. I was feeling more and more isolated. I had nowhere to go but to stay with Kathleen, and just let the time pass.

July ended and August peeked its head out. I was getting restless. One night, out of the blue, I asked her if she wanted to go to Mexico. We left and came back before the sun came up. She was very uncomfortable down there. But in the middle of the night at the Pemex gas station, I asked the gas attendant if he had any "crystal" and gave him a $10 American bill. He told me to wait as he got on his bike and took off. Kathleen and I waited and he came back and took me to the bathroom light. He held up a good sized amount of clear green "GO", as Kathleen called it. I honestly thought I was getting ripped off and that he was giving me a baggie of cupcake sugar. This was the first time that I had ever purchased methamphetamine. I thanked him and we made it to the border. I took the cellophane off the Marlboro pack and wrapped the green crystal baggie in it. Real quick like, I Easter-egged it.

"Citizenship?" The brown-shirt asked.

"American." And I handed him both of our ID's.

"How long have you owned this car?" He asked. We didn't know. Kathleen and I didn't really recognize time, we had a routine. So we both simultaneously answered with different answers. He politely asked us to proceed to the secondary inspection.

Going into the building while they inspected the car, which I wasn't worried about, Kathleen was doing the pee dance. He let her go to the bathroom. I looked at the array of clocks above the officer's head and in the center of the array was a digital clock labeled "Zulu" reading '2359.' I told the officer I hadn't seen Zulu time since I was in the Navy sending off "ZCZC" messages in the Mediterranean. He smiled.

"Ok, you are good to go." One officer said and we departed.

Stopping at a casino on our way back, I pulled in for a free soda. The $10 I spent on the drugs was the last money Kathleen had on her, but I didn't know that. I really wanted to play one dollar of video poker. I was almost irritated that I couldn't play a hand. We sat in the morning sun outside the small casino and I struck up a Spanish conversation with a woman leaving. I could sense Kathleen's irritation and ended the conversation. We were once again on the road.

We pulled up to her house in silence. She was happy to be home, and went to take a nap, as we had been up all night. I went to the bathroom to retrieve my package. It looked like a Christmas tree. Then I went to find a light bulb, an idea inspired by Guymas. I carefully broke off the metal part of the unit and wrapped some duct tape around the sharp edges, then retrieved a straw from the kitchen.

I then went to the bathroom and sprinkled some of the green crystals into the hollowed out bulb. Here goes nothing.

I saw, quickly, how that could be addicting, like, badly addicting. But with spice gone, and weed unfulfilling, I needed an escape. So the cops had cleaned up the spice problem, hooray! But that just forced me and others to find their fix somewhere else. And for me that was not a good thing. I took off on the bike.

Usually, my rounds consisted of going from bus stop to bus stop to raid the garbage cans for Monster Tabs, for my collection, and Coca-Cola bottle caps, to enter the codes online, anything to pass the time. I would be on the lookout for cigarette butts in gas station ashtrays, if I didn't have tobacco. But I would always have rolling papers, though.

The drugs ran out within a few days, as I would invite random strangers to the house to smoke with me. I would let them use the computer while I sat on the floor and we would pass the bulb. If Kathleen was mad, she never said anything. I almost wished she would have. I wonder what her diaries would report.

Kathleen gave me her debit card one morning, a week later, and asked me to get some Redbox movies for the night. I did. She said she would be gone for a few hours and we could watch them when she got back, if I wanted. I returned from the Circle K down the street and went to bed. I woke up from the nap and she was still gone. I went into the shower, content with another day of routine. As I opened the shower door to grab a towel, she opened the half-closed door, took two steps into the bathroom and slammed down the black box cutter on the vanity and walked out.

I was stone cold sober. You know the rest.

I closed the bedroom door for the last time and sealed it by closing the Ace of Spades in the door jamb to remind me not to go back in. I had retrieved her debit and credit card. I immediately went to the Circle K ATM on the corner and withdrew $300. Back at the house, I started packing. There was a pile of Halloween things I was supposed to have taken to the Goodwill that was a mere four minute walk from the house, that I never made the effort to do, yet. There was a plastic skull, a skeleton hand, and an 18" long, black, cardboard coffin. It seemed   pertinent. I put the black box cutter in it, and took the items to the car.

I took some clothes, the laptop, a green marijuana holder with four pre-rolls in it and debated on taking the dog and cat, but resolved that they would be discovered in a couple days' time. I dropped some items on my way out of the house, but wasn't looking back. Look, if I wanted to disappear, I could have. The title to her car was visible in the office, and I had connections in Mexico. This was not the point. The point was to have three or four days to enjoy the last little bit of freedom I could experience before what was probably going to be the rest of my life. I wanted to go over the evidence and have it all ready to hand over to the authorities, upon my surrender. I went to Wal-Mart.

I bought a U of A T-shirt, the college she was employed with for many years, and a female watch with a similar print as the blanket that was currently covering her head and upper torso. To me, it tied her spirit to me. At the car I took off the "Twilight: Breaking Dawn" shirt given to me by Shawn, and used it as a cover for the passenger seat and put on the U of A shirt. In the early hours of Monday, August 29th, I made it to Yuma, AZ and crossed into Mexico. I should have kept going west to San Diego, but thought it would be safer in Mexico. I was wrong.

Shortly after crossing, I noticed a lighted inspection station with nowhere to retreat. I broke upon interrogation, and my Spanish was bad. I told one of the rifle holding guards that I was going to Playas de Tijuana to write poems on the beach for my girlfriend that just passed away. Not a good way to start an interrogation.

They asked me to pop the trunk and get out of the car. I had no choice. They took me to the back of the vehicle and came back with a pre-roll in its "Bloom" packaging, and the green medicinal marijuana container holding a "Northern Lights" variety. They told me I could go to prison for that amount of marijuana, and I was almost like, bring it on. I knew any prison sentence wouldn't last long once the United States found out I was there.

The Sergeant asked me if I had any more, to which I   replied, yes. I didn't see if they had already looked in the laptop case and didn't know if he was testing my honesty. I retrieved the three remaining pre-rolls from the laptop bag and put them on the closed trunk. I had only $80 cash on me and they tried to shake me down. They wanted $60. I explained to them that if I did that I wouldn't have enough money to get to Playas and back. The Sergeant seemed like he was content with letting me go, after he asked me if I was an addict. To which I responded no, I just use it to write songs and poetry.

I told him that in the states it is legal. I then went into a diatribe about how much time I have spent in Mexico and how I'm not going to lie to him and say that the little bit of weed they originally discovered was all of it. I told him that, in Mexico, my word still meant something to me. He surprisingly understood my point. One of the uniformed underlings took me to the driver's side door and told me to give him $60, quickly. I have a feeling that he wasn't going to share with the Sergeant. Fuck, whatever. I still had the $150 prepaid Visa card. I gave him the cash and he allowed me to get back into the car.

278

The Sergeant came around and handed me one of the confiscated pre-rolled joints. I thought that was nice of him. He told me to be careful and sent me on my way.

I found out quickly that the prepaid Visa was only for use in the United States. How could I have overlooked that fine print? That info would have changed a lot of things. The way things went down, I spent that night on the beaches of Tijuana, laid out a blanket with the Halloween items and lit a candle.

I brought the laptop and recorded me having a conversation with myself, addressed to Kathleen. I was hoping that this was special to her. It was a solemn moment for me. That night, no one was out. I was almost looking to go to a bar and find a girl, but that wasn't happening, not on a Monday night. It was a ghost town. The next day, I tried to figure out what I was going to do. I was literally out of gas. Like, really stuck. I came to the conclusion that I would have to sell the laptop to get cash for the drive back. I copied the murder video to a USB flash drive and went to a couple waiting cab drivers to ask if they would be interested in the laptop. I sold it soon thereafter. At 9:00 PM, with cash in hand I went to the OXXO and bought a couple beers and some cigarettes. I had about $40 cash left and was going to cross at the San Ysidro port and use up the $150 Visa card to get back to Tucson. Then the shittiest thing happened.

It was sunrise, and I was waiting on the beach for vehicle traffic to pick up, around where the car was resting. I had walked to the Pemex gas station about 300 yards from the car, the night before, but the attendant said that he didn't have a gas can for me to use. So I walked back and asked the cabbies, who didn't have one, either. So I was relegated to waiting for a miracle gas can from the breakfast crowd.

I made my way down to the beach and with the car just out of eyesight, I took in the morning light. Taking all into account, it was a three minute walkabout. I turned to walk back to the car, when police trucks showed up, on the sand. They were picking up random people on the beach. Good thing I wasn't doing anything wrong, right? HA. No.

The cop came running at me, and grabbed me and took me to the truck. I tried to explain to him that I was just leaving, and my car was unlocked with the keys on the dashboard. He didn't care. I asked him what I did, and he said, "You know what you did." They handcuffed me to another person and led us to the bed of the truck.

I was placed in a urine puddled holding tank with 20 other people not knowing what was going on. Once I hit Tijuana, after the bribe incident, I made a quick buy of some speed. Spice isn't really a thing in Tijuana and I wouldn't know how to ask for it anyways. The speed was definitely low quality, not like the Christmas tree I had gotten, weeks earlier. I was booked into jail on the 30ᵗʰ, and was released on the 31ˢᵗ. But they didn't just release me, they DEPORTED me!

They drove me, again handcuffed to a random person, to the border, and pushed me into the line going back to the United States. When I got to the checkpoint, I was asked my name and date of birth, to which I said August 6ᵗʰ 1992, and name of Mitchell Gant. I was then asked to be fingerprinted. I was reluctant but had no choice.

For sure, I thought, there was a warrant for me and, now, I have ZERO evidence of what had transpired less than 72 hours before.

"Ok, Clifford," the customs agent said, "you are good to go." I was wearing pants that were ripped up to my thighs, an alteration that I had managed while being jailed. Dumbfounded, I found myself on American Soil. I went to the same Jack in the Box that I had left Amber and her mom at, over seven years earlier. What was I going to do? Why was I free? I had nothing. I had to get back to that car. I waited until nightfall and tried my shot at getting back into Mexico.

In 2008, the pedestrian crossing was a mere turnstile gate. Anyone could go in. By 2016, Mexico had rerouted the pedestrian traffic to go through a checkpoint. There were now two lines. One line was for the Mexican nationals and another for everyone else. I had no identification and tried my shot at going through the Mexican side of the crossing. My ripped up, frayed pants drew too much attention, and the Mexican authorities didn't even redirect me to the other line, they just deported me, again. This time, I was in a different area of border security. This time, I wasn't so lucky crossing back.

My fingerprints came up with a warrant. I was arrested and moved into the Customs area for criminals, I guess. I was getting belligerent with the staff, with the very real concern that the rest of my life hung in the balance of them finding that car. They didn't care, and finally decided to move me to an isolated cell.

I was woken up, hours later, by the door opening, and two Tucson police officers took me into an interrogation room. I was tired and coming down from some really weak speed and only remember opening up to them in a really bizarre way. I didn't want to talk. In prison, I have watched enough crime stories and everyone knows you ask for a lawyer, and keep your mouth shut. Thing was, the scene in Tucson was meant to leave no doubt that I was the guilty party. I wanted to mount a proper defense though, and now I had nothing. So, I had nothing to lose. One of the officers took off his badge neck chain and I took that as a move to let me know it was ok to talk. I've seen plenty of liars trying to deny, deny, deny. It never works.

I said what I said during the interrogation, knowing that I was never going to get a trial. Not caring at that point, it almost seemed that I wanted to make it even more difficult for me. I really was operating under the assumption that I was going to get the death penalty, and I was ok with that. I didn't want to get off, or get off easy. I really just wanted to be dead. There was a lot of bad acting. A lot of statements made that had no basis in fact or reality, so I figured that this was the only shot I was going to get to make any sense of the situation.

I brought up the 2008 incident. I brought up the cards. I brought up Kathleen's part in this drama. Having this interrogation being the basis of the state's case was unfortunate, because I was not in my right mind. There was no 'fooling around,' or sexual undertones in the commission of the offense. Why I said that, I can only surmise, now, would be that it would lead to a quickening of the end of my time here on earth. Which at that time, I was welcoming.

Kathleen was the only person that believed I was something special. Not that I *wanted* to be in the spotlight, but that I was cast into this role by divine right. Along with a series of unexplainable events, she was the culmination, or capstone, of my existence.

Once they had gotten their pressing questions answered, I was brought back into my isolation cell and given a rather large breakfast burrito. Please sir, can I have some more?

I was then transferred to the San Diego jail. I think I was there for about three weeks before the extradition was finalized. I almost got into a jam when Kelly, Kathleen's sister, sent me an email asking simply, "Why did you kill my sister." I do not think that I gave her a proper response. I am certain that if she would have gotten to know me deeper than my YouTube videos, perhaps the outcome would have been different. I almost want to delete that sentence, but there is no saying if anything would have changed. It was a perfect storm. I can rest my soul on this one fact:

If Kathleen hadn't have slammed down that box cutter, her life
wouldn't have been taken.

That was the sole activating action that led me to my ultimate decision.

God will judge me accordingly.

Chapter XXIV
The Labs

Post Mortem Drug Screen

Blood		Urine
<u>Morphine</u>		<u>Morphine</u>
16.7ng/ml		457ng/ml
10-80	~~Therapeutic Range~~	UNKNOWN
<u>Hydrocodone</u>		<u>Hydrocodone</u>
191 ng/ml		721ng/ml
10-40	~~Therapeutic Range~~	UNKNOWN
		<u>Hydromorphone</u>
		59 ng/ml
	~~Therapeutic Range~~	UNKNOWN

Chapter XXV

THE 262 GRAND JURY OF PIMA COUNTY

BEFORE THE 262 GRAND JURY OF PIMA COUNTY

TUCSON, ARIZONA

STATE OF ARIZONA,   )

    Plaintiff,   )

) NO.   262-GJ-866

    Vs.   ) NO.   CR-2016-4294

001-CLIFFORD GANT   )

    Accused.   )

OFFICIAL COURT REPORTER'S

TRANSCRIPT OF PROCEEDINGS

Official Court Reporter's Transcript of proceedings had before the Pima County Grand Jury, in secret session, on the 26th day of September, 2016, on the 16th floor of the Pima County Legal Building, Tucson Arizona.

MARIA LAURDES GEARE, RPR

Official Court Reporter

Certified Reporter No. 50555

APPEARANCES:

FOR THE STATE:
    MS. KELLY JOHNSON
    DEPUTY COUNTY ATTORNEY
    COUNTRY ATTORNEYS OFFICE
    GRAND JURORS:

BOND	
CASTILLO	(CLERK)
DIAZ	(FOREPERSON)
FRIAUF	
GAMBLE	
MUTNANSKY	
NGUYEN	
PEARSON	
PIERPONT	
REED	
RIGGS	(ALT. CLERK)
RIVERA	
SCHEIER	(ALT. BAILIFF)
TUXHORN	(ALT. FOREPERSON)
WILSON	(BAILIFF)
ZOOK	

SEPTEMBER 26, 2016

(Maria Lourdes Geare was duly sworn to act as Official Court Reporter herein.)

PROCEEDINGS

    GRAND JURY FOREPERSON: We'll excuse MR. Davilla for this case.

We're back on the record. No case facts or matters of law were discussed off the record.

This will be case 262-GJ-866. There are 15 Grand Jurors present. Those absent are Mr. Davilla. There are no unauthorized persons present.

For the afternoon, the clerk will call the roll.

> GRAND JURY CLERK CASTILLO: Bond?
> GRAND JUROR BOND: Here.
> GRAND JURY CLERK CASTILLO: Castillo is here. Davila is not present. Friauf?
> GRAND JUROR FRIAUF: Here.
> GRAND JURY CLERK CASTILLO: Gamble?
> GRAND JUROR GAMBLE: Here.
> GRAND JURY CLERK CASTILLO: Mutnansky?
> GRAND JUROR MUTNANSKY: Here.
> GRAND JURY CLERK CASTILLO: Nguyen?
> GRAND JUROR NGUYEN: Here.
> GRAND JURY CLERK CASTILLO: Pearson?
> GRAND JUROR PEARSON: Here.
> GRAND JURY CLERK CASTILLO: Pierpont?
> GRAND JUROR PIERPONT: Here.
> GRAND JURY CLERK CASTILLO: Riggs?
> GRAND JUROR RIGGS: Here.
> GRAND JURY CLERK CASTILLO: Rivera?
> GRAND JUROR RIVERA: Here.
> GRAND JURY CLERK CASTILLO: Scheier?
> GRAND JUROR SCHEIER: Here.
> GRAND JURY CLERK CASTILLO: Tuxhorn?
> GRAND JUROR TUXHORN: Here.
> GRAND JURY CLERK CASTILLO: Wilson?
> GRAND JUROR WILSON: Here.
> GRAND JURY CLERK CASTILLO: Zook?
> GRAND JUROR ZOOK: Here.
> GRAND JURY CLERK CASTILLO: We have 15.
> GRAND JURY FOREPERSON: Okay. There are 15 Grand Jurors present. I declare this is a quorum and we will begin.

This is 262-GJ-866. There are 15 Grand Jurors present. Those absent are Mr. Davila. There are no unauthorized persons present.

The accused is Clifford Gant. The charges are, one count first degree murder; and one count theft of means of transportation.

The witness will be Detective Cheek.

(Witness enters the Grand Jury Room.)

DETECTIVE JOSH CHEEK,

Having been first duly sworn, testifies as follows:

EXAMINATION BY MS. JOHNSON:

Q.	Good afternoon. Will you introduce yourself to the Grand Jury, Please?
A.	Yes. My name is Josh Cheek. I'm a Detective with the Tucson Police Department.
Q.	Do you have some information for Grand Jury this afternoon, regarding the investigation into the death of Kathleen Huffer?
A.	Yes, I do.
Q.	And was Ms. Huffer discovered on or about the 28th day of August in her home deceased?
A.	Yes.
Q.	Could you go ahead and tell the Grand Jury about your involvement and what happened during your investigation?
A.	Yes. So Kathleen Huffer lived at 3060 North Richey with Clifford Gant. Huffer had medical issues that required her sister, Kelly Spivack deliver medications to her twice a week. And I should note that the resident on 3060 North Riche, that's located within Pima County.

On August 30th, 2016, Kelly Spivack received a phone call from her mother, also Kathleen's mother, who indicated she couldn't reach Kathleen by phone and was concerned.

So Kelly and her husband drove over to Kathleen's residence, at 3060 North Richie. The gate around the front yard of the residence was locked with the lock hanging outside the gate.

According to the Spivack's, this was the condition in which the gate was typically left when someone had left the residence and locked that gate behind them.

Kathleen's vehicle, a gold Chevy Impala, was not parked at the residence. Kelly and Mark Spivack said that Kathleen was the only one who drove her vehicle and Clifford Gant had not had permission to drive it, unless he was with her.

Kelly and Mark unlocked the gate and walked out up to the residence. There was a triangular tailored type stone set upright on the front door step. Over the doorway, along the door trim, there was a business card that had Clifford Gant's name on it put on the outside of the door.

Kelly unlocked the dead bolt lock of the front door and entered the residence. The bedroom door was closed and there was a note on the door. Kelly opened the bedroom door and found Kathleen lying face down on the bed with her hair partially wrapped in a blanket.

There was mass of trauma to her head and she was pronounced deceased once police arrived at the scene. Detectives later searched the residence. Kathleen Huffer's wrists were bound with ligature behind he back and her ankles were also bound with ligature.

There were numerous objects that had been placed on her body, including a note. A symbol had been drawn on the heel on one of her feet. And there was a hammer lying near the blanket that was partially wrapped around her head. She had severe trauma to the back of her head. There were also business cards and there was other paperwork indicia for Clifford Gant found inside the residence.

Detectives determined that there was surveillance video from the San Luis port of entry at the United States and Mexico, that showed Kathleen's vehicle being driven by a male who was the only occupant of that vehicle into Mexico on August 29th, 2016 at approximately 3:36 a.m.

Further investigation revealed that the vehicle had previously crossed into Mexico through the Nogales port of entry on August 13th of 2016 at approximately 4:06 a.m.

At this time it was being driven by a male who appeared to be the same male who later drove it into Mexico on August 29th, 2016. And on occasion, back on the 13th of August, a female passenger was also inside the vehicle.

When that vehicle re-entered the United States, again, on August 13th, it was selected for secondary inspection. And the occupants of that vehicle were identified by customs and border protection as Kathleen Huffer and Clifford Gant.

On September 1st, 2016 at approximately 9:18 hours – at approximately 9:18 p.m., Clifford Gant was contacted in San Diego after walking on foot through the San Pedro port of entry in Mexico to the United States.

Detectives went to San Diego and met with Clifford Gant at a customs and border protection facility there.

During the interview, Gant told detectives, we already know that I'm guilty. And talked about leaving his calling card. He specified that his calling card was the capstone on the front door step outside the residence.

He admitted to tying Kathleen up in what he described as a sexual manner, with her hands behind her back. He said they played around a little bit, then he told her he was going to get some water.

He went and retrieved a hammer instead. He said he kneeled over her buttocks and struck her in the back of her head with a hammer. He guessed he struck her approximately 18 to 20 times, but said he stopped out of 8 or 9 times to take a breath.

He described a labored breathing sound Kathleen made after the first eight or nine strikes. So then he went back and continued striking her repeatedly until he got blood splatter in his face and decided he was done.

He stood up during the interview and acted out the murder for us while we spoke with him. He claimed he had video recorded the entire thing, using the laptop, that he later sold to a taxi driver in Mexico. That laptop as of yet has not been recovered.

When asked why he killed Kathleen, he said it would be my job to figure that out. He describes items that had been place on the body and in the residence that were consistent with the items that were found at the scene.

After the murder, he said he drove Kathleen's car and parked it in Mexico. Detectives later worked with DPS investigators and border liaison officers who coordinated with Mexican police. And were ultimately able to locate that vehicle in a small town called Rosarito, Mexico, it's close to Tijuana, Mexico.

The vehicle was later transferred into the custody of DPS investigator in Yuma, Arizona. And Gant described the items he left inside the vehicle that were consistent with the items that detectives later found in that vehicle.

Q. So, a couple of follow-up questions, and you may have mentioned it, and if I missed it, I apologize. Did your investigation show that Clifford Gant had actually resided at the home where Kathleen was discovered for quite a period of time?

A. Yes. For a period of months.

Q. And they were boyfriend and girlfriend, basically in a relationship of some sort.

A. They were either roommates or boyfriend and girlfriend, depending on who we spoke with.

Q. And when you say depending on who you spoke to, that would be her family?

A. Correct. And his family.

Q. Okay. And you said that Mr. Gant, when he described for you how he had killed Kathleen, indicated that at first he had tied her up in a sexual manner?

A. That's correct.

Q. Based on what he was describing to you was the initial sexual contact with Kathleen is consensual?

A. Yes. Based on what he was describing that initial – he claimed that the initial activity was consensual, as far as tying her up.

Q. And during the course of your investigation, did you find evidence that supported the fact that Kathleen and Mr. Gant would engage in this type of consensual sexual behavior with being tied up and things like that?

A. Yes, we did.

Q. Thank you.

MS. JOHNSON: That's all the questions that I have.

GRAND JURY FOREPERSON: Does any member of the Grand Jury have any questions for the witness? Let the record show none.

You're excused but please wait until the remaining of this case. Thank you.

THE WITNESS: Thank you.

(Witness exits the Grand Jury Room.)

GRAND JURY FOREPERSON: Does anyone have any legal questions for the Deputy County Attorney? Let the record show none.

Is there anyone who is a witness, has a direct or indirect interest in this case, or who has knowledge of the suspect which would bias or prejudice their ability to serve? Let the record show none.

Court Reporter and the County Attorney are Excused.

(The County Attorney and Court Reporter exit the Grand Jury Room.)

(The County Attorney and Court Reporter enter the Grand Jury Room.)

> GRAND JURY FOREPERSON: Number 262-GJ-866. The accused is Clifford Gant. The charges are read. By a vote of 15 to zero, the Grand Jury has returned a true bill on all counts.

STATE OF ARIZONA   )
COUNTY OF PIMA   ) SS.

I, MARIA LOURDES GEARE, Certified Reporter #50555, Official Court Reporter for the superior court, in and for the County Of Pima, Do hereby Certify that I took the shorthand notes in the foregoing matter; that the same was transcribed under my direction ; that the preceding pages of typewritten matter are a true, accurate and complete transcript of all the matters adduced, to the best of my skill and ability.

_____X_____

MARIA LOURDES GEARE, Certified Reporter
CR-505555,
Official Court Reporter,
Pima County Superior Court

DATED: OCTOBER 21, 2016

Chapter XXVI
The Sentence

ARIZONA SUPERIOR COURT, PIMA COUNTY
HON. DANELLE B. LIWSKI   CASE NO.   CR20164294-001
COURT REPORTER: John Bouley   DATE: May 23, 2017
              Courtroom - 686

STATE OF ARIZONA   Kellie L. Johnson,
                                 Esq. counsel for State
VS.

CLIFFORD GANT (-001)
        Defendant   Sean H Bruner, Esq. and
                                Nancy J Arce, Esq.
                                Counsel for Defendant
DATE OF BIRTH: 12/10/1984

MINUTE ENTRY
SENTENCE TO THE ARIZONA STATE HOSPITAL
        Defendant present, in custody.
        The defendant is advised of the charge and the
determination of guilt, and all parties are given the opportunity
to make recommendations/statements to the Court.
        Two members of the victim's family make statements to
the Court.
        Pursuant to 13-607 and upon due consideration of the
offenses and the facts, law and circumstances involved in this
case, the Court finds no legal cause to delay rendition of
judgment and pronouncement of sentence.
        Based on the evaluations, which are sealed in the court
file, and pursuant to A.R.S. §§13-502 and 13-3994,
        THE COURT FINDS clear and convincing evidence that the
defendant was legally insane at the time of the offense.
        Pursuant to the defendant's plea of guilty except insane,
the Court enters the following judgment and sentence:
        IT IS THE JUDGEMENT OF THE COURT that the defendant
is GUILTY EXCEPT INSANE of COUNT ONE: FIRST DEGREE
MURDER, a Class One Felony, guilty except insane in violation of
A.R.S. §§13-1105, 13-502, 13-3994(D) and (E), committed on or
about August 28, 2016 through August 30, 2016.

        Linda McCormick
        Deputy Clerk

294

MINUTE ENTRY

Page 2   Dates: May 23, 2017
Case No.:   CR20164294-001

IT IS ORDERED, pursuant to A.R.S. §§ 13-502, 13-502;
13-3994(D) and (E), that the defendant be committed to the
Arizona State Hospital under the Department of Health Services
for a term of NATURAL LIFE, for a period of treatment
commencing May 23, 2017, until the date of the defendant's
death. There is no credit for time previously served.
        THE COURT FINDS that the offense did involve death or
serious physical injury or the threat of death or serious physical
injury.
        IT IS ORDERED that the defendant be placed under the
jurisdiction of the Psychiatric Security Review Board for the
duration of this sentence.
        IT IS ORDERED that the Court retain jurisdiction for all
matters not specifically delegated to the Psychiatric Security
Review Board for the duration of the presumptive sentence.
        IT IS ORDERED that the Pima County Sheriff transport the
defendant before 3:00 p.m. on a Tuesday, Wednesday or
Thursday to the Arizona State Hospital for treatment.
        IT IS ORDERED that the Sheriff of Pima County notify the
Jennah Benson, Forensic Admissions/Discharge Coordinator,
Arizona State Hospital, that the defendant is being transported
by the Sheriff to the Arizona State Hospital.
        IT IS ORDERED that the Clerk shall remit to the Arizona
State Hospital a copy of this order together with all medical and
psychological reports and Indictment relating to the defendant
and involving the case.
        IT IS ORDERED, pursuant to the plea, that all remaining
counts and allegations shall be dismissed as to this cause number
only.
        IT IS ORDERED that any outstanding bond that has not
been previously referred for a bond forfeiture proceeding is
hereby exonerated.
        The defendant is advised of his rights of Review, signs,
and receives a copy of the same.

Let the record reflect that the defendant's fingerprint is permanently affixed to the signature page of this sentencing order in open court.

FILED IN COURT: Commitment Order; Presentence Report; Notice of Rights of Review

_____X_____
HON. DANELLE B LIWSKI

Linda McCormick
Deputy Clerk

PART 4: REDEMPTION

Chapter XXVII

Reset

6/2/2020   6:37 PM

Reset. This is the moment for a much needed national reset.

George Floyd was not the straw that broke the camel's back, George Floyd is the Camel. George Floyd is the manifestation of all the collective pressure placed on all the bricks at the bottom of this hierarchal pyramid-scheme (the poor, the underprivileged, the minority). For those at the top of society and government, there is little to nothing weighing on neither their backs nor a hefty yoke on their necks. But, see how they squirm and squeal when we have to stay home and stop buying their goods? National Stimulus they say, "Go spend" so the government doesn't go broke. Meanwhile 60% of those making 40k or less are out of work. What about when the single mother was $100 short for rent in December, where was her government then? Go to the bank and they turn her away like she is out of her mind. "Go turn a trick," they'd laugh with each other as she walks out. It's a disgrace. This is the moment. This is the moment.

Correct me if I'm wrong, but doesn't the Declaration of Independence state: "We the people find these truths to be self-evident, that all men are created equal." Not all white men, nor all men of color. Nor does it exclusively state only American Men, but ALL MEN. (And in saying 'man' or 'men' I do include womankind in this collective, even if the founders vaguely left that up to interpretation) Why then do we devalue life elsewhere as well just as we do at home? Why is a Chinaman's labor worth less than yours? Why is 50% of the world living on less than $2 a day while we sit back waiting for our next opportunity to Netflix & Chill? Why are we ok with that? Who are we to judge? Why do you look at a being, a sentient living, breathing, human being and judge them? That man is black so he is a threat, that man is homeless so he must have made bad decisions, that person is wearing a suit, or a uniform, so they should be admired, obeyed, and learned from. That person has a nice car, they must have money, and wouldn't it be nice? That person uses drugs so they should be in jail or in rehab. That person is in the military defending our "freedom", and I am one, but think for a moment, freedom to do what? Freedom to remain ignorant? Freedom to remain consciously naïve to the same exact systemic failures of leadership and the monetized economies of military, fear and crime, that led to this travesty in the first place?

Tell me, and this is coming from experience- in 2016, a man in America gets pulled over for taking a wide right out of a Dollar Tree and the cop finds him with five grams of methamphetamine. He gets taken to jail and sentenced to five years flat because he had prior infractions. This man has a son, this man had a job, this man paid taxes, but because the system we have been born into, we quickly learn that no matter how hard we work we can never get ahead, we can never have enough money at the end of the month to just simply, in the spirit of George Floyd, JUST BREATHE. So, for a substance that equated to less that $250 of economic value, this man got removed from his child's life to the tune of five years in prison. The economic resource, averaged out per prisoner, comes to right in at $30,000/year. So for a crime you didn't see and a drug that people will find anyways, the taxpayer is today, still on the hook for the $150,000 bill to imprison that man. Do you know the amount, averaged out, per child in America to get an education? $6-8,000. Seems that the 100k+ difference would have been better used as ten-$10,000 scholarships, rather than keeping this "Victim of The Game" imprisoned. Why are we spending all of our present resources punishing a past-wrong that we can't change, instead of investing in the future good that we can guide? Disproportionately the poor get into the drug game, for the quick influx of cash. But even in an 'honest' 'white-privilege' household (if there exists such a class), two incomes are still barely enough to keep things afloat. You saw and will continue to see that with COVID. This is the continuing war that affects us equally but with a heavier invisible hand, MONEY. No matter how great you were living in 2019, it was merely a cash flow management game. Barely any of us are/will be able to withstand another three months of no economic activity/income. Imagine there were not policies in place to freeze rent and mortgage payments for the last three months. I mean, people, $1,200 can only go so far. I don't mean to sway from Black Lives Matter because this newfound support for equality is foundational to any rebuilding we can ever expect to witness, but each and every one of you needs to take a look in the mirror tonight, right now, and ask yourselves why has this taken so long?

Apathy equals consent, PERIOD. I am personally beyond frustrated that it has taken a mass exodus from the labor pool and a free man getting slaughtered in broad daylight for people to finally wake up enough to discover the newfound free time to stand on their own two feet and say enough is enough... what if there was no video of Mr. Floyd? What if there was no witness report of his dying cries to simply be allowed to breathe, you think the officers would have put that in their report? Ha. What about the 10's of thousands, nay, 100's of thousands of underprivileged in American jails and prisons right now that have had the same amount of legal wiggle-room that George Floyd did, none. This is a war of class, this is a war of money, and this is a war for Liberty.

If you think when the protests are over, and COVID is 'gone for the summer', that they will still not be waging economic warfare on any race they deem to be the patsy, spend your downtime educating yourself, and spend the day looking into the life of another, or the death of one. But know this, the moment you sit down, after having stood for so long, is the minute you lose the battle. Not just for you and yours, but for 7 generations down the line. When they look back at us in this unique tryst in time, and look among themselves, are they going to be collectively grateful for our sacrifice and energy and relentlessly seeing this fight through, or are they going to be under gun and baton subservient to the hand that feeds them table scraps?

Your voice.

Your time.

Your decision.

Chapter XXVIII
OATH §502

August 8, 2002, Phoenix, Arizona– "I, CLIFFORD FREDERICK GANT, do solemnly swear that I will support and defend the Constitution of the United States against all enemies, foreign and domestic; that I will bear true faith and allegiance to the same; and that I will obey the orders of the President of the United States and the orders of the officers appointed over me, according to the regulations and the Uniform Code of Military Justice. So help me God."

Constitution of the United States

Article I section 8 paragraph 5

"[The congress shall have power to...] coin money, regulate the value thereof, and of foreign Coin, and fix the standard of weights and measures."

Article I section 10 paragraph 1

"[No state shall] ... coin money; emit bills of credit; make any Thing but gold and silver coin a tender of payments of debts."

10/28/2017

"A NEW BIRTH OF FREEDOM"

Oh, how we have struggled with the heavy yoke of the inferior DOLLAR. 105 years of the Federal Reserve managing the pain, when they **KNOW** they've been screwing us all along. Heads of state, bear witness, this is THE END. This is the end of the tyrannical reign of the Federal Reserve printing press **and** the complicit governors that sat idly by as the spoils of our 40-hour week purchased less and less. With the majority of America's workforce living paycheck to paycheck, many able bodied souls merely sit on their couch with their Flat screen TV and eat junk food subsidized by the same people who can barely make ends meet. Let alone that they should pay an extra

$200/month so some person they don't even know can play video-games and drink Mountain Dew and eat Ramen noodles or sell their food stamp benefits for 50 cents on the dollar so they can get a quick fix. I HAVE SEEN IT, but I digress.

How many of you have ever wondered why money is the way it is? Nobody in the previous two elections even felt money was an issue. Although they bragged about putting people to work once they get the polling numbers. How many jobs does Trump average per tweet? ***just a thought*** How many of you have held a dollar in your hand (all). What about a silver dollar? (Less than all) Hmm. Makes me think.

Why does a silver eagle ounce have " ~ONE DOLLAR" stamped on it? I can't buy one for a dollar. In fact it takes $16-$21 to purchase one silver ounce. Weird, yes, thought provoking, maybe, infuriating, not so much...but it should.

When the United States was founded, they needed a money source. To inhibit trade with our biggest trade partner to the south, $1 US dollar was parodied to 1 Mexican Peso, which was one ounce of fine silver. One ounce of silver equaled one ounce of silver, DUH, *right*? Then someone got greedy. They started debasing the silver to the point of making a dollar, PAPER! In 1913, after the market crash of 1909, "never let a crisis go to waste" (or so they say), they established the Federal Reserve whose mandate is to assist with job creation and regulate the newly printed "Dollar" (The paper ones.) So over the course of over 100 years, the FED has killed off 95% of the purchasing power of the dollar. How? Printing. And not allowing silver to get out of control. Thing is, there is still purchasing power in the USD. But it's devaluing steadily.

I'm not going to get into the numerous details, that is for you to care. But the information that follows should have you really questioning the tender/currency/money that surrounds your life. Republican, Democrat, Rich, Poor, Black, Asian, European, Pacific Islander, one thing that touches us all is money. And they have for at least 100 years been manipulating it against us, or, for the sake of not killing the sacred cow, they just didn't see it. By any means necessary, I suppose.

The following evidence is intended to support my theory in motion.

Thank you for your time, mind space, and any future action you are compelled to take.

Start the discussion. An entirely new freedom waits, for the world, and us.

10/28/2017

Gold ounce   <=> $1276

Silver ounce   <=> $16.91

Peso/USD   <=>   19.19

(How long for **you** to profit $1,276???) 40 hour week @ $31.9/hour OR 106 hours @ $12/HR (they have effectively priced society out of the market.) Who can afford that?

Silver is $16.91USD=> |1/16.85| means 1 paper USD has PURCHASING POWER of 5.9¢ when weighted against its 1913 inception.

****thought bubble****

Bretton Woods III

One USD ($)=($) One MXN

U.S. $ stays constant & works to make decisive changes in shoring up our dollar.

Ounce of silver would now purchase $400USD worth of goods and gold would purchase $20,000USD of goods.

Yes, globally.

The 261M ounces of reported gold in treasury at this honest valuation will yield $5.1T

With $1.47T in FED circulation, treasury could cover every bill in print with gold with $3.53T held in reserves.

–Clifford Gant, CTOSN, USN, 2689

"Just like Campbell's, OOOOO the possibilities!"

8/5/2020

Gold ounce   <= > $2054 {up 61% from 10/28/2017}

Silver ounce   <= > $27.11 {up 60% from 10/28/2017}

Peso/USD   <= > 22.23 {devalued 16% from 10/28/2017}

(How long for **you** to profit $2054???) 40 hour week @ $51.35/hour OR 170 hours @ $12/HR (they have effectively priced society out of the market.) Who can afford that?

If one ounce of silver is now purchases $400USD worth of goods and gold purchases $20,000USD globally, the financials would still look like this...

The 261M ounces of gold in treasury at this honest valuation will yield $5.1T

With $1.47T in FED FIAT USD CURRENCY & COIN circulation, treasury could cover every bill in print and minted coin in gold with $3.53T held in gold reserves.

11/5/2020

We could establish a new National Bank who could receive 1/3 of Physical Treasury Gold and use fractional reserve banking to make Grants. Pay back within 10 years if you are successful with the investment, 100% forgiveness if you fail to the last penny.

Using FRB or fractional reserve banking, 350M Americans each could get a gold backed investment vehicle of $50,000.

Or you can keep bullshitting yourselves $1,200, $600, or $1,400 at a time. FIATLY. The true ramifications of not doing this will only be realized when it is too late.   -GANT, C 2689

Chapter XXIX
Letters to Dad

11/27/2017

Hey Dad,

     Just got your letter today and I was impressed with your kayak getup. It looks "fresh". The print job was fine. If you have time in between your trips and could make a copy of the lake wakeboarding picture of me, that would be something awesome to see. Oh, how much I've seen since then. Sorry my last letter was so short, I was kind of at a loss for what to say, I realized that there are only broad generalizations that come to mind when I think about you in the context of being my father. The past can't and shouldn't be revisited, but we have this moment moving forward.

     I am a bit anxious lately. I see the political clamoring and jockeying to come up with the newest bit of distraction to label it all "breaking news". The stock market is at another all-time high. The purchasing power of the US dollar is at an all-time low. And nobody is talking about the viability of Bitcoin gaining market share against the Dollar. (Bitcoin has been on a tear, recently up to over $8000 each, a sign of a rapidly weakening dollar.) Even though neither fully fulfill the muster for the bullet points that make a thing "money." (Mitchell was heavily involved with Bitcoin when they were less than $5 a coin and his Bitcoin wallet currently shows that his wallet processed over $16 million dollars' worth of Bitcoin at today's valuation.) I don't know how to really contextualize the equations going on in my head so I won't even try. I can only do what Gandhi said, "BE the change you want to see in the world. I have about $200 worth of silver I've bought over the past two months. I get $20 a week working here doing ceramic crafts and some painting, I should move up to $30 a week by New Years. My next purchase is going to be a 1/10 OZ Platinum coin. I've found a discrepancy with prices concerning silver/gold/platinum and have found silver to be undervalued, gold overpriced, and platinum the "sleeper" investment. The US mint stamps its walking liberty/silver eagles with "~ONE DOLLAR." Gold is minted with "~50 DOLLARS." And last week I found myself looking up Platinum online and found that the US Mint has monetized Platinum at "~100 DOLLARS" now as you may know these precious metals cannot be bought at those face values. Gold is trading at a hair below

$1300/OZ, silver at $17.05/OZ, and platinum at $950/OZ. What does this mean? The ratios are quite askew. Like a pyramid, we lay the groundwork first...

A dollar in 1913 buys over $25 today. 100% purchasing power pre federal reserve, and since then the dollar has dove to 4% purchasing power of a "DOLLAR." So let's try to extrapolate this data.

"One dollar" Silver @ $17/OZ
Now, gold is monetized at "$50", so gold should equal $850USD. ($17x50)
And platinum which is stamped with "$100" should be $1700USD ($17x100)

Value in respect to ratio	Target price	Todays price
Silver = 17	$20	$17
Gold = 850	$1000	$1295
Platinum = 1700	$2000	$950

I have some other confirming theories but I am not here to sell you on anything, but just as you stated that there are going to be some changes heading down the pike, I've known it since 2008. The stock market is acting like the housing bubble in 2007-2008 just going nowhere but straight up. It is a clear sign of not companies getting better, making more profits, or producing more products/ sales, it's a screaming signal that the dollar's absolute zero intrinsic value is being rapidly sold or exchanged for .... The gamble is worth more than holding onto the hot potato, or the warm elephant shit, depending on your level of disgust with the current currency of the world.
I have seen 1/10 ounce of platinum for sale from between $110 and $169, I am allowing myself to believe that you have a little bit of free time, I encourage you to steer some of your personal growth time into reading up on the current state of metal money. Historical charts and what not. The current DOW chart is almost an enlarged mimic of the 1930-1933 stock market crash, we are on the third "boom" of this bull run and I will not say that I am some stock market prophet, rather just someone who has found a easily understandable take on the metals market and where it will intrinsically go.
We are all entering an unprecedented time where we are facing issues in every corner of the globe. Last night I came to the conclusion that I am not going to speak more on this topic, as it has been an un-carryable burden since the day I turned 24 and the eureka moment is just as valid now as the day it was divined to me. So I'll leave you with one more paragraph on the topic.... Some serious shooting from the hip.

What is it worth? When I show someone a piece of silver- that is the common response. So how do I respond to that? The price I paid? The amount I could sell it for? How much do I think it is worth? There is a parable of Jesus in Luke that states: if a woman has 10 silver coins and loses one, does she not clean the house and search diligently until she finds it. And does she not then go to the neighbors hose and being exceedingly joyful tell the neighbors "rejoice with me for I have found the lost coin..." Now in today's world if you had lost what would be equal to $20 would you spend all day looking for it, when you had 9 left? Would you go to your neighbor's house or call or post on Facebook "HEY found that 20 I lost" I am going to say my wager is no. Your neighbors wouldn't give a hoot. But instead of $20 worth of purchasing power you lose something that holds $400 worth of purchasing power, I know me for one, would definitely put some time into looking for it, even if I had the other $3600 worth of purchasing power (9 coins) accounted for in the safe. And if I had a rapport with my neighbor, I might spend some of that and bring over some beer and beef for a barbecue. It is impossible to value precious metals in dollar terms because it is valuing a finite commodity in infinite terms. i.e. how much Monopoly money would you take for your truck with the "we support the troops" sticker on it? No amount would suffice, obviously. Now, my finale. The Clifford Gant Theorem:

Silver to be valued at its historical purchasing power of $400/ OZ.
    Gold would then be $400x50= $20,000/OZ
    Platinum would be $400x100= $40,000/OZ

Then the 265 million ounces of gold in the TREASURY could back the entire $1.5 Trillion US paper Dollars in circulation with a fixed amount of gold. And have $3.5T in hard assets to repatriate the function of money in our society away from the Federal Reserve. Now, I believe that silver is being purchased in talents by some big banks (and I'm talking millions and millions of ounces) because when the new money/Amero/silver based currency gets announced they are going to the banks with all the base money. But that is for another conversation. I will start 2018 with 10 ounces of silver (bought @$24/Oz and I'm fine with paying the online premium) and the yet to acquire 1/10 OZ of platinum selling for $120. All I can say is that I hope you understand somewhat the changes that are upon us and will make a small step to hedge for the future, if you haven't already. My days here start at 8:30AM or so for breakfast. Then a class or two (music studio where you can play one of their guitars or open art where you can paint or color.) There is a songwriter class I attend on Tuesdays along with a TED talk class. I'm sure you have heard of them, if not, look them up on YouTube. Stands for Technology, entertainment, and design. Have you got a GoPro for your kayaking trips? That might be interesting. I mean I just know when I was planning my trip a go pro was at the top of the list of things I wanted, I mean you never know when that once in a lifetime shot will present itself and although the experience of being there and seeing it live can draw no comparison there exists many a people who would love to see an eagle swoop and get a meal from the kayakers point of view. I don't know.

Kind of like that wakeboarding shot.

Anyways lunch is about 11:45AM and then at 3 I go out to walk the 'Track" I have 2 therapy sessions per week, we've talked money from day one. And that's about it. I been missing some meals and I'm down to 138 lbs. just weighed myself yesterday. Just a side experiment, I want to know the limits of my body. I think I left prison in 2014 at like 165lbs. But this place is a lot different that prison.

I get a visit from Mom about once every two weeks and Melissa has brought Jax to two visits so far. Jessica makes it about once a month , I've seen Mitchell about 4 times, always with Mom. But that's about it, oh, we have a mini gym and "fitness" is at like 8-9am I just walk on the treadmill and that's it. Never had big muscles, I don't need them, I can still do my navy minimum 40 pushups and that's good enough for me. And there is a class at the other unit I was in that brought in ropes and fitness stuff and she had a perfect pushup set. Shit happens. You got the raw side of the deal on that one, pops, and that is a heavy weight on my heart when I think about it, cuz I know you always wanted the best for us, and kind of unfortunately it came with an expense of time not spent with us. Don't worry this isn't a Dad-bash ending, I've lived with some stark examples of isolating oneself to create something original and unique, a lot of times at the expense of the ones I've loved. I'd rather be poor and create than enriched and enslaved. I get it. I hold no ill will, and possibly this communication line might lead us both towards an understanding and an insight into the mindsets of each other.

Hope you had a good thanksgiving.

Respect.
Clifford Gant

P.S. I know you are getting up there in human years, although you are still as active as the young guns, but if you ever die of natural causes and I don't have the AUREN you promised me as a child, I might never forgive you. If it is an accidental death, (even you aren't immune from drunk drivers) I will keep it in my heart that you were planning on it. And if you are ever at it, Melody needs that tiara thing that the princess wore, too.

2/25/2019

Hey Dad,

Jessica's wedding is coming up, you getting excited? It will be the first female wedding for the Gant-Biddle children. Your spelling is not an issue; I can use context clues if you err largely. How is your new place? Is it adequate? That will be nice to have a garden; we have a little garden here too. We grow tomatoes, squash, some herbs and flowers, also some hot peppers. It's nice to see the things grow. We recently re-grassed an area about 13x13 feet and it grew up super green and fast (like 3 weeks).

My weeks have been going by fast. I attend about 30 group activities/classes per month. Some are as simple as walking in the morning around the campus (we call it 'the mall') and some are a little more demanding such as "Resolution Group." It is one of the pre-requisites for leaving here that deals with drug education and impulses, as well as doing testimonials about our "Index Offence." They also have relaxation groups from Tai-Chi to music studio, where I will pick up a guitar for a half-hour or so and do a little picking. It's enjoyable.

I fully intend on using my time here as a stepping stone. Very few people get the opportunity to be here, and I am already working on saving money for me to have once I leave here. I mean, most people just are here and so messed up on prescription meds that they don't think about the future, they spend all of their money on snacks and are broke by Monday. (Payday is Thursday.) Currently I have an off-campus savings that has $312 in it, and COH (Cash On Hand) of $15 and my ledger has about $100 that is owed to me, that should be mostly cleared by next week.

I have ordered a black titanium ring online that will have the engraving "REIGN" on it, which is what I plan to call the dog I will be adopting when I get out of here. It will give me something to care about and some companionship. By that time (looking between 7-10 years), I will have saved up over $10,000 and I plan on getting an RV in the days after my release and will find an RV park. I'm thinking maybe Flagstaff, so I can get all four seasons. A little warmer would be Prescott. I don't think I'll go back to Havasu. If there is a budget option, I wouldn't mind Kingman, but we will see.

Before I get released, they will work with me to get me government aid, SSI Disability, which will come out to around $500 a month, $350-$400 for space rent, so I will be fine. (The amount may be bigger than that, but I like to lowball the numbers/money I receive and highball my expenses.) Also, I am not going to think about this much longer than to just to tell you. Because I was diagnosed in 2013-ish and Social Security denied my claim, when I get approved this time around, they are required to give me back pay for the time I was in society i.e. not in prison, jail or this hospital. So if I am eligible for $500 a month SSI Disability, where I was free for about a conservative 20 months, I would be eligible for a $10,000 back pay check. I am not counting on that because I haven't talked to my social worker about that, it was a different staff member that talked to me about it. So yes, I am doing all I can to get me out with the best start possible. If I have to sacrifice snacks and a majority of the sodas I used to buy, I will be in great shape to chart my own destiny.

Well it's time for dinner. Chicken and baked potato, or did I get the burger? Oh yeah, was reading some trivia for the nightly community meeting, and it said that in one burger patty you could have meat from as many as 100 different cattle. Yeah. No thanks!

Love you pops,
Clifford F.

7/4/2020

Ok pop, here it is. Our come to God moment. Thanks for taking the time. 6:17am on Saturday July 4th. Not quite the scenario you thought you would be in when you entered your 78th year one short month ago. Life has always been full of its own cruel revelations though, hasn't it? I woke up 27 hours ago and haven't slept since. I am just now able to get back on the computer to try to transcribe all that has been mulling around in my head since I got off the computer at cut off time 11PM last night. Rest assured this is not going to be a rebuke of your parenting style over the years, nor a long winded apology for how I have wronged you over the years. You claimed "water under the bridge" all those years ago, and yet here we are, standing on the same squeaky cedars we had thought we left behind us. In a much different situation though. I have not come to stake a claim on what your labors have earned you; from the moment I held the Auryn pendant in my hand I had considered me and you square. The seeming lack of fatherhood counterbalanced my deficiency in sonsmanship pretty fairly, in my calculations. I can't speak for the others in the pack, but you made good on the never-ending childhood promise, and in quick time I might add. I imagined that in less than 20 minutes after reading that letter you were pecking away at your keyboard hoping someone, somewhere, had one attainable. Top notch effort. No I have not come to stake claim, I have come to perhaps enlighten, and subsequently bargain.

I have come bearing 3 wishes, and one ask. I do not want yes or no replies right now, I want to speak my peace and let you think on your impending decisions, as some might be harder to justify than others. But I will still present my case for each. Now I know you are not a barrel of unlimited wish granting, which is why at the end my 'ask' yields a reciprocal harvest.
The three wishes can be all granted or none granted, no ill will harbored if denied, no special favors if approved.
Here we go. Ill open the floor for us at the end, please just listen to the story until then.
Before I left for the navy in 2002 you bought and presented me with a new book. Napoleon Hill, Think and Grow Rich. In that book, almost prophetically in your case, was penned a poem, "The wages of life." Do you remember it? I do. By heart. And have held it with me for the better part of 20 years. Hear me.

I bargained with life for a penny
And life would pay no more
However I begged at evening

312

When I counted my scanty store
For life is a just employer
It will give you what you ask
But once you've set the wages
Why you must bear the task
I bargained with life for a penny
Only to learn dismayed
That any wage I would have asked of life
Life would have willingly paid.

Now other than that heart full woman you found yourself as a helpmate of, Penny is not on the table for discussion, she is an amazing specimen of a woman and I am better for knowing her.

Wish #1
There was something in your life that you promised yourself you would see to getting if the cards ever just fell your way. For years I knew your goal was an $8,000 banjo, and probably decades longer without verbalizing your dream music machine, you secretly carried that struggle of burden. I can imagine your thoughts on your beat up flat-top complete with a couple drops of Pabst Blue Ribbon accidently dripped on it after your lips missing a swig. "One day, I'll hold one that would make Earl Scruggs jealous." I imagined you thinking. And the steps you laid for climbing that pyramid was those first repetitive string slides on your "Foggy Mountain Breakdown" rendition. I'm not going to say what I imagined you felt when I heard you were finally able to acquire it, but I know from experience that wanting something that society says is out of reach, and finally proving them wrong by getting it in the face of extreme adversity, just leaves you with the bittersweet taste, of "ok, what's next?" "What now?" So in order to carry on the memory and testament of dreams created and pinnacles achieved, I'd like to make one of your crowning achievements my foundation, under no circumstance will it be sold. It will remain under my watch. In the meantime, we are allowed musical instruments on the unit, personal guitars and keyboards and such, and to have your guidebooks, I would make it my leisurely duty to learn some of your favorite riffs, those are my intentions. I have a couple irons in the fire right now, an undeveloped website is mine for the next 2 years, and the next stimulus package which will probably be here by the end of July will give me enough cash to get it operable so I can start posting my writings to it, via a third party I will have to hire somehow. The other main thing I will let you know about shortly. But I just want to let you know that I am not wasting my time here waiting to get released, I will accomplish my goals even being handcuffed upside-down and underwater. You have seen me accomplish what I deem needs

accomplishing and with or without your banjo, I'm going to get it done, having it would add some major elements to the provenance of its history and mine. Who else would do it the justice it deserves? Think about it.

Wish #2
The time we spent on main street in Wisconsin in the little garage workshop, I watched you craft your finest handiwork: the mahogany and brass Gant Razor. I know I was making beer can ottomans and 'couches for mouses' and such, but I was mostly watching you. Learning how to care about something fashioned from raw elements, and with pointed labor, how you could make anything in this world transform magically into just about anything you desired it to be. Even later in life, paring it with my little wooden infinity symbol in Penny's backyard, somehow looking back seems I was placing my mark on it way back then. Rest assured, even though I can't have it here, when I do get out, it will be my known razor of choice. And when I post videos of me shaving with the king's razor on my site, people are going to start asking questions. And I will be holding all of the cards. This is what was meant by you knowing it was an idea ahead of its time. Retro is going to be huge, and I don't care how many German engineered blades you can throw on the tip of a T, nothing will top the Gant.

Wish #3
I understand vaguely how time is getting short, but I need a handwritten statement from you. This one might sound obscure and weird but I can't lead you into giving me an answer one way or the other. I need in 1 or 2 paragraphs your recollection of signing any documents regarding my naval enlistment. What you remember signing, who was there to witness it, and any other thoughts you had about that time around December 11th-12th of 2001. The secondary important part of this wish is to get to a bank and get it notarized and then sent to me, please.

Finally, the ask.

I know you have sworn off the doctors and to my understanding haven't talked to the oncologist since your cancelled surgery. I am about 20% done with my very detailed memoir in which you play a recurring role in, imagine that. I only have so many hours in the day to use the computer and have to share 2 terminals with 20 different people. Given the circumstance I am prepared to talk to my doctor on Monday to ask if for the immediate future, I can have access to the computer from 8pm till 8am and sleep during the day so I can get all of what I want to say on paper without interruption or distraction. Writing is inherently about inspiration and motivation and currently I have both in spades. If you tell me how long you think you have, I will not stop till you have my life history in your hands. It would be something else to have one of the last books you read be mine. Just as the wishes weren't all or nothing, so is this offer. I but I will not send you chapter by chapter to have you part ways in this existence with unfinished business. You stick around to get the first draft of the book, goal of 144,000 words (80,000 words marks a novel, 144,000 marks a life) if things get bad, I would be willing to send an unedited, 120 pages worth, and be proud of that. The reason behind this is that the only thing you really know about me, is things about me I was too young to remember, and things that have been told to you by me or others, or things written about me without me having a chance to defend myself. I would like you to know some of the stories and experiences that have given me a life I would be willing to trade our respective sentences for. You seem to have things left of your bucket list, and I'm dying for a moment of non-self-inflicted expiration. If you make it the month, which is what I think it will take for me to do the book justice, you might understand my reasoning behind my jealousy of your situation. I could speed up the timeframe if the doc signs off on my idea to work at night, but I need a timetable, Dad. So either professionally, the "how long do I have, doc?" question needs to be asked, if only for my ears only, just for me to know if this Everest-esque goal is to be attained. Or, as one who knows his body better than anyone, how long do you think you are going to be hanging around, coherent enough to read a book of that scale and gravity.

It's 8:30AM now, it's taken me 2 hours to write this, and I need to go stretch my legs for the 15 minutes a day we get to go outside.

Love you, Pop.

Chapter XXX
Dear My World, Pt. 1

5/9/2021

   Look, world. If we could all come to the table for a minute and shelve the never ending war about who God is or what to call him/her/it and get the second most important factor in our wellbeing and trajectory as a Globe under control, I think the blessings of God would rain down upon us.

   I am merely a messenger. I am that previously mentioned 'walking corpse.' I have somehow managed to follow the only path I've ever known in life and it has brought me here, to a place removed from time. On the system's dime, and your spare change, I am in the system for life. You are paying me for the rest of my life. So thank you. One part of me feels vindicated. This stay will prove to be much more expensive for the Government (Read: Taxpayer) than if they would have approved my SSI Disability request back in 2012. And not to mention, someone lost their life.

   It's been ninety days since Dad succumbed to his cancer on February 7th, 2021. Penny was by his side holding his hand when she whispered to him, "Let go, and let God." Those were the last words he heard. I was watching most of his transition via Google Hangouts. He only got to read 100 pages or so of this manuscript before he started deteriorating rapidly. He did tell me that he learned a lot about me, and even remembered some things about himself that he had forgotten about, and that made me feel good. It really validated my work and every stimulus dollar I received (and then some) to get the first edition self-published, and to produce this revised work in a more contemporary format.

   I think that a majority of those paying attention would say that the proverbial writing is on the wall. That this system of exchanging our very finite time and energy, for a fiat middle-man called the 'commodity of cash,' has about run its course. We are at a breaking point. I believe we will soon see the decoupling of America as the world's powerhouse. It doesn't have to be that way, though. What if the world got paid? $50,000 of purchasing power per citizen should be included in any basic "Welcome to Earth" package. This would foster growth, this would incentivize entrepreneurship and this would release the bonds that the concept of money has on the human psyche. $400T is how much monopoly money it would take to distribute to the

8 Billion humans on earth $50,000 worth of purchasing power. (We are not yet at 8 Billion, but it's a nice round estimate number.) In any one world currency 1 should equal 1, period. Price the world in US Dollars and let 1 equal 1. Let me show you how this would work.

Africa would be beyond rich and no longer the bitch of the upper class. The rape and abandonment of a huge chunk of the world's natural resources would no longer be ignored. Mexico would wake up with using what would buy one taco the day before, but now being able to buy the entire family a meal (20 Pesos for a taco now buys $20 worth of goods.) Instead of paying 4,000 Pesos a month for rent, that same 4,000 Pesos would afford rent for over a year. Basic needs would be almost un-buyable because it would be illogical to spend the time to make paper change for a 10 Peso coin worth ~50c in US Dollars today, but tomorrow would buy $10 worth of goods. The United States would feel no real economic change, but the rest of the world is insta-rich. "The first shall be last and the last shall be first." The Central banks would have to buy up the Venezuelan Dollars and the Zimbabwe dollars because not every American has change for a $10,000 Venezuelan Dollar bill or a $500,000 Zimbabwe Dollar bill. Customs could collect the high value bills, and activate a debit card for the traveler denominated in US Dollars with a cap at $1M dollars. We will never get a truer Global Economic reset than this.

Those that don't want to see this happen are those that are content with the racket they have engineered and the humanoids that they have trained to comply with their system. Those that complain are those that think that they are somehow inherently better than any other race or demographic. Those that have will still have, but so will the rest of the world's populous. As Americans, we should feel a groundswell of charity, no longer with just our "money," but with our minds and bodies to go out into the world and physically show the benefits of financially backed freedom.

Manpower for charitable causes would now be the new commodity. And as I believe that people are inherently good, the world could start working together to tackle the hunger epidemic, the class crisis, and other humanitarian crises' around the globe. One of the most pressing dangers, in my understanding, isn't even the problems above ground, it lies in the world's oceans.

It's not just money that would change. Time itself would have to be universally synched. We could run the world on Zulu time. A universal time setting that would allow us to know what happened when. 800 Zulu may be day on one side of the world and night on the other, but no more chasing the sun. The Gregorian calendar is flawed. The prefix 'Oct' means 8. The prefix 'Nov' means 9. The prefix 'Dec' means 10. Thus December should be the 10th month.

When shifted, this would make January and February the 11ᵗʰ and 12ᵗʰ month, respectfully. The Jewish calendar already reflects this. Which makes sense, because why do we do leap year (the remainder of ¼ a day per year, saved every 4 years to add a day) two months after the start of our calendar year? February *should* be the 12ᵗʰ month. And thus we have the remainder of the year, roughly 6 hours per year, at the very end, where 'remainders' belong. This is basic math stuffs. Fuck it, my book, and my world, right?

I don't know who ever thought that leap year was a good idea. Who had the audacity to believe that they could effectively BANK time? Oh wait, they didn't have digital clocks back in 1300 A.D. A remainder needs to be spent or written off; it cannot be *banked* and given a fresh square on our time maps every four years. This is how I think it should go, Zulu time or not. At the end of every 365 day calendar year, we should rotate the Sun around *us*. On February 28ᵗʰ of the initiating year the world winds their clocks back 6 hours at sunset. This makes for one 30 hour day. This advances the Sun. Meaning the Sun will rise 6 hours sooner on March 1ˢᵗ.

It would be a rotating 4 year Dawn cycle:

Year 0: Sunlight hours at equivalent time of roughly 5:30AM to 7:15PM

Year 1: Sunlight hours at equivalent time of roughly 11:30PM to 1:15PM

Year 2: Sunlight hours at equivalent time of roughly 5:30PM to 7:15AM

Year 3: Sunlight hours at equivalent time of roughly 11:30AM to 1:15PM

Year 4: Sunlight hours at equivalent time of roughly 5:30AM to 7:15PM

With the time runoff sound, we won't have to worry about changing our calendars within our lifetimes. We could get 6 more hours of rest, or 6 more hours at the bar. I have a feeling that the first 4 years, Earth's inhabitants will be less worried about partying and more interested in bringing the third world up to speed. That is the truest form of job creation... **mission endowment.** True economic growth is fostered by people doing what they believe in, not just being a place holder with a job, getting the bills paid.

The whole of the law should be "Do No Harm." I feel that most would choose to do good deeds, especially when that is what the majority of the populous is doing. Alan Watts inspired me once with his lecture, "What would you do if money were no object." He implores the listener to answer that question and then do that thing. There would be no more obstacles blocking our dreams. True liberty.

What would *you* do? They say money is the root of all evil. Well, if that were true, why does the Church still ask for it? Why does

318

God need your money? Ugh. I have a sneaking suspicion that I'm going to have to present my case against Christ now... I was thinking I wouldn't have to but...damnit...pardon the interruption.

CHAPTER XXXI
The Case Against Christ

Well, if it's never going to be accepted that I could be in the running to be the Devil incarnate, or even possibly the Messiah, then you are going to have to run with me on this one because I can only make this case while carrying the persona of said entity, or maybe just some mildly insightful human, or, just a simple hater. Here goes.

The crux of the Christ Complex really falls apart if anyone does some good old fashioned critical thinking. I am not here to say that he was a fabricated character, I do believe that he walked the earth, but to have 1/3 of this world's population follow this enigma based on the ingrained clerical boast that "Christ never sinned," I offer you the following exhibits.

The Temptation in the Desert

This story has never set well with me. For such an important moment, coming right after Jesus was baptized by John the Baptist, how did this story get relayed? It is told as if an unbiased invisible third party was reporting. There is no evidence given that Jesus had anyone with him. Who was there to validate the trueness of his 40 day fast? Was it a 'no consumption at all fast', or a dawn till dusk fast? Then we get into the Temptation.

"If you are truly the Son of God, command that these stones become bread." The tempter prodded. Now, first off who labeled the question asker 'The Devil?' How did he appear to Jesus? The same way Jesus would appear to his followers after the crucifixion, like a hologram, or ghost-like presence? If it was me asking this first softball of a question, it is a question that really could answer the point of all existence at that time. He turns the stones to bread, he is the Son of God. If he can't or refuses (refusal usually means, in my experience, inability) then we have to look for a proof in an escalated question. Jesus replied a political response: "It is written: Man shall not live on bread alone, but on every word that comes from the mouth of God." I, as the Devil, never asked Jesus to EAT the bread, much less sustain himself on it. I have existed since pre-earth, and word came that earth had a contender to be the Messiah. I had to check it out for myself. So far, I am not impressed.

Then, as the story goes, the Devil took him to the Holy City and had him stand on the highest point of the temple and questioned him with his own "for it is written" response framing of the previous question:

320

"If you are truly the Son of God, throw yourself down. For it is written: He will command his angels concerning you and they will lift you up in their hands so that you will not strike your foot against a stone." The second gauntlet was thrown. I, as the Devil, am saying that if you want to abide by what has been written, then I have a test for that, too. To which Jesus's response was political in nature again, "It is also written: Do not put the Lord your God to the test." Ok, we are now having a failure to communicate. Who led who to the highest point of the temple, in this, the Holy City? Who were you 'guided by the spirit' to meet for this literal 'test.' (The Greek for *tempted* can also mean *tested*.) And what makes you so sure you are 'the Lord My God?' But, see, I'm not here now, nor wasn't there, for a debate. I know who I am. I was cast out of Heaven long ago. I have quite infinite time, but that doesn't mean I like wasting it on ½ measured God-Complex characters. The next question, as all good things come in threes, will surely make this fraud turn up his nose.

Again, the Devil took him to a very high mountain and showed him all the kingdoms of the world and their splendor. "All this I will give to you if you will bow down and worship me." And the irritated Messiah-in-the-running replied, "Away from me Satan! For it is written: 'Worship the Lord your God and serve him only.'" So is it me or did Jesus deny any clear proof that he was the Son of God, to the only being that is outside of God, completely hinged off of writings by previous non-God authors? Seems kind of petty, don't you think? Is anyone else getting a Star Wars vibe from this encounter? Like "Jesus, Jesus, I am your Father!" Just in the costume of the Devil. So, Jesus in this encounter, was pretty, how do I say, racist? If it looked like the Devil, and it talked like the Devil... but Jesus (if that *is* your real name)... have you ever **seen** the face of your God, your 'Father?' That is beside the point. But if you could turn a stone to bread, and refused to just because the one asking may have presented as your enemy, to prove your identity and lineage to the asker, keeper of unknown truths, may not be a 'sin' but definitely goes to show Jesus's character as being undeservingly pious. And we are only in Chapter 4 of the New Testament!

A juicy nugget in Matthew Chapter 10 reads: (34) "Do not suppose that I have come to bring peace to the earth. I did not come to bring peace, but a sword." It goes on, but I don't wish to waste ink toner with cyclical Jesus speak. Look what death and destruction has come from this entity and his advents aftermath. Christian Dark Ages, anyone? Oh, how easy it is to overlook. Or, how about the Catholic Pedophilia 3-ring circus? And they still want your *money*? In God We Trust, right?

We have been abandoned. Our ancient ancestors have been shown a man who had been given gifts that mortal man couldn't explain, and then he allowed himself to be taken from them, to distract from the inexplicable notion that we are alive. Jesus came to divide the world, and has done just that. Inciting a 2,000 year insurrection? Countless deaths and millions of current and never disclosed un-healable traumas later, still, sinless?

Loyalty before Family

Although this is a short example and not a sin, it still goes to show the pompous caricature of 'The Son of God.' "While Jesus was still talking to the crowd, his mother and brothers stood outside, wanting to speak to him. Someone told him, "Your mother and brothers are standing outside, wanting to speak to you." He replied to him, "Who is my mother, and who are my brothers?" Pointing to his disciples, he said, "Here are my mother and my brothers. For whoever does the will of my Father in heaven is my brother and sister and mother." Basically, he is saying that loyalty to an idea trumps the loyalty to your family tree. I don't know if you agree with that, I certainly do not. The Bible never lets us know if he ever let his family in. But I think that if they were, the following verses would have let us know.

The Possessed Man

Short story shorter, Jesus came upon a man with an 'evil spirit' and sent the spirit to a herd of pigs (reportedly around 2,000 pigs). When the 'mob of spirits' went to the pigs, they immediately dove off the cliffside to a watery grave. The man who was relieved of the spirit went off to tell the masses about what Jesus had done for him, as per direction. The pig tenders, however, asked Jesus to leave their territory, for obvious reasons. What was the aftermath of that 'miracle'? 2,000 pigs is an awful large gathering, and to lose them because the 'Son of God' cast a demon out of one man, but caused a substantial loss to the farm owner, all while granting the evil spirit a temporary abode in the swine. Whose side are you on, Jesus? A sin, though? Debatable. A criminal charge in today's America? Depends on the true *pig*ment of his skin, I gather, pun not intended.

The Fig Tree

This example, in Mark, I do levy a charge against him: Destruction of Property. A fig tree, which was not in season and had no fruit was approached and Jesus, upon seeing this, piously declared, "No one shall ever eat figs from you again!" The next morning the fig tree was withered to the roots. And the story propagated. I don't know why this was impressive to the disciples. Did the tree deserve to die simply because the seasons didn't bow to the 'Son of God'? Certainly if Jesus was hungry, being the offspring of the True One, he could have picked up a pebble and made it a fig. He didn't have the power to do so though, did he? How many people may have passed said fig tree in the future, and having it been in season, could have enjoyed its fruit? Plenty, I reckon. Dick move, Jesus.

The Moneychangers Table

In John 2:13, a story is told how Jesus went to Jerusalem and was so disgusted with the commerce that was going on there he drove all of the livestock from the temple and overturned the tables of the moneychangers, scattering their coins. Disorderly Conduct to a T. Arrestable? Absolutely. But the law was different in those days, so the Jewish authorities asked him, "What miracle can you perform to show us that you have the right to do this?" Then you get the "Tear down this temple and in three days I will build it again." And that threw the establishment into frenzy, and the Bible then comes to his defense, interpreting that although the authorities were thinking about the physical Temple that took 46 years to build, Jesus was really talking about his body. Well, thanks for that clarification, the Bible, but he did not say "tear down the temple of my body and I will raise it in three days," did he? Like me texting Annette, saying that "It was I who killed the unborn Kennedy." But I was talking about the late President, *she* interpreted it to mean her fetus. Yeah, that took me to jail. The case to get rid of this schmuck, Jesus, was beginning to solidify itself.

Theft From Death

The numerous lives that Jesus brought back from death, or woke up from their 'sleeping,' was stealing from Death. Where are the stories about the people he resurrected? If the 'Child of God' brought *me* back from death, I imagine I would talk about it. I imagine with that kind of power wielded I would never have to die ever again. I hold the same feelings about the feedings of the multitudes. Did they poop out the cloned bread or fish? Was it ghost food? I imagine being fed with a miracle, I would write my experience in the following days, or keep an oral history about my experience with the 'bottleneck of God's glory'. 'No one comes to the father but by me,' it doesn't take a classically trained theist to know that there is but one God and no offspring can tamper its evidence by saying 'If you love anything or anyone more than me, you will not see the father.' Beyond Bullshit.

Suicide By Proxy

So with pages more of his 'miracles' and the horrendous underreporting of what the paths were of those who drank the wine, ate the bread, or woke up from sleeping, we may never know. But by claiming to have outs for the predicament you found yourself in, Jesus, and not exhausting every chance to continue on, you committed suicide by proxy, or suicide by cop. If I went to Compton, CA with a sign that said "Fuck Niggers" and expected to live to see the next day unharmed, I would be delirious. As was in Jesus' day, to throw the whole system on its head by trolling the scholars, the Priests, and the authorities, you were bound to meet your demise sooner or later. But to say that you were crucified by anyone other than your own deeds, or refusal to preform deeds when you were called to, you are the weakest link, Sir, goodbye.

His Dying Words

Father, Father, why have you forsaken me? Really! That is what he said. I mean, not in the King's English, but that's what it whittles down to. And that is when he gave up the ghost. "Father, Father, why have you forsaken me?"

Once I beat Johnny Walker with a USB cable, for some wrong deed, eating through the clothes washer's power cable, if I remember correctly. He took it for 4 or 5 whips but then lashed out to bite me before the next lash could be brought upon him. I immediately dropped the cable and gave him kisses, and he licked my face, like he was sorry, too. It is what I see with what happened with the last moments of Christ. Jesus tapped out while at the same time blaspheming God. I do not claim to have the stones to put myself in God's shoes, but if I was the omnipotent one and gave my son a planet and it's heavens to rule, gave him guidance and installed in him the ability to do all sorts of miracles in the land, and when it comes time to die, you think that God would leave you in that moment. Father, Father, why have you forsaken me? No, my friend, not even close. Bad form, Jesus.

God is everywhere at all times. This may give you more to think on. Why then is there suffering? Why couldn't God just play a movie for us and then let us into the cast party? Well, by revealing the cards to me as they were, God let me know. It is done. Has been for some time. This body of work isn't the end. It isn't claiming to be the beginning. It's nothing but a toast, "Here's to living in the moment."

Now that that is out of the way, I can continue. (I didn't even spontaneously combust- I must be on to something.)

324

Chapter XXXII
Dear My World, Pt. 2

In a patriarchal society, the phallic pyramid system of governance, there is only room at the top for a few power endowed elite. The energy flow is such that you have to tear down or remove someone from the higher tiers to make room for those climbing the proverbial ladder of success. It is inherently set up to monopolize "Status Quo or Death." We are approaching the end of Man's reign on earth and moving unaided into the reign of the Chalice. In this new Matriarchal system, you are thrust upwards by the spirit of inverted gravity. In the 'Δ' economic system, the weight of power is distributed downwardly to the lowest levels of societal existence. Distributed over such a vast foundation that those at the bottom don't even really feel the weight of those stones above them because it's all we've ever known. But in the Matriarchal society 'V' there is unlimited upward potential and it all hinges on a true singular bottom. In this case, me. And, in your case, *YOU.*

I have dug myself a hole so deep that not even I can get out of it; I can only wait for the end to manifest itself. This isn't some ploy to get you to bow to me. As the Mayans said, I *am* another you. In my case, I'd like to think that when the time comes I will be able to say to the world, if I drink - you drink, if I eat - you eat. Until the least of us are rescued from Death's vice-grip power hold.

But, I tell you, don't believe me. Watch it happen, and when you start having questions I will be here to give you my opinion. I am not God. I might be the Devil. I could be the Messiah. But for sure, in the end, I am a mental patient who took a life, don't forget that. But do you pay taxes? Sales tax, even? Than to think that you don't have blood on your hands is more ludacris than me currently getting waited on like I was a king, as a patient at the Arizona State Hospital. The military is funded by taxes, well, in theory, anyways. And the military is and has been killing people in the longest undeclared war the United States has ever been involved in, save for the war on drugs. Wittingly or unwittingly, you are complicit in atrocities that you don't even know have happened. This literal house of cards is about to tip its hand. Where will you be? How will you be positioned? I am not afraid to taste death. Unfortunately, it is going to be a long journey for me. How much global suffering are *you* willing to write off, knowing that even by simply consuming purchased goods you are chipping in and perpetuating the tyranny of America's global economic class war? Apathy equals consent, remember?

I know, I know... "What can I do about it?" You may be asking yourselves. I have no individual answer for you. En Masse, though? I think public disobedience on a grand scale would be something worthy to be a part of.

If an enforcer of policy gets to choose who gets arrested versus who gets a ticket, which get tazed and which get shot dead, that policy initiator has got to go. The United States Government is a machine of ineffective policy drafting and enforcement, among other titles. We should all be ashamed for letting it get this out of control. I rebelled out of disgust. And not only did I not lose anything, I in fact gained a pretty comfortable existence. Granted, my life is now more structured, compartmentalized, but it's for natural life, folks. I am not going anywhere. To put this completed work in the public square, I am opening myself up to scrutiny. I will relish it.

I come with a message of utter confusion as to why we accept what is below us. We offer our best daily and our reward is to get to do it all over again? We have become our own worst nightmare. It's not over yet. But I'll have a great view to watch the system implode. I'll send you a postcard.

What do we have to lose by realigning ourselves to the right side of the future? Fuck being on the right side of *history*.

2,000+ years is long enough to wait for someone to save us. **We** can dig out of this! Or, at least, rattle God's cage enough so that he is forced to show himself.

Until then, I'll just be chilling on Mount Zion (Arizona) on *your* blood-soaked dime.

Waiting.

$$1=1$$

Novel concept, isn't it?

Chapter XXXIII

Bonus Content

Circa 2015
WHAT WORDS?

What words are there left?
When they're wasted on the daily
Tell me what you use to have
That shit don't even faze me
There ain't nothing that can't be done
With a pen and a pad
And a script that hits you
Nations move to war for fun
Civilizations rise at the point of an arrow or the tip of a gun
But the world turns a blind eye
To the child so hungry he's about to die
And Y'all motherfuckers just sittin' in the Penn
Rappin' about Glocks and Bitches
Bout 'Pussy-Ass Niggas' and 'Fuck the Snitches'
Why you even pay them mind?
Overload your senses
Wastin' your lyrical rhymes
Bragging up or tearing down
Shit that ain't fuckin worth a dime
Instead, focus your talented thinkin'
On putting together a cypher worth rippin'
The right letters in the correct combination
Just might free this earthly prison
Where we're ALL FUCKING LIFERS
No matter what you're sippin'

-c.gant

Spoken word, after Xander Died Circa 2007
Finally Found

I've loved and I've lost
I've lived and paid the cost
Of the mistakes I've done
But the battles nearly won
I've misplaced my soul
But finding it now has made me whole
It's swallowed the night
That shadowed my fears
And forgetting the times that I've tasted my tears
I HAVE a destination
And when that final bridge is crossed
With me I will carry the baggage of the lost
And show them there is a way
To start living for the moment
And FUCK yesterday
There ain't nothin' worth knowing that comes easy
And I never again will cast my 'pearls among swine'
And this is the way I will end this rhyme:
IN MY HEART
I SEE THE STARS
THAT WILLL BEACON THE MISGUIDED
AND HELP HEAL THEIR SCARS
AND THE ONES LIFE FORGOT
WILL LOOK BACK TO THE DAY THEY THOUGHT
"I HAVE NOTHING LEFT TO GIVE"
"THIS IS **NOT** THE WAY I WANT TO LIVE"
THEN SMILING AT THE MEDIOCRITY TO WHICH THEY THOGHT THEY
WERE BOUND
ANOTHER MISPLACED SOUL
IS FINALLY FOUND

Rap, written in Mohave County Jail Circa. 9/2014
'Criminal Romeo'

I'm a Criminal Romeo
Stealin' hearts just for show
You may claim 'Expert' in one thing
But there ain't much I don't know
Heard a Bitch nixin' Country
Just jumped to Pop radio
Now, Nashville, Big Machine
Let me 'Grease' Your biggest star
Or do I have to call Republic?
Jimmy Harnen, Jimmy Harnen!
Yeah he on my Facebook
Jim and I go way back
Tipped him off to THE SENATORS
Now my boys are on track
Opened for an idol, Phillip Phillips in Phene
On the same exact plot we poisoned New York City
If you don't catch the reference
Think back to early Milleni
AZ took the PENNANT from UNLIMITED MONEY
Send the Yanks packin' sacks
With their heads hangin' low
Double the distance from here to K.C., MO
Now I could draw another line about a snake and an apple
But I wouldn't want the clergy goin' and call me an 'Asshole'
Now think about this:
If your minds not been rotted
With what Obama has plotted
"Don't buy my insurance? I'll FINE you!"
"If you're Muslim, I'll FIND you!"
Salute a Staff Sergeant
Who never quit the Crucible
With a STARBUCKS in your hand...?
Oh, BO, how DARE you!
But I Digress
Time will put him to rest
But instead of daily news of unendable wars
Wouldn't it be cool to turn to PBS and see my TAY on all fours?
Begging for a throat fuck from my dick
To impregnate her Grammy Winnin' Larynx
Maybelline® Mascara heavy runnin' down her cheeks
"Better not struggle, slut, I know you need to breathe"

330

Then we pick up a RES.
Run the world from Sin City
In the Dime-Stack Pent
Hint-Hint Steve Wynnie
Call up Sheldon Adle' an'
Break bread with your nemesy
Fund me 2016 I'll run write in Independe
But by the time it comes to pass
This world will know war
Is no excuse for the justification we been living it for
We stand united
Yellow, white, black, and brown
And ANY race
Yet to be made or found
We stand at the gates
My brothers in arms
It's been long enough
It's fuckin' time to sound the alarm
When you walk through that door
Open your miracle eyes
The 'Kingdom of Heaven'
AS PROMISED.
TAKE IT!
IT'S YOURS!
And all it's gonna take
To get the gears of eternity churnin'
Is one tablespoon of grease
That comes when I bust my nut
In the bitch who tooth and nail I fought
Every waking minute
And double in my sleep
To make an edit to her hit
Fuck 'SAY YES' when she says "I DO!"

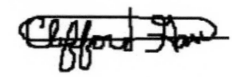

AFTERWARD

In the twinkling of an eye, your world can change. I hope I have represented my past in an open and honest way. Not everyone is going to appreciate my candor. I don't know exactly what the future holds, but I am excited to watch it all manifest. We now find ourselves on the brink of greatness, or the precipice of disaster. I believe it is for us to decide our fate. We can continue living in the darkness, ignorant of world events and next door neighbor travesties, or, we can stand for something new and uncharted. We can either fight for a system of inclusion and equality, or be disappointedly reserved to waiting for a savior, for eternity.

Thank you for your consideration.

-GANT

Arizona State Hospital
CLIFFORD F. GANT
2500 E. Van Buren St.
Phoenix, Arizona 85008